Communicating Environmental Geoscience

IUGS/GSL publishing agreement

This volume is published under an agreement between the International Union of Geological Sciences and the Geological Society of London and arises from IUGS International Commission on the History of Geological Sciences (INHIGEO).

GSL is the publisher of choice for books related to IUGS activities, and the IUGS receives a royalty for all books published under this agreement.

Books published under this agreement are subject to the Society's standard rigorous proposal and manuscript review procedures.

It is recommended that reference to all or part of this book should be made in one of the following ways:

LIVERMAN, D. G. E., PEREIRA, C. P. G. & MARKER, B. 2008. *Communicating Environmental Geoscience*. Geological Society, London, Special Publications, **305**.

ROYSE, K. R., REEVES, H. J. & GIBSON, A. R. 2008. The modelling and visualization of digital geoscientific data as a communication aid to land-use planning in the urban environment: an example from the Thames Gateway. *In*: LIVERMAN, D. G. E., PEREIRA, C. P. G. & MARKER, B. (eds) *Communicating Environmental Geoscience*. Geological Society, London, Special Publications, **305**, 89–106.

GEOLOGICAL SOCIETY SPECIAL PUBLICATION NO. 305

Communicating Environmental Geoscience

EDITED BY

D. G. E. LIVERMAN
Geological Survey of Newfoundland and Labrador, Canada

C. P. G. PEREIRA
Geological Survey of Newfoundland and Labrador, Canada

and

B. MARKER
Independent Consultant, UK

2008
Published by
The Geological Society
London

THE GEOLOGICAL SOCIETY

The Geological Society of London (GSL) was founded in 1807. It is the oldest national geological society in the world and the largest in Europe. It was incorporated under Royal Charter in 1825 and is Registered Charity 210161.

The Society is the UK national learned and professional society for geology with a worldwide Fellowship (FGS) of over 9000. The Society has the power to confer Chartered status on suitably qualified Fellows, and about 2000 of the Fellowship carry the title (CGeol). Chartered Geologists may also obtain the equivalent European title, European Geologist (EurGeol). One fifth of the Society's fellowship resides outside the UK. To find out more about the Society, log on to www.geolsoc.org.uk.

The Geological Society Publishing House (Bath, UK) produces the Society's international journals and books, and acts as European distributor for selected publications of the American Association of Petroleum Geologists (AAPG), the Indonesian Petroleum Association (IPA), the Geological Society of America (GSA), the Society for Sedimentary Geology (SEPM) and the Geologists' Association (GA). Joint marketing agreements ensure that GSL Fellows may purchase these societies' publications at a discount. The Society's online bookshop (accessible from www.geolsoc.org.uk) offers secure book purchasing with your credit or debit card.

To find out about joining the Society and benefiting from substantial discounts on publications of GSL and other societies worldwide, consult www.geolsoc.org.uk, or contact the Fellowship Department at: The Geological Society, Burlington House, Piccadilly, London W1J 0BG: Tel. +44 (0)20 7434 9944; Fax +44 (0)20 7439 8975; E-mail: enquiries@geolsoc.org.uk.

For information about the Society's meetings, consult *Events* on www.geolsoc.org.uk. To find out more about the Society's Corporate Affiliates Scheme, write to enquiries@geolsoc.org.uk

Published by The Geological Society from:
The Geological Society Publishing House, Unit 7, Brassmill Enterprise Centre, Brassmill Lane, Bath BA1 3JN, UK

(*Orders*:   Tel. +44 (0)1225 445046, Fax +44 (0)1225 442836)
Online bookshop: www.geolsoc.org.uk/bookshop

The publishers make no representation, express or implied, with regard to the accuracy of the information contained in this book and cannot accept any legal responsibility for any errors or omissions that may be made.

British Library Cataloguing in Publication Data

A catalogue record for this book is available from the British Library.
ISBN 978-1-86239-260-1
Typeset by Techset Composition Ltd., Salisbury, UK
Printed by Cromwell Press, Trowbridge, UK

Distributors

North America
For trade and institutional orders:
The Geological Society, c/o AIDC, 82 Winter Sport Lane, Williston, VT 05495, USA
Orders: Tel +1 800-972-9892
           Fax +1 802-864-7626
           Email gsl.orders@aidcvt.com

For individual and corporate orders:
AAPG Bookstore, PO Box 979, Tulsa, OK 74101-0979, USA
Orders: Tel +1 918-584-2555
           Fax +1 918-560-2652
           Email bookstore@aapg.org
           Website http://bookstore.aapg.org

India
Affiliated East-West Press Private Ltd, Marketing Division, G-1/16 Ansari Road, Darya Ganj, New Delhi 110 002, India
Orders: Tel. +91 11 2327-9113/2326-4180
           Fax +91 11 2326-0538
           E-mail affiliat@vsnl.com

Contents

Communicating environmental geoscience: introduction

DAVE LIVERMAN[1], CHRISTOPHER P. G. PEREIRA[1] & BRIAN MARKER[2]

[1]*Geological Survey of Newfoundland & Labrador, Department of Natural Resources,
PO Box 8700, St. John's, NL, Canada, A1B 4J6 (e-mail: dliverman@gov.nl.ca)*

[2]*40 Kingsdown Avenue, London W13 9PT, UK*

Abstract: This collection of papers is aimed primarily at the environmental geoscientist faced with the challenges of communicating important scientific results to those who might benefit from them, whether they are politicians, policy-makers, potential victims of geological disasters, fellow scientists or other members of the public. Environmental geoscience has grown to become one of the most important disciplines of geoscience as a whole, and scientific methods of investigation have become sophisticated and effective at addressing numerous problems that directly affect health and safety. The audience for such research thus is wide, and for such research to be used in the most effective manner requires well-developed communication skills to reach an audience that varies greatly in education and ability to comprehend scientific concepts. The implications of failing to communicate effectively may be severe: geological disasters have had a massive economic and social impact, with major loss of life.

This initiative arose out of the inaugural workshop of the 'Communicating Environmental Geoscience' working group of the International Union of Geological Sciences Commission 'Geoscience for Environmental Management', held in Nottingham in 2006.

In 2005, one of us (Dave Liverman) took part in an unusual scientific meeting, organized under the auspices of International Council of Scientific Unions 'Dark Nature' project. This project aimed to bring together scientists who worked in the field of environmental change to examine how past societies and communities reacted in the face of harmful events, and to explore the implications of rapid natural change on current environmental and public policies. This meeting was held in Mauritania, West Africa. To quote from the meeting report: 'The structure of the conference was unusual: field visits in the mornings and afternoons and oral presentations before lunch and before dinner. The participants were from north Europe, south Europe, north Africa, Australia and north America, facilitating N–S and W–E exchanges.... All the talks were translated in English and French, by bilingual volunteers. But in the vehicles, during the meals or during the three day trek across the sand dunes, the conversations were often in a curious mix of languages indicating the desire to communicate by any means.... The field conference ended on discussions on the role of scientists, what we can and should do and how to transfer our knowledge to the wider public.'

What emerged from these evening discussions in remote parts of the Sahara was a common feeling of frustration that there was so little general understanding of the scientific research, and that significant scientific work rarely affected the decisions made by policy-makers and politicians. At the same time, the International Union of Geological Sciences Geoindicators Initiative was winding up a decade of work, promoting the use of geoindicators as a way of communicating rapid geological change to those involved in managing the environment. The Geoindicators management committee proposed to the IUGS Commission 'Geoscience for Environmental Management' (IUGS-GEM) that a working group be established to address the issue of communicating environmental geoscience. The proposal to establish such a group was accepted in 2005, and one of the first activities was to convene a workshop in September 2006 in the UK in conjunction with the Geohazards Working Group of the Engineering Group of the Geological Society (London). This workshop was attended by a mixture of UK-based participants and members of the IUGS-GEM commission, and had a useful combination of presentations and discussion. One of the outcomes of the workshop was to attempt to publish a wider range of selected papers in book form. These papers form the basis of the current publication, supplemented by further contributions from members of the working group, and others interested in the general subject area.

This collection is not a comprehensive survey because it is selective in subject matter and geographical scope. Most of the authors are geoscientists, who have come to realize, through their own experiences, the importance of communication of their science, and the concerns and problems that

From: LIVERMAN, D. G. E., PEREIRA, C. P. G. & MARKER, B. (eds) *Communicating Environmental Geoscience*. Geological Society, London, Special Publications, **305**, 1–4.
DOI: 10.1144/SP305.1   0305-8719/08/$15.00 © The Geological Society of London 2008.

exist in communication across cultural, social and economic lines. The papers need to be read with the understanding that there is an extensive literature covering the general field of science communication. For example, several journals exist, including the *Journal of Science Communication*, the *Journal of Health Communication*, *Science Communication*, and, recently, *Environmental Communication*. These journals draw largely from the social sciences, and little has been written specifically by and for environmental geoscientists whose work often must be communicated to a general audience.

It might be expected that a collection of papers emphasizing communication would all be shining examples of clarity of writing style; we leave it to the reader to judge how well the authors (and editors) have succeeded but are well aware that the papers reflect a range of abilities in communication of difficult concepts to what is hoped to be a general audience (and, of course, some authors are writing in a language that is not their own).

Writing these papers posed a communication challenge for many, as their training was to write in the standard scientific style, yet their subject matter did not always lend itself to such a method of presentation. When writing on communication, much can be learned from anecdotal experiences, opinions and examples. As such, our referees also faced difficulties in evaluating manuscripts that departed from the familiar format of the scientific paper. The reader will thus find the papers presented in contrasting styles; for instance, the paper by **Ted Nield** reflects the author's background as a science journalist and communicator, and in his own words 'is not a learned paper based on exhaustive consideration of allegedly objective evidence gathered under controlled conditions ... I don't do those' (Nield, pers. comm.). Other papers are written in a style more familiar to social scientists, who have their own terminology and conventions that may challenge those without a background in this area.

The issues surrounding communication of science have been researched by social scientists, but the specific problems facing the environmental geoscientist have, as far as we know, never been addressed directly by the social sciences. There is considerable overlap, however, with social science research in natural hazards, and risk communication. In this collection several authors have used the method of describing communication problems faced in their own experience, and the degree to which these problems have been overcome. **Donnelly** describes lessons learned through his broad experience as a consultant, ranging from forensic geological investigations to natural hazards. **Di Giulio *et al.*** describe how, as a result of the lack of a communication strategy, the impact of research designed to help a community deal with lead contamination had unexpected and unfortunate consequences.

Petterson *et al.* (as does, in part, **Donnelly**) deal with the issues faced when working in areas where local society and culture is very different from that with which many scientists are familiar. The challenges of crossing cultural barriers in communication mean that scientists, in addition to dealing with issues of language, must be aware of the protocols and structure of decision-making in the society where they are working; in fact, at times have to take on the role of anthropologists. **Catto & Parewick** describe how scientists have adapted to local cultural values when working in Arctic communities to allow their science to be used constructively by the community in decision-making. The authors emphasize the value of developing partnerships, and through their own experience show how researchers must consider communication on a single community basis rather than using a generic model.

Hermelin & Bedoya show how Andean communities have been successfully engaged and involved in hazard awareness in Colombia, despite challenges in political and social structure. Local committees are run by people with little or no formal education but who understand that they must participate as a group to prevent or mitigate the effects of natural disasters. The co-operation between technical experts and trained residents represents an outstanding example of good communication and co-operation for urban populations living in areas prone to natural disasters.

A paper by **Jaramillo** and others describes a large multinational research effort in Andean South America (MAP:GAC), an area with a history of serious natural disasters. The project identified that an important first step was developing a consistent lexicon of terminology and methods at the scientific level. A variety of approaches to slope hazard analysis and classification had been taken in the countries involved in the study, and ensuring that scientists were able to effectively communicate amongst themselves was an important first step prior to working at the community level.

Decision-making structures in Australia are dealt with by **Simpson**, who points out that understanding the structure of institutional science on a national level is important. By directing efforts towards the body that has most influence on policy, science has the greatest opportunity of informing decision-making at that level.

The field of climate-change science is perhaps an example of where, over a period of time, scientists have successfully influenced policy development on local, national and global scales through their communication efforts. **Boykoff** outlines the successes and challenges faced by climate scientists as they learn to deal with the media. **Schmidt-Thomé & Kaulbarsz** deal, specifically, with the major issue of uncertainty. Scientific research only rarely can deliver the exact answers desired by planners and policy-makers. They outline a decision-support framework that handles the issue of uncertainty as it pertains to sea-level change, and show how this approach was successful in influencing policy in Poland.

Ward also discusses uncertainty as it pertains to climate change. He suggests that, in a number of cases, uncertainties have been overstated or understated by both scientists and policy-makers, relative to scientific assessments. He argues that although distortions in the expression of uncertainties are motivated by a desire to justify particular policy positions, there is evidence that they risk undermining the credibility of information sources and diminishing public support. In such cases it is important to be aware of current thinking in risk communication.

Two papers illustrate how the British Geological Survey is approaching communication issues. **Walsby** shows how the BGS has taken the traditional geology map, which requires experience and geological knowledge to interpret, and derived more accessible products that are better at providing the information required by planners and policy-makers. Geographic Information System (GIS) datasets with 'plain English' descriptions have been created for natural gas emissions, landslides, swell–shrink clays, compressible and collapsible deposits, soluble rocks, running sands, and groundwater flooding. Geological information is thus potentially brought before a wider audience and in a form that reveals to the British public and industry how geology can be used in conjunction with other information, and why it is relevant to their lives.

Royse et al. deal with the complex datasets that exist in urban settings, where extensive borehole data mean that geology can be described in three dimensions. New and innovative ways of visualizing and communicating geoscience information have been developed using computer methods. Geoscientific information is imported into standard GIS packages and queried along with other complementary ground investigation data, resulting in the creation of a powerful tool to assist in strategic planning and sustainable development.

Two of the editors have contributed to the volume, and there is considerable overlap in the conclusions they draw. **Marker** draws on 30 years of experience as an official in a central government department charged with preparing and advising on legislation, policy and guidance on minerals, waste

management and responses to geological hazards, and with specifying and managing research in support of those tasks; and in teaching adult education classes on applied geoscience topics. **Liverman** examines the published literature in science, communication and the social sciences to provide direction for environmental geoscientists trying to improve their communication skills. Both Liverman and Marker conclude that, to be effective, scientists have to understand institutional and decision-making structures; outputs must be tailored to specific audiences; experts in communication are a useful resource; dissemination of results can be as important as presentation; and that there is a need to work with social scientists. Further, Marker points out that consultation, presentation for non-specialists and dissemination are time consuming, and that staff, time and money to support these endeavours must be made available. He also suggests that it is wise to plan consultation, presentation and dissemination from the commencement of work, revising plans as a fuller understanding of systems and audience requirements is gained.

Three papers deal with, in part, the hazards associated with volcanoes. Petterson *et al.* (Solomon Islands) and Donnelly (Montserrat) use case studies to highlight communication issues. **Barclay et al.** attempt to provide a more general overview of communication issues associated with volcanic hazard. Barclay *et al.* emphasize the need for physical scientists to work with social scientists, particularly those with expertise in risk communication. Analysis of case studies suggests that scientists must endeavour to make their communication more inclusive by direct involvement with communities, and solutions driven by community needs as well as scientific evidence.

There are some areas of environmental geology that are not covered in this compilation; notably issues associated with earthquakes, a major and unpredictable hazard that has some interesting and specific communication issues associated with it. Environmental geochemistry is touched upon only in one paper, that of Di Giulio *et al.* This field is of increasing interest, and because of the implications to public health issues, communication is of vital importance. There are deficiencies in geographical distribution as well. There is good representation from Europe, North and South America, and two papers from Australia; there is little from most of the rest of the world, Africa and Asia in particular. There is much to be learned about communicating environmental geoscience in these areas. The people most vulnerable to natural hazards tend to be those of the poorest countries in the world, who lack the economic ability to adapt, build defences or move. The balance between environmental protection and development is challenging in China and India, where the intense pace of development is causing major environmental problems. Geoscientists have a role to play in the decision-making process in these areas, and require communication skills specific to the cultures and economic and political circumstances in those countries.

There are some common themes and messages that emerge from this collection of papers. Perhaps the most important is that of involvement and engagement with the community. Barclay *et al.*, Di Giulio *et al.*, Catto & Parewick and Petterson *et al.* all emphasize the importance of environmental scientists considering and engaging with the community affected by the results of their science. As Catto & Parewick state, 'Geoscience is too important to be left strictly to geoscientists'. Scientists need to re-evaluate their roles in the decision-making process, and be part of a more inclusive process, with dialogue between scientists, authorities and stakeholders at a variety of levels. The model of experts telling the uninformed what to do is ineffective, and must be re-evaluated.

Environmental geoscientists need to understand decision-making structures. Scientists must be aware of where and how to direct their communication efforts to make them most effective, whether it is through understanding institutional pathways (Simpson) or learning about how decisions are made in societies structured differently from those that geoscientists are previously familiar with (Petterson *et al.*).

Communication needs to be planned, and adequate funds and time allocated to communication in the design of projects. Communication skills can be improved through training, and working with media and communication professionals (Nield). For environmental geoscientists to become better communicators it is important that educational institutions and employers recognize the need for training, and reward efforts to transmit the results of environmental geoscience to the public.

Communication products need to be tailored to the audience they are aimed at. To provide the right product, communicators must understand the target audience, whether it is indigenous people with an unfamiliar language and society, a journalist looking for a good story, a politician unused to scientific terms, or the public faced with an impending natural disaster. Communication must flow in both directions; too often communication success is measured by provoking what the communicator considers to be an appropriate response. By listening to the audience, a better appreciation of the impact of scientific work can be gained, as well as perhaps an understanding of the factors driving responses.

There is an extensive body of literature in the social sciences dealing with science communication that many environmental geoscientists are unaware of. Although much research on risk communication exists, the one area that remains challenging, as identified by Ward and Barclay *et al.* is that of communicating uncertainty. Because of the unpredictability of natural systems, this issue will remain prominent for environmental geoscientists.

There is a need to think carefully about communication in terms of intended audiences and administrative structures throughout applied work on geoscience issues. There are an increasing number of opportunities for environmental geoscientists to improve their ability to communicate. Many research projects now involve communication planning, and the importance of appropriate communication of science is increasingly acknowledged.

Much can be learned from previous efforts to communicate and there have been important initiatives, particularly in the area of hazards. The US Geological Survey Professional Paper '*Nature to be Commanded: Earth Science Maps Applied to Land and Water Management*' (Robinson & Spieker 1978) was a pioneering effort in communicating the importance of Earth sciences to planners, and provided guidance to other projects including the Geotechnical Area Studies Programme in Hong Kong and the ZERMOIS mapping in France (reviewed by Cascini *et al.* 2005).

However, there is much room for improvement and it is hoped that this collection of papers provides some direction to environmental geoscientists facing these issues for the first time as well as pointing to areas for future research.

We are most grateful to the numerous reviewers who volunteered their time to improve the papers collected here; we do not acknowledge all of them by name here, but their efforts and insight were greatly appreciated. The authors for the most part kept to the deadlines and schedules imposed on them, and helped our efforts considerably. We are grateful to the British Geological Survey, and the Geological Society Geohazards working group for their assistance in organizing the 2006 workshop that led to this book, and to the IUGS Commission on Geoscience for Environmental Management for their support.

References

CASCINI, L., BONNARD, C., COROMINAS, J., JIBSON, R. & MONTERO-OLARTE, J. 2005. Landslide hazard and risk zoning for urban planning and development. *In*: *International Conference on Landslide Risk Management*. Balkema, Rotterdam, 199–235.

ROBINSON, G. D. & SPIEKER, A. M. 1978. *Nature to be Commanded: Earth Science Maps Applied to Land and Water Management*. US Geological Survey Professional Papers, **950**.

Altered priorities ahead; or how to develop fruitful relationships with the media

Geological Society of London, Burlington House, Piccadilly, London W1J 0BG, UK
(e-mail: ted.nield@geolsoc.org.uk)

Abstract: This paper examines the conflict between scientists' usual conception of the media and the reality of working successfully with them when transmitting research findings. It suggests that if scientists rid themselves of some common misconceptions, they can begin to engage more effectively with the news media. By always bearing in mind two crucial facts (that the news media are not going to change the way they work to please scientists, and that they should be approached as a branch of the entertainment industry) all subsequent decisions and behaviours on the part of scientists and their companies or institutions will be more likely to be blessed with success. It concludes by reporting some case histories, as worked examples of how scientific institutions can promote themselves through their research by harnessing the potent power of enlightened self-interest.

Let me first be clear about what this paper isn't. First, it is not meant to be a complete course in media relations. Interactions with journalists take on many different forms, depending on circumstances. Also, dealing with specialist science correspondents (which is what I shall assume in this paper) is a very different business from dealing with unknown folk from other beats or with general news reporters who don't owe you any allegiance.

So here is a health warning: trying to promote yourself in the media because you want publicity is a completely different activity from trying to make the best of an unfortunate situation in which the news media have you under siege. In all circumstances, and especially the latter, you should never act alone and should always liaise with your company or institution's media relations office.

What I intend to discuss in this paper are the particular problems that many scientists and engineers tend to have when trying to get publicity for their work. These difficulties derive from the preconceptions and misapprehensions scientists tend to hold about journalists, and the industry they work in; errors that can be fatal to any hope of putting up a good performance.

It is based mainly on UK examples, for the usual reason that *c'est ce que j'ai vu*. However, I would qualify my apology by saying that the UK perspective is a salutary one for other countries, for two reasons. First, there are hardly any difficulties facing a scientist or an institution in the media spotlight that are not hugely exacerbated simply by being British. Reserve, understatement, politeness, rigidity, hierarchies, snobbery, bad teeth; you name it, we British suffer from it. Second, the UK

also boasts perhaps the world's most crowded, competitive, tough-minded, aggressive, persistent and even rapacious media organizations in the world. So, to echo the song, 'if you can make it there, you'll make it anywhere'.

Part 1: Right in principle, or open your mind (but not so wide that your brains fall out)

Scientists are supposed to be more capable than most of opening their minds to impossible notions. So I encourage you now to open your mind to the possibility that everything you probably think you know about the media is completely wrong.

Folkloric tales

'Live and don't learn, that's me' *(Bart Simpson)*

Scientists share with educated people the world over the curious misconception that the media solely exist for the edification of the masses; that their whole purpose is to inform and educate; that they convey facts about the world to the reader, viewer or listener in a process I call 'education-lite'.

In this strangely distorted world-view, the scientist plays the role of lecturing professor; the journalist plays the role of postgraduate teaching assistant, interpreting and disseminating the words of the Great Man for the benefit of the unwashed undergraduate horde, upon whom the light of reason then miraculously dawns. Hurrah for another triumph of enlightenment. By virtue of

From: Liverman, D. G. E., Pereira, C. P. G. & Marker, B. (eds) *Communicating Environmental Geoscience*. Geological Society, London, Special Publications, **305**, 5–10.
DOI: 10.1144/SP305.2   0305-8719/08/$15.00 © The Geological Society of London 2008.

this activity, a few people come to know a bit more science, and hence the world is made a better place (especially for scientists).

All people interpret the world using metaphors derived from what they know best. What educated people such as scientists know better than anything else is education. That they should therefore interpret the media's role and function solely in terms of an education-like process is not that surprising, because it does have some compelling superficial similarities. As an approximation to reality, however, this picturesque myth is about on a par with the traditional Balinese explanation for earthquakes; the one involving a giant turtle and a pair of snakes. It is a fantasy.

Journalists are not even peripherally part of the education racket. Journalism is a branch of the entertainment industry. Granted, some forms of media have nobler pretensions, but they still need volunteers to buy them, so in truth they all need to entertain.

Understanding deficit

The second misconception under which scientists tend to labour is that the public hate them. In fact, the overwhelming majority of the public think that scientists mean well and that their work makes the world a better place. But perception is reality in this game and scientists are unaware of the research.

Their third big misconception is believing that the secret of making the public love them and all their works is to teach them. In the science communication industry this is called the 'deficit model', whereby the human race is pictured in terms of how full up with scientific facts individuals are. Scientists are very full, and hence ecstatically happy about science, whereas the public tend to be not as full, which explains why they may be less happy and are therefore correspondingly less likely to think that science is A Good Thing. In other words, the public, wrongly conceived of as anti-science (or perhaps as 'insufficiently pro-science'), are thought to hold these low opinions out of ignorance.

If the idea that 'educating people makes them love you' is nonsense, then the deficit model is nonsense on stilts, and among those whose job it is to theorize about such matters it has long been completely discredited. Rumours of its extinction, however, are grossly exaggerated, for although science communicators as a profession may think it extinct, it remains alive and well among scientists themselves.

Think about it; it's obvious really. To know all may be to forgive all, but how grateful were you, when they made you learn the Krebs Cycle by heart? What education can and does achieve is a better-informed debate. It doesn't make your enemies agree with you. For the purposes of this paper, and of improving your dealings with the media, the mantra to repeat to yourself in your bath for the next few weeks is 'education is not public relations'.

Joy of learning? Give me a break

Now, don't get me wrong. I do not deny the importance of science education. I merely deny its usefulness in making friends and influencing people, which is what we are interested in. In fact, the attempt to educate people by stealth through the media is, if detected, in my view quite likely to be resented and to make the situation worse.

Here is another impossible notion for you. The 'joy of learning' of which we hear so much, and on which so many hopes are pinned, is a myth, largely created by those few people for whom it is true. For them, it is a form of whistling in the dark, because it gives the illusion of company. But alas, it is another comfortable fiction. For most people, education is the last place they will go in search of joy. We should apply the principle of 'a place for everything and everything in its place'. The place for scientific education is in school, college and university. After then, what 'learning activities' people at large choose to engage in is up to them. But anyone who tries cynically to force education upon an unsuspecting public by consciously manipulating the news media and other legitimate forms of entertainment deserves to be fed on their own press releases.

The other thing to remember when dealing with science journalists is that they are journalists. Like any other kind of specialist reporter, they are there to act as informed, independent, and (above all) critical commentators on their subject, not to be its mouthpieces, cheerleaders or spin-doctors. It is likely that a science journalist will be interested in science, and hence more likely to be broadly pro-science in outlook. But you should not bank on it, just as you shouldn't bank on their possessing specialist knowledge.

This is not to deny that people do receive education via the news media; we are all immeasurably better educated about the world we live in today than we were 60 years ago, thanks to the mass media. But this is a byproduct. But you would do well to believe that the only reason people engage with the media in the first place is that they wish to be entertained. You will have fewer failures that way. All the customers of the media are volunteers. As my friend and colleague Tim Radford (former Science Editor of The Guardian) is fond of saying, 'the democratic imperative laid on scientists to communicate with the public is not met by a corresponding public obligation to listen'.

This is why so much greater skill is required when dealing with the 'paying volunteer' public than with captive pupils who, wanting to learn, will willingly apply themselves to overcoming the inadequacies of their teachers.

Touchy feely catchee monkey

The news media are an inefficient way of conveyancing fact, and we see the evidence of this all around us every day. However, they are a very efficient way of manipulating the emotions. Manipulating people's emotions is something that scientists tend not to be good at, but it is the very stuff of public relations. In the PR world, which is what we are now entering, the priorities are somewhat different from those in the world of science. In the PR world, 'being right' may be important, but it can just as easily count for nothing. In this world, perception is reality. Where education conveyances facts and ideas, scientists' stock-in-trade, from one person's brain to another, public relations exists to engender warm feelings, such as trust, and to create affective bonds.

The relative powerlessness of 'being right' is nowhere better illustrated than by the infamous Brent Spar farrago, where Shell was consistently wrong-footed and outmanoeuvred by Greenpeace. I did say I would not cover 'firefighting' PR, but in this respect only, Brent Spar is a germane piece of evidence that should be admitted here. Greenpeace later admitted they had used inaccurate and misleading data in their arguments and suffered some PR damage themselves as a result; but this did almost nothing to help Shell out of its hole, because the whole argument had from the start been driven not by facts or science, but by emotion. Dumping the Spar at sea was just not on, chaps, whatever the evidence. 'Being right' was irrelevant.

Scientists can deplore this situation all they like; but it doesn't help, and it will never change. Scientists often imagine that this situation (where emotion plays such a powerful role in public debate) could be corrected by the injection of proper scientific rational argument; and it is true that accurate science can be very important in winning PR battles. The organization Sense About Science exists to spread reliable information about science issues and subscribes to this idea of spreading rational thought and enlightenment. What use are arms if your soldiers do not know how to deploy them?

Campaigning organizations, even those that (when it suits them) put on the trappings of science to push their causes, are much better at doing this than large companies or governments. They are nimbler, for a start, and they are also less worried about being footloose with the science. Their relatively free-and-easy attitude towards the sacred facts and scientific scruple gives them an extraordinary, and unfair, PR advantage. Combine this with the public's proven tendency to place more faith in scientists who work for green pressure groups than those who work for industry or government (though not universities, interestingly), it is a very difficult job to beat them at this game.

That said, however, it wouldn't be hopeless did not scientists then tend to hand their opponents victory on a plate by refusing to play the media game. They are perfectly entitled to do this of course, but sadly, in stalking off the field in protest (a tactic that many find tempting and often cave in to) they forfeit the right to complain about the result. In all of this, the media dictate everything. The media are more powerful than any pressure group, including science. They own the ball. Therefore they make the rules, and always will. (I have more to say about the 'refusal to speculate', a particular form of 'refusing to play the game', below.)

After one or two bruising encounters of this kind, scientists and scientific organizations tend to approach the media in a spirit of suspicion and fear (that they may be traduced) and with a mission to 'set the record straight' (i.e. prove that they are 'right', as though anybody cared, when arguments are often won or lost not on facts but on style).

The only genuine excuse for burdening the world with even more information is that by doing so, someone else passes a few moments less dully than otherwise. If the result of your communication is dull, however, the world is not improved, and it had been better not to try. If your communication fails this crucial test, that it has transcended teaching and become entertainment, then what you have done is no better than commit the sin perpetrated upon university students every day (but which is there absolved because the victims signed up for it).

By attempting to perpetrate education upon the unwilling, you commit a cynical attack upon freedom, the right of all free adult citizens not be bored against their will by special interest groups.

To sum up:

(1) News media do educate but their prime directive is to entertain.
(2) Education, the conveyancing of fact and idea, makes bad public relations.
(3) Public relations exists to engender warm feelings such as trust.

Once these points of principle are truly understood and accepted, then all your subsequent decisions about how to handle a particular media situation will stand a much better chance of being the right ones.

Take the following scenario. If a TV crew from *Wales Today* announces that it wishes to film at your HQ because you are building the Aberdrewi by-pass through the sacred burial grounds of the Ancient Welsh, rather than taking a more costly route underlain by the difficult and treacherous Boggy Beds, what will you do?

Will you now think: 'Ah, we need to put up Professor Droning Moonbat, consultant to our London-based Geotechnical Directorate, because he's the expert in the engineering geology of the Boggy Beds and will be certain to get all his facts right?' Or, guided by those points above, will you think: 'It's TV—we need to put up the young graduate trainee Annwyl Pritchard (loyal daughter of Aberdrewi)—who can hardly be accused of racial insensitivity, who is fresh, bilingual, fully supplied with teeth, and bursting with a radiant hope for the economic and environmental gains that the by-pass will bring to Aberdrewi's people, without once becoming embroiled in the Boggy Beds (about whose geotechnical fine points nobody cares, and none will remember)?'

Part 2: Do it right; are you hard or soft?

There can only ever be one innocent reason for communicating science to adults via the media, and that is the possibility that some of them might enjoy it. And the evidence is, they do.

However, apart from Moon landings, a cure for cancer or decoding the human genome, nearly all of what scientists have to tell other people through the media is inessential information, also known as soft news. Soft news still has to be topical (in order to be news at all) but it is news whose absence from the paper does not make the paper look incompetent, and hence doesn't get the science correspondent sacked. Another useful thing to remember here is that, typically, hard news comes at you; soft news has to be pushed. Hard news is also in all papers. Soft news usually has to be exclusive to be in any.

So the conclusion of this is that if you have soft news to sell, the very worst thing to do with it is put it in a press release. Why? Because then everyone has it, and that often kills it stone dead. Unfortunately, this is exactly what most institutions tend to do with their soft news, and the reason they do it is that the press officer is either badly trained or overworked (or both). Also, these rules are not inflexible. It may be a slow news day when you issue your flabby news release; you may get lucky. Now and then a soft news story does get covered from a press release, perhaps in specialist periodicals where the news values are rather lower. All this reinforces bad practice. The brutal truth is that putting out a news release is relatively quick and easy. Actually getting good coverage by building personal relationships with journalists and farming out exclusives to individuals to whom each story is deemed to be best suited is time-consuming and requires creative thought. Hence it tends to happen rather rarely.

The interfaces

The only real route to the hearts and minds of non-scientific folk lies not through 'engagement', 'consultation' and certainly not education, but effective public relations. For that alone, scientists need to be able to work with the media.

There are not very many interfaces that really matter in science communication. They are: (1) scientists directly to the public as authors and TV or radio front men (very rare); (2) scientists via journalists; (3) scientists via journalists through the medium of institutional public relations.

The second interface in this list relies simply on science journalists doing their jobs, and in the UK, science writing is not only in a better shape than anywhere else in the world, it is in better shape today than ever before, with more writers filling more space, bandwidth and airwaves than ever. More science makes the news; more scientists are doing science writing; there are more scientific documentaries on TV (though 'more', in this case, has indeed meant 'worse' in most cases). Overall, it is boom time. As Shakespeare never said about media relations, the problem lies not among our star performers but in our institutions, that they are underlings.

Few UK universities with marketable science research stories fund the effective science PR that those stories need to get out there. All is by no means darkness, and there are pockets of bright, effective talent. But, to my knowledge, very few UK universities employ a science writer or even a specialist science PR officer on its PR staff. In the USA, however, this is the standard model for science-strong universities and companies, and (moreover) one that works just as well here in the UK, as I proved over 20 years ago (more of which in a moment).

One has only to look at Penn State University, for instance, for a PR office based on this model that clearly works and actually results in real coverage, promoting the university's reputation through its research, and promoting public admiration for science as a by-product. I pick that example almost at random. Ask any science journalist about the quality of science stories that come out of US universities, and they will say the same thing.

The Warwick Experiment

In the late 1980s, Warwick University's former PR supremo Geoffrey Middleton and I researched and proved this model for university PR officers to promote their science and scientists. I have frequently held up The Warwick Experiment, as I have rather pompously named it, to conference after conference of PR officers from universities and learned societies. Although its practical success was undeniable, it has never really been duplicated because it depends on two factors that occur together in almost no press office: (1) sufficient in-house journalistic training or experience to recognize news (a knack that may be learned, but can never be taught); (2) time to devote to interviewing scientific colleagues within the university, and writing story ideas based upon those interviews for offer to locally based freelance science journalists.

Geoffrey Middleton, himself a sometime contributor to *The Guardian*, and with a reasonably well-resourced external relations office under his command, did have these things. For the purposes of the experiment I acted in the role of 'available local freelance' to whom he offered the ideas. I then went off and pitched to editors, returning, after successfully selling these ideas, to interview the scientists involved. It was a great success, achieving coverage for Warwick in *New Scientist* and *The Independent* in eight out of ten cases.

A similar method, though differently organized, produced another successful and cost-effective way of promoting a university through its science. This technique involved nothing more complex than commissioning a freelance science journalist to write the university's annual research report. I sold my services in this way for a number of years and wrote annual research reports for several science-strong universities and medical schools, including Newcastle, Salford and the Hammersmith (a postgraduate medical school) in London.

The experience of conducting back-to-back interviews for 3 or 4 days solid is gruelling; but in the course of collecting material for the official publication, I also stumbled over many stories that could form the basis of news that I could then sell into the pages of national newspapers, or of opinion or editorial pieces ideal for *New Scientist* or the (then) multiplying weekly science pages of the nationals. So, even if nobody ever read the resulting research prospectus, at least they read about the university's research in the newspapers.

I realized then that all a university need do for this process to happen universally is to develop a relationship with one or more freelance journalists, and give them similar work. The subsequent steps in the process would take care of themselves and would need little or no further management beyond the occasional helping hand. The reason for this is that everyone in the process is engaged in doing what he or she does best; reasons of self-interest ensure that each step gets done. Even better, no extra staff need be permanently employed.

If university management is nervous that the journalists thus let loose upon them will sniff out (or invent!) embarrassing scandal that will damage the institution, then it needs a good slap, which it is the media relations manager's job to administer. Freelance journalists would (of course) be failing in their professional duty if they ignored a true scandal, but universities and research institutions are really not that interesting, to be frank. Moreover, few freelances could afford to bite the hand that was feeding them, for anything other than a very good public interest reason.

However, The Warwick Experiment, in which everyone worked to their own strengths (and self-interest) to the wider benefit of science and sponsoring institutions, will only ever work when universities give the correct powers to external relations managers who really understand the media (preferably after having worked in them), and (crucially) resource them appropriately. This happens in the USA. It tends not to happen in Europe, and shows little sign of doing so because those who might do most to help it along are wasting their time 'engaging' people in public debates about science they never asked for and don't want.

Epilogue: speculation and the 24 hour news world

One of the things scientists most dislike about the media has got a lot worse since we entered the world of 24 hour news. With the Internet and 24 hour channels on satellite and cable, 'rolling news' (or 'rolling bollocks' as cynical old hands tellingly dubbed it in its early days) is insatiable in its appetite for comment and analysis. This has opened up a huge opportunity to the willing pundit; unfortunately, it is not hugely popular with scientists, who tend to want to know all the facts before they say anything.

It is also true that their reluctance to speculate about wider implications frequently betrays a simple failure to have thought about the issue properly. Very often such speculations need not stray into ineffable realms, and the invitation by a journalist to broaden out the subject is entirely reasonable. Sadly though, many scientists regard themselves as responsible for the technical details but not the wider social implications of what they do. This doesn't come across well.

Absolute refusal to speculate, unfortunately, is to stalk off the pitch and refuse to play the game, once again. It is much better for a proper scientist to go onto a programme and to explain why it is not proper to speculate, than to refuse to appear. So, if you get asked to appear prematurely, please do not misunderstand the motives of the press officer asking you. You are not being asked to do anything against your beliefs or will. You are being asked to deliver an 'informed refusal to speculate'. It sounds odd; but if you don't do it, someone else will do what you had too much scruple to do. They will then use the opportunity to peddle their own agendas, of which you will most definitely not approve.

Finally I would like to leave you this, possibly rather romantic, thought. Like research itself, if it is going to work, science promotion via the media has to be done willingly and with joy. It can be extremely hard work, but it should be fun. If it isn't, you've missed the point and you're doing it wrong.

I would like to thank the reviewers of this paper for perceptive comments that greatly improved the manuscript. I should also like to single out colleagues T. Radford and V. Parry, for our many entertaining discussions about science in the (truly) popular media, and F. Fox for her always refreshing and clear-sighted views of how science and the media engage (or, occasionally, fail to).

Suggested further reading

Fox, F. 2007. Why scientists need to speculate without speculating. http://fionafox.blogspot.com/. Leaderene of the Royal Institution's Science Media Centre makes a compelling case for scientists to participate in 24 h news speculation.

Nield, T. (various dates). *Media Monitor* articles at http://www.geolsoc.org.uk/gsl/geoscientist/media, especially 'Oh no, they love us after all', which was inspired by the OST/Wellcome Report listed below.

Nield, T. 2006. The Madness of Scientists; the pseudo-blog, at http://themadnessofscientists.blogspot.com.

OST/Wellcome Trust 2000. *Science and the public: a review of science communication and public attitudes to science in Britain*. ISBN 1 841290 25 4. Available free as PDF at www.wellcome.ac.uk or from the Marketing Department, Wellcome Trust, 183 Euston Road London NW1 2BE. E-mail marketing@wellcome.ac.uk. Essential reading; the first (and so far last) exhaustive survey of what the British public really does think about science and scientists.

Parry, V. 2002. Scientists as Communicators—how to win friends and influence people. *Journal of Molecular Biology*, **319**, 973–978. An experienced science journalist distils the experience of a lifetime spent coaxing news and good performances out of reluctant scientists.

Penn State. Take a look at the website of a truly effective university media relations operation. http://www.psu.edu/ur/presspass/.

Sense About Science. Lucretian rationalism from this worthy organization's site. http://www.senseaboutscience.org.uk/. 'Sense About Science is an independent charitable trust. We respond to the misrepresentation of science and scientific evidence on issues that matter to society, from scares about plastic bottles, fluoride and the MMR vaccine to controversies about genetic modification, stem cell research and radiation'.

Media and scientific communication: a case of climate change

MAXWELL T. BOYKOFF

Environmental Change Institute, Oxford University Centre for the Environment,
Dyson Perrins Building, University of Oxford, South Parks Road, Oxford OX1 3QY, UK
(e-mail: maxwell.boykoff@eci.ox.ac.uk)

Abstract: This paper explores how media representational practices shape and affect current international science and policy or practice communications, through a focus on climate change. Many complex factors contribute to these interactions. The norms and pressures that guide journalistic decision-making and shape mass-media coverage of anthropogenic climate science critically shape current discourses at the highly politicized climate science–policy interface. This paper investigates the multifarious journalistic, political, cultural and economic norms that dynamically influence media coverage of climate science. It explores the case-study of climate change to also work through factors shaping the translation of uncertainty in climate science. This project demonstrates that mass-media coverage of climate change is not simply a random amalgam of articles and segments; rather, it is a social relationship between scientists, policy actors and the public that is mediated by such news packages. Moreover, this research shows how mass media play a significant role in shaping the construction and maintenance of discourse on climate change at the interface of science and policy.

It can often feel like an insurmountable challenge to effectively communicate environmental geoscience via mass media. To do so, one must compress the complexities of time and spatial scales into succinct yet accurate 'sound bites' as well as crisply worded commentary. These portrayals are what are typically valued by policy actors, mass media and public citizens. Although this process can seem akin to trying to adequately summarize the contours of biogeochemistry in the space of a picture postcard, this is the challenge at hand.

In the spirit of writer John McPhee, science communication can be situated within the larger landscape of this geological time and space that is represented and described. In *Annals of the Former World*, McPhee provides the well-known analogy that the 4.6 billion year history of time on Earth can be considered like distance from fingertip to fingertip with one's arms spread wide. He writes that, 'the Cambrian begins at the wrist . . . all of the Cenozoic is in a fingerprint, and in a single stroke with a medium-grained nail file you could eradicate human history' (McPhee 1998).

Thus, perhaps it would merely take a fine-grained nail file to remove the history of science communications and mass media. Organized studies of the art of communications, called Rhetoric, began in ancient Greek and Roman times. However, it was not until the 1920s that scholars actually began to speak of such activities as 'media', as they are now widely dubbed in contemporary society (Briggs & Burke 2005). Since these early roots and through the Middle Ages and

Renaissance, media representations have encompassed a wide range of activities and modes of communication. From performance art, plays and poetry to news and debate, media portrayals have drawn on narratives, arguments, allusions and reports to communicate various themes, information, issues and events. The increasing reach of modern media communications has led to the term 'mass media'. Mass media have played an important role in translation (of information, concepts, developments, debates) between communities, such as science and the public. 'Mass media' are now commonly referred to as the publishers, editors, journalists and others who constitute this communications industry, and who translate information, through production, interpretation and dissemination, through outlets such as newspapers, magazines, television, radio and the Internet. Through human time scales, mass-media coverage has proven to be a key contributor, among a number of factors, that has shaped and affected continuing interactions between science, politics and the public. These media communications unfold within larger contexts that include elements such as regulatory frameworks, technical capacity challenges, cultural and institutional pressures, as well as journalistic norms.

This paper surveys some of these interacting factors in the production of mass-media representations, through this focus on communicating science via mass media. It explores the case-study of climate change to work through political, economic, social, cultural and journalistic pressures,

From: LIVERMAN, D. G. E., PEREIRA, C. P. G. & MARKER, B. (eds). *Communicating Environmental Geoscience*. Geological Society, London, Special Publications, **305**, 11–18.
DOI: 10.1144/SP305.3   0305-8719/08/$15.00 © The Geological Society of London 2008.

and how these influence media 'framings'. The paper then illustrates salient features of these communications through a discussion of factors shaping the translation of uncertainty in climate science. The focus here is on the production of media portrayals and associated factors, and thus does not centrally take up the complex and non-linear connections to public uptake and/or resistance as well as issues of individual (dis)engagement. However, these framing processes provide explicit links to these other arenas. Once news texts, segments and messages (from television or radio broadcasts, to printed newspapers or magazines, and Internet communications) are assembled, they compete in public spaces for attention. Moreover, these public discourses permeate and integrate to varying degrees into personal understanding and behaviour. Precisely how this information is interpreted and translated into decisions and potential behavioural change is complex, dynamic and contested, and feeds back into continuing production processes. Discussing these connected issues in detail is beyond the scope of this contribution.

Communicating (climate) science through mass media

In recent decades, studies have consistently found that the public garners much of its knowledge about science from the mass media (e.g. Nelkin 1987). In the case of climate change, research has also shown that accurate knowledge of its causes is the strongest predictor of a person's stated intentions to act (Bord et al. 2000). Thus, it is important to consider the role of mass media in current climate science, policy and practice, and examine drivers of as well as effects from these media portrayals. In other words, media representations are an important factor in public understanding and engagement with climate science, and thus deserve critical consideration.

Figure 1 tracks the quantity of 'climate change' or 'global warming' coverage in 40 of the most influential English-language world newspapers since 1987. The sample was compiled by using the *Lexis Nexis* database, and selecting articles where at least one of these terms appeared in the headline or somewhere in the first three paragraphs. These newspapers cover 17 countries across five continents, and thus provide a proxy for media attention paid to the issue over the last two decades. Media coverage of climate change or global warming increased substantially in Western Europe and North America beginning in 1988. Many factors contributed to this rise in coverage. Among them was a newsworthy speech by UK Prime Minister Margaret Thatcher to the Royal

Society of London, where she spoke out about the threat of climate change, among a host of environmental issues. She asserted, 'we may have unwittingly begun a massive experiment with the system of the planet itself' (Leggett 2001, p. x). Across the Atlantic, NASA scientist James Hansen testified to the US Congress that summer, and said he was '99 percent certain' that warmer temperatures were caused by the burning of fossil fuels and not solely a result of natural variation (Shabecoff 1988, p. A1). This was also an election year in the USA, where the issue of climate change permeated campaign promises, such as George H. W. Bush's vow to 'fight the greenhouse effect with the White House effect' (Peterson 1989, p. A1). Moreover, the summer of 1988 was one marked by extreme drought and high temperatures throughout North America. These concomitant events were thought to sensitize many, including the media community, to the issue. In the science and policy spheres, 1988 was also the year in which the United Nations Environment Program (UNEP) and World Meteorological Organization (WMO) created the Intergovernmental Panel on Climate Change (IPCC), and the WMO held a landmark international conference in Toronto, Canada called 'Our Changing Atmosphere' (Gupta 2001). Coverage increased through 1990, the year in which the IPCC First Assessment Report on climate change was released. In looking into the content of news coverage over these years of ebbs and flows in the quantity of coverage, certain events garnered particular media attention. For instance, the 1992 UN Framework Convention on Climate Change (UN FCCC), the 1997 Kyoto Protocol, and the releases of IPCC Second and Third assessment reports in 1995 and 2001 were covered heavily in Western European and North American media. Coverage in Australia, New Zealand, the Middle East, Asia, Eastern Europe and South Africa remained low overall until 1997, the year in which the Kyoto Protocol was negotiated. At the negotiations in Kyoto, Japan, registrants included 3500 journalists from over 400 media organizations in 160 countries and discussions took place regarding phases of mandatory commitments to reduce greenhouse gas emissions throughout the world (Leggett 2001).

However, the most evident increases in media attention throughout all the regions came in 2005 and 2006. Again, through examinations of the content of these news articles it is evident that specific single as well as linked events contributed to this. For instance, in 2005 the Group of Eight (G8) Summit in Gleneagles, Scotland attracted media attention, as climate change was one of the key items on the policy agenda. Moreover, Hurricane Katrina, which made landfall in August

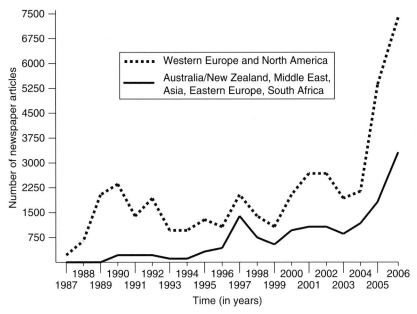

Fig. 1. Newspaper coverage of climate change or global warming. This notes the increases in quantity of coverage of climate change or global warming over time. The newspapers covered were the *Sydney Morning Herald, The Age* (Melbourne), the *Courier-Mail* (Brisbane), *The Australian*, the *Daily Telegraph* (Sydney), *Globe and Mail* (Toronto), the *Toronto Star*, the *South China Morning Post* (Hong Kong), the *Prague Post*, the *Irish Times* (Dublin), the *Jerusalem Post*, the *Jerusalem Report*, *Yomiuri Shimbun* (Tokyo), the *Japan Times* (Tokyo), *Mainichi Shimbun* (Tokyo), the *Korea Herald*, the *Korea Times* (Seoul), the *New Straits Times* (Wilayah Persekutuan), *Het Financieele Dagblad* (Eindhoven), the *New Zealand Herald* (Auckland), the *Dominion Post* (Wellington), *The Press* (Christchurch), the *Moscow News*, the *Moscow Times*, *The Straits Times* (Singapore), *Business Day* (Johannesburg), the *Financial Mail* (Johannesburg), the *Sunday Times* (Johannesburg), *The Nation* (Bangkok), *The Guardian* (London), the *Observer* (London), *The Independent* (and *The Independent on Sunday*) (London), *The Times* (and *Sunday Times*) (London), the *Financial Times* (London), *The Herald* (Glasgow), *The Scotsman* (and *Scotland on Sunday*) (Edinburgh), the *Los Angeles Times, The New York Times, U.S.A. Today* (McLean, VA), the *Wall Street Journal* (New York) and *The Washington Post*.

2005 in the Gulf Coast of the USA, garnered considerable media coverage, as the event tapped into many related issues of risk, hazards and vulnerability, as well as questions regarding what the causes were, who was responsible, and what needed to be done. In 2006, the release of the influential film *An Inconvenient Truth* with Al Gore, and the media coverage of the UK 'Stern Review' on the economic costs of climate-change mitigation, impacts and adaptation further spurred media coverage across the world.

Shifting attention more centrally to the factors shaping the content of news reports, influences are complex, non-linear and dynamic. Although climate-change science, policy and ecological–meteorological events have shaped media reporting and public understanding, journalism and public concern have also shaped climate science and policy decisions. Within the mass media, a number of intersecting political, economic, cultural, social and journalistic factors shape what is seen

as the news or Internet article and television or radio segment.

Mass-media editors and reporters must navigate through many pressures and challenges while reporting the news. These are very difficult to disentangle, as factors interact and feed back through time, as well as re-embed themselves in macro-relations (such as decision-making within the capitalist political economy) and micro-processes (such as everyday journalistic practices). For instance, micro-level journalistic decisions are made in the context of macro-level pressures, where journalist's constraints on time-to-deadlines and space exist within a predominantly corporate-controlled media environment (Bagdikian 2004). This can unavoidably limit the depth of reporting, by editors and journalists, and this situation can be particularly troubling when covering a complex issue such as climate-change science and policy (Weingart *et al.* 2000). Research has documented that deadlines and space considerations constrain

journalists (Schudson 1978), and editorial preferences and publisher pressures can affect news
reporting (Schoenfeld et al. 1979). Moreover, the
amount of exposure and placement (front page or
buried deep in the newspaper), as well as the use
of headlines and photographs, which are often
editorial decisions, can also affect how events and
situations are construed by the public.

Although many of these multifarious pressures
and norms are codified and explicit, others are
implicit, and shaped by social convention. Factors
such as access and power to affect public discourse
through ownership and media control are more
readily apparent, whereas other influences, such as
a journalist's background and training, are more
concealed. Economic considerations have led to
decreased mass-media budgets for investigative
journalism (McChesney 1999), and have led to
more journalists working as 'generalists' by covering many areas of news, rather than 'specialists' on
a particular news beat (Gans 2004). In climate
science and policy reporting, generalists are at a distinct disadvantage in terms of detailed scientific
knowledge. A lack of science training among journalists can serve as a detriment to translations of
climate-change science and policy information
(McComas & Shanahan 1999; Wilson 2000). Moreover, in the case of climate change, the biophysical
agency of the environment is centrally important, as
dramatic environmental events such as the breaking
off of a large piece of the disintegrating Larson
B ice shelf in 2003 can affect media coverage of
that and other related climate-change issues.
Above all, these multiple pressures shape and
affect the continuing process of media production.

A key function of mass-media coverage of
environmental issues has been to 'frame' them for
policy actors and the public. Generally, framing
is employed to contextualize and organize the
dynamic swirl of issues, events and occurrences. It
can be defined as the ways in which elements of
discourse are assembled that then privilege
certain interpretations and understandings over
others (Goffman 1974). Media framing involves an
inevitable series of choices to cover certain
events within a larger current of dynamic activities.
Through journalistic norms and values, certain
events become news stories, thereby shaping public
perception (Tuchman 1978; Iyengar 1991).
According to Entman, 'Framing essentially involves
selection and salience' and it 'plays a major role in
the exertion of political power, and the frame in a
news text is really the imprint of power—it registers
the identity of actors or interest that competed to
dominate the text' (Entman 1993, pp. 52–55). Asym-
metrical influences also feed back into these social
relationships and further shape emergent frames of
'news', knowledge and discourse.

Overall, various actors, both individuals and
collective, seek to access and utilize mass-media
sources to shape perceptions of environmental
issues contingent on their perspectives and interests
(Nisbet & Mooney 2007). Earlier work in media
studies of the environment has looked at the
increasing attention paid to environmental issues
through varying roles of 'interest group entrepre-
neurs', or claims-makers in constructing environmental issues as social problems (Schoenfeld
et al. 1979). Mass media represent a key arena
where such claims are communicated as well as
contested and negotiated. In this mix of pressures
and influences, a particular challenge to media coverage of climate-change science and policy, along
with many associated factors, gains salience and
thus warrants further discussion: dealing appropriately with uncertainty.

Communicating (climate) uncertainty through mass media

Uncertainty is not inherent only to scientific
inquiry; it also appears in places such as business,
marketing, and insurance endeavours, informing,
yet not prohibiting action. Inquiry contains uncertainty by definition, as it operates past the bounds
of certainty in examinations, critiques and analyses
of the unknown. Translated by mass media at the
science–policy interface, uncertainty often garners
a great deal of attention, and is a battlefield for
meaning. In past research, uncertainty has been
explored more generally in relation to media
coverage (Boffey et al. 1999; Dunwoody 1999;
Gee 2000).

Some observers regard strategic insertions of
uncertainty in anthropogenic climate-change discourse in science, as well as in the media, as a
tactic deployed by intransigent policy actors to
'invalidate the overall public concern for global
warming as an environmental–social problem'
(Williams 2000, p. 70). In this more deliberate
and often nefarious form, uncertainty can be
reframed as scientific incompetence. In the case of
climate change, oppositions have arisen primarily
in a cohesive group of 'climate contrarians',
dubbed 'climate sceptics' or the 'carbon club',
who have gained significant discursive traction
through the media, and, as a result, have
significantly affected public understanding. In
terms of environmental issues more broadly,
Freudenberg has discussed constructions of 'non-
problematicity'. Through embedded power and
leveraged legitimacy, 'if one person or social
group is able to obtain privileged access to valued
resources without having other persons or groups
challenge that privilege—or perhaps even notice

it—so much the better' (Freudenburg 2000, p. 106). Research by McCright & Dunlap has focused on this opposition movement, and has examined how climate contrarians have developed competing discourses that challenge top climate scientific evidence, and effectively gain a foothold in national and international discourse on the causes of climate change (McCright & Dunlap 2000). These researchers also examined links between contrarians and conservative think tanks, anti-environment movements and carbon-based industry (McCright & Dunlap 2003). Climate contrarians include scientists S. Fred Singer, Robert Balling, Sallie Baliunas, David Legates, Sherwood Idso, Frederick Seitz, Richard Lindzen and Patrick Michaels.

Contrarian voices, although heterogeneous in some ways, have garnered media coverage and have thus amplified uncertainty regarding various aspects of climate science, from questions of anthropogenic climate change to validity of modelling research. Research has revealed that scientific uncertainty has been a key ingredient inserted into discourse, to raise the perception of debate (Wilkins 1993; Zehr 2000). This perception of debate has often been seized upon by policy actors to justify resistance to various climate policy approaches. Policy-makers such as James Inhofe and Chuck Hagel have received extensive media coverage for their contrarian comments on climate change. Inhofe (Republican, Oklahoma), former Chair of the Senate Environment and Public Works committee, has said, 'could it be that man-made global warming is the greatest hoax ever perpetrated on the American people? It sure sounds like it' (Inhofe 2003). Senator Chuck Hagel (Republican, Nebraska) has said, 'The scientific community has simply not yet resolved the question of whether we have a problem with global warming. They have not been able to definitively conclude if the warming that has occurred in this century is due to human action or natural variations in the earth's atmosphere' (Hagel 1997).

In the summer of 1998, the Nebraska newspaper *Omaha World Herald* posed the question, 'What do Ginger Spice, Chuck Hagel and global warming have in common?' Part of the answer was that Hagel had recently held up the 'Oregon Petition', assembled by Frederick Seitz and signed by 17 000 'scientists', on the US Senate Floor. This petition questioned scientific evidence that greenhouse gases cause global warming, and stated that the USA should pull out of international climate agreement negotiations. The other part of the answer was that a number of the names listed on the petition were not actually scientists, and some were not even real people. The list included people such as Ginger Spice of the Spice Girls,

listed as 'Dr. Gerri Halliwell' as well as characters from the popular US television show MASH (Johansen 2002). None the less, this 'scientist's petition' has recirculated many times in opinion or editorial columns, interviews and commentaries in subsequent years through mass-media channels. For instance, religious leader Pat Robertson held up this petition in February 2006 on the *700 Club* program to undercut the authority of the IPCC as a 'radical environmental group that want to shut America down … [and] that have an agenda that is far beyond just helping the environment' (Robertson 2006). One can dismiss this banter as nonsense, but the discursive sway that such assertions have over their viewers warrants attention.

Organizational entities have also used aspects of uncertainty to stage disinformation campaigns via the media. Moreover, the media have at times served as a watchdog rather than a conduit for such activities, despite deliberate efforts to the contrary. Prominently illustrating both these points is the 1998 leak of a draft of an industry proposal that was developed by carbon-based industry. *The New York Times* revealed that opponents of mandatory international action regarding climate change, such as the Kyoto Protocol, put together a plan with a $600 000 budget to recruit scientists 'who share the industry's views of climate science and to train them in public relations so they can help convince journalists, politicians and the public that the risk of global warming is too uncertain to justify'. This plan was to be directed at science writers, editors, columnists and television network correspondents, and was to raise questions about and undercut the 'prevailing scientific wisdom'. Moreover, the leaked proposal stated that it would measure success 'by counting, among other things, the percentage of news articles that raise questions about climate science and the number of radio talk show appearances by scientists questioning the prevailing views'. This campaign was reportedly crafted and assembled at American Petroleum Institute offices in Washington, DC by a range of interests from major oil companies, conservative policy research organizations and trade associations (Cushman 1998, p. A1).

In 2003, a memo from US Republican strategist Frank Luntz was leaked to the press (e.g. Burkeman 2003). This memo focused on 'winning the global warming debate' and emphasized key messages that Republicans should convey to the public via mass media. Among them, the memo outlined: 'Voters believe there is *no consensus* about global warming within the scientific community… Therefore, *you need to continue to make the lack of scientific certainty a primary issue in the debate* … the scientific debate is closing (against us) but not yet closed. There is still a window of opportunity to challenge the science' (Luntz 2003, p. 142, italics in original).

Another example of policy and carbon-based industry relations' attempt to highlight uncertainties in climate science was reported through the mass media in 2005. Documents regarding the US Climate Science Program drafts in 2002 and 2003 were leaked to the press. These showed that White House Council on Environmental Quality (CEQ) Chief of Staff Phillip Cooney made edits to these documents, after they had undergone multiple drafts of peer review from experts in climate science, to weaken stated links between greenhouse gas emissions and climate change. Of note, Cooney had worked as a lobbyist for the American Petroleum Institute on climate issues before his time at the CEQ (Revkin 2005a). Cooney, who has no background in science, made subtle changes to wording and tone in many passages in the draft, and thus raised uncertainty and debate in aspects of the climate research that scientists working on the project found relatively certain, including that of anthropogenic climate change. For instance, Cooney inserted the words 'significant and fundamental' before the word 'uncertainties' in the document, thereby changing the communicated meaning (Revkin 2005a). Two days after these edits were leaked, Cooney resigned from the CEQ. Three days after that, it was announced that Cooney was hired as a consultant for ExxonMobil (Revkin 2005b).

Overall, these examples demonstrate the multifarious challenges faced when translating scientific uncertainty via mass media. Focusing on communications from scientists, it is often very difficult to place the uncertainty associated with one's research into a familiar context, through an appropriate analogy; in other words, 'translating error bars into ordinary language' (Pollack 2003, p. 77). Frankly, it is unavoidably challenging to accurately distil years of iterative research into media-friendly sound bites. As a result, most scientists need not look far, to colleagues or a mirror, to realize that climate scientists have often shied away from media interactions, thus leaving sourcing for stories to other communities for interpretation. When subject to interpretation primarily from policy actors, and interest groups (from non-governmental organizations to carbon-based industry spokespeople), there are risks that inaccurate amplification or diminution of uncertainty can obfuscate or confuse rather than clarify many important aspects of the subject. In other words, the 'battlefield' of communicating and understanding environmental geoscience is not well served by scientists reluctant to acknowledge and act on what is an integral piece of one's contemporary responsibility: interacting with mass media.

Conclusion

The focus on media and science communication of climate change, arguably the most heavily politicized scientific issue at the turn of the new millennium, provides a number of opportunities. Among them, examinations of these amplified interactions can inform and anticipate other current science issues, such as continuing concerns for toxic materials or genetically modified organisms in the environment, nanotechnological risks, and increased threats to water quality. By unpacking and analysing interactions that focus on climate science and media interactions, representative challenges ranging from extrinsic issues (e.g. political economics) to intrinsic issues (e.g. uncertainty) can inform perceptions and decision-making.

Although this case-study has focused on the challenges in science and mass-media interactions, there are also a number of opportunities for improvements. With a focus on science and media communities in this case of climate change, these opportunities also apply across other arenas of science. Beginning with the scientific community, there are many more opportunities to develop skills to more effectively work with the media. In past decades, it is well known that most reward systems within science (and academia more broadly) were structured such that little was gained professionally through increased 'non-academic' pursuits, such as media outreach (Boykoff 2007a). In fact, the opposite was true, as much could be lost, such as time spent in these endeavours. It was also widely sensed that much could be risked if one were misquoted about the implications of their research. Such impediments contributed to troubled interactions between science and media communities.

However, some argue that the situation is changing and that increased visibility through media coverage has increased public understanding of and engagement with scientific issues, increased collegial or social status, and even enhanced funding possibilities for researchers and scholars. These last benefits also hold for the university where they may be employed, thus providing a new and positive feedback loop. Although media outreach may continue to be ranked routinely below many other pressures (such as grant funding and publishing) the increasing recognition of its importance has proven to be an encouraging sign for effective communication of environmental geoscience via mass media. In addition, there are now more workshops and conferences that bring together scientists to discuss these issues (e.g. the Aldo Leopold Leadership Program) and others that bring together scientists and journalists (e.g. US National Science Foundation-funded projects).

These opportunities for discussion and critical reflection or diffraction bode well for more consistent and improved communications into the future.

In terms of media communities on the larger scale, there have been many movements in recent years for broader reforms of journalistic freedom (e.g. McChesney 1999) within the constructs of corporate media pressures (outlined above). In addition, there have been vibrant independent media movements to circumvent some of the political economic pressures of corporate control. There has also been evidence of improvements on the individual level in terms of better contextualization of the complexities of the scientific issues covered, and more precise and accurate descriptions of those quoted within stories (Boykoff 2007b). Previous research has found that situating controversial information in the larger context of the scientific issue has helped to mitigate perceived uncertainty and confusion (Corbett & Durfee 2004). In terms of the latter, *The New York Times* environment reporter Andrew Revkin has described this improvement as better capturing 'truth' through labelling. Although scientific research and scientific consensus are not 'truths' necessarily, they signify aspects of science where there is clear understanding.

Overall, this paper has sought to complement others in this volume by first delineating various challenges faced in interactions between science and mass media, and then briefly outlining some opportunities for more focused communications of environmental geoscience. By describing some of the multifarious pressures that shape interactions between climate science and mass media, this essay endeavours to more clearly identify key points of resistance and possibility as we collectively proceed with caution. Returning to McPhee, he has written, '[T]he human mind may not have evolved enough to be able to comprehend deep time' (McPhee 1998). In other words, human understanding of long-term geological time scales remains a core challenge. Thus, there are many thorny difficulties that make this endeavour a tricky one overall. However, this is the necessary task at hand in communicating environmental geoscience in the future.

References

BAGDIKIAN, B. 2004. *The Media Monopoly.* Beacon Press, Boston, MA.

BOFFEY, P. M., RODGERS, J. E. & SCHNEIDER, S. H. 1999. Interpreting uncertainty: a panel discussion. *In*: FRIEDMAN, S. M., DUNWOODY, S. & ROGERS, C. L. (eds) *Communicating Uncertainty: Media Coverage of New and Controversial Science.* Lawrence Erlbaum, Mahwah, NJ, 81–94.

BORD, R. J., O'CONNOR, R. E. & FISCHER, A. 2000. In what sense does the public need to understand global climate change? *Public Understanding of Science*, **9**, 205–218.

BOYKOFF, M. T. 2007a. From convergence to contention: United States mass media representations of anthropogenic climate science. *Transactions of the Institute of British Geographers*, **32**, 477–489.

BOYKOFF, M. T. 2007b. Flogging a dead norm? Media coverage of anthropogenic climate change in the United States and United Kingdom from 2003–2006. *Area*, **39**, 470–481.

BRIGGS, A. & BURKE, P. 2005. *A Social History of the Media: from Gutenberg to the Internet.* Polity Press, Cambridge.

BURKEMAN, O. 2003. Memo exposes Bush's new green strategy. *The Guardian*, 4 March, 1.

CORBETT, J. B. & DURFEE, J. L. 2004. Testing public (un)certainty of science: media representations of global warming. *Science Communication*, **262**, 129.

CUSHMAN, J. H. 1998. Industrial group plans to battle climate treaty. *The New York Times*, 26 April, A1.

DUNWOODY, S. 1999. Scientists, journalists, and the meaning of uncertainty. *In*: FRIEDMAN, S. M., DUNWOODY, S. & ROGERS, C. L. (eds) *Communicating Uncertainty: Media Coverage of New and Controversial Science.* Lawrence Erlbaum, Mahwah, NJ, 59–80.

ENTMAN, R. M. 1993. Framing: toward clarification of a fractured paradigm. *Journal of Communication*, **434**, 51–58.

FREUDENBURG, W. R. 2000. Social construction and social constrictions: toward analyzing the social construction of 'the naturalized' and well as 'the natural'. *In*: SPAARGAREN, G. MOL, A. P. J. & BUTTEL, F. H. (eds) *Environment and Global Modernity.* Sage, London, 103–119.

GANS, H. 2004. *Deciding What's News.* Northwestern University Press, Evanston, IL.

GEE, D. 2000. Communicating complexity and uncertainty: a challenge for the media. *In*: SMITH, J. (ed.) *The Daily Globe: Environmental Change, the Public and the Media.* Earthscan, London, 208–222.

GOFFMAN, E. 1974. *Frame Analysis: An Essay on the Organization of Experience.* Harvard University Press, Cambridge, MA.

GUPTA, J. 2001. *Our Simmering Planet: What to Do About Global Warming?* Zed Books, New York.

HAGEL, C. 1997. Countdown to Kyoto: the consequences of mandatory global CO_2 emission reductions, Canberra. World Wide Web Address: www.corpwatch.org/trac/corner/worldnews/other/355.html.

INHOFE, J. 2003. The science of climate change Senate Floor statement. US Senate, Committee on Environment and Public Works, 28 July.

IYENGAR, S. 1991. *Is Anyone Responsible?* University of Chicago Press, Chicago, IL.

JOHANSEN, B. E. 2002. *The Global Warming Desk Reference.* Greenwood Press, Westport, CT.

LEGGETT, J. K. 2001. *The Carbon War: Global Warming and the End of the Oil Era.* Routledge, New York.

LUNTZ, F. 2003. *The Environment: A Cleaner, Safer, Healthier America.* The Luntz Research Companies–Straight Talk, Washington, DC, 131–146.

MCCHESNEY, R. W. 1999. *Rich Media, Poor Democracy: Communication Politics in Dubious Times*. University of Illinois Press, Urbana, IL.

MCCOMAS, K. & SHANAHAN, J. 1999. Telling stories about global climate change: measuring the impact of narratives on issue cycles. *Communication Research*, **261**, 30–57.

MCCRIGHT, A. M. & DUNLAP, R. E. 2000. Challenging global warming as a social problem: an analysis of the conservative movement's counter-claims. *Social Problems*, **474**, 499–522.

MCCRIGHT, A. M. & DUNLAP, R. E. 2003. Defeating Kyoto: the conservative movement's impact on US climate change policy. *Social Problems*, **503**, 348–373.

MCPHEE, J. 1998. *Annals of the Former World*. Farrar Straus Giroux, London.

NELKIN, D. 1987. *Selling Science: How the Press Covers Science and Technology*. W. H. Freeman, New York.

NISBET, M. C. & MOONEY, C. 2007. Framing science. *Science*, **3166**, 56.

PETERSON, C. 1989. Experts, OMB spar on global warming: 'greenhouse effect' may be accelerating, scientists tell hearing. *The Washington Post*, 9 May, A1.

POLLACK, H. 2003. Can the media help science? *Skeptic*, **102**, 73–80.

REVKIN, A. 2005a. Bush aide edited climate reports. *The New York Times*, 8 June, A1.

REVKIN, A. 2005b. Former Bush aide who edited reports is hired by Exxon. *The New York Times*, 15 June, A21.

ROBERTSON, P. 2006. Evangelism and environment. *700 Club*, 9 February.

SCHOENFELD, A. C., MEIER, R. F. & GRIFFIN, R. J. 1979. Constructing a social problem: the press and the environment. *Social Problems*, **271**, 38–61.

SCHUDSON, M. 1978. *Discovering the News: A Social History of American Newspapers*. Basic Books, New York.

SHABECOFF, P. 1988. Global warming has begun, expert tells Senate. *The New York Times*, 24 June, A1.

TUCHMAN, G. 1978. *Making News: A Study in the Construction of Reality*. Free Press, New York.

WEINGART, P., ENGELS, A. & PANSEGRAU, P. 2000. Risks of communication: discourses on climate change in science, politics, and the mass media. *Public Understanding of Science*, **9**, 261–283.

WILKINS, L. 1993. Between the facts and values: print media coverage of the greenhouse effect, 1987–1990. *Public Understanding of Science*, **2**, 71–84.

WILLIAMS, J. 2000. The phenomenology of global warming: the role of proposed solutions as competitive factors in the public arenas of discourse. *Human Ecology Review*, **72**, 63–72.

WILSON, K. M. 2000. Communicating climate change through the media: predictions, politics, and perceptions of risk. *In*: ALLAN, S., ADAM, B. & CARTER, C. (eds) *Environmental Risks and the Media*. Routledge, London, 201–217.

ZEHR, S. C. 2000. Public representations of scientific uncertainty about global climate change. *Public Understanding of Science*, **9**, 85–103.

Good and bad practice in the communication of uncertainties associated with the relationship between climate change and weather-related natural disasters

ROBERT E. T. WARD

Risk Management Solutions, Peninsular House, 30 Monument Street, London EC3R 8NB, UK (e-mail: bob.ward@rms.com)

Abstract: There is evidence that climate change is affecting the frequency, intensity and geographical distribution of weather-related natural disasters. However, the exact details of this relationship are subject to varying degrees of uncertainty. Scientists, policy-makers and others have recognized how this connection could influence public support for decisions and policies around climate change, such as measures to reduce greenhouse gas emissions. This has led to a number of cases in which stakeholders in the public policy debate about climate change have overstated or understated uncertainties, relative to the scientific assessments of the Intergovernmental Panel on Climate Change. Although such distortions in the expression of uncertainties are motivated by a desire to justify particular policy positions, they could instead undermine the credibility of, and trust in, information sources and diminish public support.

Uncertainty is a fundamental feature of research in the geosciences. Indeed, it is often the fact that our knowledge and understanding is incomplete and uncertain that provides the impetus for research. But uncertainties take on added importance in research on natural disasters because of its implications for public policy. In this case, the effective and appropriate communication of uncertainties by scientists to other groups such as policy-makers, the public and the media, is vital to allow informed decision-making about limiting the exposure and vulnerability of people and their property to natural hazards.

One of the most significant public policy issues relating to natural disasters at present is the potential impact of climate change on millions of people worldwide through its influence on the frequency, intensity and geographical distribution of extreme weather events, such as floods, droughts and tropical cyclones. These effects are particularly important in the context of the public policy debate about the options for mitigating and adapting to climate change.

For instance, Christiansen (2003) suggested that 'owing to the somewhat intangible link between for instance road traffic and increasing temperatures, extreme weather events like flood and heat waves could have a greater impact than increased scientific evidence in terms of increasing public demand for policy action'. This echoed the statement by Crispin Tickell, the former representative for the UK at the United Nations, who is widely credited with having persuaded Margaret Thatcher during her period as Prime Minister to take climate change seriously as a

political issue, pointing out that 'apart from where there is suffering from unexpected heat or cold, flood or drought, it is always hard to give climate change the appropriate urgency' (Tickell 2002).

With the relationship between climate change and weather-related natural disasters having such an influence over the public policy debate, clear communication of the nature and extent of uncertainties has become vital. This paper considers how uncertainties have been communicated by the research community and by various other stakeholders in the public debate in the UK and the USA, in the period between the publication by the Intergovernmental Panel on Climate Change (IPCC) of its Third Assessment Report in 2001 and its Fourth Assessment Report in 2007.

IPCC assessments of the relationship between climate change and weather-related natural disasters

The work of the IPCC is recognized by scientists around the world as representing the research community's consensus on the causes and consequences of climate change. In May 2001, 17 national academies of science published a statement (Australian Academy of Sciences *et al.* 2001), supporting the IPCC and endorsing the main findings of its Third Assessment Report (IPCC 2001*d*). Given the support from the researchers for the IPCC, it is considered appropriate for the purposes of this study to use its assessments of the relationship between climate change and weather-related

From: LIVERMAN, D. G. E., PEREIRA, C. P. G. & MARKER, B. (eds) *Communicating Environmental Geoscience*. Geological Society, London, Special Publications, **305**, 19–37.
DOI: 10.1144/SP305.4   0305-8719/08/$15.00 © The Geological Society of London 2008.

natural disasters as the standard work against which to compare the communication activities of others.

The IPCC Third Assessment Report was published in four separate volumes during the course of 2001, representing the findings of three working groups, together with a synthesis of the conclusions of all three groups. Working Group I focused on the science of climate change, Working Group II considered impacts, adaptation and vulnerability, and Working Group III concentrated on mitigation. Each of the four volumes consisted of two main parts: a technical report and a 'summary for policymakers'. The IPCC Fourth Assessment Report followed the same broad procedure with the publication of four volumes during 2007. In both of the assessment reports, information about climate change and weather-related natural disasters was contained in the volumes on the science and on impacts, vulnerability and adaptation, as well as the synthesis report. As the primary focus here is on communication within the context of the public policy debate, the 'summary for policymakers' from the synthesis reports of both the Third and Fourth Assessment Reports are the most relevant, given that they were aimed at a wider audience than the research community and received widespread coverage from the media.

'Summary for policymakers' from the synthesis report of the IPCC Third Assessment Report

This 34 page document (IPCC 2001*d*) was launched at a press conference on 1 October 2001 and accompanied by a press conference. One of the key features of it, and the other parts of the Third Assessment Report, was the use of qualitative descriptors of uncertainty accompanied by quantified ranges. The following explanation appeared in a box on page 5 of the document under the title 'Confidence and likelihood statements': 'Where appropriate, the authors of the Third Assessment Report assigned confidence levels that represent their collective judgment in the validity of a conclusion based on observational evidence, modeling results, and theory that they have examined. The following words have been used throughout the text of the Synthesis Report to the TAR [Third Assessment Report] relating to WGI [Working Group I] finding: *virtually certain* (greater than 99% chance that a result is true); *very likely* (90–99% chance); *likely* (66–90% chance); *medium likelihood* (33–66% chance); *unlikely* (10–33% chance); *very unlikely* (1–10% chance); and exceptionally *unlikely* (less than 1% chance). An explicit uncertainty range ($\pm$) is a *likely* range. Estimates of confidence relating to WGII [Working Group II]

findings are: *very high* (95% or greater), *high* (67–95%), *medium* (33–67%), *low* (5–33%), and *very low* (5% or less). No confidence levels were assigned in WGIII [Working Group III]'.

The document used these qualitative descriptors in its discussion of the connection between climate change and extreme weather events, and the consequences. It noted that it was 'likely' that, during the 20th century, heavy precipitation events increased at mid- and high latitudes, and that there was increased summer drying and associated incidence of drought in a few areas, with the frequency and intensity of droughts increasing in the last decades in some regions, such as parts of Asia and Africa. It also indicated that global mean sea level rise at an average annual rate of 1–2 mm during the 20th century. But it pointed out that 'there are conflicting analyses and insufficient data to assess changes in intensities of tropical and extra-tropical cyclones and severe local storm activity in the mid-latitudes'.

In relation to the impact of extreme weather events, the document indicated that global inflation-adjusted economic losses rose an order of magnitude over the last four decades of the 20th century, but noted that '[p]art of the observed upward trend is linked to socio-economic factors and part is linked to climatic factors'. It also stated: 'Preliminary indications suggest that some social and economic systems have been affected by recent increases in floods and droughts, with increases in economic losses for catastrophic weather events. However, because these systems are also affected by changes in socio-economic factors such as demographic shifts and land-use changes, quantifying the negative impact of climate change (either anthropogenic or natural) and socio-economic factors is difficult'.

The document also indicated that 'changes in frequency, intensity, and duration of extreme events, such as more hot days, heat waves, heavy precipitation events, and fewer cold days' were projected under the six scenarios generated by models for the evolution of greenhouse gas concentrations in the atmosphere that were described in the IPCC *Special Report on Emissions Scenarios* (SRES; Nakićenović *et al.* 2000). It presented examples of climate variability and extreme weather events, and their projected impacts (listed in Table 1). The notes accompanying the table pointed out that the impacts 'can be lessened by appropriate response measures'.

'Summary for policymakers' from the synthesis report of the IPCC Fourth Assessment Report

This 23 page document (IPCC 2007*a*) was launched at a press conference on 17 November 2007. Unlike

Table 1. *Climate variability and extreme climate events and examples of their impacts cited by the IPCC (2001d)*

Projected changes during the 21st century in extreme climate phenomena and their likelihood	Representative examples of projected impacts (all high confidence of occurrence in some areas)
Higher maximum temperatures, more hot days and heat waves over nearly all land areas (very likely)	Increased incidence of death and serious illness in older age groups and urban poor Increased heat stress in livestock and wildlife Shift in tourist destinations Increased risk of damage to a number of crops Increased electric cooling demand and reduced energy supply reliability
Higher (increasing) minimum temperatures, fewer cold days, frost days and cold waves over nearly all land areas (very likely)	Decreased cold-related human morbidity and mortality Decreased risk of damage to a number of crops, and increased risk to others Extended range and activity of some pest and disease vectors Reduced heating energy demand
More intense precipitation events (very likely, over many areas)	Increased flood, landslide, avalanche, and mudslide damage Increased soil erosion Increased flood runoff could increase recharge of some floodplain aquifers Increased pressure on government and private flood insurance systems and disaster relief
Increased summer drying over most mid-latitude continental interiors and associated risk of drought (likely)	Decreased crop yields Increased damage to building foundations caused by ground shrinkage Decreased water resource quantity and quality Increased risk of forest fire
Increase in tropical cyclone peak wind intensities, mean and peak precipitation intensities (likely, over some areas; changes in regional distribution of tropical cyclones are possible but have not been established)	Increased risks to human life, risk of infectious disease epidemics and many other risks Increased coastal erosion and damage to coastal buildings and infrastructure Increased damage to coastal ecosystems such as coral reefs and mangroves
Intensified droughts and floods associated with El Niño events in many different regions (likely)	Decreased agricultural and rangeland productivity in drought- and flood-prone regions Decreased hydro-power potential in drought-prone regions
Increased Asian summer monsoon precipitation variability (likely)	Increase in flood and drought magnitude and damages in temperate and tropical Asia
Increased intensity of mid-latitude storms (little agreement between current models)	Increased risks to human life and health Increased property and infrastructure losses Increased damage to coastal ecosystems

the corresponding document from the Third Assessment Report, it did not include information about the qualitative descriptors of uncertainty, but instead referred to details contained in the technical report (IPCC 2007b). The descriptors were very similar, but not identical, to those used in the Third Assessment Report. It noted that the findings of Working Group I primarily employed 'likelihood assessments': 'Where uncertainty in specific outcomes is assessed using expert judgment and statistical analysis of a body of evidence (e.g. observations or model results), then the following likelihood ranges are used to express the assessed probability of occurrence: *virtually certain* >99%; *extremely likely* >95%; *very likely* >90%; *likely* >66%; *more likely than not* >50%; *about as likely as not* 33% to 66%; *unlikely* <33%; *very unlikely* <10%; *extremely unlikely* <5%; *exceptionally unlikely* <1%'.

The findings of Working Group II used a combination of likelihood assessments and confidence: 'Where uncertainty is assessed more quantitatively using expert judgement of the correctness of underlying data, models or analyses, then the following scale of confidence levels is used to express the assessed chance of a finding being correct: *very high confidence* at least 9 out of 10; *high confidence* about 8 out of 10; *medium confidence* about 5 out of 10; *low confidence* about 2 out of 10; and *very low confidence* less than 1 out of 10'.

In terms of assessing the impact of climate change on weather-related natural disasters, the document concluded: 'It is *likely* that: heat waves have become more frequent over most land areas, the frequency of heavy precipitation events has increased over most areas, and since 1975 the incidence of extreme high sea level [the highest 15 of hourly values of observed sea level at a station for a given reference period] has increased worldwide'. It also noted that there is 'observational evidence of an increase in intense tropical cyclone activity in the North Atlantic since about 1970, with limited evidence of increases elsewhere', although there is 'no clear trend in the annual numbers of tropical cyclones'.

It also indicated that there was 'medium confidence' that regional effects of climate change on natural and human environments are 'emerging', but 'many are difficult to discern due to adaptation and non-climatic drivers'. But it concluded that research since the publication of the Third Assessment Report (IPCC 2001*d*) showed that 'discernible human influences extend beyond average temperature to other aspects of climate', and that '[h]uman influences have:

1. very likely contributed to sea level rise during the latter half of the 20th century;
2. likely contributed to changes in wind patterns, affecting extra-tropical storm tracks and temperature patterns;
3. likely increased temperatures of extreme hot nights, cold nights and cold days; and
4. more likely than not increased risk of heat waves, area affected by drought since the 1970s and frequency of heavy precipitation events'.

In terms of potential future impacts, the document indicated that there is 'now higher confidence' than expressed in the IPCC Third Assessment Report in projected patterns of warming and other regional-scale features, including a 'very likely increase in frequency of hot extremes, heat waves, and heavy precipitation'; a 'likely increase in tropical cyclone intensity; less confidence in global decrease of tropical cyclone numbers'; and a 'poleward shift of extra-tropical storm tracks with consequent changes in wind, precipitation, and temperature patterns'.

The document concluded: 'Altered frequencies and intensities of extreme weather, together with sea level rise, are expected to have mostly adverse

effects on natural and human systems'. It provided a table (see Table 2) bearing details of potential impacts, identifying examples of extreme weather, climate and sea-level events that are expected to become, as a result of climate change, more frequent, more widespread and/or more intense during the 21st century, based on the projections from the *Special Report on Emissions Scenarios* (SRES; Nakićenović & Swart 2000).

The notes accompanying the table stressed that these impacts do not take into account 'any changes or developments in adaptive capacity'. The document suggested that there is 'high confidence that neither adaptation nor mitigation alone can avoid all climate change impacts; however, they can complement each other and together can significantly reduce the risks of climate change'. However, it also pointed out that '[r]esponses to some recent extreme events reveal higher levels of vulnerability' than documented in the Third Assessment Report (IPCC 2001*b*), and that there was 'higher confidence in the projected increases in droughts, heatwaves, and floods as well as their adverse impacts'.

Criticisms of the communication of uncertainties by the IPCC

Although the work of the IPCC is supported by national science academies (Australian Academy of Sciences *et al.* 2001) and other scientific organizations around the world, it has also been criticized for, among other things, its communication of uncertainties. For instance, the National Research Council (2001) of the US National Academies identified discrepancies in the way that uncertainty was covered by different parts of the contribution by Working Group I to the IPCC Third Assessment Report. It suggested that the 'summary for policymakers' (IPCC 2001*a*) differed from the 'technical summary' (Houghton *et al.* 2001) because it 'frequently uses terms (e.g. likely, very likely, unlikely) that convey levels of uncertainty; however, the text less frequently includes either their basis or caveats'. The National Research Council (2001) warned that, as a result, the IPCC (2001*a*) 'could give an impression that the science of global warming is "settled", even though many uncertainties remain'.

Patt & Dessai (2005) recommended that the text of IPCC reports should both use qualitative descriptors and 'remind readers of the probability ranges the specific language represents'. Patt & Schrag (2003) concluded that the use of qualitative descriptors in the IPCC Third Assessment Report had the advantage that laypeople would find them easier to relate to than numerical expressions of

Table 2. *Examples of possible changes in extreme weather, climate and sea-level events during the 21st century; their likelihoods, and their impacts on four broad sectors (after IPCC 2007b)*

Phenomenon and direction of trend	Likelihood of future trends based on projections for 21st century using SRES scenarios	Examples of major projected impacts by sector			
		Agriculture, forestry and ecosystems	Water resources	Human health	Industry, settlement and society
Over most land areas, warmer and fewer cold days and nights, warmer and more frequent hot days and nights	Virtually certain (warming of most extreme days and nights each year)	Increased yields in colder environments; decreased yields in warmer environments; increased insect outbreaks	Effects on water resources relying on snow melt; effects on some water supply	Reduced human mortality from decreased cold exposure	Reduced energy demand for heating; increased demand for cooling; declining air quality in cities; reduced disruption to transport owing to snow, ice; effects on winter tourism
Warm spells or heat waves Frequency increases over most land areas	Very likely	Reduced yields in warmer regions owing to heat stress; wild fire danger increase	Increased water demand; water quality problems, e.g. algal blooms	Increased risk of heat-related mortality especially for the elderly, chronically sick, very young and socially isolated	Reduction in quality of life for people in warm areas without appropriate housing; impacts on elderly, very young and poor
Heavy precipitation events Frequency increases over most areas	Very likely	Damage to crops; soil erosion; inability to cultivate land because of waterlogging of soils	Adverse effects on quality of surface and groundwater; contamination of water supply; water scarcity may be relieved	Increased risk of deaths, injuries, infectious, respiratory and skin diseases	Disruption of settlements, commerce, transport and societies because of flooding; pressures on urban and rural infrastructures; loss of property
Area affected by drought increases	Likely	Land degradation, lower yields or crop damage and failure; increased livestock deaths; increased risk of wildfire	More widespread water stress	Increased risk of food and water shortage; increased risk of malnutrition; increased risk of water- and food-borne diseases	Water shortages for settlements, industry and societies; reduced hydropower generation potentials; potential for population migration

(Continued)

Table 2. *Continued*

Phenomenon and direction of trend	Likelihood of future trends based on projections for 21st century using SRES scenarios	Examples of major projected impacts by sector				
		Agriculture, forestry and ecosystems	Water resources	Human health	Industry, settlement and society	
Intense tropical cyclone activity increases	Likely	Damage to crops; uprooting of trees; damage to coral reefs	Power outages cause disruption of public water supply	Increased risk of deaths, injuries, water- and food-borne diseases; post-traumatic stress disorders	Disruption by flood and high winds; withdrawal of risk coverage in vulnerable areas by private insurers; potential for population migrations; loss of property	
Increased incidence of extreme high sea level (defined as highest 1% of hourly values of observed sea level at a station for a given reference period; excludes tsunamis)	Likely	Salinization of irrigation water, estuaries and freshwater systems	Decreased freshwater availability owing to saltwater intrusion	Increased risk of deaths and injuries by drowning in floods; migration-related health effects	Costs of coastal protection versus costs of land-use relocation; potential for movement of populations and infrastructure	

probability, but warned that they tended to be misinterpreted because they were thought to relate to risk (i.e. probability and consequence). The authors noted that people tend to assume 'a certain amount of exaggeration about the likelihood of high magnitude events', and corrected for this effect during interpretation. As a result, people underestimated the probability of extreme impacts of climate change described by the report.

One further potential criticism of the 'summary for policymakers' from the synthesis reports of both the IPCC Third Assessment Report and Fourth Assessment Report is that they did not include any discussion of the extent to which individual extreme weather events could be attributed with any certainty to anthropogenic climate change. As will be shown in later sections, this issue has caused confusion among some stakeholders in the public policy debate. Instead, the 'technical summary' (Solomon et al. 2007) from the contribution of Working Group I to the Fourth Assessment Report tackled this issue, noting: 'People affected by an extreme weather event (e.g. the extremely hot summer in Europe in 2003, or the heavy rainfall in Mumbai, India in July 2005) often ask whether human influences on the climate are responsible for the event. A wide range of extreme weather events is expected in most regions even with an unchanging climate, so it is difficult to attribute any individual event to a change in the climate'. Solomon et al. (2007) also pointed out that 'several factors usually need to combine to produce an extreme event, so linking a particular extreme event to a single, specific cause is problematic'.

Despite the criticisms, the 'summary for policymakers' from the synthesis reports of the IPCC Third Assessment Report and the Fourth Assessment Report provide a good baseline against which to judge the accuracy and appropriateness of contributions by stakeholders in the public policy debate about climate change.

Good practice in communicating uncertainties about the relationship between climate change and weather-related natural disasters

This section summarizes the findings of research on good practice in communicating uncertainties about climate change generally, and specifically in relation to extreme weather events, particularly within the context of the public policy debate.

Moser & Dilling (2004) asked whether 'those communicating climate change to the public and to decisionmakers set in motion a sufficiently strong momentum that policy and social changes will now take their due course', and echoed Tickell (2002) by concluding that 'there is arguably an insufficient sense of urgency about climate change'. Moser & Dilling (2004) identified as one of the barriers that 'scientists frequently emphasize the complexities and uncertainties in academic and public communications'. The authors indicated that '[e]xperience and observations of people's reactions to statements about scientific uncertainty show, however, that a first message about uncertainty gives listeners the permission to dismiss or turn attention away from what follows'. They recommended that the most important option for increasing the persuasiveness of communication is 'to lead with the strongest argument—that is, with the greatest scientific certainty and confidence'.

Leiserowitz (2006) recommended talking openly about uncertainties over the impacts of climate change, but warned that communicators should never overstate certainty: 'Definitive claims based on uncertain science are vulnerable to attack, potentially mislead the public, and can irrevocably destroy trust and credibility'. He recommended that explanations should be offered for why uncertainties exist and to 'recognise that scientific uncertainty alone is not an adequate justification for inaction or business-as-usual'.

Leiserowitz (2006) outlined five strategies for climate-change communications, and pointed out that 'extreme events happen each year and thus provide recurring "teachable moments" to explain the potential impacts of climate change'. He noted that no specific events could be said to be caused by global warming, but that these events 'are consistent with scientists' projections of the future impacts of global warming and may be harbingers of things to come'.

Marx et al. (2007) described evidence that people generally use both experiential processing, which relates current situations to memories of experience, and analytic processing, which includes mechanisms to relate the current situation to ordered collections of past relevant experience, to understand information about uncertainties and risks associated with climate change. Marx et al. concluded that although most communications sought to engage analytic processing, '[v]icarious experiential information in the form of scenarios, narratives, and analogies can help the public and policy makers imagine the potential consequences of climate variability and change, amplify or attenuate risk perceptions, and influence both individual and behavioral intentions and public policy preferences'. They warned, however, that experiential processing is subject to biases, limitations and distortions.

Examples of bad practice in communicating uncertainties about the relationship with natural disasters caused by extreme weather events

The preceding section outlined good practice in communicating the uncertainties surrounding the connection between climate change and weather-related natural disasters. However, there are numerous examples from the past few years where key stakeholders in the public policy debate about climate change have inadvertently or deliberately disregarded good practice. Bad practice has included direct attribution of single natural disasters (e.g. the European summer heatwave in 2003; Hurricane Katrina in 2005; UK summer floods in 2007) to climate change, and exaggerating uncertainty in the relationship between climate change and weather-related natural disasters.

Below we consider examples of bad practice by the following stakeholders: scientists; policy-makers and politicians; environmental lobby groups; 'free market' lobby groups; energy companies; the media.

Scientists

Although the IPCC has made efforts through its assessment reports in 2001 and 2007 to exercise good practice in communicating to policy-makers the uncertainties in the relationship between climate change and weather-related natural disasters, there are a number of examples of scientists displaying bad practice during the intervening period.

One example has been the direct attribution of the European summer heatwave in 2003 to climate change. According to the International Federation of Red Cross and Red Crescent Societies (2004), the heatwave (primarily between 1 and 15 August) caused between 22 000 and 35 000 deaths and economic losses of US$13 billion. Allen & Lord (2004) pointed out that the immediate cause of the heatwave was a persistent anticyclone over NW Europe, and the authors stated that 'no one could sensibly claim that greenhouse gases caused that particular anticyclone'.

However, the press release accompanying the publication of a paper by Stott et al. (2004) made exactly that claim. The paper itself considered how the probability of a heatwave of a magnitude comparable with that which occurred in Europe in summer 2003 had changed as a result of human activities. Stott et al. estimated that the probability of the mean temperature exceeding the second warmest summer on record, in 2001, had increased from less than one in 1000 years to one in 250 years

as a result of anthropogenic warming. After calculating a 'fraction attributable risk', the authors concluded that '[u]sing a threshold for mean summer temperature that was exceeded in 2003, but in no other year since the start of the instrumental record in 1851, we estimate it is very likely (confidence level >90%) that human influence has at least doubled the risk of a heatwave exceeding this threshold magnitude'.

Those researchers also emphasized that '[i]t is an ill-posed question whether the 2003 heatwave was caused, in a simple deterministic sense, by modification of the external influences on climate—for example, increasing concentrations of greenhouse gases in the atmosphere—because almost any such weather event might have occurred by chance in an unmodified climate'. Yet the title of the paper, 'Human contribution to the European heatwave of 2003', appeared to offer an answer to this 'ill-posed question', as did the headline of the accompanying media release ('Man mostly to blame for 2003 heatwave') that was issued by the Met Office (2004).

Other researchers have also fallen into the trap of attributing the 2003 heatwave at least partially to anthropogenic climate change. For instance, the Royal Society for the Encouragement of Arts, Manufactures and Commerce produced a booklet by David King, the Chief Scientific Adviser to the UK Government, to introduce the science of climate change (King 2007). It included a warning that '[w]e have always experienced extreme events and one of the traps in talking about climate change is to attribute a given extreme event as part of a global trend'. However, in the following paragraph, King referred to the 2003 European heatwave and stated '[i]t has been subjected to a very detailed statistical analysis and as a result, with 90% certainty, we can say that half the severity of that heat wave can be attributed to global warming'.

There is also evidence of researchers attributing Hurricane Katrina to climate change in the public policy arena. The hurricane formed as a tropical storm off the coast of the Bahamas on 23 August 2005. Over the next week, the storm developed into a hurricane, reaching landfall first in Florida, and then along the Gulf of Mexico in Mississippi, Louisiana and Alabama. According to the Katrina Lessons Learned Review Group (2006), Hurricane Katrina is known to have caused 1330 deaths and estimated damage of $96 billion in the USA, with 2096 people still considered missing at 17 February 2006. The Katrina Lessons Learned Review Group (2006) described Hurricane Katrina as 'the most destructive natural disaster in US history', in terms of damage to property.

Some researchers claimed that Hurricane Katrina, or at least some characteristics of the storm, could be attributed to climate change. For instance, a news report (Eilperin 2005) in the *Washington Post* on 30 August 2005 stated: 'Kevin E. Trenberth, who heads the climate analysis section at the nonprofit National Center for Atmospheric Research, said all of these environmental factors help explain why flooding from Hurricane Katrina may stretch as far north as Canada. "There's a clear signature of global warming in this", he said. "While it's not the dominant factor, in some things it becomes the straw that breaks the camel's back."'

Similarly, Trenberth was quoted in another news report (Dye 2005) published on the Web on 14 September, stating: 'Global warming didn't create Katrina. But research indicates it enhanced it. "Our estimate is that rainfall from Katrina was about 7 percent enhanced by global warming," says Kevin Trenberth, head of the climate analysis section of the National Center for Atmospheric Research in Boulder, Colo'. In addition, in a public seminar on 25 October 2005 for the American Meteorological Society, Trenberth (2005) included a slide on 'How big is the effect from global warming', which suggested that climate change would lead to 'Increases in rainfall and latent heat release in storms: order 8%' and 'Implies $1''$ extra rain near New Orleans in Katrina'.

Other scientists publicly acknowledged that attribution could not be made with any certainty, but suggested that there might be some benefit if members of the public did so mistakenly. Judith Curry, a researcher at the Georgia Institute of Technology, commented on a web log that 'Hurricane Katrina, even tho [sic] there was no direct causal link with global warming, has served as a huge wakeup call to the American public that global warming might actually have some seriously adverse impacts if we were to see such storms more frequently in the future (this issue seems to have a much greater impact on the public than melting of polar ice caps)' (Curry 2006).

But it was not only in the USA that attempts were made by scientists to attribute single hurricanes in 2005 to climate change. An article published on 23 September 2005 in *The Independent* newspaper in the UK, about the progress of Hurricane Rita towards the coastline of the USA, was given the headline 'This is global warming, says environmental chief', with the subheading: 'As Hurricane Rita threatens devastation, scientist blames climate change' (McCarthy 2005). The article included the following statement in its second paragraph: 'The growing violence of storms such as Katrina, which wrecked New Orleans, and Rita, now threatening Texas, is very

probably caused by climate change, said Sir John Lawton, chairman of the Royal Commission on Environmental Pollution'. The fourth paragraph included a quote from Lawton about the perceived effect of Hurricane Rita being attributed to climate change: 'Referring to the arrival of Hurricane Rita he said: "If this makes the climate loonies in the States realise we've got a problem, some good will come out of a truly awful situation."'

It is interesting to contrast these comments with the remarks attributed in an online news report (BBC 2001) to Peter Ewins, when chief executive of the Met Office, about attempts by some policymakers to link individual extreme weather events to climate change: 'My criticism is reserved for some people in Brussels and elsewhere in Europe who seem to suggest that one-off severe weather events are in themselves proof of global warming. These statements do damage the case, which we think is so strong. It is easy for the Bush administration to rubbish the idea that a one-off severe event, like a flood or a drought, is caused by global warming, and therefore it makes it easier for them to refute the whole European stance'. Thus Ewins (BBC 2001) expected opposite political consequences, compared with those anticipated by Lawton (McCarthy 2005) and Curry (2006), from attempts to directly attribute single weather-related natural disasters to climate change.

It should be acknowledged that some members of the research community attempted to counter the mistaken assertion that climate change could be conclusively confirmed, or ruled out, as the cause of Hurricane Katrina. For instance, the web log realclimate.org posted an entry by Rahmstorf *et al.* (2005), stating that 'there is no way to prove that Katrina either was, or was not, affected by global warming'. Rahmstorf *et al.* went on to point out that the uncertainty is so great that '[f]or a single event, regardless of how extreme, such attribution is fundamentally impossible', and used the excellent analogy of a 'loaded' dice to illustrate the concept clearly: 'The situation is analogous to rolling loaded dice: one could, if one was so inclined, construct a set of dice where sixes occur twice as often as normal. But if you were to roll a six using these dice, you could not blame it specifically on the fact that the dice had been loaded. Half of the sixes would have occurred anyway, even with normal dice. Loading the dice simply doubled the odds'.

Policy-makers and politicians

On 5 March 2001, the IPCC published the 'summary for policymakers' (IPCC 2001*c*) from the contribution on mitigation by Working Group

III to the Third Assessment Report. The document outlined a number of options for reducing emissions of carbon dioxide and other greenhouse gases with the aim of stabilizing atmospheric concentrations.

Yet the immediate responses from the political leaders of the UK and the USA showed very different approaches to the careful assessment by the IPCC of uncertainties associated with the relationship between climate change and weather-related natural disasters.

The Prime Minister of the UK, Tony Blair, delivered a speech on 6 March 2001 in which he discarded the conditional statements of the IPCC reports in favour of assertions such as 'climate change will also mean ever more extreme rainfall and flooding, and increasingly severe tropical storms' (Blair 2001). He went on to warn that it 'would be irresponsible to treat these predictions as scare-mongering'. Other parts of his speech included praise for the Kyoto Protocol as 'a monument to enlightened global diplomacy' because it meant '[f]or the first time, developed countries agreed to take on legally binding targets to cut their emissions'. The Protocol was introduced in 1997 to provide binding targets for industrialized countries to reduce emissions of carbon dioxide and other greenhouse gases.

In contrast, the President of the USA, George W. Bush, wrote a letter to a group of Senators, published on 13 March 2001, in which he expressed his opposition to the Kyoto Protocol because it 'would cause serious harm to the US economy' (Bush 2001). The letter did not acknowledge the potential impacts of climate change, such as changes in extreme weather events, that were outlined in the IPCC Third Assessment Report, but emphasized instead 'the incomplete state of scientific knowledge of the causes of, and solutions to, global climate change'.

Hence, Prime Minister Blair highlighted extreme events as one of the impacts of climate change, while expressing less uncertainty than the IPCC Third Assessment Report, partly to justify his support for the Kyoto Protocol. President Bush, on the other hand, did not refer to extreme events, while expressing greater uncertainty than the IPCC Third Assessment Report, partly to justify his opposition to the Kyoto Protocol.

Dessler & Parson (2006) noted similarities between the argument first put forward by President Bush in March 2001, to explain why his administration would not ratify the Kyoto Protocol, and the communication strategy advocated in a document produced by Luntz Research Companies (2002), which was aimed at Republican Party supporters, and reported by the *New York Times* newspaper (Lee 2003). In a section on 'Winning the global warming debate—an overview', the document produced by Luntz Research Companies (2002) advised readers to keep in mind five 'communication recommendations as you address global warming in general, particularly as Democrats and opinion leaders attack President Bush over Kyoto', of which the first was: '*The scientific debate remains open*. Voters believe that there is *no consensus* about global warming within the scientific community. Should the public come to believe that the scientific issues are settled, their views about global warming will change accordingly. Therefore, *you need to continue to make the lack of scientific certainty a primary issue in the debate*, and defer to scientists and other experts in the field'.

One of the proposed messages, presented in a text box headed 'Language That Works', was: 'We must not rush to judgment before all the facts are in. We need to ask more questions. We deserve more answers. And until we learn more, we should not commit America to any international document that handcuffs us either now or into the future'.

Overall, the argument put forward by President Bush and by Luntz Research Companies (2002) was that there is uncertainty about what impacts climate change will have on the environment, and that therefore it would be better not to take action that could potentially damage the economic interests of the USA by introducing measures to limit greenhouse gas emissions. As Dessler & Parson (2006) pointed out: 'the central point of this argument—that certainty about climate change is required to justify taking costly mitigation actions, or alternatively, that some higher level of confidence is required than is provided by present scientific knowledge—is not a scientific argument at all, but a normative judgement about when it is appropriate to make costly efforts to forestall an uncertain risk'.

There are other examples where politicians have expressed greater certainty about the impacts of climate change on natural disasters, possibly to gain public support for particular policies.

During the period of May–July 2007, England recorded the highest levels of rainfall for those 3 months since measurements began in 1766 (Met Office 2007). The heavy rain included particularly intense downpours which resulted in flooding during June and July in various parts of the UK, primarily in NE and SW England. The flooding led to several deaths and, according to the Association of British Insurers (2007), more than 50 000 claims were made for insured properties, at a total cost in excess of £2.5 billion.

On 23 July 2007, following flooding in parts of SW England, the UK Prime Minister, Gordon Brown, held a press conference at which he was asked (Prime Minister's Office 2007): 'Prime Minister, you had plenty of warning of these floods, given the floods in the north of England and also the weather forecasts here. Are you confident that everything was as ready as frankly it should have been given the stories that we have heard of flood barriers stuck on motorways and infrastructure not ready?'

In his response, Prime Minister Brown (Prime Minister's Office 2007) stated that 'I am satisfied that people are doing everything they can', and then added: 'Obviously, like every advanced industrial country we are coming to terms with some of the issues surrounding climate change'. He was then asked 'what scientific advice you are getting as to what really is going on with the climate and the weather in the United Kingdom', to which he replied: 'Well what we had was a month's rainfall in some places in an hour. So this was unusual. It was something that obviously we have got to look at for the future'.

The attempt by Prime Minister Brown to link the rainfall and flooding in summer 2007 with climate change was subsequently contradicted by the Operations and Customer Services Director of the UK Met Office in a letter to the *Financial Times* (Noyes 2007): 'Our current wet summer (the wettest start, so far, since records began in 1766) is associated with a jet stream that is further south than normal. It is not possible to say whether this is a result of climate change or not. The position of the jet stream, which steers frontal systems, can vary naturally in response to changing patterns of ocean surface temperatures. But climate change can also cause the position of atmospheric circulations such as the jet stream to shift. We do not know why it is further south this year but we do know that, in general, warmer climates experience more intense rainfall'.

This was similar to a case outlined by Carvalho & Burgess (2005), who noted after river floods in the UK in 2000 that '[c]ausal links between these extreme "natural events" and climate change were prominent in press reports, an interpretive tendency reinforced by senior government politicians perhaps keen to deflect attention from other, more immediate potential contributory factors such as inadequate planning controls over development in floodplains and changing farming practices'.

Environmental lobby groups

Some environmental lobby groups have drawn attention to the link between climate change and weather-related natural disasters. Doyle (2007) noted that since 2002 'Greenpeace UK climate campaigns have also been increasingly focused upon the human impacts of a changing climate and the need

for action on both a UK governmental and personal level'. This has included the release of statements into the public domain that attribute single weather-related natural disasters to climate change.

For instance, the home page of the section on climate change on the website for Greenpeace UK in February 2006 stated: 'it is likely that the heat wave of 2003 which killed 30 000 people across Europe was caused by climate change' (Greenpeace 2006). This was accompanied by the following advice: 'By switching to clean forms of energy such as wind, wave and solar we can prevent the worst effects of climate change'.

Similarly, in a section headed on its website as 'Cause for concern: extreme weather and climate change explained' in November 2007, Greenpeace stated: 'Europe's continent-wide heat wave and fatal forest fires has [sic] focussed attention on global warming' (Greenpeace 2007a). It continued: 'But climate change is not just about hotter weather. Last summer Europe was suffering heavy flooding, and the heat waves are already giving way to floods in Asia this summer'.

Greenpeace also directly attributed extreme weather events to energy companies. A section on its website about 'The impacts of global warming' stated (Greenpeace 2007b): 'The fossil fuels produced by the oil industry are affecting people around the world. Extreme weather events are becoming more frequent, and in the last 3 years have killed 100 000 people'.

Some environmental groups in the USA also publicly linked hurricanes Katrina and Rita to climate change. In a web log posting on 6 October 2005, Carl Pope, executive director of the Sierra Club, urged his members to 'ride the waves of existing public urgency, rather than waiting for information and education to create a new current of concerns about global warming itself' (Pope 2005). He added: 'Ride the wave of public concern created over extreme weather by [hurricanes] Katrina and Rita. Force the country to seriously consider the costs and consequences of preparing for such disasters. Invest heavily in disaster preparedness. *Preparedness for extreme weather will prime the public to demand prevention of global warming*'.

On 28 August 2006, Carl Pope used the first anniversary of Hurricane Katrina's landfall to link it to climate change, declaring in a web log posting: 'One year ago, Hurricane Katrina offered terrible evidence that our society had failed to respond to the challenge of global warming' (Pope 2006).

'Free market' lobby groups

The campaigns of environmental groups for action to mitigate climate change and its impacts through reductions in greenhouse gas emissions have been countered to some extent by the efforts of lobby groups that are opposed to such measures. According to McCright (2007), a 'coordinated anti-environmental countermovement has mobilized in the United States since the 1980s to challenge the legitimacy of climate change as a problem on which society should act'. This has included 'concerted efforts by American conservative think tanks to question the necessity of dealing with climate change'. The tactics of these 'conservative think tanks', many of which publicly promote 'free market' ideologies, have included the funding and promotion of climate change 'sceptics' or 'contrarians' who 'proclaim their strong and vocal dissent from the growing consensus by criticizing mainstream science in general and pre-eminent scientists more specifically' (McCright 2007). These 'climate change sceptics' 'routinely deny the evidence of environmental problems by exploiting scientific uncertainties'.

Many of these 'free market' lobby groups have highlighted uncertainties in climate change science as a tactic within their public communication campaigns, which are sometimes funded by energy companies. For instance, the George C. Marshall Institute (2007) claims on its website that its 'intent is to promote a clear understanding of the state of climate science and assess the implications for public policy' and that a 'major component of this effort is communicating the findings to policy makers, the media and the public policy community'. In 2004 it received $145 000 from ExxonMobil for 'public information and policy research' on climate change (ExxonMobil Corporation 2005). In January 2004, the president of the Institute wrote a newspaper article in which he criticized efforts to promote renewable energy alternatives to fossil fuels to mitigate climate change (O'Keefe 2004). He stated: 'Neither I nor anyone else knows whether over the course of this century the climate will be a scientific curiosity or a serious ecological threat. If it becomes a serious threat, today's so-called renewable energy sources may not be the best solutions'. The article concluded: 'Our nation should not be frightened into adopting unknown and unproven technologies until they can contribute to healthy economic growth and until we better understand the impact of human activities on our climate system'.

Also in 2004, the Institute published a document called *Twenty-four Frequently Asked Questions on Climate Change* (George C. Marshall Institute 2004), which included a section on 'Climate change impacts'. It omitted any references to scientific papers or the findings of the IPCC, and provided the following answer to a question about the potential impacts of climate change: 'Increased precipitation and increases in flood and droughts are a common prediction about future climate. However, climate model predictions, even if one is willing to accept them, do not show consistent changes in precipitation. Floods and droughts are affected by so many other factors that determining the affect [sic] of climate change is very difficult'. This agreed partially with the findings outlined by the IPCC (2001*d*), but ignored the conclusion that there is a 90–99% chance of more intense precipitation events over many areas in the 21st century, and a 66–90% chance of increased summer continental drying and associated risk of drought over most mid-latitude continental interiors. Overall, the document produced by the George C. Marshall Institute (2004) highlighted the acknowledgements of uncertainty that occur in the scientific literature, but omitted any accurate reference to the quantification of uncertainty that researchers have assigned to potential impacts.

Campaign organizations in the UK have also copied these tactics in promoting similar positions on measures to limit and reduce greenhouse gas emissions. For instance, the Centre for Policy Studies, which claims to have played a 'global role in the dissemination of free market economics', published a document on 'Climate change: a guide to the scientific uncertainties' (Livermore 2007), including the following statement: 'Current energy policy is driven by the reduction of carbon emissions. However, in light of the uncertain science on which this is based, more effective policies, focussed on long-term energy security, should be pursued (each of these policies which will also, incidentally, reduce carbon emissions)'.

Livermore (2007) drew attention to many of the uncertainties that have been acknowledged in scientific research about the impact of climate change on natural hazards, particularly flooding, but stopped short of giving a full and accurate representation of the literature. For instance, he pointed out that '[s]ea level changes are both complex and difficult to attribute with certainty' and stated: 'Sea levels, we are told, are set to rise faster and cause severe flooding in some parts of the world. Catastrophic rises of several metres have been suggested. In actual fact, even the latest IPCC report gives a range of only 28 to 43 centimetres average rise by the 2090s, down from the figures issued five years ago'.

This comparison between figures published in the IPCC Third Assessment Report in 2001 and the Fourth Assessment Report in 2007 is misleading. As Solomon *et al.* (2007) emphasized, the range of projected sea-level rises reported in the Fourth Assessment Report would have been similar to those presented in the Third Assessment

Report if the uncertainties had been as large. In particular, the ranges cited by Solomon *et al.* (2007) excluded the potential contribution from rapid dynamic ice flows in the future, but the authors noted that '[i]f recently observed increases in ice discharge rates from the Greenland and Antarctic Ice Sheets were to increase linearly with global average temperature change, that would add 0.1 to 0.2 m to the upper bound of sea level rise'.

Energy companies

Energy companies that rely commercially on the production or consumption of fossil fuels have an obvious vested interest in policy debates about measures to limit emissions of carbon dioxide and other greenhouse gases. For instance, the signing of the Kyoto Protocol in 1997 provoked opposition from some energy producers and users, particularly in the USA, on the grounds that compliance through limiting the consumption of fossil fuels would be potentially damaging to both their commercial interests and the economic interests of the country as a whole.

However, Levy & Kolk (2002) pointed out a difference in the approaches of energy companies on either side of the Atlantic. The authors indicated that 'U.S.-based companies such as Exxon and Chevron have aggressively challenged climate science, pointed to the potentially high economic costs of greenhouse gas controls, and lobbied against mandatory controls'. But they also noted: 'By contrast, BP and Shell, the two largest European companies, have accepted the scientific basis for precautionary action, expressed support for the Kyoto Protocol on greenhouse gases, and announced substantial investment plans for renewable energy'.

The Global Climate Coalition (GCC) was set up in 1989 by a group of industrial energy producers and users to oppose mandatory measures to cut greenhouse gas emissions. Initially, it included energy companies from both sides of the Atlantic, although European companies such as Shell and BP ceased to be members in the late 1990s. The GCC announced that it had been 'deactivated' in 2001, once President George W. Bush had made clear that his government would not ratify the Kyoto Protocol.

One of the most prominent members of the GCC, ExxonMobil Corporation, has continued to play an active role in the public policy debate about climate change, and, according to Levy & Kolk (2002), has 'taken the firmest stand' against regulation of greenhouse gases, by 'citing scientific uncertainties and the exclusion of developing countries from emission controls' as well as warning of the 'dire economic consequences of Kyoto commitments'. Among the tactics used by ExxonMobil has been the publication of advertisements in newspapers in the USA and of other promotional materials, which draw attention to various uncertainties in the science of climate change, including the potential impact on extreme weather events.

For instance, on 22 January 2004, ExxonMobil placed an advertisement on its website and in a number of newspapers and magazines in the USA on the topic of 'weather and climate'. It began by stating (ExxonMobil Corporation 2004): 'In the debate over climate change, there is an understandable tendency to use recent weather events to draw conclusions about global warming. However, weather and climate are not the same—climate is far more complex.' It drew attention to the fact that single weather events cannot be attributed to climate change: 'Thus, the recent record cold weather in the Northeast U.S. does not indicate a cooling climate, just as last year's record summer heat in Europe does not confirm a warming world'.

Much of the advertisement (ExxonMobil Corporation 2004) emphasized complexity in the study of climate change and its impacts on weather, as well as the role of natural variability: 'Observations and theory both indicate that weather and important aspects of climate, for instance El Niño events, behave in a chaotic fashion that may never allow for definitive, long-term predictions. These and other fluctuations produce significant natural climate variability'. It also highlighted difficulties in attributing climate change to human activities, noting that 'scientific uncertainties continue to limit our ability to make objective, quantitative determinations regarding the human role in recent climate change or the degree and consequences of future change'.

In 2006, the company also published a document (ExxonMobil Corporation 2006) that included a 748 word section on 'Climate science: what we know', in which the words 'uncertain' and 'uncertainties' appeared eight times, along with a number of other statements that conveyed a lack of certainty. In its comments on the projected scenarios published by the IPCC (2001*d*), the document stated: 'When climate models are used to analyze the implications of these emissions scenarios, they project more severe consequences at the high end—including sea level rises, droughts and polar ice melting—and relatively benign climate changes at the low end'. In fact, IPCC (2001*d*) reported that some sea-level rise is forecast in all projections, even those with the lowest estimates of greenhouse gas emissions: 'Global mean sea level is projected to rise by 0.09 to 0.88 m between the years 1990 and 2100, for the full range of SRES [Special Report on Emissions Scenarios (Nakićenović 2000)] scenarios, but with significant regional variations'. IPCC (2001*d*) also concluded from the projections that it was 'likely' (i.e. 66–90% chance) that there would be increased summer continental drying and associated risk of drought over most mid-latitude continental interiors. However, the content of the ExxonMobil Corporation (2006) document has been publicly defended by some members of the research community. Pielke (2006) suggested on a web log that it did not contain 'anything factually inaccurate or inconsistent with the IPCC'.

ExxonMobil also provided financial support to a number of 'free market' lobby groups for public communication campaigns on climate change, because of their opposition to the Kyoto Protocol, according to Ken Cohen, the company's Vice-President for Public Affairs (reported by Wynn 2007). These lobby groups have continued to oppose any measures to regulate greenhouse gas emissions and their production through the consumption of fossil fuels, even though President George W. Bush announced in 2001 that his government would not ratify the Kyoto Protocol.

The tactics of ExxonMobil in relation to greenhouse gas emissions from fossil fuel consumption and climate change are similar to those adopted by opponents of the regulation of other products that have potentially harmful impacts on human health and/or the environment. Michaels & Monforton (2005) documented a number of examples relating to the manufacture of products, such as cigarettes, in which attempts have been made to delay regulation by highlighting the uncertainties surrounding epidemiological and laboratory studies. Michaels & Monforton concluded that by 'magnifying and exploiting these uncertainties, polluters and manufacturers of dangerous products have been remarkably successful in delaying, often for decades, regulations and other measures designed to protect the health and safety of individuals and communities'.

Media

The media in the USA and the UK have played an important role in communicating information about the relationship between climate change and weather-related natural disasters. Bostrom & Lashof (2007) suggested that both scientists and the media 'appear to have perpetuated a dissociation between extreme weather events and climate change in the 1990s' in the USA. Carvalho & Burgess (2005) suggested that since the end of the 1990s in the UK, there has been 'a new sense of urgency attached to the risks from climate change', because 'the impacts of climate change

are brought into audiences' everyday experience by news professionals reporting dramatic weather-related events in the discursive frame of accelerating climate change'. The authors suggested that 'the extreme weather events of the last few years provided an excellent hook for the new interpretive round of stories'. Corfee-Morlot *et al.* (2007) noted that there has been a significant increase since 2003 in the number of newspaper reports worldwide that have linked extreme weather events to climate change.

However, the various media outlets have adopted different approaches in reporting the link between climate change and weather-related natural disasters, and the associated uncertainties. Carvalho & Burgess (2005) pointed out that 'the media build particular images of scientific knowledge and uncertainty on climate change, and emphasize or de-emphasize forecasts of impacts, in order to sustain their political preferences regarding the regulatory role of the state, individual freedom, and the general economic and social status quo'.

This was illustrated by the coverage by newspapers in the UK of the flooding in Boscastle, Cornwall, in August 2004. In an end of year leading article, *The Independent* (2004) suggested that 'we live at a time when our influence on the natural environment is greater than at any time in history', and 'the destruction visited on the Cornish town of Boscastle this summer ... has shown the extent of our dependence on the natural environment—and what a profound responsibility we have to ensure its stability'. The article also called for Prime Minister Blair to 'persuade the Bush administration to sign up to an agreement to limit America's use of fossil fuels'.

However, the science editor of the *Daily Mail* (Hanlon 2004) on the same day insisted that 'no, last autumn's floods in Boscastle, North Cornwall, were *not*, as some people insisted, proof that climate change is here, merely just another reminder of the awesome power of nature'. He declared that 'as for global warming: the jury is, to my mind, still out' and 'Earth could simply be going through a climatic blip, a result of naturally occurring temperature change'.

These two opposite views are consistent with the conclusions of Ward (2007), who indicated that newspapers such as *The Independent* 'adopted editorial and opinion lines that were strongly consistent with the scientific consensus and supported urgent action to tackle greenhouse gas emissions', whereas newspapers like the *Daily Mail* 'appeared to have editorial and opinion lines that persistently opposed action to cut greenhouse gas emissions and expressed doubt about their contribution to climate change'.

However, not all newspapers exaggerated or downplayed the possibility of a link between climate change and the flooding in Boscastle. A leading article in *The Guardian* (2004) just after the event pointed out that 'it would be simple to blame climate change for the extreme weather conditions' but more accurately concluded: 'The honest answer, in this case at least, is that no one can say for certain: Boscastle's flash-flood appears to have had more to do with topography as any other particular cause'.

Hurricane Katrina exposed similarly polarized views in the US media. On 30 August 2005, the day after the hurricane struck New Orleans, the *Boston Globe* published an article by the journalist Ross Gelbspan, which began with the statement: 'The hurricane that struck Louisiana yesterday was nicknamed Katrina by the National Weather Service. Its real name is global warming.' The article by Gelbspan (2005) also linked a number of other extreme weather events in the USA and elsewhere with climate change.

In contrast, *Capitalism Magazine*, on 3 September 2005, published an opinion article by James Glassman, then host of the 'free market' website TechCentral Station, which dismissed any connection between the hurricane and climate change (Glassman 2005): 'Katrina has nothing to do with global warming. Nothing. It has everything to do with the immense forces of nature that have been unleashed many, many times before and the inability of humans, even the most brilliant engineers, to tame these forces'.

Media other than newspapers can also make an important contribution to the public policy debate about climate change. Lowe (2006) examined the portrayal in the film *The Day After Tomorrow* of the link between climate change and catastrophic events, and warned that 'whilst shocking images have been found to have an effect upon perceptions of climate change, the change is negative if, for example, the aim is to engage the public in efforts to reduce individual energy consumption'. He recommended that '[i]n the case of the UK and other developed countries, the willingness for the public to act should not rely upon fears over catastrophic storms, massive tidal waves and threats to human survival'.

Conclusions

There has been discussion within the research community about the benefits and problems of expressing uncertainties associated with the connection between climate change and weather-related disasters. There is recognition that uncertainty should be accurately and appropriately conveyed, even when the aim of communication is to promote particular actions rather than just to inform.

Yet the examples described here make clear that a wide range of stakeholders in the public policy debate, including scientists, policy-makers, lobby groups and the media, in both the UK and the USA, have, on occasions, overstated or understated uncertainties to make particular decisions or policies seem more appealing. Viscusi & Zeckhauser (2006) noted that there were many sources of uncertainties surrounding the science and politics of climate change and that '[d]iffering sides in the policy debate have used this massive uncertainty as a rationale for aggressive policy action or policy inaction, depending in part on whether they interpret the uncertainty as posing a risk of dire consequences, or an opportunity to learn whether there is a real problem'.

When scientists, policy-makers, environmental lobby groups and some media have directly attributed single weather-related natural disasters to climate change, their actions appear to have been primarily motivated by a desire to create a sense of immediacy about the potential adverse consequences of climate change, and to attract public support for mitigation measures. However, in some cases, this attribution has been used by some politicians to justify an inability to deal with the consequences of a natural hazard, by emphasizing an unanticipated change in risk that has been caused by climate change.

On the other hand, some policy-makers, 'free market' lobby groups, energy companies and parts of the media have sought to rule out any contribution from climate change to weather-related natural disasters, to resist calls for climate change mitigation measures. They have tended to emphasize uncertainties as part of an apparent hedging strategy to avoid incurring financial or economic costs by placing limitations on greenhouse gas emissions without being sure of the potential benefits.

Some researchers have acknowledged the exploitation of uncertainty in climate change science in communication campaigns against greenhouse gas regulations and other climate change mitigation measures. Dilling & Moser (2007) suggested that '[o]pponents of action on climate change have successfully organized and hired "their" experts (often called sceptics or contrarians) whose modus operandi has been to raise doubts about the overwhelming consensus on the state of the science while disproportionately highlighting the remaining unknowns'.

Ward (2007) pointed out that scientists often find themselves competing for media coverage against both environmental and 'free market' lobby groups, who tend to polarize the public policy debate, because '[s]ome of these groups accept the scientific consensus and even seek to present the science as more certain than it is, and some reject the consensus to varying degrees and seek to present the science as more uncertain than it is'.

It is also interesting to consider the possible impact of these examples through indicators of public opinion about the extent of a relationship between climate change and weather-related natural disasters, and the associated uncertainties. A review of public opinion surveys carried out after previous widespread flooding in the UK in 2000 pointed out that residents of affected areas appeared to be less likely than the rest of the population to make a link with climate change, concluding that 'the majority of the public associates extreme weather events with climate change only so long as they do not directly experience them' (Andrew Darnton Research & Analysis 2004). It remains to be seen what impact the 2007 floods have upon the UK public's perceptions of climate change.

Ereaut & Segnit (2006) suggested that the 'climate change discourse' in the UK has been 'confusing, contradictory and chaotic' and that it 'seems likely that the overarching message for the lay public is that in fact, nobody really knows'. They recommended that, for communications activities designed to persuade people to participate in actions to tackle climate change, the 'interested agencies need to treat the argument as having been won' and the '"facts" need to be treated as being so taken-for-granted that they need not be spoken'.

Leiserowitz (2006) suggested that although the majority of the public in the USA recognize that climate change is a problem, it 'lacks a sense of urgency'. He acknowledged that '[p]ublic risk perceptions can fundamentally compel or constrain political, economic and social action to address particular risks', and he highlighted the results of a survey that showed that very few members of the public in the USA readily associated climate change with direct consequences for them, or with impacts on human health. The survey also found that 'very few Americans associate global warming with extreme weather events, like heat waves, hurricanes, and droughts—all of which may increase in severity due to global warming'.

However, Bostrom & Lashof (2007) suggested that the public debate about the causes and consequences of the summer heatwave in Europe in 2003, and of the 2004 and 2005 Atlantic hurricane seasons, appeared to have triggered a shift away from the previous 'public dissociation' of climate change and extreme weather events in the USA. The linking of climate change and Hurricane Katrina has had a discernible effect on public opinion in the USA. According to Zogby International (2006), 68 per cent of those surveyed between 11 and 15 August 2006 agreed that 'global warming has had a major influence, or at least some influence, on more intense hurricanes like Katrina'.

However, a crucial consideration appears to have been disregarded by those stakeholders who have exaggerated or downplayed the link between climate change and weather-related natural disasters. As Leiserowitz (2006) stressed, the credibility of, and trust in, sources of information can be significantly undermined if the public detect that expressions of uncertainties are distorted. In these circumstances, public support is likely to be diminished for any decisions or policies that are promoted alongside.

The author gratefully acknowledges helpful reviews by J. Handmer, T. Lowe and R. Pielke, Jr. The views expressed in this paper are those of the author and not of Risk Management Solutions.

References

ALLEN, M. R. & LORD, R. 2004. The blame game. *Nature*, **432**, 551–552.

ANDREW DARNTON RESEARCH & ANALYSIS 2004. *Public Understanding of Climate Change*. Desk Research—Final Report for COI/Defra Communications Directorate/FUTERRA.

ASSOCIATION OF BRITISH INSURERS 2007. 50 000 and rising—insurers pulling out all the stops to deal with flood claims. News Release 80/07. World Wide Web Address: http://www.abi.org.uk/Newsreleases/viewNewsRelease.asp?nrid=14922.

AUSTRALIAN ACADEMY OF SCIENCES, ROYAL FLEMISH ACADEMY OF BELGIUM FOR SCIENCES AND THE ARTS, BRAZILIAN ACADEMY OF SCIENCES, ET AL. 2001. The science of climate change. *Science*, **292**, 1261.

BBC 2001. Prescott pressures US on climate treaty. BBC News website. World Wide Web Address: http://newsvote.bbc.co.uk/1/hi/uk_politics/1278749.stm.

BLAIR, T. 2001. Environment: the next steps. Speech by the Prime Minister, 6 March. World Wide Web Address: http://www.number10.gov.uk/output/Page1583.asp.

BOSTROM, A. & LASHOF, D. 2007. Weather or climate change? *In*: MOSER, S. C. & DILLING, L. (eds) *Creating a Climate for Change: Communicating Climate Change and Facilitating Social Change*. Cambridge University Press, Cambridge, 31–43.

BUSH, G. W. 2001. Text of a letter from the President to Senators Hagel, Helms, Craig, and Roberts. 13 March. World Wide Web Address: http://www.whitehouse.gov.edgesuite.net/news/releases/2001/03/20010314.html.

CARVALHO, A. & BURGESS, J. 2005. Cultural circuits of climate change in the UK broadsheet newspapers, 1985–2003. *Risk Analysis*, **25**, 1457–1469.

CHRISTIANSEN, A. C. 2003. Convergence of divergence? Status and prospects for US climate strategy. *Climate Policy*, **3**, 343–358.

CORFEE-MORLOT, J., MASLIN, M. & BURGESS, J. 2007. Global warming in the public sphere. *Philosophical Transactions of the Royal Society of London, Series A*, doi: 10.1098/rsta.2007.2084.

CURRY, J. 2006. Judy Curry in the comments. 21 August. World Wide Web Address: http://sciencepolicy. colorado.edu/prometheus/archives/climate_change/000906judy_curry_in_the_co.html.

DESSLER, A. E. & PARSON, E. A. 2006. *The Science and Politics of Global Climate Change: A Guide to the Debate*. Cambridge University Press, Cambridge.

DILLING, L. & MOSER, S. C. 2007. Introduction. *In*: MOSER, S. C. & DILLING, L. (eds) *Creating a Climate for Change: Communicating Climate Change and Facilitating Social Change*. Cambridge University Press, Cambridge, 1–29.

DOYLE, J. 2007. Picturing the clima(c)tic: Greenpeace and the representational politics of climate change communication. *Science as Culture*, **16**, 129–150.

DYE, L. 2005. Did global warming boost Katrina's fury? ABC News, 14 September. World Wide Web Address: http://abcnews.go.com/Technology/DyeHard/story?id=1121948.

EILPERIN, J. 2005. Shrinking La. coastline contributes to flooding. *Washington Post*, 30 August. World Wide Web Address: http://www.washingtonpost.com/wp-dyn/content/article/2005/08/29/AR2005082901875.html.

EREAUT, G. & SEGNIT, N. 2006. *Warm Words: How are We Telling the Climate Story and Can We Still Tell it Better?* Institute for Public Policy Research, London.

EXXONMOBIL CORPORATION 2004. Weather and climate. World Wide Web Address: http://www.exxonmobil.com/Corporate/news_opeds_climate.aspx.

EXXONMOBIL CORPORATION 2005. Public information and policy research. *In*: *ExxonMobil Corporation 2004 Worldwide Contributions and Community Investments*. ExxonMobil Corporation, Irving, TX.

EXXONMOBIL CORPORATION 2006. *Tomorrow's Energy: A Perspective on Energy Trends, Greenhouse Gas Emissions and Future Energy Options*. ExxonMobil Corporation, Irving, TX.

GELBSPAN, R. 2005. Katrina's real name. *Boston Globe*, 30 August. World Wide Web Address: http://www.boston.com/news/weather/articles/2005/08/30/katrinas_real_name/.

GEORGE C. MARSHALL INSTITUTE 2004. *Twenty-four Frequently Asked Questions on Climate Change*. George C. Marshall Institute, Washington, DC.

GEORGE C. MARSHALL INSTITUTE 2007. Climate change. World Wide Web Address: http://www.marshall.org/subcategory.php?id=9.

GLASSMAN, J. K. 2005. Hurricane Katrina and global warming. *Capitalism Magazine*, 3 September. World Wide Web Address: http://www.capmag.com/article.asp?ID=4391.

GREENPEACE 2006. Choose clean energy—climate change. World Wide Web Address: http://www.greenpeace.org.uk/climate/climatechange/index.cfm.

GREENPEACE 2007a. Cause for concern: extreme weather and climate change explained. World Wide Web Address: http://www.greenpeace.org.uk/climate/extreme-weather-and-climate-change-explained.

GREENPEACE 2007b. The impacts of global warming. World Wide Web Address: http://www.greenpeace.org.uk/climate/the-impacts-of-global-warming.

GUARDIAN, THE 2004. Boscastle's warning. *The Guardian*, 18 August 2004. World Wide Web Address: http://www.guardian.co.uk/environment/2004/aug/18/guardianleaders.environment.

HANLON, M. 2004. Forget global warming … it's the awesome power unleashed by our own planet that we should fear and respect the most. *Daily Mail*, 27 December 2004, 14.

HOUGHTON, J. T., DING, Y., ET AL. (eds) 2001. *Climate Change 2001: The Scientific Basis. Contribution of Working Group I to the Third Assessment Report of the Intergovernmental Panel on Climate Change*. Cambridge University Press, Cambridge.

INDEPENDENT, THE 2004. A natural disaster, but also a terrifying demonstration of the fragility of mankind. *The Independent*, 27 December 2004, World Wide Web Address: http://environment.independent.co.uk/article26244.ece.

INTERNATIONAL FEDERATION OF RED CROSS AND RED CRESCENT SOCIETIES 2004. *World Disasters Report 2004*. International Federation of Red Cross and Red Crescent Societies, Geneva.

IPCC 2001a. Summary for policymakers. *In*: HOUGHTON, J. T., DING, Y. ET AL. (eds) *Climate Change 2001: The Scientific Basis. Contribution of Working Group I to the Third Assessment Report of the Intergovernmental Panel on Climate Change*. Cambridge University Press, Cambridge, 1–20.

IPCC 2001b. Summary for policymakers. *In*: MCCARTHY, J. J., CANZIANI, O. F., LEARY, N. A., DOKKEN, D. J. & WHITE, K. S. (eds) *Climate Change 2001: Impacts, Adaptation and Vulnerability. Contribution of Working Group II to the Third Assessment Report of the Intergovernmental Panel on Climate Change*. Cambridge University Press, Cambridge, 1–17.

IPCC 2001c. Summary for policymakers. *In*: METZ, B., DAVIDSON, O., SWART, R. & PAN, J. (eds) *Climate Change 2001: Mitigation. Contribution of Working Group III to the Third Assessment Report of the Intergovernmental Panel on Climate Change*. Cambridge University Press, Cambridge, 1–13.

IPCC 2001d. Summary for policymakers. *In*: WATSON, R. T. & THE CORE WRITING TEAM (eds) *Climate Change 2001: Synthesis Report. A Contribution of Working Groups I, II, and III to the Third Assessment Report of the Intergovernmental Panel on Climate Change*. Cambridge University Press, Cambridge, 1–34.

IPCC 2007a. Summary for policymakers. *In*: IPCC (eds) *Climate Change 2007: Synthesis Report. A Contribution of Working Groups I, II, and III to the Fourth Assessment Report of the Intergovernmental Panel on Climate Change*. Cambridge University Press, Cambridge, 1–22.

IPCC 2007b. *Climate Change 2007: Synthesis Report. A Contribution of Working Groups I, II, and III to the*

Fourth Assessment Report of the Intergovernmental Panel on Climate Change. Cambridge University Press, Cambridge.

KATRINA LESSONS LEARNED REVIEW GROUP 2006. *The Federal Response to Hurricane Katrina: Lessons Learned.* Katrina Lessons Learned Review Group, Washington, DC.

KING, D. 2007. *The Science of Climate Change: An Introduction by Sir David King.* Royal Society for the Encouragement of Arts, Manufactures and Commerce, London.

LEE, J. 2003. A call for softer, greener language. *The New York Times,* 2 March. World Wide Web Address: http://select.nytimes.com/gst/abstract.html?res=F3061EF73A580C718CDDAA0894DB404482.

LEISEROWITZ, A. 2006. Communicating the risks of global warming: American risk perceptions, affective images, and interpretive communities. *In:* MOSER, S. C. & DILLING, L. (eds) *Creating a Climate for Change: Communicating Climate Change and Facilitating Social Change.* Cambridge University Press, Cambridge, 44–62.

LEVY, D. L. & KOLK, A. 2002. Strategic responses to global climate change: conflicting pressures on multinationals in the oil industry. *Business and Politics,* **4,** 275–300.

LIVERMORE, M. 2007. Climate change: a guide to the scientific uncertainties. Centre for Policy Studies, London, UK. World Wide Web Address: http://www.cps.org.uk/cpsfile.asp?id=681.

LOWE, T. 2006. *Vicarious experience vs. scientific information in climate change risk perception and behaviour: a case study of undergraduate students in Norwich, UK.* Tyndall Centre for Climate Change Research, Technical Report, **43.**

LUNTZ RESEARCH COMPANIES 2002. The Environment: a cleaner, safer, healthier America. *In:* Straight talk. Luntz Research Companies. World Wide Web Address: www.luntzspeak.com/graphics/Luntz-Research.Memo.pdf.

MARX, S. M., WEBER, E. U., ORLOVE, B. S., LEISEROWITZ, A., KRANTZ, D. H., RONCOLI, C. & PHILLIPS, J. 2007. Communication and mental processes: experiential and analytic processing of uncertain climate information. *Global Environmental Change,* **17,** 47–58.

MCCARTHY, M. 2005. This *is* global warming, says environmental chief. *The Independent,* 23 September. World Wide Web Address: http://news.independent.co.uk/world/americas/article314510.ece.

MCCRIGHT, A. 2007. Dealing with climate change contrarians. *In:* MOSER, S. C. & DILLING, L. (eds) *Creating a Climate for Change: Communicating Climate Change and Facilitating Social Change.* Cambridge University Press, Cambridge, 200–212.

MET OFFICE 2004. Man mostly to blame for 2003 heatwave. Met Office news release. World Wide Web Address: http://www.gnn.gov.uk/Content/Detail.asp?ReleaseID=137680&NewsAreaID=2.

MET OFFICE 2007. Record-breaking rainfall figures. Met Office news release, 26 July. World Wide Web Address: http://www.metoffice.gov.uk/corporate/pressoffice/2007/pr20070726.html.

MICHAELS, D. & MONFORTON, C. 2005. Manufacturing uncertainty: contested science and the protection of the public's health and environment. *American Journal of Public Health,* **95,** S39–S48.

MOSER, S. C. & DILLING, L. 2004. Making climate hot: communicating the urgency and challenge of global climate change. *Environment,* **46,** 32–46.

NAKIĆENOVIĆ, N. & SWART, R. 2000. *IPCC Special Report on Emissions Scenarios. A Special Report of Working Group III of the Intergovernmental Panel on Climate Change.* Cambridge University Press, Cambridge.

NATIONAL RESEARCH COUNCIL 2001. *Climate Change Science: An Analysis of Some Key Questions.* Committee on the Science of Climate Change, Division on Earth and Life Studies, National Research Council, Washington, DC.

NOYES, S. 2007. Be reassured, FT: the forecast is more rain *and* sun. *Financial Times,* 27 July. World Wide Web Address: http://www.ft.com/cms/s/678e4888-3bd9-11dc-8002-0000779fd2ac.html.

O'KEEFE, W. 2004. Climate debate isn't about action, it's about knowledge. *The Atlanta Journal-Constitution,* 6 January, World Wide Web Address: http://www.marshall.org/article.php?id=186.

PATT, A. G. & DESSAI, S. 2005. Communicating uncertainty: lessons learned and suggestions for climate change assessment. *Comptes Rendus Géoscience,* **337,** 425–441.

PATT, A. G. & SCHRAG, D. P. 2003. Using specific language to describe risk and probability. *Climatic Change,* **61,** 17–30.

PIELKE, R., JR. 2006. More on Royal Society's role in political debates. Prometheus, 6 October. World Wide Web Address: http://sciencepolicy.colorado.edu/prometheus/archives/the_honest_broker/000951more_on_royal_societ.html.

POPE, C. 2005. Taking the initiative: global warming after Katrina. Carl Pope's blog, 6 October. World Wide Web Address: http://www.sierraclub.org/carlpope/waves.

POPE, C. 2006. Taking the initiative: one year after Katrina—the good, the bad, and the clueless. Carl Pope's blog, 28 August. World Wide Web Address: http://www.sierraclub.org/carlpope/2006/08/one-year-after-katrina-good-bad-and_28.asp.

PRIME MINISTER'S OFFICE 2007. The PM has said that the review the Environment Secretary, Hilary Benn, is due to carry out will look into the causes and lessons learnt of the recent floods in many parts of the UK. Downing Street Press Conference, 23 July, transcript. World Wide Web Address: http://www.number10.gov.uk/output/Page12590.asp.

RAHMSTORF, S., MANN, M., BENESTAD, R., SCHMIDT, G. & CONNOLLEY, W. 2005. Hurricanes and global warming—is there a connection? 2 September. World Wide Web Address: http://www.realclimate.org/index.php?p=181.

SOLOMON, S., QIN, D. ET AL. (eds) 2007. Technical summary. *Climate Change 2007: The Physical Science Basis. Contribution of Working Group I to the Fourth Assessment Report of the Intergovernmental Panel on Climate Change.* Cambridge University Press, Cambridge, 19–91.

STOTT, P. A., STONE, D. A. & ALLEN, M. R. 2004. Human contribution to the European heatwave of 2003. *Nature*, **432**, 610–614.

TICKELL, C. 2002. Communicating climate change. *Science*, **297**, 737.

TRENBERTH, K. E. 2005. How are hurricanes changing with global warming? World Wide Web Address: http://www.ametsoc.org/atmospolicy/documents/October252005KevinTrenberth.pdf.

VISCUSI, W. K. & ZECKHAUSER, R. J. 2006. The perception and valuation of the risks of climate change: a rational and behavioral blend. *Climatic Change*, **77**, 151–177.

WARD, R. E. T. 2007. The Royal Society and the debate on climate change. *In*: BAUER, M. W. & BUCCHI, M. (eds) *Journalism, Science and Society: Science Communication between News and Public Relations*. Routledge, Abingdon, 159–172.

WYNN, G. 2007. Exxon says it never doubted climate change threat. Reuters news report, 14 June. World Wide Web Address: http://www.reuters.com/article/environmentNews/idUSL1441452220070614.

ZOGBY INTERNATIONAL 2006. Zogby International/National Wildlife Federation Survey. World Wide Web Address: http://www.zogby.com/wildlife/NWFfinal report8-17-06.htm.

Community participation in natural risk prevention: case histories from Colombia

M. HERMELIN & G. BEDOYA

Departmento de Geologia, Universidad EAFIT, Medellín, Colombia
(e-mail: hermelin@eafit.edu.co)

Abstract: More than 75% of Colombia's 42 million people live in urban areas located in the mountains and are exposed to numerous natural hazards: floods, flash floods, landslides, earthquakes and volcanism. The Armero disaster of 1985 triggered the creation of the National System for Disaster Prevention and Relief. National, regional and local committees started to operate across the country, accompanied by education commissions that produced diverse audiovisual materials to help educate people living in these areas. The experiences of working with local committees gained during the last two decades are presented here. Case histories are from cities such as Pereira, Manizales and Medellín, where the local committees are run by people with little or no formal education but who understand that they must participate as a group to prevent or mitigate the effects of natural disasters. The co-operation between technical experts and trained residents represents an outstanding example of good communication and co-operation for urban populations living in dangerous areas. Although many problems have yet to be resolved, these case histories show that this type of organization seems to be more effective than direct intervention from national government agencies. The models of community participation and communication developed and refined here may have application to similar social environments in other countries.

Over 150 years ago, the first Colombian geologist, Joaquin Acosta (1846, 1851), published in two well-known French scientific journals detailed descriptions and analyses of a lahar that occurred in 1845, on the eastern slope of the Nevado del Ruiz volcano; it caused the death of more than 1000 people and enormous destruction. About two centuries earlier, Friar Pedro de Simon (1625) had written a good description of the Nevado del Ruiz 1595 eruption. Later, in 1870, in complete ignorance of these facts, a group of Colombian peasants and businessmen founded the town of Armero, which was completely destroyed on 13 November 1985 by a lahar that killed about 23 000 people. This clearly demonstrates that historical and scientific knowledge that has not been communicated to a broad public audience is little more than worthless, at least for natural disaster prevention.

As a result of this tragedy, the Colombian National System for Disaster Prevention and Relief (SNPAD) was created by legislation in 1988. Although this system is by no means a panacea for solving the problems of disseminating information on the natural hazards in the Colombian Andes, it fostered important changes in how the country would avert similar future occurrences. The organization set about to identify and analyse areas of potential natural hazards, to form and establish committees with local and regional duties, and to integrate scientific knowledge with practical, pragmatic decisions

and the acceptance of risk-based restrictions by city planners, amongst others.

Much has been accomplished since the inception of the organization in 1988 and from these many achievements, which were, of course, accompanied by many mistakes and omissions, several valuable case histories and experiences are presented here. These detail the participation of local communities in natural risk prevention, on the basis of projects carried out in several Colombian urban areas.

Geographical and social conditions

Colombia has a geographical area of about 1 150 000 km^2 and stretches from 12°N to 4°S latitude, in the northwestern corner of South America. The western part of the country, about two-fifths of the total land area, is dominated by the Andes cordilleras, which run northeastward from the Ecuador border (Fig. 1) in three parallel mountain systems that have several ice-capped massifs. Most of the population lives within the central and eastern cordilleras and Sierra Nevada de Santa Marta but the eastern part of the country is occupied by savanna and rainforests and is sparsely populated.

Colombia has a complex geological history, expressed by the presence of Precambrian to Quaternary rocks. Its present tectonic setting includes

From: LIVERMAN, D. G. E., PEREIRA, C. P. G. & MARKER, B. (eds) *Communicating Environmental Geoscience*. Geological Society, London, Special Publications, **305**, 39–51.
DOI: 10.1144/SP305.5   0305-8719/08/$15.00 © The Geological Society of London 2008.

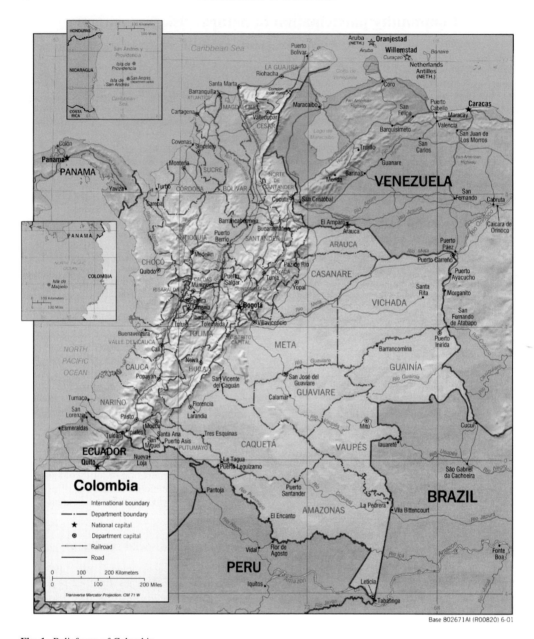

Fig. 1. Relief map of Colombia.

active subduction of the Pacific Nazca Plate under the west coast of Colombia and a relatively slower subduction of the Caribbean Plate under the northern coast (INGEOMINAS 2006). As a result of these tectonic movements, the country is subject to frequent earthquakes and volcanic eruptions (Table 1). Tsunamis have occurred along the Pacific and Caribbean coasts, and most of Caribbean coast is exposed to mud volcanism. The Colombian lowlands are mostly covered by rainforest, and the slopes of the cordilleras, up to altitudes of about 3200 m, are also mantled by Andean forests because of the predominantly humid climate (Espinal 1977). Other than the inherent hazards of this region and because of its tectonic instability, the mountainous countryside

Table 1. *Main catastrophic events of natural origin in Colombia, 1974–2007*

Year	Place	Type	Victims
1974	Quebrada Blanca (E.C)	Landslide	Several hundred
1979	South Pacific coast	Tsunami	500
1983	Popayán (CC)	Earthquake	283
1985	Nevado del Ruiz (CC)	Lahars	23 000
1987	Villa Tina (Medellín)	Landslide	500
1990	San Carlos (CC)	Flash flood, landslides	10
1992	Murindó (WC)	Earthquakes, landslides	20
1993	Río Tapartó (CC)	Flash flood	120
1994	Rio Paez (CC)	Earthquake, landslides	1100
1999	Armenia (CC)	Earthquakes	1185
2000	La Estrella (CC)	Flash flood, landslides	2
2005	Bello (CC)	Flash flood	23
2007	Medellín (CC)	Landslide	8

Abbreviations: EC, Eastern Cordillera; CC, Central Cordillera; WC, Western Cordillera.

is also susceptible to numerous landslides and frequent torrential floods.

Before the Spanish conquest, religious beliefs and taboos precluded any misuse of the Earth surface by native people. Several indigenous cultures have indeed left convincing proof that relatively large populations could live in harmony with their environment without causing irreversible destruction; for example, the Tayronas in the Sierra Nevada de Santa Marta, the Sinues in the Cauca–Magdalena lowlands, and the Calimas in the Western Cordillera (Mora 1990).

The invading Spaniards had nothing but contempt for an environment that they considered to be both their enemy and their booty; they had a similar contempt for the native indigenous populations they enslaved. The Spanish introduced cattle brought in from Europe and forced the indigenous tribes, who survived the slaughter, to change their agriculture practices to methods not suitable for the mountainous region; they forced the cultivation of the mountain slopes, which produced in several susceptible areas the complete destruction of soils (Molano 1990).

Independence from Spain did not change the relationship between the population and the

Table 2. *Change in the Colombia population (DANE 2005) in the last 40 years*

Year	Population
1964	17 484 510
1973	20 666 920
1985	27 853 435
1993	33 109 840
2005	43 593 075*

*Includes about 2 million people living abroad.

landscape. However, the large demographic increase during 20th century (Table 2) has been accompanied by a disproportionate growth of cities. At the beginning of the 20th century, Bogotá, the largest city, had about 100 000 inhabitants. The current population of the largest 15 cities is shown in Table 3. Colombia has over 42 million inhabitants (DANE 2005), of whom about 76% live in urban areas (Hermelin 1992).

Most of the cities are located in the mountains, and many of their new inhabitants live in areas vulnerable to natural hazards (Hermelin 2007). Several catastrophes (Table 4) led the legislators to enact urban reform laws for the protection of the inhabitants. For instance, Law 09 of

Table 3. *Colombia's main cities*

	City	Population
1	Bogotá	6 778 691
2	Medellín	2 223 660
3	Cali	2 075 380
4	Barranquilla	1 113 016
5	Cartagena	895 400
6	Cúcuta	585 919
7	Bucaramanga	509 918
8	Ibagué	495 246
9	Pereira	428 397
10	Santa Marta	414 387
11	Pasto	383 846
12	Montería	381 525
13	Manizales	368 433
14	Valledupar	348 990
15	Neiva	315 322
16	Armenia	272 574
17	Popayán	258 653
18	Sincelejo	236 780

Source: DANE (2005).

Table 4. *Recent disasters of natural origin in the Medellín Valley*

Location	Year	Type
Aná (Medellín)	1875	Flood
Media Luna (Medellín)	1954	Landslide
Santo Domingo (Medellín)	1974	Landslide
Villa Tina (Medellín)	1987	Landslide
Q. La Ayurá (Envigado)	1988	Torrential floods
La Estrella	2000	Landslides and floods
Q. La Sucia (Bello)	2005	Landslides and torrential flood
La Cruz (Medellín)	2007	Landslide

1989 (República de Colombia 1989, Ley 9[a], de Reforma Urbana) placed on the city authorities the responsibility to assist people living in insecure areas; that is, areas that were dangerous zones were mapped and their inhabitants had to be relocated to a safe area, and the future use of the dangerous zones was forbidden.

This law was, of course, relatively easy to enforce in the smaller towns, but in the larger cities their budgets were too exiguous to cover the costs. The cruel reality is that most of the affected population had to stay where they were because many of the housing settlements had already been connected to the public electric supply and the public water network.

For reasons that lie in the history of Colombia, most of the population lives in the mountains where, because of geographical and geological conditions, the population is often adversely affected by natural hazards. To keep the natural adversity to a minimum, the authorities have had to seek and successfully communicate an equilibrium between the unavoidable hazardous mountain environments and providing the resident population with a relatively secure standard of living.

National System for Disaster Prevention and Relief (SNPAD)

The 1985 Armero–Chinchiná catastrophe changed completely the country's perception of natural risks and on how to deal with them. For the people who directly participated in the rescue operations, the breakdown of effective communication and the apparent lack of organization at the different levels of government made a bad situation worse.

Three years later, in 1988, the executive national government led the legislature to approve a law that created an organization called the National System for Disaster Prevention and Relief (SNPAD; Fig. 2). It was conceived as a national body overseeing the interests of the whole country; it consisted of national technical committees and had a relief fund to assist with the financial burden in emergencies. It also consisted of regional and local organizations, where the national government and non-governmental organizations (NGOs) were represented.

Of course, the whole structure depended on several unpredictable variables: leadership and commitments of officials in charge of the system; motivation of local, provincial and national governments, which reached high levels after a catastrophic event; and continuation of well-trained people in their jobs, but who were often replaced by new, untrained people after elections, etc.

Large differences have been observed within local communities in how such emergencies are handled. Part of the explanation for this is that large cities have greater financial and educational resources and tend to fare better than the poorer rural areas, where local politicians rule without much community control on how they organize the relief efforts.

In 1993, as a parallel, but sometimes much more effective national web, the Ministry of Environment and Social Housing established regional corporations to be in control of environmental affairs in each of the departments; several cases were observed in which regional problems related to natural risk prevention operation were taken over by corporation special offices for several years.

Medellín and Valle de Aburra

Medellín and nine smaller municipalities are located along a 50 km mountain valley, of tectonic origin, situated at 1500 m and surrounded by mountains reaching as high as 3000 m. At present, the population consists of about 3.3 million inhabitants, a tenfold increase in the last 50 years (Fig. 3). The natural hazards present in this mountain valley area are landslides, torrential floods and earthquakes. Many of the inhabitants (mostly illegal settlers) who live on the upper slopes and near rivers, in most cases are often exposed to these phenomena. Table 4 illustrates the number

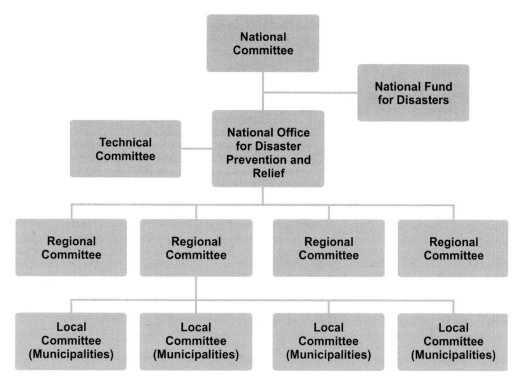

Fig. 2. Organization of the Colombian National System for Disaster Prevention and Relief.

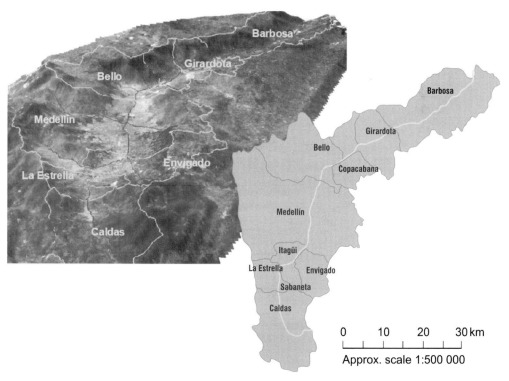

Fig. 3. Populated areas in the Aburra (Medellín) Valley.

of recent disasters that have occurred in the Aburra Valley.

The municipality of Medellín created the Metropolitan Committee for Disaster Relief in 1984, which became operational only when the Villa Tina disaster occurred in September 1987. As in the case of the Armero–Chinchiná catastrophe, this tragedy led to the preparation of preventive plans largely financed by the United Nations Development Programme (PNUD Proyecto Col. 88/010, Alcaldía de Medellín 1993), which included an educational project for communities living in dangerous areas. Unfortunately, the lack of technical support and local improvization led to the production of poorly prepared educational documents and their distribution was not reinforced by a serious educational campaign. Medellín municipality created a new office in 1994, called SIMPAD (Spanish acronym for Municipal System for Disaster Prevention and Relief), which in 1995 became part of the Office for Environment.

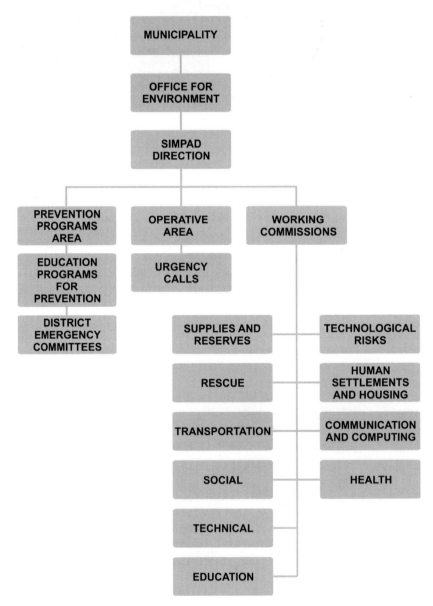

Fig. 4. SIMPAD organization.

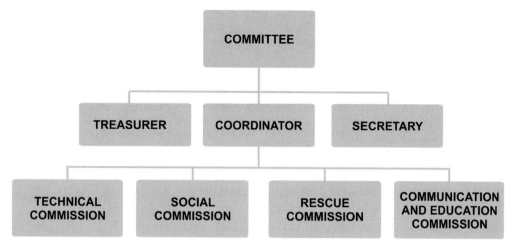

Fig. 5. Emergency district committees.

Its organizational scheme (Fig. 4) shows that, at the city district level, committees exist for the prevention and relief of emergencies (CPRE; Fig. 5); they are serviced and managed by unpaid volunteers; a remarkable feat in a city where unemployment has traditionally been very high and where political influences have proved to have a disastrous effect on such organizations. These volunteer participants are selected by SIMPAD using community support, because of the confidence they inspire in their neighbours. Their main motivation is the recognition they receive from the district inhabitants for their unselfishness and dedication to the community. They receive a distinctive uniform and the co-ordinator receives a walkie-talkie, and they are responsible for the co-ordination of all activities related to prevention and rescue. Committee members participate periodically in training and special courses organized by SIMPAD. At present, there are 186 of these committees, all located in high-risk areas and integrated in the local organization of communities. An important distinction exists between these committees and the Communal Action Councils, another organization at district level; the committees do not participate in political activities. They depend on SIMPAD, a recognized non-political organization, which gives them independence and the respect of their communities. Because of this independence they continued to work even during violent armed confrontations between the leftist guerrilla militia and the 'paramilitaries' organizations (Comites Barriales 2007).

The municipal government spends about US$1 000 000 per year for support and equipment of CPRE. Furthermore, these committees work in close co-operation with local School Prevention Committees, which are responsible to the educational and training activities of the children attending the primary level local schools. They have proved to be invaluable supporters of the municipal Emergency Prevention and Relief System, and their intervention and co-operation in case of emergency is highly appreciated both by communities and SIMPAD officials. There is no doubt that the people who work for CPRE (Fig. 4) fully deserve the reliance that their communities place upon them: they are respected and in return their advice is taken. Their effectiveness in transmitting basic knowledge and in organizing their neighbourhood is considered successful by SIMPAD. This behaviour is considered remarkable because the inhabitants are mostly migrants and refugees from diverse backgrounds, who have been living in the area for a relatively short time in extreme poverty, but nevertheless have come together as a community to support each other in emergencies.

At present, a new type of committee is being organized for the entire Aburra Valley authority. These Environmental Committees will be responsible for the entire area and will not only assume the functions of present committees on emergency but also cover environmental aspects. The selection and permanent training of people have already commenced and it is expected that they will achieve the same results as that observed for the Medellín municipality.

Slope watchwomen in Manizales

Manizales is a city of 368 000 (2005 census) inhabitants located on the western slope of the Central Cordillera, at an average altitude of 2100 m. It is underlain by several rock formations of different ages, affected by fractures and faults and partially covered by a layer of unconsolidated pyroclastic deposits of variable thickness (from the Nevado del Ruiz volcano, located only 10 km away). These materials are generally deeply weathered because of the humid climate, with rainfall of about 2500 mm per year. The city has been affected by several earthquakes but was not damaged by the 1985 lahars, which killed about 23 000 people. The expansion of the city population led to the occupation of steep slopes, particularly by illegal settlements. Triggered by high rainfalls, landslides destroyed many houses and caused hundred of victims.

Initiatives to control the situation started in 1971, with the creation of the 'Corporación CRAMSA', an entity dedicated to manage the erosional processes in Manizales and two neighbouring towns. The measures consist mainly of the engineering treatment of slopes, slum relocation and new housing projects for evacuated families. Since its inception, the 'Corporación' has evolved into a much larger organization, but in cities such as Manizales it retains its original focus on slope management. As in Medellín, people who squat and live on these steep slope areas are mostly very poor families or refugees from 'violencia' areas.

Several years after the beginning of the slope amelioration treatment, which definitely reduced the occurrence of landslides and casualties, the town corporation engineers realized the necessity to carry out maintenance work on some of the earlier civil constructions. The channels and drains had became clogged with garbage thrown away by neighbours and small fractures in the concrete quickly became hazardous gullies and vegetation grew so rapidly blocking the drains that permanent remedial action was needed. It must be stressed that for Manizales, a total area of 280 h of rehabilitated slopes means an important effort.

To solve these problems and to help the communities, corporation officials, in agreement with the municipality, decided to launch a novel programme called the 'slope watchwomen' (Guardianes de la Ladera 2003). These women were selected from communities living near the protected slopes. They are family heads with low incomes, they work only half time and receive 50% of the

Fig. 6. Slope watchwomen at work, Manizales.

minimum wage, are given a colourful uniform, and are trained in basic environmental education, first aid and also in self esteem (Fig. 6).

There are, at present, 1230 women working on the slopes of Manizales, under the supervision of several corporation managers and a civil engineer supervisor. Among their duties are the maintenance of the grass covered slopes, but also the inspection of civil works and an obligation to notify the civil authorities of the presence of any additional new settlements. They have been very well received by neighbours of all social classes and act as community representatives or even envoys to the Corporation and to the Municipality. One of the benefits for the city is that the local government receives daily reports of what is going on in the most vulnerable areas of the city (i.e. the slopes).

In conclusion, this seems to be a successful programme that involves social assistance, low-cost technology and education for the preservation of the city of Manizales. For some corporation agents, these women even deserve a new name: Manizales guardian angels.

Risaralda Department

Risaralda, one of the smallest departments of Colombia, has an area of about 4000 km² (3% of Colombia) and stretches westward from the Central Cordillera divide to the Atrato watershed, crossing the Cauca river and the Western Cordillera with a very irregular shape (Fig. 7).

Elevations vary from 4500 m at the snow-capped extinct volcano Santa Isabel (Central Cordillera) to about 500 m in the Cauca River valley, 4000 m in the Western Cordillera divide and again about 500 m in the westernmost part in the valley of the San Juan River, which empties into the Pacific Ocean. This range in elevations controls both temperatures and rainfall and thus gives rise to a variety of climates and life zone distributions.

Most of the native population was annihilated by the Spanish during and immediately after the conquest of the region. As a result of this destruction of the population the region remained practically unpopulated until the first half of 19th century, when several waves of Antioquenos peasants arrived from the Medellín area, about 150 km to the north, driven by local population increase, agricultural soil impoverishment and the closing of the gold mines. They built new villages, and using the traditional method of slash and burn started destroying the original forest to grow coffee and raise cattle, which are still the main rural activities in the region, together with sugarcane planting in the central area.

Five examples of community participation will be briefly discussed for Risaralda but three of them relate to Pereira, the capital of the department.

Environmental planning for Risaralda department towns

In 1988, in compliance with the national requirement of environmental planning, CARDER, the regional corporation, contacted a group of geologists and requested that they map each of the 13 municipalities of Risaralda (Table 5). The available information included 1:25 000-scale, 50 m contour topographic maps, recent 1:20 000-scale airphotos, and regional geological maps having a scale of 1:1 000 000.

Airphotos of the urban and surrounding suburban areas were processed at the National Geographical Institute to obtain orthophotographs. Once the photo interpretation was completed, teams of two geologists were assigned to each of the towns and each team spent about 1 month in the field doing detailed field work and interacting with local people to obtain as much information as possible about past geological processes. The information obtained included data on the rock lithology, structural geology, slope characteristics present and past, geological and geomorphological processes, as well as information on land use by the present tenants. The geological report also included studies to select suitable garbage disposal sites, examine the management of river basins that supplied the city or town with water, and preliminary analysis of sites to provide suitable building materials. Technical maps were produced that had scales of approximately 1:7000. Combining these data with field observations led to the compilation of a simplified multipurpose map designed to be understood and used by local civil servants. The maps had the following zonal scheme: (1) urbanized areas with no restrictions; (2) urbanized areas with restrictions, appropriate for recovery; (3) urbanized areas with insoluble restrictions; (4) surrounding areas with no restrictions (suitable for urban use); (5) surrounding areas with soluble restrictions; (6) surrounding areas that require intervention.

This kind of nomenclature was explained to communities and was well assimilated, and the simplified map became the basic document for municipality planning decisions (Hermelin 1990; Hermelin & Montalescot 1991). A survey carried out amongst villagers 5 years after the mapping project showed that many of them remembered perfectly what the maps meant and even considered that the relocation of some houses remaining in dangerous areas was still a priority for the community.

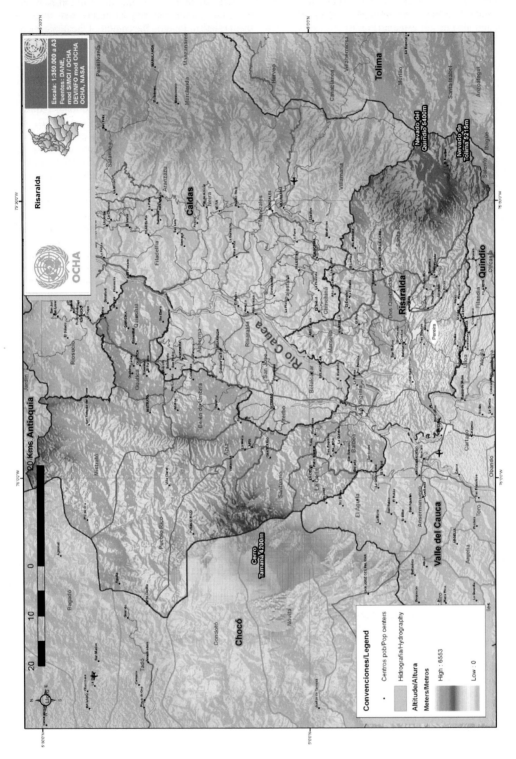

Fig. 7. Map of the Risaralda Department.

Table 5. *Municipalities of the Risaralda Department excepting Pereira and Dosquebradas*

Name	Urban population (1988)	Altitude above sea level (m)
Apía	5260	1630
Balboa	2031	1560
Belén de Umbría	9198	1364
Guática	2684	1530
La Celia	2885	1480
La Virginia	24721	920
Mistrató	3086	1900
Pueblo Rico	2049	1560
Quinchía	6600	1825
Santa Rosa de Cabal	38487	1766
Santuario	6525	1575

Botanical gardens in Risaralda towns

As a second example for Risaralda, a further development in CARDER policies was the fostering of botanical gardens in each village and simultaneously involving the communities in the development of protected areas for the preservation of natural resources (Londoño 2002). These programmes have been established in close co-operation with local schools and are supported by the education authorities. Primary and secondary schoolchildren are often invited to visit the areas and to participate in protection and conservation programmes, particularly in those areas near the river basins from which water is used for municipal aqueducts.

Relocation of families in areas exposed to natural risks

Pereira, the capital of the Department of Risaralda, at present has a population of about 428 000 inhabitants (DANE 2005) and is located on the southern bank of the Otún River, on a large,

partially dissected, alluvial fan that forms where the river leaves its canyon before reaching the Cauca plain. From 1984 to 1986, CARDER, as an environmental authority, succeeded in relocating 840 families living in areas exposed to mass movements and floods in the vicinity of the Otún River. This is a difficult task to undertake in a country such as Colombia, where once built, slums established on government-owned land cannot be evacuated if the owner refuses to do so. To carry out this project, CARDER engineers and social workers developed a meticulous plan, which included the followings steps: (1) determining the 15 critical zones; (2) identifying housing in danger (900 houses, approximately 2000 families); (3) evaluating the houses and plots; (4) notification by CARDER and beginning of negotiations; several alternatives being offered to each family; (5) purchase of the houses by CARDER; the owner purchases a new house, following several possibilities; (6) the start of a community development and social integration programme for relocated families. Surveys carried out after the process had been completed showed that most of the relocated families were satisfied (Gomez 1987; Gomez & Bautista 1989) with their new homes and location.

Landslide prediction

Another example of positive community participation in Pereira is related to the prediction of landslide occurrence in areas affected by the January 1999 earthquake (magnitude 6.2, depth 10 km), which partially destroyed the city of Armenia, located 50 km south of Pereira. In Pereira, several houses were destroyed, particularly those located on uncontrolled landfills, and more than 250 landslides were observed. After the earthquake, monitoring of land stability was carried out with the participation of the local community (Ríos & Hermelin 2004). Monitoring of mass movements included: topographical surveys; water table variation monitoring; daily visual monitoring. These permanent observations,

Table 6. *List of predicted landslides in Pereira*

District	Evacuations	Slide occurrence
El Danubio Mz 26 casa 18	23 December 1999	15 January 2000
Caracol La Curva Mz 4	4 January 2000	24 February 2000
San Fernando Mz 18	24 February 2000	7 April 2000
Nuevo Mexico–El Camionero	6 April 2000	7 March 2000
La Dulcera Calle 28. Casa 28	3 May 2000	19 May 2000
La Libertad Cra 11 calle 66	10 May 2000	1 June 2000
Chicó Monserrate (entire talus)	28 March 2000	22 June 2000
Nuevo México Calle 25 No 14B–18	30 May 2000	23 June 2000

in which the residents of the affected areas played a very important role, permitted the successful prediction of landslide occurrence and previous evacuation (Table 6).

Environmental education and risk prevention

The experiences described here demonstrate how, for a north Andean country, with strong communication between the various interested parties, the local communities can become an integral part of minimizing the risks involved with natural hazards. The following are brief considerations of the evolution of environmental communication concepts in Colombia.

The first wave of 'ecological' concern that reached Colombia in the 1970s was dominated by the necessity to protect nature, following the inspiration of the 1972 United Nations Stockholm Conference on Human Environment. The first law on environment (República de Colombia 1974, Código Nacional de Recursos Naturales Renovables y de Protección del Medio Ambiente) completely ignored that in humid mountainous countries located near the equator and exposed to active tectonism and volcanism, nature might not be the docile and resigned mother exposed to human greed. No mention was made of the numerous natural hazards to which population and constructions are exposed, an omission that can be explained only by a biased or incomplete vision of the local natural environment.

Catastrophes caused by different natural factors (earthquakes, tsunamis, volcanic eruptions, hurricanes, flooding, mass movements, etc.) during the last two decades of the 20th century obliged the Colombian people to realize that their environment was comparable with Janus, the two-faced Roman god who exposed alternatively his smiling or his furious mood. Similarly, nature also has two faces: a wealthy collection of climates, landscapes and species but also a hazardous source of all natural threats, which could suddenly cause havoc and claim many casualties. Fortunately, more recent laws (República de Colombia 1989, Ley 9ª, de Reforma Urbana; 1993, Ley 99, del Medio Ambiente; 1998, Ley 388, de Ordenamiento Territorial) recognize the importance of natural disasters in environmental management.

The experiences and the solutions described are by no means a panacea. They are complemented by more classical educational actions designed for children. For instance, Medellín has installed 80 pluviometers in schools, managed by students under the supervision of teachers, and measurements are reported periodically. Illustrated booklets have been written and distributed to show the role of water in nature and the danger it may represent in mountainous areas (Bernal et al. 2001a, b). At present, a major effort is being undertaken across the entire country to record each of the destructive events in a computer program freely distributed by the National Office for Disaster Prevention and Relief (DESINVENTAR; Observatorio Sismico del Suroccidente Colombiano–Universidad del Valle). This will improve data collection and also help to establish the real importance of natural disasters in the economy of the country (Hermelin 2003) and hopefully to focus more attention on these problems from policy- and decision-makers.

The authors gratefully acknowledge the collaboration of L. J. Mejía from SIMPAD, Medellín; G. Duque, Universidad Nacional and R. Spaggiari from Corporacion para el Desarrollo de Caldas, Manizales; C. Gómez, E. Londoño and J. I. Orozco, from Carder; and A. Alzate, Municipio de Pereira, Pereira.

References

ACOSTA, J. 1846. Relation de l'éruption boueuse sortie du Volcan de Ruiz et de la catastrophe de Lagunilla dans la République de la Nouvelle Grenade. *Comptes Rendus de l'Académie des Sciences*, **22**, 709–710.

ACOSTA, J. 1851. Sur les montagnes de Ruiz et de Tolima et les éruptions boueuses de la Madeleine, Lettres à Elie de Beaumont. *Bulletin de la Société Geologique de France, 2éme Série*, **8**, 489–497.

ALCALDÍA de Medellín 1993. *Sistematizacion de la intervención de la administración municipal en dos barrios localizados en zonas de riesgo*. Estudio contratado por la Alcaldía de Medellín, PNUD Proyecto Col. 88/010. Universidad Nacional, Sede de Medellín.

BERNAL, M., LOPEZ, J., MEJÍA, L. J., HERMELIN, M. & BEDOYA, G. 2001a. *El viaje del agua, Cartilla de manejo*. Universidad EAFIT, Corantioquia, Mi Rio, SIMPAD, Medellín.

BERNAL, M., LOPEZ, J., MEJÍA, L. J., HERMELIN, M. & BEDOYA, G. 2001b. *El viaje del agua, Manual para instructores*. Universidad EAFIT, Corantioquia, Mi Rio, SIMPAD, Medellín.

COMITES BARRIALES 2007. *La prevención en la cultura de los ciudadanos SIMPAD*. Secretaria Medio Ambiente Alcaldía de Medellín.

DANE 2005. World Wide Web Address: www.dane.gov. co/index.php?option=com_content&task=section.

ESPINAL, L. S. 1977. *Zonas de vida o formaciones vegetales de Colombia Memoria Explicativa*. IGAC, Bogotá.

GÓMEZ, C. 1987. *Evaluación del programa de reubicación*. CARDER, Pereira.

GÓMEZ, C. & BAUTISTA, C. A. 1989. *Participación comunitaria en el plan de ordenamiento y saneamiento ambiental del tramo urbano del río Otún*. CARDER, Pereira.

GUARDIANES DE LA LADERA 2003. Programa de la Protección de laderas del Municipio de Manizales.

World Wide Web Address: http://www.reddesastres. org/fileadmin/documentos/ExperienciasCompiladas _ Andino/Colombia/GUARDIANAS LADERA.

HERMELIN, M. 1990. Bases físicas para los planes de desarrollo de los municipios de Risaralda. *Environmental Geology and Natural Hazards in the Andean Region*. AGID Report, **13**, 269–274.

HERMELIN, M. 1992. El medio ambiente redefinido. *In*: HERMELIN, M. (ed.) *Memorias, II Conferencia Latinoamericana sobre Riesgo Geológico Urbano, y II Conferencia Colombiana de Geología Ambiental, Pereira, Colombia, INGEOMINAS*, **2**, 225–236.

HERMELIN, M. 2003. New trends in prevention of geological hazards. *In*: MOHRIAK, W. (ed.) *31st International Geological Congress, Memoirs, Río de Janeiro (Invited Papers Volume)*.

HERMELIN, M. 2007. Introducción: Colombia, un país de ciudades. *In*: HERMELIN, M. (ed.) *Entorno natural de 17 ciudades de Colombia*. Sociedad Colombiana de Geología, Academia Colombiana de Ciencias Exactas, Físicas y Naturales, Fondo Editorial EAFIT, Medellin, 17–21.

HERMELIN, M. & MONTALESCOT, J. 1991. Utilización de los estudios de geología ambiental en la elaboración de los planes de desarrollo municipales. *Environmental Geology and Applied Geomorphology in Colombia*, AGID Report, **16**, 49–60.

INGEOMINAS 2006. *Mapa geológico de Colombia*. INGEOMINAS, Bogotá.

LONDOÑO, E. 2002. *Áreas naturales protegidas de Risaralda*. CARDER, Pereira.

MOLANO, J. 1990. *Villa de Leyva: ensayos de interpretación social de una catástrofe ecológica*. Fondo FEN Colombia, Bogotá.

MORA, S. 1990. *Ingenierías Prehispánicas*. Fondo FEN Colombia, Instituto Colombiano de Antropología, Bogotá.

RÍOS, D. A. & HERMELIN, M. 2004. Prediction of landslide occurrence in urban areas located on volcanic ash in Pereira, Colombia. *Bulletin of Engineering Geology and the Environment*, **63**, 77–81.

SIMON, FRIAR PEDRO DE 1625. *Noticias historiales de las conquistas de tierra firme en la Indias Occidentales, Bogotá* (2nd edn, 1882–1892). Casa Editorial de Medardo Rivas, Bogota.

Guidelines for landslide hazard mapping in the Andes: speaking one language

MULTINATIONAL ANDEAN PROJECT: GEOSCIENCES FOR ANDEAN COMMUNITIES GEMMA—LANDSLIDE HAZARD STANDARDS GROUP

Geological Survey of Canada, MAP:GAC Project, 625 Robson Street, Vancouver, BC, Canada, V6B 5J3 (corresponding author Monica M. Jaramillo, e-mail: mmjaramillo@rodus.com)

Abstract: To maximize the use of geoscience information across institutions and international borders, data must be collected and stored in a uniform manner so that they are readily accessible and understandable. There is seldom consistency in the representation of these data delivered to users between countries (and, sometimes, even within institutions in the same country). The Multinational Andean Project: Geosciences for Andean Communities (MAP:GAC (2002–2008)), identified the need to research, design and develop a common terminology, techniques, classification system, cartographic symbols and databases for landslide studies. MAP:GAC produced regional guides for landslide studies and mapping, through the first regional group for landslide studies (GEMMA). It is expected that these guides will facilitate the transfer and appropriation of information, and that the generation of products will be more easily understood and applied by land-use planners, emergency-management planners and other users. The standards have been adopted by the seven Andean countries (Argentina, Bolivia, Chile, Colombia, Ecuador, Peru and Venezuela) and were published in the book *Movimientos en Masa en la Región Andina: Una Guía para la Evaluación de Amenazas* (*Landslide Hazards in the Andes*) in 2007.

Landslides are associated with some of the greatest natural disasters in history. In the Andes, the hill and mountainous terrain is susceptible to landslides in areas that are subject to high levels of precipitation and meteorological phenomenon such as the El Niño rains, frequent seismic activity and volcanic eruptions along the subduction zone where the Nazca Plate meets the South American Plate. With more than 160 million inhabitants, the Andean region is densely populated and thus represents an area of high vulnerability that often results in high-risk conditions and the occurrence of disasters. Two of the five most devastating landslide disasters in the last millennium have occurred in the Andes (Evans 2006). One of these was the lahar caused by snow melt and the eruption of the Nevado del Ruiz volcano in Colombia in 1985, which left more than 23 000 people dead (Montero 2007). The other was a landslide in 1970, which originated in Nevado Huascaran in the Peruvian Andes; it was triggered by an earthquake and killed over 18 000 people (Evans *et al.* 2007). In addition to these significant events, hundreds of small landslides interrupt normal activity in cities, towns and on highways every year, causing damage and death as well as serious economic losses.

With the goal of reducing the negative effects of geological hazards, such as volcanic eruptions, earthquakes and landslides in the Andes, the Multinational Andean Project was initiated by the geological surveys of Canada and the seven countries of the Andean region (Argentina, Bolivia, Chile, Colombia, Ecuador, Peru and Venezuela). It was recognized that there were some communication issues that needed to be addressed in landslide studies and these included the following: (1) the lack of consensus on the terminology being used between specialists in the study of landslides, and some local terms that have only limited local application and thus impair communication; (2) a lack of consensus among experts in the use of technical concepts and their graphical representation, which makes effective collaboration between the various regional institutions and countries difficult; (3) difficulties in the communication of information on geological hazards between the institutions that produce this information within countries (geological surveys, provincial governments, universities) and the users of this information (land-use planners, government institutions, emergency-management planners, and policy- and decision-makers) who require standardized and easily understandable language; (4) lack of common procedures and methods for the evaluation of hazards, making hazard and risk map comparisons difficult; (5) differences in the analysis of criteria for acceptable risk between countries, within regions, and even within single institutions.

It was understood that facilitating the understanding and communication between the concerned institutions and specialists in geological

From: LIVERMAN, D. G. E., PEREIRA, C. P. G. & MARKER, B. (eds) *Communicating Environmental Geoscience*. Geological Society, London, Special Publications, **305**, 53–61.
DOI: 10.1144/SP305.6   0305-8719/08/$15.00 © The Geological Society of London 2008.

hazards was an important step when it came to reducing the impact of natural hazards in the countries of the Andean region. With this objective in mind, the Multinational Andean Project: Geosciences for Andean Communities (MAP:GAC) formed multinational working groups in the areas of volcanology, landslide investigations, hazard mapping and neotectonics. The goal of these groups was to establish guidelines and standards for the Andean region that would be consistent and complement the advances already existing in these fields.

The Grupo de Estándares para Movimientos en Masa (GEMMA) working group gathered landslide specialists from the eight project countries, university researchers and emergency-management planners, as well as international experts from other countries. The group identified the need to establish a common 'language', apart from Spanish and English; a specialist's language, which would enable them to understand landslide processes and to select methods appropriate for their study and presentation of results, methods that would be consistent, reproducible and that would allow the production of materials easily comprehensible to the end-users. Hence, the early proposal for the group's name, GEMMA (Spanish acronym for Landslide Standards Group).

However, earlier on, the group reached the conclusion that, with the exception of a few aspects, it was not practical to establish general standards for assessing landslide hazards. There was also a danger of proposing a set of seemingly clear solutions for complex and still evolving assessment problems. Therefore, the group decided to develop a reference text, a common guide for all the Andean region countries, to be complemented and added to, as needed, to suit Andean conditions. It would also take into consideration those aspects that are well established and accepted by the specialists in each field of interest.

GEMMA worked for 3 years on the development of a series of guides for landslide hazard assessment. These guides are specific to Andean region cases and cover five aspects: (1) terminology related to landslides; (2) landslide classifications; (3) procedures for the selection of hazard analysis methods; (4) an inventory for data collection; (5) cartographic symbols. These documents were supported by the senior management of the project institutions and were adopted as an institutional guide and standard reference for landslide hazard assessment at the geoscience agencies of all seven Andean region countries.

Methods

The procedures followed by GEMMA to reach its goals included several steps. These are as follows.

Diagnosis and terms of reference

The needs of each geological survey were analysed to achieve the goal of producing these standards and guides; a detailed process for co-ordinating the development of the guides was established. The work plan and group structure were defined to include international reviewers and consultants external to the project.

Document production

The production of the guides was the result of more than 3 years of work, including three multinational meetings and field trips in Venezuela, Colombia and Peru, e-mail communications, telephone conferences and a continuing information exchange on Geosemantica (http://can.geosemantica.net). Geosemantica is a web application developed by MAP:GAC with the purpose of facilitating communication and decision-making in risk management. With nodes in all eight project countries, Geosemantica offers a digital library and tools that allow users to create, edit and share geospatial and non-geospatial information.

Designing an inventory format and database

A landslide inventory is an ordered record of the location and characteristics of all the events that have occurred in a given area. Often, inventories are the necessary starting point for landslide hazard studies. Therefore, once agreement was reached on basic aspects such as terminology and types of landslides, an inventory format and database were designed and tested in two pilot regions of Colombia.

Final document

The documents drafted by the group were compiled and published in 2007 in the book *Movimientos en Masa en la Region Andina* (*Landslides in the Andes*; MAP:GAC 2007), which includes a CD with SIGMA, the landslide information system developed from the inventory format. As a result of this long process, these standards and guides represent the consensus reached by the international group.

Results

The main products resulting from hazard studies are the hazard-zone maps that constitute the basis for decision-making in risk management (whether in reference to land-use regulations, development of building standards, implementation of instability-control measures and/or emergency management). It is, therefore, important that these studies be scientifically sound and consistent, so that both the technical community and non-technical users can interpret and apply the results.

The elements represented by the final version of a hazard-zone map as well as those aspects analysed at the preliminary stages require a certain degree of standardization. An ideal hazard-zone map must show characteristics such as the spatial and temporal probabilities, type, magnitude, velocity and run-out zone of landslides predicted for a certain area. To produce a hazard-zone map it is essential (in the majority of cases) to prepare an inventory map. This requires the clear identification of the various types of landslides, past and present, in the area of interest. Each landslide (type) occurs under specific conditions and its occurrence also produces a certain impact. If the types of landslides to affect an area are not clearly identified, then it is difficult to implement appropriate mitigation measures.

Terminology: glossary

During GEMMA's active phase, setting up a landslide glossary was identified as a prerequisite before proceeding with the study. The objective was to have, at hand, the terminology that would ease communication between the specialists, but that would also be useful for non-specialists. This arose from the finding that the landslide literature contains many identical terms that have different meanings, and many different terms that have the same meaning. Also, it is common for countries to adopt certain terms for their local use, all of which leads to a confusion of meanings when researchers discuss the various aspects of landslides. The reasons for this phenomenon vary, such as, for example, a specific worker's point of view when referring to some aspect of a landslide. In Latin America, it derives from the fact that most of the terms in use are translations, mainly from English, which are subject to each translator's interpretation and often do not correspond to that from other countries. Also, the development of areas of science involved in landslide studies has brought new terms with it, as well as the revisions and modifications of older terms (MAP:GAC 2007).

For example, the word 'huayco' is broadly used and accepted in Peru, but it is unknown by most people in the other Andean countries. Therefore, even though it is so well entrenched in Peru, it can hardly be used as a standard term in regional landslide information systems. Huaycos are landslides that have great destructive potential and therefore must be included in hazard studies. The same processes are labelled 'avenidas torrenciales' in Colombia and Venezuela. The features and characteristics of huaycos correspond to processes widely documented in the North American and European scientific literature and known as debris flows. The term debris flow, however, was not known to many people in the Andean region. The unintended result was that a great quantity of scientific literature was not being taken into account when these processes were studied in Latin America. Similarly, Peruvian literature concerning huaycos was not easily accessible to the international community.

Terms related to landslides form a substantial list if one takes into account the fact that these form part of the field of study of geology, geomorphology, geotechnical and mining engineering, and other fields of research. Therefore, landslide-related terminology is a mixture of terms derived from classical use in these sciences as well as common usage and others that one might call 'custom-made'. The focus for the production of the glossary was on compiling the terms most frequently used or those deemed most relevant for the consolidation of terms at the level of the geological surveys in the Andean countries participating in the MAP:GAC project.

With the this objective in mind, 265 terms were proposed as standard and definitions were adopted. For convenience, some terms appear in the glossary with more than one definition and its equivalent English term. Synonyms and local expressions are listed and the reader is referred to their meaning, given in the entry for the standard term. Definitions are also given for some local terms not documented in the literature; these terms describe processes typical to particular areas in the Andean region.

It is worth noting that not everyone will be in agreement with the choice of terms and their meanings. As is often the case, someone's favourite terms or meanings may have been omitted. As it is, the glossary is a starting point for improving communication, and interested persons are invited to build on it, so that an improved edition may be produced in future.

The glossary of landslide-related terms was used as a base for the development of the other aspects of the guides proposed by MAP:GAC.

Landslide classification systems

Landslide studies require the identification of landslide types (past, present and potential) and their causes. Both the types and the causes are the basis for hazard analysis and the choice of appropriate hazard mitigation measures.

The types or classifications used must empha- size aspects of practical importance related to the hazard. For example, the distinction between debris flows and debris avalanches has major impli- cations. In the case of debris flows, the hazard is concentrated in a limited zone along a channel and in the fan or deposit area. In contrast, debris avalanches may affect whole slopes without being limited to a channel. Thus, the potential area affected differs considerably between these types. This type of distinction is of great importance for hazard management and must be recorded consist- ently, using clear terms and concepts to facilitate communication between geoscientists, and between them and the users of the information.

Besides using a consistent terminology, com- munication is very much enhanced by the avail- ability of formal definitions that describe the unique aspects of each type of landslide and may be used to differentiate one from another. There are a number of systems for classifying landslides in the published literature. Those of Varnes (1958, 1978), Hutchinson (1968, 1988) and Cruden & Varnes (1996) are the most widely accepted classi- fication systems in the English-speaking world. Nevertheless, in literature searches one commonly encounters inconsistent terminology and ambigu- ous definitions for the various types of landslides (MAP:GAC 2007). In the Andean region, the most frequently used classification systems are adopted and often modified from those developed in North America or Europe, frequently leading to various interpretations and confusion of terms and meanings. There are also local terms, some of which originate in aboriginal languages that lack clear definitions, and are unknown in other regions.

GEMMA's objective was to present the various landslide types in a simple, unified manner, keeping the established concepts in the classification systems most used in the Spanish-speaking world and contributing further additional definitions. The aim was to compile a classification scheme with the equivalent local terminology, and standardized concepts that can be used to develop interactive applications such as computer-assisted landslide information systems.

Considering that the most used classification systems are conceptually related, the approach was to encourage their use, as this facilitates the correlation of the different systems and those preva- lent in other languages. The classification used in the guides is an adoption of the various above- mentioned classification systems; in the case of flow-type landslides, the proposal was to adopt the classification scheme of Hungr et al. (2001).

Part of the process of adoption of classification systems included the documentation of Andean examples; this helps to link processes that occur in the Andes to those already well documented in the international literature. The different landslide types and classification systems were discussed at international workshops with the occasional partici- pation of some of the proponents of the established systems. A total of 29 known Andean case histories are included in the guides; some cases contain orig- inal information not previously published, and in other instances the information was produced as a part of the MAP:GAC project. These case histories were documented so as to show the nature and scale of landslide hazards in the Andean region and their potential destructive effects. These were also com- piled with the objective of guiding the documen- tation of other cases.

The landslide types and the standard terms in the glossary were used to design the format and inven- tory database and various aspects of the guides.

Landslide assessment methods

From the outset of GEMMA, it was clear that it would not be possible to define a unique hazard analysis method for all the landslide types that occur in the study region. However, it is possible to improve the quality of research and communi- cation between the technicians and users through reference texts and guides.

A typical Andean basin presents every possible type of landslide, and many hazard analysis methods exist in the literature; furthermore, others are still being developed. However, assessing the combined hazard for all processes that may occur is often very demanding, costly and impractical. If combined, the resulting products may be very con- fusing for the user, thus hindering the effective application of the hazard analysis.

Therefore, hazard analysis must be directed to highlight aspects of practical importance. For example, one of MAP:GAC's pilot basins in Vene- zuela has experienced rock avalanches, debris flows, slides, rock falls and debris floods, amongst other slope failures. Assessing hazards requires the application of a different method for each case, which is costly and demanding. Combining the various hazards resulting from these processes in a single map may result in a fairly complex and confusing product, one that would be difficult for users, such as planning authorities, civil defence, etc., to apply. Thus, it is important to determine the priority of the hazards to be studied and select the best method to be applied. This will help ensure that the final product or hazard-zone map is directed at the relevant problems and is as under- standable as possible for its users.

In approaching this topic, the objective was to aid professionals in choosing effective methods for the study and mapping of landslide hazards, and to facilitate the establishment of more standardized products for users. During the development of the MAP:GAC project, emphasis was placed on giving priority to the analysis of the highest risk processes. This method is particularly valuable for use in South America, where many of these studies are done by junior geoscientists or engineers who have relatively little experience.

The cases that may occur in landslide studies are grouped into six classes. For each case, a description of the procedure recommended for its study and analysis was prepared. This helps with the selection of methods for studying and mapping landslide hazards and the production of maps that allow comparisons with other hazard or risk maps or tolerable-risk criteria maps.

These classes are as follows:

Type A case: assessment of the stability of a single slope;

Type B case: hazard zoning of a specific, already existing landslide;

Type C case: landslide susceptibility zoning;

Type D case: hazard zoning for determining setback distances;

Type E case: hazard zoning in the run-out area, based on deposit analysis;

Type F case: hazard zoning in the run-out area, based on material source analysis.

Landslide inventories

A typical inventory in the Andean region (even for small basins), contains hundreds or thousands of landslides. These inventories, which are the starting point for landslide hazard studies, are often made by people with varying levels of training and experience. Consequently, a geological survey of the Andean region will have records of thousands of landslides, the level of reporting of which reflects the different levels of training and experience of the observers, from the level of a junior geoscientist to that of a specialist. Therefore, these records require a level of consistency and standardization so that they may be used in a storage system, permitting research and analysis; in this way, the inventory fulfils its objective as a base reservoir of data for hazard-assessment studies.

The features that are recorded in an inventory vary in accordance with the type of instability problem being studied, and, to date, there is no unified scheme for inventory records. This logically led GEMMA, with MAP:GAC's objectives in mind, to propose (as the next step) the design and establishment of an inventory form as a complement to earlier work in the region.

The proposed form (Fig. 1) is for use as a tool for the systematic collection of basic information about landslides. The form is in two parts; the first part must be compiled in the field and the second part

may require office work. The format that has been developed is divided into 14 major information themes about landslides; these are further divided into sub-themes. A guide was also developed to assist in processing the data on the form.

Although it would be desirable to have at hand complete and precise information on all aspects of a landslide, an experienced landslide investigator will know that any proposed inventory model is not in itself a detailed study of such aspects. It is a compilation of basic facts for locating, in space and time, a set of landslides and synthesizing its most characteristic features in accordance with its geological, geomorphological and geotechnical attributes as well as its impact. The intention is to contribute to the building of a reliable database for hazard and risk assessment, given that the absence of these facts is found to be critical, in particular, when the intent is to create zones for landslide hazards and risks (MAP:GAC 2007).

The inventory format was tested by INGEOMINAS, Colombia's geological survey, an agency with a mandate to provide the country with geohazard information, including landslides. INGEOMINAS used the inventory format in two pilot zones in the centre and NE of Colombia, where it recorded about 500 landslides in total; this allowed a refinement of the information-gathering format. In the NE region of the country, a database designed around the inventory form was used and it proved to be very useful to the technical staff. Also, computer applications were designed to present the information to the community; that is, applications that allow the people affected to visualize and understand the problem, thus making it easier to take action. Both experiences were very positive in the sense that they supplied large amounts of information for the development of the final version of SIGMA (the database and landslide information system). SIGMA was launched in 2007 and was put to the test in taking an inventory of the landslides that took place during, and after, the 15 August 2007 earthquake (with an epicentre beneath the Pacific Ocean along the central Peruvian coast).

The SIGMA information system allows for the organized, codified storage of landslide inventory information. It allows searches by any stored parameter, category or theme, facilitating information analysis. An important feature of the information system is that it allows the visualization of the data in GIS (geographic information system) environments. For example, data may be exported in digital layers in easily handled formats, known as GML and KML, and may be spatially viewed in systems such as Geosemantica and GoogleEarth. This makes it easy to work in other GIS applications commonly used to produce the final products.

Through SIGMA, the scientific community and the users can consult data stored by the geological

FORMATO PARA INVENTARIO DE MOVIMIENTOS EN MASA
Proyecto Multinacional Andino: Geociencias para las Comunidades Andina

IMPORTANCIA DEL EVENTO
☐ Alta ☐ Media ☐ Baja

Nombre del Encuestador: _____ Fecha ___ Día: ___ Mes: ___ Año: ___ Institución: _____ Código del Evento: _____

LOCALIZACION GEOGRAFICA Y DOCUMENTAL DEL EVENTO

POR DIVISION POLITICA
País: _____
Dpto./Prov./Edo.: _____
Municipio/Ciudad: _____
Localidad: _____

COORDENADAS
Sitio: _____
Norte/Lat.: _____
Este/Long.: _____
Proyección: _____
Altura sitio (m.s.n.m.): _____

REFERENTES GEOGRAFICOS
Mapa/Plancha No.: ___ Año: ___ Escala: ___ Editor: _____

DOCUMENTACION
Fotografía No.: ___ Año: ___ Escala: ___ Editor: _____

ESPACIAMIENTO (m)
>2 | 2 - 0,6 | 0,6-0,2 | 0,2-0,06 | <0,06

ACTIVIDAD DEL MOVIMIENTO

FECHAS DE OCURRENCIA
DD / MM / AA
Primer Movimiento: ___ / ___ / ___
Edad (años): ___
___ / ___
___ / ___

ESTADO
Activo
Reactivado
Suspendido
Latente
Abandonado
Estabilizado
Relicto

ESTILO
Complejo
Compuesto
Múltiple
Sucesivo
Unico
Enjambre

DISTRIBUCION
Retrogresivo
Avanzando
Ensanchando
Confinado
Creciente
Decreciente
Móvil

LITOLOGIA Y ESTRATIGRAFIA

DESCRIPCION

ESTRUCTURA
DB | BZ
DB: Dirección de buzamiento BZ: Buzamiento

ORIENTACION
DB | BZ

CLASIFICACION DEL MOVIMIENTO

TIPO DE MOVIMIENTO
1 | 2 | %1 | %2
Caída
Volcamiento
Deslizamiento rotacional
Deslizamiento traslacional
Propagación lateral
Reptación
Flujo
Deformaciones gravitacionales profundas

NOTAS: 1 = Primer movimiento
2 = Segundo movimiento

MATERIAL
1 | 2
Roca
Detritos
Tierra
Suelos Ingeniería:
Bloques
Cantos
Grava
Arena
Finos
M.O.
M.O. Materia orgánica, turba

Humedad del suelo
1 | 2
Seco
Lig. Húmedo
Húmedo
Muy húmedo
Mojado

Plasticidad
1 | 2
Alta
Media
Baja
No plástico

Origen del Suelo 1
Residual
Sedimentario (*)
* Tipo suelo sedimentario:

Clasificación USCS:

OTRAS CARACTERISTICAS
Movimiento canalizado
Movimiento no canalizado
Licuación
Otra ... Describir

Sistema de Clasificación:
NOMBRE DEL MOVIMIENTO:

VELOCIDAD
DESCRIPCION	VELOCIDAD TIPICA
Extr. Rápido	(>5 m/s)
Muy rápido	(>3 m/min)
Rápido	(>1,8 m/h)
Moderado	(> 13 m/mes)
Lento	(> 1,6 m/año)
Muy lento	(> 16 mm/año)
Ext. Lento	(< 16 mm/año)

Vmáx.: _____
Vmedia: _____
Mr. Medida C. Calculada E. Estimada

CLASIFICACION DEL MOVIMIENTO

MORFOMETRIA

GENERAL
Diferencia de altura corona a punta (m): _____
Longitud horizontal corona a punta (m): _____
Fahrböschung (°): _____
Pendiente ladera en post-falla (°): _____
Pendiente ladera en pre-falla (°): _____
Dirección del movimiento (°): _____
Azimut del talud (°): _____
Profundidad de la superficie de falla, Dr (m): _____
Ancho de la superficie de falla Wr (m): _____
Longitud de superficie de falla Lr (m): _____
Espesor de la masa desplazada Dd (m): _____
Ancho de la masa desplazada Wd (m): _____
Longitud de la masa desplazada Ld (m): _____
Longitud total, L (m): _____

DIMENSIONES
Volúmen inicial (m3): _____
Volúmen desplazado (m3): _____
Area inicial (km2): _____
Area total afectada (km2): _____
Distancia de viaje (km): _____
Runup (m): _____

DEFORMACION DEL TERRENO
Modo
Ondulación
Escalonamiento

Severidad
Leve
Media
Severa

GEOFORMA

CAUSAS DEL MOVIMIENTO

C | D
Material plástico débil
Material sensitivo
Material colapsible
Material meteorizado físicamente
Material meteorizado químicamente
Material fallado por corte
Material fisurado o agrietado
Orientación desfavorable de discontinuidades
Contraste de permeabilidad de materiales
Contraste de rigidez de materiales
Meteorización por congelamiento/deshielo
Meteorización por expansión/contracción
Deforestación o ausencia de vegetación

Movimiento tectónico
Sismo: M ___ E ___ De ___ P ___
Erupción volcánica
Lluvias: mm24h= ___ mm48h= ___ mm72h= ___
Viento
Deshielo
Avance/retroceso de glaciares
Rompimiento de lagos en cráteres
Rompimiento de presas
Desembalse rápido de represas
Embalse
Erosión del pie del talud por glaciares
Erosión superficial

C | D
Socavación del pie del talud por corriente agua
Socavación del pie del talud por oleaje
Excavación del pie del talud
Carga en la corona del talud
Erosión subterránea (disolución, tubificación)
Irrigación
Mantenimiento deficiente sistema de drenaje
Escapes de agua de tuberías
Minería
Disposición deficiente de esteriles/escombros
Vibración artificial (tráfico, explosiones, hincado de pilotes)
Otros

NOTAS: C, Condicionantes; D, Detonante mm24h: lluvia acumulada en las 24 horas antes del sismo Mt: magnitud del sismo, E: Escala del sismo (ML, Ms, mb, Mw), De: Distancia al epicentro (km), P: Profundidad (km)

COBERTURA Y USO DEL SUELO

TIPO COBERTURA | %
Veg. Herbácea
Bosque/Selva
Matorrales
Cuerpo agua
Cultivos
Construcciones
Sin cobertura

TIPO USO | %
Ganadería
Area protegida
Agrícola
Recreación
Zona arqueológica
Zona industrial
Vivienda
Vías
Minería

DOCUMENTOS DE REFERENCIA

Autores	Año	Título	Revista/libro/Informe	Editor/Institución	Ciudad	Volumen Páginas

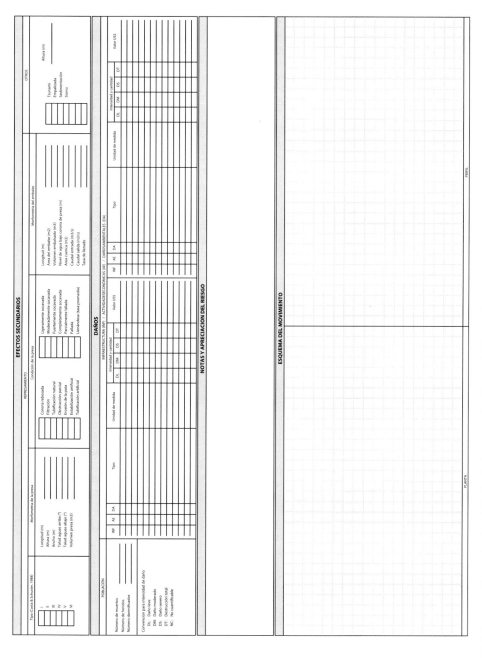

Fig. 1. Landslide inventory format developed for the Andean countries. The model format displayed in this illustration is divided into 14 fields: (1) geographical and documentary location of the event; (2) landslide activity; (3) lithology and stratigraphy; (4) landslide classification; (5) morphometrics; (6) landslide causes; (7) soil coverage and land use; (8) documentary references; (9) secondary effects; (10) importance of the event (in the upper right corner of the first page); (11) damage; (12) notes and assessment of risk; (13) sketch map; (14) photographic register.

surveys of the Andean countries. Similarly, the geological surveys may feed their database with information compiled by other agencies using the same format.

Cartography

Cartography has as its main purpose the presentation of information in a simplified graphic format as it relates to different hazardous events for a given area in a single map. It offers a view of the natural processes, with their differing characteristics, such as magnitude, frequency and impact area.

The effective use of landslide hazard information for managing emergencies or regulating land use requires a considerable effort from those who generate the information and also from those who use it. If the scientific and engineering data are not converted to a common, easily understandable language, communities cannot make effective use of the information and it will be of limited value for other scientists and engineers. Furthermore, such information will probably be misused or set aside in the process of planning for development (MAP:GAC 2007).

The main achievement of GEMMA was to encourage the use of standardized cartographic symbols for landslides, in accordance with the agreed-upon types and definitions, displaying this information in map form.

Distribution of the guidelines

The guidelines produced by MAP:GAC are distributed free in the Andean countries through their national geological surveys. In addition, they were distributed to many of the affected countries and relevant institutes in Central America and the Spanish-speaking regions of the Caribbean; there the guidelines may represent examples that do not fit completely with local conditions but nevertheless can be used as a guide for carrying out a similar effort in these regions.

Also, the guidebook and inventory database are available free in PDF format through each country's Geosemantica nodes and through the Web pages of the geological surveys of the Andean nations. Also, printed copies may be purchased for the cost of printing, from each of the geological surveys.

Outlook

Over the past few decades, numerous landslide risk-management strategies have been designed and implemented. The experience gained by many countries has encouraged the use of hazard- and risk-zoning maps for land-use regulations and emergency management; this clearly shows that there is a need for standardized, reproducible hazard assessment and zoning methods, particularly as regards to the definition of classes of landslides (Cascini *et al.* 2005).

In an effort to communicate clearly with the various levels of users of the landslide inventories (and thus minimize a potential catastrophe) the preparation of these guides for landslide hazard studies is a contribution to the geological surveys of the Andean countries and other organizations involved in risk management. It is hoped that these guides will help to create more understandable products for users, such as land-use authorities, emergency management offices and civil defence.

GEMMA's experience at the multinational level has been very positive and rewarding. The group quickly focused its efforts toward the production of standards and guides, in part because of the needs in this field that had been identified earlier by many previous reseachers. In addition, some efforts had already been made to resolve them; the group enjoyed full institutional support from the outset of its work.

The experience with the pilot studies in Colombia, where the inventories were put to the test, had a positive impact on the multinational effort. The topical developments made in this country prior to GEMMA's work constituted a good starting point. Also, the need identified in Colombia for a landslide information system made it easier to test GEMMA's developments. The success of this Colombian initiative is expected to have a positive impact on the implementation of these standards and guides in the neighbouring countries.

For the future, it is important to consider that initiatives such as GEMMA are subject to the typical issues of projects undertaken in these regions. Problems such as the high rates of staff turnover, changes to institutional mandates, the short lives of some geosciences institutions and the fluctuating levels of political currency in the agencies and ministries on which the continuity of these activities depend all affect outcomes.

It is important for future projects to evaluate the lessons learned here, reporting both successes and failures. Prior to its disbanding in July 2008, the project will produce reports in that spirit, not only of the MAP:GAC pilot zones but also of the thematic areas described in this paper; these published reports will be a guide for future projects in the Andean region.

The MAP:GAC project acknowledges the financial support of the Canadian International Development Agency (CIDA), as well as the support of the seven geological survey partners: SEGEMAR (Argentina), SERGEOTECMIN (Bolivia), SERNAGEOMIN (Chile), DINAGE (Ecuador), INGEMMET (Peru), INGEOMINAS (Colombia) and INGEOMIN (Venezuela). Reviews by D. Liverman, S. McCuaig, C. P. G. Pereira, and C. J. Hickson improved the manuscript.

Authors of the guidelines

The following are the members of GEMMA and main contributors and authors of the book *Movimientos en Masa en la Región Andina* (in alphabetical order).

Argentina (SEGEMAR). Valerie Bauman, Luís Fauqué, Maria A. González, Omar Lapido and Alejandra Tejedo.

Bolivia (SERGEOTECMIN). Miguel Blacutt and Gonzalo Quenta.

Canada (Geological Survey of Canada). Reginald L. Hermanns, Lionel Jackson, Jr and Mónica M. Jaramillo, GEMMA Group leader. (*University of British Columbia, UBC*) Oldrich Hungr, Advisor to the GEMMA Group.

Chile (SERNAGEOMIN). Renate Wall and Luis Lara.

Colombia (INGEOMINAS). Yolanda Calderón, Edgar Carrillo, José H. Carvajal, Gloria L. Ruiz Peña and Jacobo Ojeda-Moncayo, South American GEMMA leader.

Ecuador (DINAGE). Elías Ibadango and Aracelly Lima.

Peru (INGEMMET) Lionel Fídel and Bilberto Zabala.

Venezuela (INGEOMIN) Jesús Guerrero.

References

CASCINI, L., BONNARD, CH., COROMINAS, J., JIBSON, R. & MONTERO-OLARTE, J. 2005. Landslide hazard and risk zoning for urban planning and development. *In*: HUNGR, O., FELL, R., COUTURE, R. & EBERHARDT, E. (eds) *Landslide Risk Management Proceedings of the International Conference on Landslide Risk Management, Vancouver, Canada.* Balkema, Rotterdam, 199–235.

CRUDEN, D. M. & VARNES, D. J. 1996. Landslide types and processes. *In*: TURNER, K. & SCHUSTER, R. L. (eds) *Landslides Investigation and Mitigation.* Transportation Research Board, Special Report, **247**, 36–75.

EVANS, S. G. 2006. Single event landslides resulting from massive rock slope failure: Characterizing their frequency and impact on society. *In*: EVANS, S. G., SCARASCIA MUGNOZZA, G., STROM, A. & HERMANNS, R. L. (eds) *Landslides from Massive Rock Slope Failure.* NATO Science Series IV, Earth and Environmental Sciences, **49**, 53–73.

EVANS, S. G., FIDEL, L. & ZEGARRA, J. 2007. Los movimientos en masa de 1962 y 1970 en el Nevado de Huascaran, Valle del Rio Santa, Cordillera Blanca, Peru. *In*: MAP:GAC (ed.) *Movimientos en Masa en la Región Andina: Una Guía para la Evaluación de Amenazas.* Servicio Nacional de Geología y Minería, Publicación Geológica Multinacional, **4**, 386–403.

HUNGR, O., EVANS, S. G., BOVIS, M. & HUTCHINSON, J. N. 2001. Review of the classification of landslides of the flow type. *Environmental and Engineering Geoscience*, **VII**, 221–238.

HUTCHINSON, J. N. 1968. Mass movements. *In*: FAIRBRIDGE, R. W. (ed.) *The Encyclopedia of Geomorphology.* Reinhold, New York, 688–695.

HUTCHINSON, J. N. 1988. Morphological and geotechnical parameters of landslides in relation to geology and hydrogeology. *In*: BONNARD, C. (ed.) *Proceedings, 5th International Conference on Landslides, Vol. 1, Lausanne,* A. A. Balkema, Rotterdam, 3–35.

MAP:GAC (ed.) 2007. *Movimientos en Masa en la Región Andina: Una Guía para la Evaluación de Amenazas.* Servicio Nacional de Geología y Minería, Publicación Geológica Multinacional, **4**.

MONTERO, J. 2007. Flujos de detritos (lahares) catastróficos del Volcán Nevado del Ruiz, Colombia, 11 de noviembre de 1985. *In*: MAP:GAC (ed.) *Movimientos en Masa en la Región Andina: Una Guía para la Evaluación de Amenazas.* Servicio Nacional de Geología y Minería, Publicación Geológica Multinacional, **4**, 369–385.

VARNES, D. J. 1958. Landslides types and processes. *In*: ECKEL, E. B. (ed.) *Landslides and Engineering Practice.* Highway Research Board, Special Report, **28**, 20–47.

VARNES, D. J. 1978. Slope movements, types and processes. *In*: SCHUSTER, R. L. & KRIZEK, R. J. (eds) *Landslides Analysis and Control.* Transportation Research Board, Special Report, **176**, 9–33.

Lead contamination, the media and risk communication: a case study from the Ribeira Valley, Brazil

GABRIELA MARQUES DI GIULIO[1], NEWTON MÜLLER PEREIRA[2] &
BERNARDINO RIBEIRO DE FIGUEIREDO[2]

[1]*Environmental Studies Center, NEPAM, University of Campinas, R. dos Flamboyants,
155, Cidade Universitária Zeferino Vaz, 13084-867, Campinas, SP, Brazil*

[2]*Institute of Geosciences, University of Campinas, R. João Pandiá, Calógeras, 51,
Cidade Universitária Zeferino Vaz, 13083-970, Campinas, SP, Brazil*
(e-mail: berna@ige.unicamp.br)

Abstract: This paper discusses the importance of risk communication in studies of public health issues, and analyses the roles of scientists and the media in communicating scientific data, and their influence on risk perception. The findings are based on a case study from Adrianópolis in the Ribeira Valley (Brazil), conducted between 2005 and 2006, where residents were exposed to lead contamination that originated from a smelter and a sulphide mine. This study had two goals: (1) to understand the impact of information regarding lead contamination on the daily lives of the local inhabitants; (2) to understand and analyse the consequences of an absence of a strategy for risk communication by the researchers involved in the study. Besides drawing attention to the need for studies concerning passive environmental issues, the Adrianópolis case study showed that there was a lack of adequate planning for dissemination of information to local inhabitants that seriously undermined the relationships between researchers, the community and the media, and this caused damage to the various stakeholders.

In the last few years, many people in industrialized and developing countries have become more concerned about risks present in their daily lives. Consequently, people require a commitment from the scientific community that reflects a higher awareness of its responsibilities in evaluating, as well as managing, environmental risks and risks to public health. For this reason, scientists need to consider the implications of using communities as subject areas in their research. They must examine means of public communication of the results obtained, particularly when these results have implications for health risk. Researchers need to recognize that public participation in the decision-making processes that are part of the risk management phase is as important as the release and dissemination of information. As a process, 'risk communication' includes strategies that ensure that information is divulged in a clear manner, so that the local population can understand the results and its implications. The local population should be encouraged to actively participate in the solution to problems or in mitigation of risk.

The US National Research Council (NRC) defines risk communication as the exchange of information about the nature, magnitude, interpretation, acceptability and management of risk. The concept of risk communication mainly developed following the Chernobyl nuclear accident, which occurred in the Ukraine in 1986. This accident illustrated the communication problems that researchers were faced with in disseminating adequately information to the public about the risk and the uncertainty in the estimation of the risk. Since then, scientists, communicators and public administrators, mainly from developed countries, have emphasized the need to put an interactive communication process into practice. This involves the exchange of opinions among the various social actors, and examines their reactions to messages about risk or the legal and institutional measures related to risk management. Today, 20 years after the Chernobyl incident, the discussion about risk communication has gained ground in the public agenda, as a result of the perception of risk involved with situations that range from natural and environmental disasters, infectious diseases (such as the recent 'bird flu') to the threat of bombs, bioterrorism and epidemics of chronic diseases.

This paper discusses risk communication as it relates to a study that took place between 2005 and 2006 in the town of Adrianópolis, located in Paraná State in the Ribeira Valley, Brazil (Di Giulio 2006). This valley is known for its intense mining activity during the 20th century, which focused on the production of lead, zinc and silver. The Ribeira Valley encompasses 32 towns from São Paulo and Paraná States (southeastern

From: LIVERMAN, D. G. E., PEREIRA, C. P. G. & MARKER, B. (eds) *Communicating Environmental Geoscience*. Geological Society, London, Special Publications, **305**, 63–74.
DOI: 10.1144/SP305.7   0305-8719/08/$15.00 © The Geological Society of London 2008.

Fig. 1. Ribeira Valley, Brazil.

and southern regions of Brazil) and has an estimated population of 400 000 inhabitants (Fig. 1). The town of Adrianópolis, in the Upper Ribeira Valley, was the main centre for lead ore production that was processed at the Plumbum Mineração e Metalurgia Ltda plant between 1945 and 1995. During most of this period, mining and processing activities were developed in a manner inconsistent with modern mining standards, with little control of environmental and human health impacts. The plant, in its 50 years of operation, must have released a large quantity of gases and lead-rich particulate matter into the atmosphere, and the latter was deposited on the soil surfaces near the refinery, particularly in the Capelinha and Vila Mota neighbourhoods in the rural area of Adrianópolis (Paoliello *et al.* 2002, 2003; Cunha *et al.* 2005; Figueiredo 2005, 2007).

These areas are home to around 100 families at a distance of 1500 m from the processing plant, along an unpaved road that passes in front of the facility and connects the Capelinha and Vila Mota neighbourhoods (Fig. 2). Analysis showed that most of the greens and vegetables produced from residential gardens near Plumbum, and consumed by residents, exceeded the lead concentration limits recommended by the Brazilian Ministry of Health (Lamoglia *et al.* 2006).

In 2001, during studies of environmental contamination and human exposure to lead in Adrianópolis, the media had access to part of the research findings and extensively covered the subject. The first story was broadcast on *Jornal Nacional*, from TV Globo (one of the programmes most watched by Brazilian audiences). This piece, shown on 28 February 2001, served as a catalyst for other media outlets, which published several articles and broadcast news about the case in March 2001. As a result, Adrianópolis, albeit inadvertently, came to be known as 'lead town.'

To understand the communication process that resulted from the initial research projects at Adrianópolis, a second study was carried out in 2005 and 2006. This study had the aims of documenting the impact of information on lead contamination on the daily lives of local inhabitants, and of analysing the consequences of the absence of a strategy for risk communication by researchers involved in the initial studies.

Methods

Two methods were used in the present study: (1) research on published material; (2) empirical

Fig. 2. Vila Mota residents, who were exposed to contaminated soil and dust that originated from unpaved roads.

research based on interviews. The results were compared with the existing literature on evaluation, administration, perception and communication of risk; scientific and media publications; the role of the media in the popularization of science; and questions related to environmental risk and public health.

News reports from between February and March 2001 were studied, a period in which the lead contamination problem in Adrianópolis was extensively communicated through the media. From various stories about the subject, three articles from three prominent national news outlets and 21 articles published in two prominent regional newspapers from Parana State were chosen for detailed analysis.

The empirical research consisted of visits to Adrianópolis and collection of statements from important actors in the case (Fig. 3). These were initially subdivided into five social categories or groups: local residents, government officials (local and state), ex-employees of Plumbum, journalists, and environmental and health researchers. The statements and information collected during the interview process supported the grouping of the respondents according to their occupations, responsibilities, behaviour during past studies, and

the impact felt as a result of media coverage. The interviews with the local inhabitants, government officials and Plumbum ex-employees illustrated their perception of risk, the relationship with the researchers during and after the studies, how they analysed the media's influence on communicating the issue, and the impacts of this communication. The interviews with journalists who covered the subject in 2001 allowed reflection on how the case was communicated and its impacts, and the consideration of possible failures and successes during their work. Statements collected from researchers had the goal of recognizing how this group perceived the role of the media in risk communication and the consequent amplification of risk perception, and how they evaluated the involvement of the residents of Adrianópolis in the research performed.

To analyse the statements that were collected, in addition to taking the division of the interview subjects into established groups into consideration, interviews were evaluated in four areas: perception of risk, media coverage of the case, the relationship between the social actors, and improvements in risk communication in the future.

Fig. 3. One of the interviews that took place in Adrianópolis, Curitiba (capital of Parana State), Campinas, and São Paulo city.

Results

News analysis

The first stories, published in 2001, had a warning tone and focused on the seriousness of the situation. In those stories, sensational expressions such as 'contaminated inhabitants', 'extremely serious', 'warning state', 'leaded', 'lead-hunt' and 'Adrianópolis savages' were used (Fig. 4). For example, in one of the stories published, in *Gazeta do Povo* on 1 March 2001, the headline focused people's attention on the lead contamination of children: '70% of Adrianópolis' children are contaminated'. The article noted that 70% of the children in the town had levels of lead in their bodies that were three times higher than the level considered safe by the World Health Organization (WHO). It also explained that a study of the town showed that the soil, animals and river water near Adrianópolis were contaminated with lead. The article was factually inaccurate on two points: the contamination of the river water was not verified by the studies of the area (Cunha *et al.* 2005) and the percentage of children who were contaminated was incorrect.

The studies (Paoliello *et al.* 2002, 2003) showed that 60% of the blood samples (from both children and adults) had lead levels above 10 μg dL^{-1}, the internationally accepted value considered as the maximum limit for good health, and only 13% of the samples had lead concentrations above 20 μg dl^{-1}.

The analysis also showed that the media tried to reinforce political involvement in the Adrianópolis case; for example, backing the proposal of an inquiry to investigate the matter at the Brazilian parliament. Headlines such as 'The Adrianópolis case may lead to a parliamentary inquiry' and 'Adrianópolis lead contamination case to be examined by the Senate', and phrases such as 'The senator is sure that the Adrianópolis case should have repercussions in the Congress' illustrated that the case reached the political arena.

Twenty-five days after the first story about the Adrianópolis case was published, it could be seen that the media changed their focus to criticism of the way the research was conducted (emphasizing the complex relation between the media and researchers that characterized this case). The news media attempted to show the public that there had

Fig. 4. The Plumbum smelter that was responsible for lead pollution in Adrianópolis, which attracted media attention in 2001.

been a pattern of warnings in the stories that had been broadcast.

Sentences such as 'the revelations contained in preliminary studies from São Paulo State universities fell into a black hole. They didn't reach the doctors from the State Secretary of Health. Jealousy from the professional world and academic competition obstructed information exchange' and 'it was all a scare', and 'the story that lead was poisoning Adrianópolis' seven thousand inhabitants appears to be the product of fertile imaginations and an excess of zeal on the part of the Deputy-Mayor ...' are examples that confirm this suggestion.

Interviews and analysis of statements

Risk perception. Analysis of the interviews showed that the local community (local residents, government authorities and Plumbum ex-employees) perceived the lead contamination risk in different ways. Some inhabitants and authorities pointed out that part of the community believed that to live with this daily risk could mean a chance of receiving a court-awarded settlement. This quote from one resident teacher is an example: 'Many people think that if they are actually contaminated,

they will go to court and request monetary compensation. This is the general thought of the people around here. If you die, you'll pass it on to your kids.'

The group made up of Plumbum ex-employees associated the risk exclusively with occupational activity. This came from the idea that the former workers of the mining company were expected to suffer from contamination problems, whereas the current inhabitants (years after the company had closed), would not have any problem simply because they lived nearby. A quote from one former employee illustrates this analysis: 'I'm going to turn 80 and I've spend almost all my life here ... and I don't feel a thing. Thank God I've never had a health problem. I think many people who worked in the factory have died, but they died because their time had come. But not from poisoning.'

Some residents and local authorities associated the risk only with the presence of spoil heaps that were the result of mining activities. These respondents suggested that if the spoil heaps were removed, the contamination problem would cease to exist (ignoring the results from studies regarding contamination of soil and food crops planted in gardens in the backyards of houses next to Plumbum). This perception may be illustrated by the following statement from the Agriculture and the Environment Secretary: 'The present owners of Plumbum have started to worry about the environmental issue and are finishing a project to mitigate the environmental damage, covering the tailings and residue with soil and vegetation. This solves the problem. Lead is an inert material. As to the residue, there were problems with visual pollution from the dust. Putting the two materials together and covering them with soil and grass will take care of the problem.'

Media coverage of the case. With regard to the media approach and the impacts that resulted from this coverage, the local residents pointed out that the sensational way in which the media covered the story contributed to the stigmatization of the town. A school director stated: 'For the residents, the actions of the media were damaging. They defiled the town.'

According to the statements collected, the inhabitants themselves were stigmatized and had problems with their social acceptance. The stigma was noticed in the daily routine of the residents and, in addition to incurring harmful feelings such as shame, it also resulted in economic losses, including unemployment, devaluation of private properties and local land, and the rejection of local products sold in the free markets. Statements such as this one from the principal of the town school confirm such problems: 'some students that finished their high school and went to Curitiba to look for work couldn't get it when they wrote down on the application form that they were from Adrianópolis. People said that they were sick'.

The authorities' opinions were divided. Even though all agreed that the news coverage produced negative consequences for the town, some pointed out that they noticed, at least initially, a hope that the media coverage would achieve improvements for the town. The former Deputy-Mayor's statement illustrated this: 'The press is the scream of the person who is not heard.' Another local official pointed out the problems brought to the community that resulted from the media coverage: 'Adrianópolis has come to be known as lead town. Everybody thinks that there's only contamination here, that everyone was contaminated.'

Researchers thought that the media acted improperly by releasing the story prematurely and proceeding with alarmist coverage of the problem. The comment by one of the health area researchers demonstrates this impression: 'After the subject was broadcast through the media, these people [the inhabitants] became poisoned, they could not find work because they come from this region. I think this was a negative repercussion to which the media contributed.' One researcher, also from

the health area, mentioned the media exposure: 'The press only exposed the problem. It did not come back later to say if the situation got better or worse. It only frightened the town.' For another researcher in the same area, the problem with the news broadcasts was that they were 'distorted and mistaken', and were generated from the lack of understanding by the journalists about what was happening in Adrianópolis.

The journalists recognized that the theme that was being communicated had human interest and presented dramatic situations, which is why the media coverage expanded so rapidly. 'The news fitted into our profile: it had human interest and the most susceptible people in that situation were the children ... and let's confess, journalists like this and such news sells more', said one of the journalists interviewed.

Even though they defended the coverage, journalists pointed out that the coverage was somewhat exaggerated, sensational, fragmented and shallow; and that the repercussions were negative for the town. According to one of the journalists, 'the repercussions of the case did not bring anything positive to the town and had a negative impact on the company'. Another interviewee mentioned that 'the impacts were economically negative'. One of the journalists defended his own coverage of the subject, but felt that the media in general had treated the case frivolously.

In coverage of similar themes the journalist group pointed out the importance of not over-emphasizing the human interest aspect coverage, and to be more attentive to scientific research, including more contact with the researchers. The statement of one journalist interviewed summarizes such perception: 'We are producing more and more news about human cases and not about environmental and health impacts. We are tied to human impacts and we do not go after the real causes of the problems ... It is necessary to deal more with the issue and less with people.'

Relations among social actors. As far as the relationship between the scientific community and the local community is concerned, the statements obtained from the researchers showed that they believed that the relation with the residents was good; 'cordial and friendly' as one researcher stated. However, one of the researchers in the environmental area recognized the need for meetings and seminars for the local residents before starting research in the area, to explain what will be done and to avoid creating false expectations.

One of the health area researchers emphasized the positive contact established with local authorities: 'The first approach was always towards the Mayor and/or the Town Health Secretary. We were greeted by the Deputy-Mayor in Adrianópolis. We explained the objectives of the research and the return of data to the town ... after contacting the Town Hall we went to speak with school directors. We also explained the objectives of the research and the need to have a meeting with student's parents [or close relatives] ... [we acted in this way] so that the community leaders could acknowledge our research and support us in several steps.'

According to town inhabitants, the relationship with groups of researchers was focused on providing support to the study. For example, one director of a municipal school stated that a single researcher from the health area had made contact, asking for her help, which was promptly provided: 'We prepared communication slips [asking parents' permission for students to participate in the research campaigns] ... we spent a whole day helping with blood collection. I appreciated their work [researcher's work]. We helped as much as possible.' Another educator also emphasized his role in the research project: 'I was a director of a school in Ribeira [a town close to Adrianópolis] at that time and I selected some students from there to participate in the research, with the blood collection campaign.'

The residents pointed out the need to access the products (e.g. reports, academic papers) from the research projects completed in Adrianópolis. The director said: 'I would like the researchers to send me all published material so I can place it in the school library. It would be very nice for us since we experienced a negative image from the media. It will be good for the town to have the research more publicly available ... we need to have this information, about the findings and what are the measures to be taken by the residents, so that the school can do its work.'

The authorities, however, were divided and some of them demonstrated discomfort with the impression that their town is a 'study nursery' for the universities. One of the local authority staff even questioned the real need for the studies that took place in Adrianópolis by saying: 'If the problem does not have a solution, then do not come to research over here. I respect your work [researchers]. I also have a son who is in college. I have nothing against you [researchers], but you come here, research and don't do anything. The things only got worse for us.'

The state authorities noted that the researchers failed to contact them before beginning the studies and also pointed out the difficulty in maintaining a close relationship between public servants and academics. 'We believe that there is a lack of commitment from universities regarding society. Research ends up being broadcast by the media and serves to compromise the public trust in

public agencies, such as the Health Secretariat and the Environmental Secretariat. The university goes there, raises the problem, but it doesn't offer an answer for anything. And it is up to the Secretariats to provide answers to whatever is raised by the researchers.'

The relationship between researchers and journalists was one of conflict and tension, which emphasizes the different goals of these two groups. On one side, the scientific community tries to develop a long-term strategy (based on theoretical references and empirical results) and it is reluctant to release preliminary results to the media. On the other hand, the media deal in the short term. They want a constant flow of information, they work with short deadlines, and they emphasize data that suggest a crisis or tragedy to get the public's attention on an issue, as in the Adrianópolis case, even if this attitude may compromise the quality of the media coverage.

Statements from two interviewees illustrated the tension in this relationship. 'I felt at first that the researchers were available to speak about the subject and were very worried about the broadcasting of information and the direction the news was going. After the first report was published by the newspapers, I felt that the relationship with them became harsher; they always emphasized that the situation was not a disaster', said one of the journalists. 'The relationship with the media was unilateral since the beginning ... because the media predicted the contents of official data releases. That is, it forced a release that was not planned yet, since we only had partial data', complained one of the researchers from the health area.

There was also some tension in the relationship between the local Adrianópolis community and the journalists who covered the subject, as shown by a statement from a local government official: 'The journalists came to Adrianópolis to produce news about lead and told a couple to get a blood test. The newspaper would pay for the exam to verify if there was lead in their blood. The couple took the test and there was lead only in the husband's blood. But nobody came back to talk about any action. Therefore, I tell the people: Do not grant interviews to anyone. If they come here, say that you will not talk about this subject.'

Another local official claimed to have been asked by journalists for interviews, but they failed to report his statements accurately. 'The journalists came looking for me to know what was happening, because there is no one else that had and have more interest in that subject than me ... and suddenly, another reporter from the newspaper showed up, very stylish, and I innocently trusted him. One day he showed up, asked several questions, spoke to a doctor that was in Adrianópolis, who was from the contamination area and coordinated the work over there ... interviewed several people, and saw what was happening. The journalist didn't report anything he observed. He came up with his own story ... said that the doctor looked like a Spiritualist Pastor [Pai de Santo] in the middle of poor people and that I was the Apocalypse prophet. That got to me ... I think the news was corrupted.'

Future care with risk communication. The statements collected showed that the two groups of researchers recognized the failures that resulted from lack of planning, and pointed out that the information needed to be communicated carefully, within a pre-established communication plan (including communication with the media), and that it is necessary to include trained people who know how to communicate risks in the research group.

One of the health care researchers pointed out that public information has to be carefully communicated: 'the care with which information is released is also important because the mention of toxicology tends to alarm people. The language related to toxicology is always alarming, having negative connotations, sometimes even pejorative or stigmatizing.' One of the environmental researchers even suggested that a federal agency should be responsible for the release of information, to avoid political problems and those related with the misinterpretation of data.

Statements such as: 'We would need to have the media already briefed about what is being investigated, the possible implications of results, along with the presentation of data designed for institutions and local residents' and '[in future research], I believe we would release data quickly in order to avoid confusion and misinterpretation, as it happened in Adrianópolis', clearly indicate the care to be taken in the future in similar circumstances.

Discussion

The Adrianópolis case demonstrates that the media placed most importance on news that involved conflicts, human plights, drama and strong images with children. It also illustrated that the sense of urgency that has become an inherent characteristic of the journalistic process produces fragmented and superficial coverage without revealing the underlying causes of the situations that are presented. Similar conclusions on the role of the media in reporting risks associated with health and environmental issues were reached by Hannigan (1995), Ramos (1995), Covello & Sandman (2001) and Lhulier & Miller (2001).

The case study showed that an event gains great media coverage if there is some sort of social drama, such as the possibility that children were contaminated. The greater the media attention, the more attention people give to the risk that is being communicated, and the greater the perception that people have about the seriousness of the risk; Adrianópolis came to be known as 'lead town' and, even today, the local inhabitants have problems related to this title.

It is necessary to consider that the divergent opinions from the groups of respondents regarding the risk from lead exposure are directly related to the factors that influence risk perception, which is an intuitive judgement that people have regarding a certain risk. Acceptance or non-acceptance of the existence of such risk is determined by the individual's familiarity, control, the media coverage, beliefs, personal feelings, and the level of knowledge (Smith 1992; Weyman & Kelly 1999; Duncam 2004; Sturloni 2006).

The case showed that the media, with the justification that they were providing a public service and were functioning as a spokesperson for the citizens, did not adequately consider the local economic impacts from their coverage of the story. Their coverage may have contributed to stigmatism of the local residents through the use of terms such as 'contaminated', 'leaded' and 'intoxicated'.

When the concept of risk communication was evaluated in this case, it can be argued that the researchers lacked any plan about how to release the information obtained to the local residents or the media. This planning should have included specialized communication professionals, as the goal is to transmit information that will contribute to the formation of public opinion that can trigger, depending on its content and the manner by which it is communicated, attitudes and behaviours that may be favourable or contrary to the goal of involving citizens in the risk management process (Moreno 2003).

Preliminary visits to Adrianópolis indicated that there was some concern from the scientific community regarding communication of the information obtained to the local residents. However, actions that were implemented, such as meetings with local residents and officials (e.g. Fig. 5), seemed to not have been sufficient. Information bulletins were distributed that contained results of lead analysis of soil and food (Fig. 6). These bulletins included tables in which the lead contents in foods clearly exceeded maximum limits established by Brazilian regulations. These bulletins were easy to interpret from the researchers' point of view, but this apparently positive strategy had problems. Some residents could not read or, if they could, did not understand what was written and seemed to be suspicious of what was explained by the scientists.

Fig. 5. Meeting at Vila Mota, April 2001, where geologists and medical doctors presented their results to residents and local authorities.

This suspicion also resulted from the 'distance established among the actors' that came from the unilateral style of communication established between researchers and the community. The researchers released information without consultation, and the residents did not perceive that they were involved in the research process or problem resolution. As a consequence, even though most of the local population knew about the existence of the research and knew some (or all) of the results obtained, collected statements showed that most of Adrianópolis's inhabitants are still far from aware of the implications of the research.

These observations show that researchers need to be aware of community concerns. It is necessary to listen to the issues that the community would like to have resolved, and the studies that it believes to be important. If this relationship of trust and commitment is not established early in the process, the entire risk management process will be compromised, because the community and local authorities will neither comprehend nor support it. As in the Adrianópolis case, the town may have the feeling that its problems and its lands only make up a 'study nursery' for researchers.

It therefore is necessary to set up partnerships with local communities in environmental and public health research, not only because local knowledge is important, but also because local environmental preservation will be greater if the community is involved in decision-making processes, and resistance to official environmental policies will be smaller (Davis 1996).

Public involvement includes the participation of several social actors in the decision-making process acting together with government authorities. It is produced by information dissemination, public consultation and public participation (Rowe & Frewer 2004). Participation will depend on institutional context, the transparency with which the process occurs, and the level of communication with the local residents. It is important that participative communication be implemented to achieve effective public involvement. This assumes that those people affected by decisions have to be involved in the planning process and choices of solutions (Mosquera 2005).

Participative communication is one of the seven guidelines for risk communication established by the US Environmental Protection Agency (EPA). These include careful planning and evaluation of efforts during the research and communication process; listening to public specific concerns; acting with honesty and sincerity; taking the communication vehicles' needs into consideration; articulating and collaborating with other agencies

Fig. 6. Adrianópolis revisited for soil and food sampling in 2005.

and reliable groups (conflicts and disagreements among organizations make communication with the public more difficult); and communicating messages in a clear way with empathy. It is clear that these guidelines were not followed in the Adrianópolis case. The main omissions were an open dialogue with the local community and authorities, as well as their involvement in the research process. A communication strategy and relationship with state agencies, other agencies and institutions involved in the matter did not exist. There was also a failure to establish a media communication plan, taking the media's specific interests into

consideration to avoid the inappropriate release of data.

Issues related to media coverage were not confined to Adrianópolis. Other similar cases such as Love Canal (USA), Chernobyl (Europe), and Bhopal (India) were covered by the media in such a manner as to emphasize negative asapects as well as creating a mood of 'collective psychosis' (Sturloni 2006).

A case that received considerable attention in Brazil was the Goiania (Goias State capital) accident involving radioactive material, in September 1987. The accident involved a caesium-137 capsule that was part of hospital equipment used for radiotherapy, which had been abandoned in a building belonging to the Goias Radiotherapy Institute. Two scrap collectors entered the building, took the lead block in which the capsule was encased and sold it to a junk dealer. To dismantle the equipment to reuse the lead, the owner of the junkyard exposed caesium-137, which radiated a blue light in the dark. After noticing the beautiful light emission, the owner distributed the material to relatives, neighbours and friends. The accident was initially broadcast by only one local paper, receiving little media attention, but was picked up by a TV station on 1 October 1987. The resulting press coverage was characterized by dramatization and exaggeration of the incidents and findings after the accident. An army of journalists took over the town to cover the event and details of the accident were released, even by US papers, which used headlines such as 'mortal glitter', 'a carnival of poisonous glitter' and 'playing with radiation'. The media raised extraordinary public interest, with perceptions of an enormous apparent risk, even among people who did not have any contact with the material or with contaminated individuals (Kasperson *et al.* 2005).

Conclusion

This study demonstrates that the lack of adequate planning regarding communication of information (to the press, to the studied community, and to authorities or governments) can seriously compromise the relationship between researchers, the community and the media, as well as cause damage to the actors involved.

The sense of urgency and the desire of the media to report news that generates attention and attract a larger audience results in the broadcast of erroneous or misleading information that compromises journalistic quality. This attitude also serves to damage the relationship established between the public, the media and its information sources (which includes the scientific community and people affected by hazardous situations).

As a result of economic and social damage from 'sensationalist' coverage, the community at risk may not wish to participate or collaborate with future research. A barrier is thus created to hamper scientists, impeding or damaging the development of future studies that could assist the community in mitigating its problems.

The barrier to future studies may be worsened if there is no strategy to involve local residents in them. As in Adrianópolis, the absence of a local community involvement plan can create false expectations among residents; for example, the expectation that the studies will help the residents to receive monetary compensation for living in a risky situation. The lack of a plan for community involvement may also produce a feeling of exclusion from the decision-making process, as if the thoughts and desires of the local community for the area are not important, and therefore should not be taken into consideration. The damage from this 'distance' between scientists and inhabitants can be even more serious if remediation plans are not formulated, contextualized or implemented.

The Adrianópolis experience showed that the researchers need to be conscious that, during the evaluation and risk management process, the individual and collective perceptions of risks are taken into account. Furthermore, they must allow the citizens who are directly and indirectly involved in these situations to actively participate in the decision-making processes to solve or mitigate the diagnosed risks. To accomplish this, risk communication strategies must be established that take into account the main difficulties that exist in the process, such as the high level of scientific illiteracy, the complexity and characteristics of scientific studies, and the fact that the scientists and decision-makers do not agree about how to characterize risks.

This study shows an urgent need to standardize the procedures related to risk communication and to guarantee community involvement in the formulation and application of risk management measures. The following risk communication strategies are proposed to avoid repetition of the communication failures during the Adrianópolis case study.

1. Public meetings should be held during the research period, so that people can express their emotions and concerns and feel that they are participating in an open dialogue and negotiation process.
2. A system should be developed that promptly answers the concerns of local residents, as well as providing honest and forthright information regarding the rationale behind decisions.
3. It is important that the term 'planning' is part of the communication process. It is necessary to plan how and what information will be released, choose the people who will act as spokespeople in this process, and anticipate possible questions and answers from inhabitants and local authorities, as well as from the media. It is fundamental to keep the media as a partner, keeping in mind the time and space requirements that the media have to report the news.
4. It is also necessary to understand the cultural, social and economic customs of the community being studied. To do that, it is necessary to perform an evaluation to identify the

different public interests, expectations and cultural agendas existing in that community.

5. It is essential to recognize that because there are different public factions involved, a variety of risk communication strategies must be established to reach the whole spectrum of social groups.

6. It is important to maintain constant contact with some community representatives, such as neighbourhood association presidents, teachers and health care workers, and explain step by step the studies performed, as well as providing details of the results obtained. These representatives may work as volunteers and help with communication, as they are trusted by the local population.

7. It is also useful to develop publications and resource material to be released to newspapers and TV stations, as well as local radio stations. It is necessary to understand the media habits of the local population, to be effective in this area.

8. As a communication strategy, a positive message should always be used (to avoid creating panic), which must be adapted to the target audience. The message should contain a description of the problem, its potential impact, alternatives for remediation, and the importance of taking precautions. These messages must be simple, direct and realistic; the broadcast information should also be brought to the public with objectiveness, clarity and efficiency.

This study benefited from the financial support provided by FAPESP (Grants 2002/00271-0, 2005/52239-0 and 2006/57720-1) and the Brazilian National Research Council—CNPq (Grant 304338/2005-2). The authors wish to express their gratitude to M. Batterson, J. Cripps and O. Selinus, who contributed greatly to improvement of the manuscript.

References

COVELLO, V. & SANDMAN, P. M. 2001. Risk communication: evolution and revolution. *In*: WOLBARST, A. (ed.) *Solutions to an Environment in Peril*. Johns Hopkins University Press, Baltimore, MD, 164–178.

CUNHA, F. G., FIGUEIREDO, B. R., PAOLIELLO, M. M. B., DE CAPITANI, E. M. & SAKUMA, A. M. 2005. Human and environmental lead contamination in the Upper Ribeira Valley, southeastern Brazil. *Terrae*, **2**, 28–36.

DAVIS, S. H. 1996. *Public Involvement in Environmental Decision Making—Some Reflections on the Western European Experience*. The World Bank, Washington, DC.

DI GIULIO, G. M. 2006. *Divulgação científica e comunicação de risco: um olhar sobre Adrianópolis, Vale do Ribeira*. MSc dissertation, Institute of Geosciences, University of Campinas.

DUNCAM, B. 2004. Percepción pública y comunicación eficaz del riesgo. World Wide Web Address: http://www.jrc.es/home/report/spanish/articles/vol82/welcome.html.

FIGUEIREDO, B. R. 2005. A Contaminação Ambiental e Humana por Chumbo no Vale do Ribeira (SP-PR). *Revista Eletrônica Com Ciência SBPC/LABJOR*.

FIGUEIREDO, B. R. 2007. Geoindicators as a tool for epidemiological studies in lead contaminated areas in Brazil. *In*: *II Hemispheric Conference on Medical Geology, XICBGq, Atibaia, Brazil, October, 2007, Proceedings* (CD ROM).

HANNIGAN, J. 1995. *Sociologia Ambiental—a formação de uma perspectiva social*. Instituto Piaget, Lisbon.

KASPERSON, R. E., JHAVERI, N. & KASPERSON, J. X. 2005. Stigma and the social amplification of risk: towards a framework of analysis. *In*: KASPERSON, J. X. & KASPERSON, R. E. (eds) *The Social Contours of Risk: Publics, Risk Communication and the Social Amplification of Risk*. Earthscan, London, 161–180.

LAMOGLIA, T., FIGUEIREDO, B. R., SAKUMA, A. M., BUZZO, M. L., OKADA, I. A. & KIRA, C. S. 2006. Lead in food and soil from a mining area in Brazil and human exposure. *Chinese Journal of Geochemistry* (Supplementary Issue dedicated to the 7th International Symposium on Environmental Geochemistry, Beijing, September), 66.

LHULIER, L. & MILLER, D. S. 2001. Contextual information and the political economy of environmental risk communication. *In*: AEPLI, M. F., DELICATH, J. W. & KASPERSON, R. E. (eds) *Proceedings of the 6th Biennial Conference on Communication and Environment, Cincinnati, Center for Environmental Studies and Department of Communication, University of Cincinnati, Ohio, 27–30 July*.

MORENO, A. R. 2003. La comunicación de riesgos en salud y ambiente. *Revista Salud Pública y Nutrición*, **4**, http://www.respyn.uanl.mx/iv/1/invitado/index.html, accessed Nov. 14, 2005.

MOSQUERA, M. 2005. Communicación en Salud: Conceptos, Teorías y Experiencias. World Wide Web Address: http://www.comminit.com/la/pensamientoestrategico/lasth/lasld750.html.

PAOLIELLO, M. M. B., CAPITANI, E. M., CUNHA, F. G., MATSUO, T., CARVALHO, M. F., SAKUMA, A. & FIGUEIREDO, B. R. 2002. Exposure of children to lead and cadmium from a mining area of Brazil, *Environmental Research, Section A*, **88**, 120–128.

PAOLIELLO, M. M. B., CAPITANI, E. M., CUNHA, F. G., CARVALHO, M. F., MATSUO, T., SAKUMA, A. & FIGUEIREDO, B. R. 2003. Determinants of blood lead levels in an adult population from a mining area in Brazil. *Journal de Physique IV*, **107**, 127–130.

RAMOS, L. F. A. 1995. *Meio ambiente e meios de comunicação*. Annablume–Fapesp, São Paulo.

ROWE, G. & FREWER, L. J. 2004. Evaluating public participation exercises: a research agenda. *Science, Technology and Human Values*, **29**, 512–556.

SMITH, K. 1992. *Environmental Hazards—Assessing Risk and Reducing Disaster*. Routledge, London.

STURLONI, G. 2006. *Le mele de Chernobyl sono buone: mezo secolo di rischio tecnológico*. SIRONI, Milano.

WEYMAN, A. K. & KELLY, C. J. 1999. *Risk Perception and Risk Communication: A Review of Literature*. HSE Books, Broad Lane, Sheffield.

Communicating uncertainty in climate-change adaptation and decision support; further development of the Gdańsk case study

PHILIPP SCHMIDT-THOMÉ[1] & DOROTA KAULBARSZ[2]

[1]*Geological Survey of Finland, PO Box 96, 02151 Espoo, Finland*
(e-mail: philipp.schmidt-thome@gtk.fi)

[2]*Polish Geological Institute, Branch of Marine Geology, Kościerska 5, 80-328 Gdańsk, Poland*

Abstract: The impact of climate change on European society is an issue of increasing concern on the agenda of European regional development policy. Using sea-level rise and changing flood-prone areas as an example of climate-change impact, this paper reviews an approach to stakeholder communication developed in the Baltic Sea Region. The application of climate- and sea-level change scenarios in spatial planning, as well as the communication between scientists and stakeholders, was integrated into a set of tools called the 'decision support frame' (DSF), which focuses especially on uncertainty aspects. By specifically addressing the communication process the DSF distances itself from pure computer-based decision-making. The city of Gdańsk is a good example where a combination of climate-change models, maps and various discussion rounds led to a communication process that has integrated several planning authorities and decision-makers.

Climate-change adaptation has entered climate policy relatively recently and is quickly growing in importance (Schmidt-Thomé 2006*a*). For example, the new Territorial Agenda of the European Union, signed by all European ministers responsible for spatial planning, mentions climate change as an important issue for European regional development (Territorial Agenda 2007). Nevertheless, the linkages from climate change to planning and decision-making are still not well developed despite the growing need for both appropriate adaptation and mitigation strategies (e.g. Lewis *et al.* 2006; Schmidt-Thomé 2006*a*; Hecimovich 2007). Climate-change adaptation is still often mentioned simultaneously, or even confused with, climate-change mitigation. Generally speaking, the difference between adaptation and mitigation is that the latter aims to reduce global warming, whereas adaptation focuses on the possibilities of developing appropriate strategies to cope with the effects of a warming climate. Climate-change adaptation and mitigation are not mutually exclusive strategies but it can often be observed that mitigation attracts stronger attention, especially in the media. Although climate-change mitigation plays an important role in, and should be mainly handled on, national and international scales, there is a growing tendency to focus on mitigation activities on regional and local scales. Climate-change adaptation, on the other hand, can be planned and implemented on all levels, including local and micro levels, as, for example, every village or even house-owner can design their own adaptation strategies.

Regional development and climate-change adaptation in the Baltic Sea Region

The BSR INTERREG IIIB projects 'Sea level change affecting the spatial development of the Baltic Sea Region' (SEAREG) and 'Developing policies and adaptation strategies to climate change in the Baltic Sea Region' (ASTRA), both co-financed by the European Regional Development Fund (ERDF), concentrated on the integration of climate-change impact scenarios in local decision-making processes (e.g. land-use planning). Whereas SEAREG (2002–2005) had the aim of implementing connections between climate change induced sea-level rise and planning concerns at local and regional levels in the Baltic Sea Region, ASTRA (2005–2007) focused on a broader view of climate-change effects (e.g. including the effects of droughts and heatwaves on regional development).

The SEAREG project downscaled climate-change scenarios of the Intergovernmental Panel on Climate Change (IPCC) to the Baltic Sea Region. The resulting local scenarios of potential future coastlines and flood-prone areas were then analysed in co-operation with stakeholders. This communication process resulted in a set of tools, the decision support frame (DSF; see www.gtk.fi/slr), that bridges the gap between climate-change models and spatial planning by specifically addressing uncertainty issues and integrated scenario interpretation. The DSF specifically addresses uncertainty of climate-change model results. It

From: LIVERMAN, D. G. E., PEREIRA, C. P. G. & MARKER, B. (eds) *Communicating Environmental Geoscience*. Geological Society, London, Special Publications, **305**, 75–79.
DOI: 10.1144/SP305.8   0305-8719/08/$15.00 © The Geological Society of London 2008.

uses geographic information system (GIS) applications and models but this is only one part of the entire DSF process. It also contains a vulnerability analysis, a knowledge base and a discussion platform. The vulnerability assessment and the discussion platform particularly focus on the communication process and thus distance the DSF from pure computer-based decision-making. Both the vulnerability analysis and the discussion platform not only help to identify the specific stakeholders to be addressed but also seek to identify and clarify climate-change impacts taking uncertainties of the models into account (Schmidt-Thomé 2006b).

Climate-change communication and uncertainty aspects

Both projects, SEAREG and ASTRA, found from experience that the integration of climate-change scenarios into planning processes is dependent on two main factors, communication and uncertainty. The SEAREG project team consisted of natural scientists (mainly geoscientists and meteorologists), social scientists and planners. Even though the target of the project (supporting regional development with information on changing sea levels) was well described, the first obstacle lay in reaching an understanding on the use of terms and concepts within the project team. The most critical points of discussion concentrated on: (1) the definition and applicability of climate-change models, including underlying forcing scenarios; (2) the plotting of model and scenario results into thematic maps; (3) how to integrate uncertainty and how to interpret the resulting scenarios; (4) the communication of the scenarios to those not involved in the project. This internal communication process lasted for nearly two-thirds of the entire project duration. One main problem appeared to be the demand to simply explain the creation, application and uncertainty of complex climate models on the one hand and the inclusion of social sciences into applicable communication and application frameworks for climate-change adaptation strategies on the other hand.

Even though this problematic setting of interdisciplinary co-operation between several actors seems to be trivial, it is actually very complex (Schmidt-Thomé & Peltonen 2006a). The exchange of experience with other projects has yielded the information that, rather often, certain sciences or fields of expertise are deliberately excluded from projects to avoid such difficult discussions. There are examples of climate-change projects that exclude stakeholders or even climatologists, with the reasoning that result-oriented interdisciplinary co-operation would be basically impossible, mainly because of the above-mentioned misunderstanding of terms as well as exhaustively long discussion rounds that do not yield the clarification needed. Other projects included the potential effects of climate change without analysing or even mentioning climate change itself, simply to avoid the problem of uncertainty.

When observing the lengthy discussions within the SEAREG project it soon became clear that, despite the excellence of scientific knowledge and implementation of leading climate-change modelling technology, the crucial problem was how to communicate the uncertainty (Lehtonen & Peltonen 2006). It was not possible to reach an agreement on the use of one forcing scenario, nor on one model. The compromise that was reached consisted of using two forcing scenarios and developing three sea-level change scenarios for the Baltic Sea Region (Meier et al. 2004; Schmidt-Thomé & Peltonen 2006b). The advantage in developing three scenarios was to display the minimum (low-case) and the maximum (high-case) sea-level change, including a step in the middle (ensemble average). The three scenarios were developed for all case-study areas and used to show that at minimum sea level will not stay where it is now but will rise at least by a small amount. It was also possible to show that there is an upper limit of sea-level rise. It was clearly stated that the ensemble average scenario showed only a step between the low and the high case but that it was by no means the most probable (see also Schmidt-Thomé 2006a). This approach proved to be reasonably successful, as it was an excellent tool to explain the range of uncertainty to stakeholders.

Often it seemed, decision-makers frustrated by waiting for scientific results opt for an educated guess to determine, for example, lowest building-ground elevations above flood-prone areas. Therefore, the stakeholder communication process in the SEAREG project was structured in the so-called discussion platform of the DSF. It was used to analyse the uncertainty behind the models, and to find ways of deriving conclusions from climate-change models that can be applied in planning. This discussion platform specifically endorsed dialogue via seeking the interests, possibilities and restrictions of each of the actors involved in this project. For instance, it was of great importance for the natural scientists to learn what kind of information is actually demanded by planners; and planners also learned about the possibilities and limitations of scientific research (Lehtonen & Peltonen 2006; Schmidt-Thomé & Peltonen 2006b).

In the beginning of the SEAREG project it was very difficult to make meaningful contact with stakeholders from the case-study areas, in part because of the long time-range of the scenarios (100 years). However, the winter storm Gudrun–Erwin, which struck the Baltic Sea Region in January 2005, led to record sea-level and storm-surge heights. This gave a hint that the models used by the SEAREG project were not catastrophic predictions of a distant future but rather displayed the current range of extreme events fairly well. Particularly in Pärnu, one of the SEAREG case-study areas in Estonia, sea level rose during the storm surge to the level of the high-case scenario of the SEAREG project (Schmidt-Thomé 2006a). The effects of this storm, as well as several high river floods that occurred in the beginning of the 21st century in several parts of Europe, triggered wide media coverage, and eased the science–stakeholder communication process. The uncertainties remained as high as they had been previously but the willingness to discuss the range of uncertainties (including upper and lower limits) certainly rose. An important factor in risk analysis and planning is the debate between reactive and proactive response; that is, adaptation, strategies and their integration into policies (Lehtonen & Peltonen 2006; Schmidt-Thomé & Schmidt-Thomé 2007). The SEAREG project and its DSF have managed to put climate change, especially sea-level rise and changes in flood-prone areas, on the agenda of the stakeholders involved in the project. So far the project cannot trace which recent decisions on climate-change adaptation can be directly accredited to the project, but it certainly contributed to raising awareness. However, it has at least resulted in stakeholders involved in the SEAREG project stating often that two important factors were addressed by the DSF: (1) the uncertainty, by using three scenarios instead of one; (2) that the models displayed rather conservative, or cautious effects of climate change and avoided the use of extreme scenarios.

Based on these positive experiences, the SEAREG project team then planned a follow-up project to analyse the impacts of climate change on a broader scale than just sea-level rise and changing flood patterns. While setting up the ASTRA project team the response from stakeholders to participate in, and to co-finance the project was much stronger than during the setting up of the SEAREG project team.

The methodological approach of the SEAREG project was to explain the potential effects of climate change to stakeholders and to develop adaptation strategies in interdisciplinary co-operation. The approach of the ASTRA project was to ask stakeholders what they perceive as the biggest potential impacts caused by climate change (Eisenack et al. 2007). Several inland case studies were taken up in the project to avoid a strong influence of sea-level rise on the project. Nevertheless, once

the project started and stakeholders involved were asked to express their main concerns about climate-change impact, basically all those involved mentioned sea-level rise and changing flood-prone areas. This suggests that although the SEAREG project thought that it had developed techniques on communication, in reality it mainly contributed to raising of awareness. In fact, ASTRA, which aimed to go beyond the intentions of SEAREG, is also still used as an awareness-raising project, which is now also fulfilling the previous SEAREG goals; that is, the development of adaptation strategies on changing flood-prone areas and sea-level rise. For example, the city of Kokkola in northern Finland is planning to adapt land-use plans, particularly the outlining of new housing development sites, to the sea-level change scenarios of the SEAREG project (see www.astra-project.org).

This delayed reaction is an interesting outcome and shows that regional development projects can trigger certain aspects among stakeholders, but that the real implementation of new ideas takes very much longer.

Case study: Gdańsk

Gdańsk is one of the ASTRA case studies already involved in the SEAREG project. The development of the DSF in this city has been documented comprehensively by Schmidt-Thomé et al. (2005, 2006) and Staudt et al. (2005), and discussed by Schmidt-Thomé (2006a). The integration of Gdańsk into SEAREG's follow-up project ASTRA led to an improvement of the SEAREG scenarios and also an improvement in the stakeholder communication process. The local partners were now able to initiate a dialogue between relevant planners and the regional authorities responsible for flood protection. In October 2006 a conference on climate-change adaptation and flood risks in coastal areas was organized in Gdańsk, joined with a workshop dedicated to climate-change adaptation (see www.astra-project.org for documentation). These events aroused significant interest among a large group of invited guests and resulted in a subsequent meeting in the Gdańsk local development agency. As a result of the excellent co-operation with the Gdańsk Municipality a new high-quality digital terrain model (DTM) could be applied in the evaluation of areas potentially affected by climate change. Planned directions of spatial development of Gdańsk (Gdańsk Development Agency 2007) were then compared with the three SEAREG sea-level rise scenarios. As a first result it was possible to overlay planned land use with sea-level rise and flood scenarios (Fig. 1).

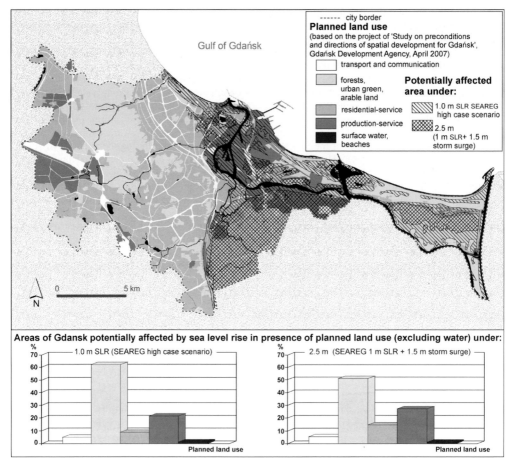

Fig. 1. Overlay of planned land use, sea-level rise scenarios and flood-prone areas (modified from Kaulbarsz *et al.* 2007).

As a further development of this communication process, representatives of local and regional spatial planning and water management authorities from Gdańsk participated in the 3rd ASTRA conference on climate change and water in Riga, in May 2007 (see www.astra-project.org). The representatives took part in a stakeholder panel discussion that focused on the integration of climate-change adaptation issues into existing development policies. The panel discussion, which included stakeholders from several countries surrounding the Baltic Sea Region, functioned as a platform to exchange ideas and develop processes around decision-making in climate-change adaptation. This panel discussion was probably the first time in the Baltic Sea Region that planners and other representatives from relevant planning authorities met in such an international environment to present and discuss the potential effects, and planned adaptation strategies, for their respective areas in front of a public audience.

Because of its location between the Baltic Sea and a hilly hinterland, Gdańsk is especially prone to storm surges, flash floods and river floods. According to an act under the Polish law, the indication of flood risk areas is currently the responsibility of regionally corresponding authorities on water management and coastal management. Simultaneously, these areas should be considered in local spatial development plans. Because it was possible to raise interest in the two projects' activities by those persons who actually decide on marking the flood-prone areas in official planning documents, the scenarios developed under SEAREG and ASTRA should now be taken into account for indicating flood-prone areas. It was mentioned by the authorities that the uncertainty factor is one of the most important issues in decision-making and they expressed their strong desire to learn more about the SEAREG and ASTRA approaches. In addition to the flood plans, the ASTRA partners from Gdańsk are currently preparing a groundwater vulnerability map, which will function as a tool for further analysis and support the integration of climate-change impact issues and flood-protection aspects into planning and decision-making in Gdańsk.

Conclusions

The positive response of the authorities in the Gdańsk case-study area can be seen as a milestone in the further application of the decision support frame. It shows not only that it was possible to continue successful project work over 5 years but also that there is a prospect of future continuation of this process. It seems that both the SEAREG and the ASTRA project contributed to placing the problem of climate-change impacts on the agenda of decision-makers and also to positively influencing land-use planning processes by the integration of geo-scientific knowledge and uncertainty aspects. It has to be seen to what extent it will be possible to defend appropriate climate-change adaptation strategies in future land-use plans against other, short-term, financial interests. The ASTRA project will closely follow this further development, probably also under the umbrella of further follow-up projects. As an overall first result, it can already be stated at this stage that the initial purpose of the INTERREG initiative, transnational co-operation to ensure sustainable development, was not only addressed but it was also implemented by the projects presented here.

References

EISENACK, K., TEKKEN, V. & KROPP, J. P. 2007. Stakeholders' perceptions of climate change in the Baltic Sea Region. *In*: SCHERNEWSKI, G., GLAESER, B., SCHEIBE, R., SEKŚCIŃSKA, A. & THAMM, R. (eds) *Coastal Development: The Oder Estuary and Beyond*. Coastline Reports, **8**, 245–255.

GDAŃSK DEVELOPMENT AGENCY. 2007. Study on preconditions and directions of spatial development for Gdańsk, 2007. Project of actualization of existing spatial development plans, state as in April 2007.

HECIMOVICH, J. 2007. Climate change and planners, 2007. Bettman Symposium Session. World Wide Web Address: http://www.planning.org/conferencecoverage/2007/sunday/climatechange.htm.

KAULBARSZ, D., KORDALSKI, Z. & JEGLIŃSKI, W. 2007. Climate change impact in the Gdańsk region—vulnerability of water system and spatial planning. Presentation during 3rd ASTRA Conference: Climate Change and Waters, Riga, 11–12 May. www.astra-project.org

LEHTONEN, S. & PELTONEN, L. 2006. Risk communication and sea level rise: Bridging the gap between climate science and planning practice. *In*: SCHMIDT-THOMÉ, P. (ed.) *Sea Level Changes Affecting the Spatial Development of the Baltic Sea Region*. Geological Survey of Finland, Special Paper, **41**, 61–69.

LEWIS, M., FRIEDMAN, N. & ROSS, L. 2006. The role of planning in the new energy era: results of a survey. World Wide Web Address: http://www.planning.org/energy/06mar/index.htm.

MEIER, H. E. M., BROMAN, B. & KJELLSTRÖM, E. 2004. Simulated sea level in past and future climates of the Baltic Sea. *Climate Research*, **27**, 59–75.

SCHMIDT-THOMÉ, P. 2006a. *Integration of Natural Hazards, Risk and Climate Change into Spatial Planning Practices*. PhD thesis, University of Helsinki.

SCHMIDT-THOMÉ, P. 2006b. *Sea Level Changes Affecting the Spatial Development of the Baltic Sea Region*. Geological Survey of Finland, Special Paper, **41**.

SCHMIDT-THOMÉ, K. & PELTONEN, L. 2006a. Actors, networks and actor–networks in coping with sea level rise. *In*: SCHMIDT-THOMÉ, P. (ed.) *Sea Level Changes Affecting the Spatial Development of the Baltic Sea Region*. Geological Survey of Finland, Special Paper, **41**, 51–59.

SCHMIDT-THOMÉ, P. & PELTONEN, L. 2006b. Sea level change assessment in the Baltic Sea Region and spatial planning responses. *In*: SCHMIDT-THOMÉ, P. (ed.) *Sea Level Changes Affecting the Spatial Development of the Baltic Sea Region*. Geological Survey of Finland, Special Paper, **41**, 7–17.

SCHMIDT-THOMÉ, P. & SCHMIDT-THOMÉ, K. 2007. Natural hazards and climate change: stakeholder communication and decision-making processes: an analysis of the outcomes of the 2006 Davos conference on disaster reduction. *Management of Environmental Quality*, **18**, 329–339.

SCHMIDT-THOMÉ, P., STAUDT, M., KALLIO, H. & KLEIN, J. 2005. Decision support frame to estimate possible future impacts of sea level changes on soil contamination. *In*: LENS, P., GROTENHUIS, T., MALINA, G. & TABAK, H. (eds) *Soil and Sediment Remediation: Mechanisms, Technologies and Applications*. Integrated Environmental Technology Series, London, 409–417.

SCHMIDT-THOMÉ, P., VIEHHAUSER, M. & STAUDT, M. 2006. Climate change impacts on sea level and runoff patterns: application of a decision support frame for spatial planners in case study areas. *Quaternary International*, **145–146**, 135–144.

STAUDT, M., KORDALSKI, Z. & ZMUDA, J. 2005. Assessment of modelled sea level rise impacts in the Gdańsk region, Poland. *In*: SCHMIDT-THOME, P. (ed.) *Sea Level Changes Affecting the Spatial Development of the Baltic Sea Region*. Geological Survey of Finland, Special Paper, **41**, 121–130.

TERRITORIAL AGENDA 2007. Territorial Agenda of the European Union: Towards a More Competitive and Sustainable Europe of Diverse Regions—Agreed on the Occasion of the Informal Ministerial Meeting on Urban Development and Territorial Cohesion in Leipzig on 24–25 May 2007. World Wide Web Address: http://www.bmvbs.de/Anlage/original_1005295/Territorial-Agenda-of-the-European-Union-Agreed-on-25-May-2007-accessible.pdf.

GeoSure; a bridge between geology and decision-makers

JENNIFER C. WALSBY

British Geological Survey, Kingsley Dunham Centre, Nicker Hill, Keyworth, Nottingham, NG12 5GG, UK (e-mail: jcw@bgs.ac.uk)

Abstract: How many people understand a geological map and use it to assess the ground on which they live or plan to develop? How many town planners, house owners or insurers know that geologists can identify areas prone to flooding, radon gas emissions, landslides and subsidence? Do decision-makers understand the relevance of geology? Concerned about these questions, geological and geographic information system (GIS) professionals at the British Geological Survey (BGS) have created datasets that make information about geological hazards ('geohazards') easy to obtain, use and understand. The term 'geohazard' is emotive. Many people think of natural hazards as being large-scale disasters, such as tsunami and major earthquakes. Appropriate terminology is required to explain the relevance of factors such as the potential cost and health implications of the usually less dramatic British geohazards. Using the vast data holdings and geoscientific knowledge within BGS and building on past thematic mapping activities, a series of national geohazard datasets has been developed. GIS datasets with 'plain English' descriptions have been created for natural gas emissions, landslides, swell–shrink clays, compressible and collapsible deposits, soluble rocks, running sands and groundwater flooding. Geological information is thus brought before a wider audience and in a form that reveals to the British public and industry how geology can be used in conjunction with other information and why it is relevant to their lives.

Geological information has been used in Britain for many decades to aid decision-making in regard to land use and property, in particular by central and local government, engineers, builders and farmers. Historically most of the reports, maps and verbal communications were provided using expert language, mainly for use by people with geoscientific knowledge, and with limited 'translation' into lay terms. Scientists at the British Geological Survey (BGS) have increasingly recognized the need to provide information in different ways as different user groups have acknowledged the importance of geology to their activities.

During the 1980s and 1990s a diverse set of mainly hard-copy outputs evolved. Examples of these were sets of more customer-focused and less geologically oriented maps and reports, including assessments of foundation conditions, landslip potential, aquifer vulnerability and mineral resources. These thematic maps were provided mainly to restricted audiences, including government departments and local authorities, and their consultants, for planning and exploitation purposes. The language used in these outputs was less geological, but full understanding of their implications still required some expert knowledge. The maps provided for the Stoke on Trent planning report (Wilson *et al.* 1992) are a good example, with communication styles ranging from detailed geotechnical information on the foundation conditions map to simple explanations of landslip potential on the environmental geology map.

As personnel in organizations change the knowledge of how to use specialist products such as BGS thematic maps can be lost and subsequently the information holding falls into disuse. It is therefore important to provide a product that has longevity from a communication point of view, but at the same time currency of information is also vital. Digital maps and reports allow regular updates to be created and made available by various means. Many government and private organizations use digital systems (e.g. geographic information systems; GIS) to collate and report on environmental issues such as ground stability. Use of a digital GIS allows access to corporate and departmentally held datasets by a wide group of people, including managers, non-specialists and others, who might need additional information to help them understand specialist data and their relevance to their working practices.

BGS has acknowledged that such information needs to be accessible to a wider audience in a variety of delivery formats. An example of this enlightened approach involves Internet report generation, whereby digital information for a user's specified area is extracted into a PDF report and the selected geoscience topic is described in user-friendly terms. Map data from which report extracts are created are also available as GIS data and each point, line and polygon is attributed with its geological description. Thematic information is provided where the geology has been reclassified in terms of geohazard properties.

From: LIVERMAN, D. G. E., PEREIRA, C. P. G. & MARKER, B. (eds) *Communicating Environmental Geoscience*. Geological Society, London, Special Publications, **305**, 81–87.
DOI: 10.1144/SP305.9   0305-8719/08/$15.00 © The Geological Society of London 2008.

This paper looks at a process by which geologists are trying to make their information understandable to decision-makers. The thinking and technical process are described for which mapped geology and sample data have been collated, interpreted and classified in terms of geohazard potential and described in lay terms; and how the move from paper maps and reports to digital data and thematic output was driven by technological change and user demand. Growth in demand for easy-to-use reports that collate national datasets for use by solicitors, insurers, house buyers and development consultants was a leading driver.

Building a dataset to characterize ground stability: GeoSure

During the 1990s, BGS transformed its map output into a fully digital production system. Map production methods were further developed in line with the growth in use of GIS technology and cartographic data developed into spatially referenced geological data items that could be viewed, manipulated and queried in GIS and modelling software. By 2000 GIS use was commonplace both in the geoscience community and within many of the non-science communities with which BGS needed to communicate.

Once in place BGS's digital map information system allowed the capture of archive maps and the presentation of all new mapping in digital form. By 2001 the first nationwide 1:50 000-scale digital geological map dataset was produced: DiGMapGB-50 (which includes four layers: bedrock, superficial deposits, mass-movement and artificial deposits). This opened the door for further national datasets based upon the digital geology. With knowledge of a growing demand for geoscience information to aid land-use planning and property transactions, BGS initiated the GeoSure programme to generate 1:50 000-scale ground stability characterization of Great Britain. Geological point, line and polygon data are reclassified using geologists' knowledge in combination with various datasets, including mapped and modelled surface geology, boreholes, terrain models and groundwater, to produce potential hazard assessments for six ground stability geohazards. These are swell–shrink, landslides, compressible and collapsible deposits, running sands, and soluble rocks. Database records of hazard incidents then are used to validate these geohazard assessments.

There has been an international emphasis on monitoring and creating inventories of hazard events. However, records of past events are variable and monitoring is rare in the UK (ESFS 2004). As a result, BGS developed a deterministic rather than probabilistic approach, whereby the influence of various causative factors is assessed and used to classify the six ground stability geohazards. For example, in simple terms:

$$clay + steep\ slope + water = landslide.$$

Each geological polygon (that is, an area of ground identified as having specific geological characteristics) is labelled in DiGMapGB-50 with its stratigraphical name 'LEX' code (e.g. Wasperton Sand and Gravel Member = WAT) and its main lithology 'RCS' code (e.g. sand and gravel = XSG); creating a LEX_RCS code for each polygon (e.g. WAT_XSG). Geologists with knowledge of the rock units, their lithology and their regional characteristics identified the geohazard propensity for each LEX_RCS combination. For example, parts of Britain are underlain by Permian and Triassic rocks containing gypsum that can dissolve quickly and cause subsidence. Other datasets, such as surface slope, were incorporated to enhance the capacity for defining engineering characteristics.

A database table of the geohazard classification details for each LEX_RCS combination is created and the geological polygons are converted into 25 m grid squares. GIS software is then used to translate the data automatically, to give a hazard rating for each 25 m grid square. The ratings range from null, through 'A' (low hazard potential) to 'E' (high hazard potential) (Figs 1 and 2). The output data are then compared with available records of hazard occurrences, and checked by experienced geologists who have working knowledge of specific areas. Anomalies are identified and corrected where possible, feeding new information back into the classification method.

Data into products

Once the GIS maps are created for the six ground stability geohazards, additional text attributes can be added to each of the null and A–E classification areas to enhance users' understanding of the data. For example, Figure 1 shows how brief but informative descriptions can be provided of the implications for land use in areas of potentially unstable ground. This text can be updated regularly along with the underlying geometries, as understanding progresses and as data are improved. The text descriptions can also be taken further to meet the requirements of particular groups of end users, as in Creath's (1996) booklet, where, for a described geohazard, advice is given on what to do about each hazard and who to consult.

CLASS	COLLAPSIBLE GROUND	RUNNING SAND	COMPRESSIBLE GROUND	LANDSLIDES (SLOPE INSTABILITY)	SOLUBLE ROCKS (DISSOLUTION)	SHRINK-SWELL
NULL	Collapsible ground not thought to be present.	No NULL class in this data layer.	No NULL class in this data layer.	No NULL class in this data layer	Soluble rocks not thought to be present in this area.	No NULL class in this data layer
A	N/A	Running sand conditions are not thought to occur whatever the position of the water table. No identified constraints on land uses due to running conditions.	Compressible strata are not thought to occur.	Slope instability problems are not thought to occur but potential problems of adjacent areas impacting on the site should always be considered.	Soluble rocks are present, but unlikely to cause problems except under exceptional conditions.	Ground conditions predominantly non-plastic.
B	N/A	Running sand conditions may occur if the water table rises. Constraints may apply to land uses involving excavation or the addition or removal of water.	Compressibility and uneven settlement problems are not likely to be significant on the site for most land uses.	Slope instability problems are not likely to occur but potential problems of adjacent areas impacting on the site should always be considered.	Significant soluble rocks, but few dissolution features and no subsidence; unlikely to cause problems except with considerable surface or subsurface water flow.	Ground conditions predominantly low plasticity.
C	Deposits with the potential to collapse when saturated and loaded may be present in places.	Running sand conditions may be present. Constraints may apply to land uses involving excavation or the addition or removal of water.	Compressibility and uneven settlement potential may be present. Land use should consider specifically the compressibility and variability of the site.	Slope instability problems may be present or anticipated. Site investigation should consider specifically the slope stability of the site.	Significant soluble rocks, where there are dissolution features, and no or very little recorded subsidence, but a low possibility of it occurring naturally or in adverse conditions such as high surface or subsurface water flow.	Ground conditions predominantly medium plasticity
D	Deposits with the potential to collapse when saturated and loaded are probably present in places.	Running sand conditions are probably present. Constraints may apply to land uses involving excavation or the addition or removal of water.	Compressibility and uneven settlement hazards are probably present. Land use should consider specifically the compressibility and variability of the site.	Slope instability problems are probably present or have occurred in the past. Land use should consider specifically the stability of the site.	Very significant soluble rocks, where there are numerous dissolution features and/or some recorded subsidence with a moderate possibility of localized subsidence occurring naturally or in adverse conditions such as high surface or subsurface water flow.	Ground conditions predominantly high plasticity.
E	N/A	Running sand conditions are almost certainly present. Constraints will apply to land uses involving excavation or the addition or removal of water.	Highly compressible strata present. Significant constraint on land use depending on thickness.	Slope instability problems almost certainly present and may be active. Significant constraint on land use.	Very significant soluble rocks, where there are numerous dissolution features and/or considerable recorded subsidence with high possibility of localized subsidence occurring naturally or in adverse conditions such as high surface or subsurface water flow.	Ground conditions predominantly very high plasticity. NOTE: There is no Class E in this data layer in the UK.

Fig. 1. Legend for GeoSure: ground stability GIS datasets showing the null to E hazard ratings and the simple descriptions of hazard and advice for any action. N/A, not applicable.

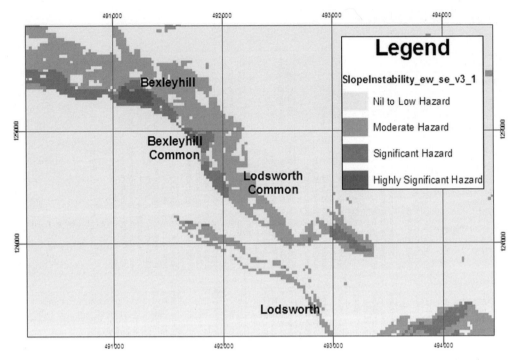

Fig. 2. Map of potential landslide hazard data north of Lodsworth, Sussex (the key gives the minimum and maximum hazard ratings in the area).

BGS was aware that previous outputs, such as thematic maps and reports, had not reached a sufficiently wide audience. To address this, BGS invested in 2000 in a report delivery system called GeoReports, fronted by an online shop (http://shop.bgs.ac.uk/georeports/). This proved a breakthrough in communication for BGS and has been very popular amongst users; in 2006–2007 BGS sold around 9000 GeoReports. It uses a semi-automated method of delivering national geoscience information in simple and understandable terms. Paper or PDF files are supplied containing extracts of the geology and geohazard maps (such as in Fig. 2), enhanced by the additional text descriptions of the hazards taken from the database tables (such as Fig. 1). Where more detailed descriptions are required by users, these reports can be expanded by manual input from BGS geologists, thereby providing a vehicle for full transfer of BGS knowledge to users; 2200 of the requested reports in 2006–2007 were for those with geologists' input. In the example extract from a GeoReport in Fig. 3, the hazard assessments are set out as a series of questions related to a client's site, and explained in simple terms for ease of use. A range of other reports is provided, tailored to meet the requirements of a range of land users, from developers to planners, property purchasers or owners.

BGS aims to match its geohazard products to the need for relevant and understandable information, through succinct but advisory attribute text with GIS data and through focused simple geohazard reports for a development site, a single house plot or a planning area. Detailed, more scientific, reports are also available. Provision of Internet access to reports has also been most helpful to members of the public looking for simple explanations, or to specialists looking for information for professional searches, output as paper or PDF. For example, a BGS report advising that 'Your home is not in an area susceptible to subsidence' might give a home owner all the information they need, but 'This site might be affected by swell–shrink damage; do not plant or remove trees without getting further advice' should lead an inquirer to seek additional information, and an engineer would normally also require more detail to make a full assessment. BGS works closely with client groups to adapt the format of geohazard reporting to meet their needs. For example, in consultation with a value-added reseller for insurance companies the GIS geohazard data were merged with postcode data to create new insurance-hazard polygons.

Added flexibility is provided for a growing number of BGS data users by supporting the

Question 1	Answer	
Is significant natural ground instability possible in the area?	*YES*	

Question 2		Answer
What is the level of hazard on a scale A to E (low to high)? NOTE: Only levels C, D and E are shown and described below, as Levels A & B are considered insignificant		Level D

Question 3	Answer
Which natural geological hazards could be contributing to the ground instability in the area? *How much ground instability each hazard may cause is indicated by the Level C to E in brackets.*	Clays that can swell when wet and shrink when dry, causing the ground to rise and fall ('Swelling Clays Hazard') (LEVEL C) Sand that can wash away or flow into holes or fissures due to water flowing through it ('Running Sand Hazard') (LEVEL C) Weak or unstable rocks that could slip downhill on steep slopes (greater than c. 5 degrees) or into excavations ('Landslide Hazard') (LEVEL C) Very soft ground that might compress and progressively sink under the weight of a building ('Compressible Ground Hazard') (LEVEL D)

Question 4	Answer
What action should be taken?	If natural ground instability has been indicated, then this means there is potential in your area for some properties to suffer subsidence damage. However, it does not necessarily mean that your property will be affected, and in order to find out if this is the case or not, you should obtain further advice from a qualified expert, such as a building surveyor. Show them this report and ask them to evaluate the property and its surroundings for any signs of existing subsidence damage as well as advise on the likelihood for subsidence to occur in the future. The notes at the end of this report may be useful in this regard. Note that the type of building and its surroundings (e.g. the presence of trees) are also very important when considering subsidence risk. Many types of properties, particularly newer ones, are very well constructed and unlikely to be affected by subsidence, even in areas of very significant ground movements.

Fig. 3. Extracts from ground stability GeoReport for the BGS Keyworth office site.

incorporation of geohazard (and many other) data-sets into their own decision-support and reporting systems. This facility is especially useful for local planning and environmental health officers, and for commercial companies that provide reports to development consultants and conveyancing solicitors via the Internet. Provision of geohazard information via a third party, such as a commercial reporting company, has many advantages for BGS, including wider and more focused communication and market research.

Communication issues

Language

The understanding of the terms hazard and geohazard is highly dependent on a person's life experience and education. For many, a hazard indicates potential danger such as a hole in the road or a warning for floods or bad weather; but they may not be sure which of these is a geohazard.

However, if geohazards are listed, many words would be recognized by the general public and related impacts readily envisaged. Those reading terms such as earthquake, landslide, volcanic eruption or mining collapse would immediately be aware of potential outcomes even if the underlying conditions and mechanisms were not understood. Other user-perspectives must also be considered; an insurance company, for example, might view a geological hazard as being the cause of a problem, but see the symptom as a financial cost (hazard).

General assistance to geoscientists eager to share their knowledge is still lacking in terms of clear guidance on how best to communicate in a form that is accessible to a variety of audiences. In 1996 Creath published the *Home Buyers' Guide to Geologic Hazards in America*, describing each hazard in lay terms and aiding property owners in identifying whether a hazard could affect their property. Although the level of scientific terminology used would still challenge many readers, it is written in a non-technical style and it set a good precedent for user-oriented (rather than scientist-oriented) information provision. BGS used its connections with commercial companies and educational institutes to aid understanding of their needs and to adapt its presentation styles. Improvement continues in these areas thanks to this kind of market intelligence. Other geoscience organizations have also embraced the need for appropriate presentation of scientific ideas; Geoscience Australia in particular, and a number of American institutes have good records in producing geohazard leaflets suitable for a broad-spectrum technical audience and also informative to members of the lay public who have some technical knowledge (Forster & Freeborough 2006).

The study by Forster & Freeborough (2006) advocated the use of good visual material, clear simple language and consideration of the knowledge and needs of the intended audience. They also highlighted that successful communication is an emotional rather than a technical skill, in which many scientists might need training.

Although plain English might be understandable to most British citizens, some business sectors will look for their own professional terminology (jargon) before identifying a dataset as being relevant to them. For example, planning officers will look for references to legal or government requirements such as Planning Policy Guidance relating to unstable land for geohazard information (Anonymous 1990, 1996). These documents are aimed specifically at the planning community and associated professionals, and are written in a style that includes planning terminology with reference to other regulations familiar to planners and conveys the information in a precise manner. It is human nature to respond positively to recognized terminology and look for easy ways to meet such policy requirements. The more easily an individual can identify with a piece of information the more readily they will accept and use it. BGS's association with some insurers, and their guidance on expected information format and content, has allowed better BGS communication and a more positive reception of geohazard information in the insurance arena.

The message

Following any geohazard-related event such as a landslide on the British coast, awareness of potential hazards in the affected area is raised, but this might not increase awareness of the term 'geohazard'. More important, and of greatest interest to those affected, is gaining an understanding of what has happened and why, what can be done to prevent repetition or how to be prepared for future events. Long-term impacts and any related safety implications must also be communicated.

Organizations such as BGS that traditionally are linked with central government commonly are called upon to provide definitive information and to offer explanations and advice. Therefore, maintaining user confidence in any data provided and taking care with the language used to describe geohazard data are issues of paramount importance.

Public outreach

For many decades the relevance of earth-science research results to decision-makers, politicians, industry and the lay public has been promoted by prominent bodies such as the Royal Society (1985, 2006). More recently, the International Geographical Union's Commission on Hazards and Risks has reported on the role of science in public policy decision-making, reviewing who uses information, what information is used, and the purposes for which it is used (ESFS 2004). Emphasizing the importance of widespread dissemination of scientific knowledge, the Royal Society also acknowledged the difficulties caused by lack of guidance for scientists and the perceived professional stigma associated with communicating their results to a lay audience. Any such stigma associated with interacting with the media and promoting public dissemination of science has diminished markedly, thanks partly to the many radio and television programmes that have been presented during the past 10 years. Nevertheless, peer disapproval of publication in popular rather than scientific journals and of the use of lay terms continues to be identified as a barrier to 'popular' communication (Van Loon 2003).

Conclusions

Many personal, public and business decisions have a scientific aspect that might include geohazards. In response, geoscientists have to be increasingly focused on societal vulnerability to natural hazards as much as the scientific causes and physical consequences of such hazards.

The provision of geohazard information to non-geologists and the creation of thematic output are not new ideas. More novel are considerations of users' understanding of geology and the provision of such information using formats and language that are recognizable to particular groups. To communicate well there must be comprehension of the topic's relevance to the recipient. To allow a good understanding of scientific information that is being presented, minimal scientific jargon should be used and when focusing on a particular group, concepts and language familiar to them should be included.

Internationally there have been great steps forward in the successful communication of geohazard information by geoscientists to a broadly based audience, and the BGS contribution has been a part of that trend. The provision of GIS data for recipients to use in their own systems, supported by text that describes the geohazards in lay terms, and especially the provision of tailored reports for non-technical persons have been enormous steps forward in the development of BGS geohazard knowledge transfer.

In answer to the question: 'Can geologists make geology relevant to others?' I would say 'Emphatically yes'. However, we have yet to develop a still more versatile bridge across the gap between helping users understand that geology is relevant to them and making geological information understandable to all.

References

ANONYMOUS, 1990. *Planning Policy Guidance 14. Development on Unstable Land.* Department of the Environment and the Welsh Office. HMSO, London.

ANONYMOUS, 1996. *Planning Policy Guidance 14 (Annex 1). Development on Unstable Land: Landslides and Planning.* Department of the Environment. HMSO, London.

CREATH, W. B. 1996. *Home Buyers' Guide to Geologic Hazards.* An AIPG Issues and Answers Publication. American Institute of Professional Geologists, Arvada, CO.

ESFS 2004. Hazards—Minimising risk, maximising awareness. Earth Sciences for Society prospectus for a key theme of the International Year of Planet Earth, November 2004. Earth Sciences for Society Foundation. World Wide Web Address: http://www.iugs.org/iugs/downloads/iype/03_hazards.pdf.

FORSTER, A. & FREEBOROUGH, K. 2006. *A guide to the communication of geohazards information to the public.* British Geological Survey Internal Report, **IR/06/009**.

Royal Society 1985. *The Public Understanding of Science.* Royal Society, London.

Royal Society 2006. *Science and the Public Interest. Communicating the Results of New Scientific Research to the Public.* Royal Society, London.

VAN LOON, A. J. 2003. Towards a public-friendly publishing attitude in the earth sciences. Geological Society of America Abstracts with Programs, Vol. 35, No. 6, September, Seattle Annual Meeting, The Geological Society of America, 2.

WILSON, A. A., REES, J. G., CROFTS, R. G., HOWARD, A. S., BUCHANAN, J. G. & WAINE, P. J. 1992. *Stoke on Trent: A Geological Background for Planning and Development.* British Geological Survey Technical Report, **WN/91/101**.

The modelling and visualization of digital geoscientific data as a communication aid to land-use planning in the urban environment: an example from the Thames Gateway

K. R. ROYSE, H. J. REEVES & A. R. GIBSON

British Geological Survey, Keyworth, Nottingham NG12 5GG, UK (e-mail: krro@bgs.ac.uk)

Abstract: The Thames Gateway Development Zone is the biggest urban development project in the UK for over 50 years. Developers and planners need to understand the implications of such large-scale urbanization on the environment. Requirements for sustainable growth within the Thames Gateway region mean that developers are being required to demonstrate that proposals are based on sound scientific information. This has resulted in a growing demand for geo-environmental information to be provided in more accessible, relevant and understandable forms. Advances in the use of geographic information systems (GIS) and 3D modelling software mean that there is now far greater opportunity to develop geo-environmental information products for urban development. New and innovative ways of visualizing and communicating geoscience information have been developed. Using this new technology it is possible to predict not only the types of rocks beneath a site, but also the engineering properties (such as rock strength, shrink–swell characteristics or compressibility), hydrogeological properties (such as permeability, porosity and thickness of the unsaturated zone) and geohazard potential. Geoscientific information can then be imported into standard GIS packages and queried along with other complementary ground investigation data, resulting in the creation of a powerful tool to assist in strategic planning and sustainable development.

The importance of good quality geo-environmental information is becoming increasingly important as new guidance and legislative changes (such as the Planning Policy Statements (PPS) 9 (Department for Communities and Local Government 2006), 23 (Office of the Deputy Prime Minister 2004) and 25 (Communities and Local Government 2006), the water framework directive and part IIA of the Environment Protection Act 1990) have forced developers, planning authorities and regulators to consider the implications and impact of large-scale development initiatives on the environment. To comply with the principles of sustainable development, developers increasingly are required to demonstrate that proposals are based on the best possible scientific information and analysis of risk. Nowhere are these issues more relevant than in the context of the urban environment.

The case for using geo-environmental information to underpin preliminary site appraisal and for developing regional strategies has been made elsewhere and has been discussed in depth by Culshaw *et al.* (1994), Ellison *et al.* (1998, 2002), McKirdy *et al.* (1998), Thompson *et al.* (1998), Bobrowsky (2002) and Culshaw & Ellison (2002). In the UK, studies commissioned by the Department of the Environment in the 1980s and 1990s (Smith & Ellison 1999) promoted the use of applied geological maps to identify the principal geological factors that should be taken into account for development planning. Since this

work was completed, advances in the use of geographic information systems (GIS) and 3D modelling software have meant that there is now a greater opportunity to develop geo-environmental information systems for urban development, which can take greater account of the third dimension. As a result, new and innovative ways of communicating and visualizing geoscientific information have been developed.

The research on which this paper is based focuses on London and the Thames Gateway Development Zone, but builds on earlier work in Manchester and Salford (Culshaw 2005; Lelliott *et al.* 2006). London is one of the most densely populated cities in Europe. The Mayor of London's Plan (Mayor of London 2004) predicts that the total population of London will rise by 900 000 by the year 2016. For London to cope with such a huge increase in population, it must grow and develop fast. The only way this can be achieved is by development taking place outside London's current boundaries. As a result, a 40 mile stretch of land running eastwards from the East End of London, along both north and south banks of the River Thames towards Southend-on-Sea, forms the area known as the Thames Gateway Development Zone (TGDZ; Fig. 1). It is currently the focus of the biggest building programme to be undertaken in the UK for over 50 years.

From: LIVERMAN, D. G. E., PEREIRA, C. P. G. & MARKER, B. (eds) *Communicating Environmental Geoscience*. Geological Society, London, Special Publications, **305**, 89–106.
DOI: 10.1144/SP305.10   0305-8719/08/$15.00 © The Geological Society of London 2008.

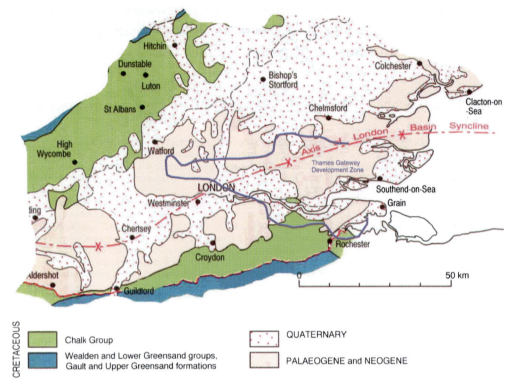

Fig. 1. Geological map of London and the Thames Gateway area.

A large proportion of the planned development projects in the Thames Gateway will necessitate construction on ground that contains highly compressible soils, shrinking and swelling clays, high groundwater levels, potentially contaminated brownfield sites and ground that is affected by other geohazards. Failure to fully appreciate the ground conditions at the planning stage of any development is likely to prove costly and may lead to project overrun (Marker 1998). A report by the Institution of Civil Engineers in 1993 found that of the 5000 industrial building projects that it surveyed, nearly all those that overran were due to problems created by unforeseen ground conditions (Site Investigation Steering Group 1993). The Thames Gateway planning framework document (RPG 9A, Anonymous 1995) recognizes numerous issues related to geology. These include such issues as dealing with existing and potential land contamination, preservation of the natural environment (including sites of geological interest) and flood risk. Yet, unlike the Environment Agency and the Countryside Agency, the British Geological Survey has not been a statutory consultee in the planning process for the TGDZ.

If sound decisions are to be made then, clearly, those organizations involved in planning and development need access to all relevant information. This paper explores new ways that geoscientists can present and communicate their information, so that regional development strategies include relevant geoscientific information and land-use planners can obtain a better understanding of the relevance of geoscientific data in planning and development.

Geological setting

The TGDZ is contained within the London Basin (Fig. 1). The London Basin is a broad, gentle synclinal fold whose axis can be traced from Marlborough to Westminster. The London Basin formed in Oligocene to mid-Miocene times during the main Alpine compressional event. Formations in this region range from Cretaceous (144–65 Ma) to Quaternary (2 Ma to present day) in age.

The Cretaceous Chalk is typically a fine-grained white limestone (Bristow *et al.* (1997) have provided a detailed description of the Chalk lithostratigraphy). It has a total thickness of between 175 and 200 m and generally thins from the west to the east. Overlying the Chalk is the oldest

Palaeogene deposit, the Thanet Sand Formation. This formation consists of a coarsening upwards sequence of fine-grained, grey sand. The formation reaches a maximum thickness of around 30 m in the area. A basal conglomerate (the Bullhead Beds) defines the base of the Thanet Sand, which consists of rounded black flint pebbles. Above the Thanet Sand Formation lies the Lambeth Group, which consists of three formations: the Upnor, Woolwich and Reading formations. The Lambeth Group is between 20 and 30 m thick in the area and lithologically the group is highly variable, consisting of variable proportions of sands, silts, clays and gravels.

Overlying this are the Eocene sediments of the Thames Group, which consists of the Harwich and London Clay formations. The Harwich Formation (formally known as the Blackheath or Oldhaven Beds) consists predominantly of sand and pebble beds up to 4 m thick. Above this is approximately 90–130 m of London Clay. The London Clay Formation consists of grey to blue–grey, bioturbated, silty clay. Quaternary deposits are encountered right across the TGDZ. These include evidence of an ancient river system and the development of the present-day River Thames valley. Deposits include alluvium, peat, brickearth and river terrace deposits (e.g. the Kempton Park, Taplow and Shepperton Gravels).

Requirements for digital geoscientific data

The essential function of land-use planning can be summarized as 'the scientific, aesthetic, and orderly disposition of land, resources, facilities and services with a view to securing the physical, economic and social efficiency, health and well-being of urban and rural communities' (Canadian Institute of Planners 2000). This requires planners to consider the social, economic and political needs of their area as well as the needs of the environment. Geological and geotechnical issues tend to appear well down the list of priorities (Paul et al. 2002). All too often it is only after problems have occurred that attention is turned towards geological and geotechnical issues.

New guidance and legislative changes such as PPS 9, 23 and 25 have forced planners and developers to consider the implications of large-scale development initiatives on the environment. Policy documents such as those published by Anonymous (1995), Thompson et al. (1998) and the Office of the Deputy Prime Minister (2004) have resulted in an increased awareness of the importance of geoscientific data in land-use planning and a requirement to base planning decisions

on the best available environmental information. This has resulted in geoscientists making increasing efforts to provide planners with relevant geological information (Smith & Ellison 1999). However, the final project output has often resulted in the work being presented in a form that does not meet the needs of planners, many of whom do not have a geoscientific background (Marker 1998). Turner (2003) suggested that most geoscientific information systems fail not because they were inadequate scientifically or technologically, but because the system did not meet the needs of the user community it was designed to serve.

Geoscientists have principally two problems to overcome. First, the traditional method of visualizing geoscientific information is to produce a geological map. Although an excellent way of recording several sets of 2D information on a flat surface, it requires a significant amount of expert knowledge to interpret its meaning. For the non-geoscientist the geological map presents itself as a confusing array of colours and lines, which have little relevance to the users' everyday working lives. Second, with changes in planning policy, there has been a significant change in the type of data-users requiring geoscience information. Data-users can be divided into two camps, 'thick' and 'thin' (Turner 2006). Traditionally, geoscientific information has been provided to 'thick' clients. 'Thick' clients are those who are happy to interpret and manipulate raw data; typically they are keen to have large quantities of uninterpreted data (e.g. academics). 'Thin' clients, in contrast, desire simple, concise data that answer precise questions (Turner 2006). 'Thin' clients make up the majority of planners and developers. This view was supported by Culshaw (2003), who suggested that academic users were no longer the most important users of geoscientific information. Therefore, if geoscience data are going to be used widely within the land-use planning sector, geoscientists need to rethink, radically, the way geoscientific data are presented and visualized.

Turner (2003) indicated that generic products are often insufficient to meet the needs of a specific user group such as planners, and suggested instead that geoscientists should concentrate on producing customized products. Therefore, before the geoscientist can produce such outputs three questions must be considered: (1) What geoscientific information do planners and developers need? (2) What type of geoscience data is required to meet these needs? (3) Why are geoscientific data not always fully used?

Urban areas require geological resources for construction and maintenance (Marker 1998). They also require geological data to ensure that sterilization of resources or contaminative activities close to vulnerable aquifers do not occur. With these views firmly in mind, several researchers such as Brook & Marker (1987), Bell & Culshaw (1998), Marker (1998), Smith & Ellison (1999), Howland (2000) and Paul *et al.* (2002) have suggested what types of geoscientific data planners and developers require: (1) lithostratigraphical geology (at site, area and regional scale); (2) geomorphology; (3) the nature and use of ground materials; (4) the availability and quality of water; (5) the susceptibility of aquifers to pollution; (6) natural and anthropogenic geohazards; (7) the engineering behaviour of the ground; (8) land that may be contaminated; (9) identification of development potential (constraints on and resources for development).

To find out why geoscientific information is not being fully used and applied, the views of around 20 stakeholders within the Thames Gateway region were sought from a variety of professions, including local and regional government, utility industries, government agencies, geotechnical and engineering companies, and local development agencies and corporations. This information was combined with information from previous studies, such as those by Nickless (1982), De Mulder (1988), Ellison *et al.* (1998), Marker (1998), Thompson *et al.* (1998) and Culshaw & Ellison (2002). All this information has been incorporated into Table 1. From these discussions it can be concluded that three distinct concerns affect the greater use of geoscientific information. These relate to its relevance, interpretation and visualization (Royse

et al. 2005). Using the Thames Gateway area as a case study this paper will show how geoscientific information can be interpreted and visualized appropriately, and hence made more relevant to planners and developers.

Responding to users' needs

Two key advances have allowed geoscientists to change the way they present data to planners and developers. (1) the availability of geoscientific data in (computer-readable) digital form (Jackson 2004; Bowie 2005); (2) advances in GIS and 3D modelling software; these have meant that there is now a greater opportunity to develop geoenvironmental information systems for the urban environment, which significantly can take account of the third dimension.

In the past, one of the main reasons why many professionals did not use 3D digital models routinely was that many modelling packages are too complex to use (Hack *et al.* 2006). A key development in changing that perception has been the advances in 3D modelling capabilities and software development, which allow geologists to construct 3D models much more easily (Hinze *et al.* 1999; Sobisch 2000; Culshaw 2005). As a result of developments in 3D viewing software (Sobisch 2000), 3D models can now be viewed and manipulated on a standard desktop computer and, more importantly, updated quickly and easily when new data become available. Models can

Table 1. *The needs of developers and planners and the types of uses to which the 3D attributed digital geological model could be used in planning and development to answer these needs*

Planners' and developers' needs	Data outputs from the attributed geological mode
To make the best use of natural resources and protect and conserve their region's natural heritage	Location, thickness and distribution of mineral-rich geological units
	Hydrogeological domain and aquifer vulnerability maps
	Improved groundwater models
	Identification of geological strata rich in archaeological finds
	Geo-diversity maps
	Potential contaminated land risk assessment maps at the level of build
To ensure that development takes place in the right place and is properly designed	Geological maps and models
	Foundation condition maps, SUDS initial assessment tools
	Geohazard maps
	Site investigation planning tools or models
	Geotechnical classification of the ground at depth of build
	Underground asset management systems
	Decision support tools
To be able to set broad polices for land use in a particular area	Regional attributed geological models
	Geohazards maps and models
	Environmental information systems
	Regional groundwater management plans
	Decision support tools

be attributed with physical, chemical or hydrogeological parameters. Once the attributed 3D model is completed, a large number of customized geoscientific outputs can be generated, with little computation (Fig. 2). These are major steps forward from previous 3D urban modelling systems; for example, that of Strange *et al.* (1998), which required a significant amount of specialist computer knowledge and access to large computing capabilities. Data outputs also tended to be static, as updating was difficult and time consuming.

In the following sections, this paper explores how the main needs of planners and developers (Table 1) can be fulfilled by the use and manipulation of digital geoscientific data and 3D geological models.

Making the best of natural resources

To manage natural resources effectively (e.g. biodiversity, soil, land and water) planners need to integrate a scientific understanding of environmental processes with an appreciation of socioeconomics. Geoscience information can help in a variety of ways, from the location and distribution of mineral-rich layers to improving groundwater management and protection plans.

Geodiversity maps. An appreciation of geodiversity is important to gain a full understanding of many aspects of biodiversity. Geodiversity offers very substantial opportunities to enhance the conservation, management and educational use of land within a region; it is, therefore, an essential part of green network planning (Office of the Deputy Prime Minister & Department of Environment, Food and Rural Affairs 2004). However, until the changes in PPS 9 in August 2005, geodiversity had received little serious consideration.

Geodiversity interests need to be integrated into management and conservation strategies for related or parallel interests, including wildlife and archaeological features. The key to doing this is providing planners with spatially registered digital geoscientific data that can then be queried with other environmental information within a standard GIS system. Geodiversity issues contribute significantly to informing a wide range of planning and environmental policies.

Geodiversity audits have been carried out by the British Geological Survey, most recently for

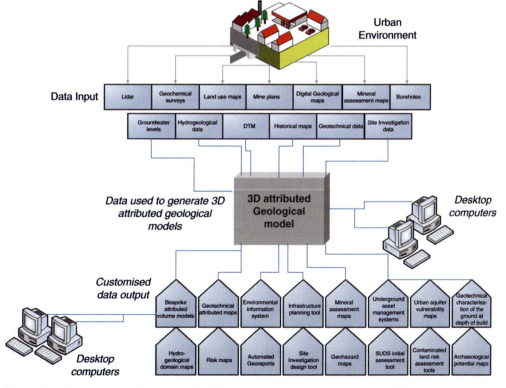

Fig. 2. Flow diagram showing the process of building and attributing the 3D geological model.

Northumberland (Lawrence *et al.* 2007). Although none have been compiled yet for the Thames Gateway, the same principles would apply. In each case a spatial database is set up, whereby geological sites and landscape features are explained and evaluated, thereby setting them in a local, regional, national and, where appropriate, international context for local authorities. These data can then be queried, along with other spatially referenced datasets. The resulting GIS system can be used to assess the number of environmental assets present within a region (Steadman *et al.* 2004).

Location and distribution of mineral-rich layers. Probably the best way to provide an indication of the geometry, distribution and spatial relationship of gravel deposits within the Thames Gateway region is to produce a 3D geological model. The Thames Gateway model was built using over 4000 borehole logs and creating over 200 north–south- and east–west-trending cross-sections. The model was then constructed using a generalized vertical section (GVS) of the lithostratigraphy, which, when combined with the generated cross-sections, created a fence diagram of the geology (Fig. 3). The geological fence diagram of the superficial and bedrock geology was 'hung' from, and constrained by, recent 1:10 000-scale digital geological mapping and a digital terrain model (DTM) of the area.

Figure 4 displays part of the 3D geological model for the TGDZ. The model provides the user with a view of the geometry and spatial distribution of each of the geological formations within the Thames Gateway region. The user is also able to visualize the variations in thickness. For example, in Figure 5 the thickness of the alluvial deposits changes from 1–5 m in the west to 20 m in the east. Using a traditional 2D paper map with borehole data, interpreting the same information would require a significant amount of time and effort by a geologist. The advantage of the digital 3D model is that this information can be more readily communicated and made available.

Identification of strata rich in archaeological deposits. The 3D model also can be used to provide information on the likelihood of archaeological remains being present within a particular site; in London and the Thames Gateway area archaeological remains can be linked to the palaeo-environment and hence the geology (Bates 1998; Bates & Bates 2000). As a result, the 3D geological model can be used by archaeological units within local governmental planning departments to provide advice on whether developments are taking place within potentially archaeologically rich strata and hence whether particular planning

conditions should be applied and specialist investigations required.

Groundwater management. The Thames Gateway 3D geological model can be used as a framework to help develop a conceptual model of the hydrogeological system, essential in understanding groundwater flow and pollution transport. There are a number of ways this can be achieved, such as: using the model to understand the geometry and distribution of hydrogeologically important units; adding hydrogeological parameters to the geological model (such as permeability or porosity); displaying water surfaces in the geological model; and the creation of geology maps from the model at a given potentiometric surface. Attributing the 3D geological model allows the user to view and analyse the vertical and lateral variation in hydrogeological properties, rather than the variation in lithostratigraphy. For example, if high-permeability units were required, say, for the assessment of aquifer storage and recovery potential, then these units, and their depth, thickness and lateral extent, can be quickly identified (Fig. 6). The 3D models also can be linked to 4D process models (such as MODFLOW and ZOOMQ3D; Jackson 2001) that show movement of groundwater through the system.

The 3D model also can be used to define areas or domains of recharge and discharge; that is, to identify sequences of rock types that are likely to be characterized by similar hydrogeological properties. The models can then be used to assist with water resource management strategies at a regional and site-specific level (e.g. Lelliott *et al.* 2006). The use of this domain style of mapping in the context of aquifer recharge or discharge is not new (McMillan *et al.* 2000; Dochartaigh *et al.* 2005). However, exporting the 3D geological model as gridded surfaces into a GIS system means that the model can be spatially queried. By identifying and describing each of the domains and by formulating a set of spatial rules, to describe each unit, a thematic recharge or discharge map in two dimensions is produced that displays complex packages of sediments, defined from the 3D model (Lelliott *et al.* 2006). The resulting thematic map (Fig. 7) simplifies what is often a complex and diverse collection of anthropogenic, superficial and bedrock deposits, by placing the information into a form that can be more easily understood.

Understanding the site

According to the UK Government's sustainable communities policy (Office of the Deputy Prime Minister 2003) '[Land-use] Planning shapes the places where people live and work and the

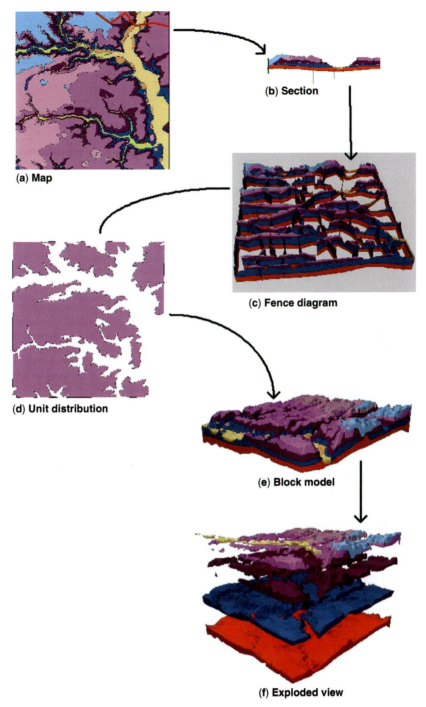

Fig. 3. Diagram of the 3D geological model building work flow (after Kessler & Mathers 2005).

Fig. 4. Three-dimensional geological model of the Thames Gateway Development Zone from Stratford in the west to Canvey Island in the east. Areas of peat (brown) are revealed beneath deposits of alluvium (yellow–green), river terrace deposits (orange) and anthropogenic deposits (grey). Bedrock is composed of Palaeogene deposits (orange, dark blue and pink) underlain by Chalk (blue–green).

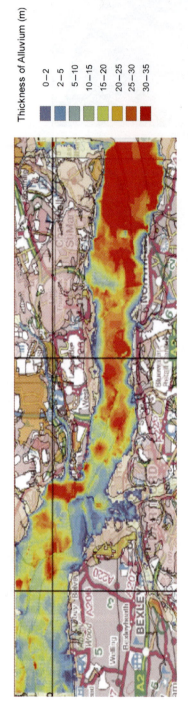

Thickness of Alluvium (m)

0–2
2–5
5–10
10–15
15–20
20–25
25–30
30–35

Fig. 5. Contour map of the thickness of the alluvium between Bexley and Tilbury displayed in ArcGIS generated from the 3D geological model. OS topography © Crown Copyright. All rights reserved. 100017897/2008.

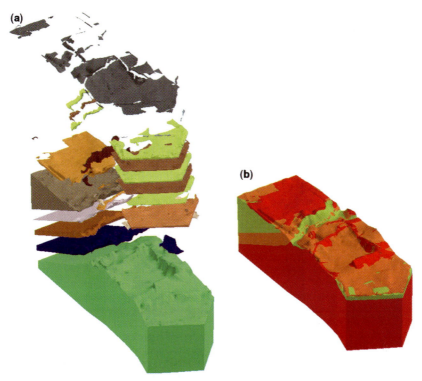

Fig. 6. Three-dimensional property and geological models for West Thurrock; (**a**) geological model (see Fig. 1 for details of the stratigraphy); (**b**) property model, displaying the differences in permeability between the geological units (high permeability in red; low permeability in green; variable permeability in orange).

country we live in. Good planning ensures that we get the right development, in the right place and at the right time. It makes a positive difference to people's lives and helps to deliver homes, jobs, and better opportunities for all, whilst protecting and enhancing the natural and historic environment'. Consequently, sustainable development is at the very core of planning policy in the UK today. The World Commission on Environment and Development (Bruntland 1987) defined sustainable development as: 'development that meets the needs of the present without compromising the ability of future generations to meet their own needs'. If such policies are to be acted upon, it is essential that land-use planners understand the significance of geoscience information in providing a better context for design of site investigations (Marker 1998). The examples below indicate how geoscientific data and 3D models, especially when attributed with property data, can provide land-use planners with a thorough understanding of the shallow subsurface.

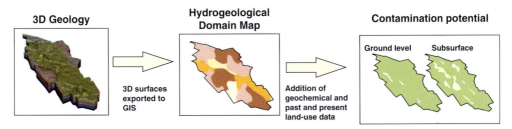

Fig. 7. Diagram indicating how a 3D geological model can be used to generate thematic 2D maps by incorporating other geo-environmental datasets and using spatial queries available within standard GIS packages.

Potential contaminated land and risk assessment. The 3D model can be used to assess the risk of a new development contaminating the local groundwater supplies. Contamination studies concentrate on the linkages between source and receptor (the 'pathway'). The 3D model can be used to assess these potential links. An example of this is the Lower Lea Valley. Here, thick sequences of superficial deposits comprising river terrace gravels and alluvium are underlain by Palaeogene deposits of the London Clay Formation with the Lambeth Group below. A detailed description has been given by Ellison *et al.* (2004). Where the London Clay is absent and the superficial deposits rest on the Lambeth Group (which consists of interbedded layers of clay and sand), for example near Stratford Marsh, there are significant implications for the development of pathways from the surface to the Chalk aquifer. As the Lambeth Group is extremely variable, it is likely that at some locations the clay layers may be thin or absent; consequently, the Chalk aquifer will be partially or wholly unconfined. A similar situation occurs in the Kempton Park Gravels, where irregularities in the rockhead surface (scour hollows) are known to exist (Berry 1979). The scour hollows can be as much as 15 m in depth; in these instances, the scouring will have removed the clay layers from within the Lambeth Group and, as a result, a direct pathway is established between surface water and the Chalk aquifer. By using the 3D geological model it is possible to locate sites where these situations are likely to occur and hence, at an early stage, identify these potentially problematical ground conditions.

Foundation conditions and geotechnical classification of ground at depth. For engineering applications, modelling provides a 3D framework in which spatial presentation and interpretation of geotechnical data can be undertaken. From this spatial information, an engineering geological classification can be formulated and hence the engineering geological ground conditions can then be visualized in three dimensions. Engineers and geologists can use this visualization to assist in the recognition and identification of problematic ground conditions, to help design more appropriate ground investigations and contribute to the most efficient foundation design.

Synthetic geological cross-sections and borehole logs can be generated along a specified route, allowing an interpretation of the subsurface geology beneath the route to be formulated. For example, a synthetic section can be generated along a given linear route such as railway track. Once a geological appraisal of a section of track has been prepared (Fig. 8), an engineering geological interpretation can be undertaken

(Fig. 8). This involves the use of different types of geotechnical test data (e.g. standard penetration test, moisture content, particle size distribution) to aid in the interpretation and assessment of the ground conditions. This assessment is undertaken in accordance with BS5930 (British Standards Institution 1999) to determine the grain size (clay, silt, sand, gravel, etc.) and strength or density, thus allowing the ground conditions to be classified into a number of engineering geological units (Table 2). In the TGDZ, the geological model was characterized using particle size distribution and standard penetration test data, held in the National Geotechnical Database (maintained by the British Geological Survey). This allowed 10 engineering geological units to be identified (Table 2). This classification was then applied to the synthetic geological cross-section and an engineering geological section was produced (Fig. 8). Visual inspection of Figure 8 allows zones of potentially difficult ground conditions to be identified.

It is now not sufficient to identify, say fine-grained soils as locations for potentially problematic ground conditions as was done in the past using 2D geological maps. More information is required about the geological structure, lithological variability, mineralogy, moisture content and geotechnical properties of the rocks and soils, much of which can be supplied from 3D geospatial databases. These databases can be interrogated at key depths to show the wide variability of geological materials and conditions beneath the ground surface. Detailed geological sections along linear routes, such as the example shown from the c2c train operating company's railway route from Purfleet to east Tilbury, can be modelled and the locations of potential problematic rocks and soils, such as alluvium and peats, can be identified (Fig. 8). Spatial attribution of geotechnical data and simple methods to recast sections in engineering geological terms are easily realized using these new techniques. Such attributed sections are an additional tool in strategic infrastructure (e.g. rail and road) maintenance and network expansion plans.

Site investigation planning tools. Once a 3D geological framework has been created, geotechnical, hydrogeological data and maps, utility maps, mine plans, etc. can be added into a GIS system where site investigation planning tools can be created. Using these tools, it is possible for ground investigations to be focused on areas where the GIS system shows data to be incomplete or where the ground conditions are problematic. These GIS systems can be viewed from a desktop PC, making the modelled data far easier to use on a day-to-day basis. It is also possible for data to be

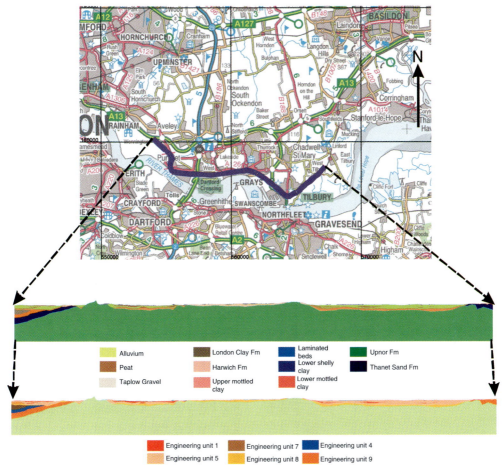

Fig. 8. Three-dimensional geological model of a railway route from Purfleet to East Tilbury, London, with automatically generated geological and engineering geological cross-sections. OS topography © Crown Copyright. All rights reserved. 100017897/2008.

updatable so that site investigation data can be used to advise developers during the construction process (Kaalberg *et al.* 2003).

Assessment of urban drainage. Sustainable Urban Drainage Systems (SUDS) are an alternative approach to conventional drainage systems and replicate, as far as possible, natural drainage systems to manage rainwater runoff effectively. The successful implementation of SUDS (which include swales, balancing ponds and porous pavements) can save money, reduce pollution and alleviate flood risk (CIRIA 2001). BGS has developed a method within the Manchester Urban Project (Lelliott *et al.* 2006) that has since been applied to the TGDZ, and allows the assessment of SUDS to be carried out quickly and simply at the site planning stage of the project. The assessment is made by reference to the 3D lithological

model (type of rock and soil), the topographic slope angle, the permeability of the near-surface deposits and the thickness of the unsaturated zone. The data are then combined into a simple tri-category map; areas more suited to infiltration techniques (e.g. porous pavements) can then be easily identified.

This system is now being developed to incorporate other issues, such as potential contamination, present-day land use and aquifer vulnerability, to provide a more realistic picture of the environmental considerations necessary for the implementation of a successful SUDS scheme.

Geohazard maps. Despite the TGDZ's low relief, lack of soluble or collapsible deposits and distance from any large seismic sources, it is actually one of the areas of Britain most affected by geohazards. As described above, most of the TGDZ is underlain by

Table 2. *Engineering classification of the geological units encountered in the central part of the Thames Gateway area (after D. Entwisle, pers. comm.)*

Engineering unit		Geological unit	Characteristics	Engineering consideration
Soil				
Organic	1	Peat	Very soft to firm, fibrous or amorphous dark brown, or black clayey peat, occasionally woody or with layers of shells	Highly compressible; even light foundation will be subject to variable and considerable settlement over long periods; dewatering produces considerable and prolonged settlement; may produce acidic groundwater
Mixed soils	2	Worked and made ground	Highly variable, very soft to stiff, uncompact to compact; loose to dense clay, silt, sand, gravel and cobble; may include man-made materials; may be compacted	Highly variable ground conditions, depending on content and whether it is engineered; may be contaminated; may produce explosive or noxious gases
	3	Engineered embankments	Highly variable generally stiff or dense compact clay, silt, sand, gravel; may include man-made materials; compacted	Mostly suitable for foundations, depending on construction methods
	4	Lambeth Group and Harwich Formation	Highly variable rock types, firm to hard clay, occasional weak claystone, compact silt, dense to very dense sand and/or flint gravel, some shelly or shell beds, occasional weak limestone, occasionally organic; lithological variation often unpredictable	Generally good foundation material; however, the lithological variability gives rise to variable groundwater conditions including lenticular water-bearing sands; variability provides difficult to very difficult tunnelling and deep excavation conditions; fissuring in clays may affect the stability of cuttings
Fine	5	Alluvium	Very soft to soft, sometimes firm, sometimes laminated, often organic, sometimes with shelly clay; top 2–3 m may be firm to stiff owing to desiccation	Generally highly compressible; bearing capacities less than 100 kPa; light foundation may be subject to variable and considerable settlement over long periods; dewatering produces considerable and prolonged settlement

	No.	Formation	Description	Engineering properties
	6	Crayford Silt and Ilford Silt Formations	Uncompact to compact, often with vertical fissures, silt or firm clay	Some parts have high porosity and open structure, which may be prone to collapse on loading and wetting; generally well drained; used in the manufacture of bricks (hence 'brickearth'); excellent agricultural land
	7	London Clay Formation	Firm to stiff becoming very stiff or hard at depth, near surface generally fissured, brown often with gypsum otherwise grey, clay sometimes compact silt, occasionally dense to very dense sand	Near surface prone to shrink–swell affecting shallow foundations; planting or removal of trees near buildings may exacerbate this; depth of weathering, and fissuring, varies
Coarse	8	Shepperton, Kempton Park, Taplow, Hackney and Lynch Hill Gravels Formations	Generally moderately dense to dense, sometimes very dense sand or gravel or mixture of the two, sometimes silty or clayey with local lenses of silt, clay or peat	Generally good foundation condition; excavations may require dewatering and are generally unstable; high water table in excavations may lead to running sand conditions
	9	Thanet Sand Formation	Very dense, slightly silty or clayey to silty to clayey fine sand, with gravel to cobble flint at base (Bullhead Beds)	Generally high bearing capacity but may be lower near surface where weathered or cryoturbated; requires dewatering in tunnelling and deeper excavation; water pressures often artesian where this formation is below clay
Rock Chalk	10	Seaford and Newhaven Formations	Comminuted to high-density chalk, variable weathering depth, sometimes karstic	Depends on degree and depth of weathering and the presence of karst; bearing capacity generally good where not highly weathered; however, both bored and driven piles have little friction

the London Clay Formation. Problems associated with this material, at surface and at depth are well known to the construction industry (see Burnett & Fookes 1974; Chandler & Apted 1988; Hight & Jardine 1993; Dimmock & Mair 2007). This overconsolidated, highly plastic clay is particularly susceptible to shrink–swell activity, and, when on a slope, is prone to mass movement and landslides (Hutchinson 1965; Forster 1999). Demonstrating, describing and quantifying the extent and impacts of shrink–swell activity is more difficult; building distress resulting from ground shrinkage is often categorized as 'subsidence' damage. Insurance claims resulting from such damage are higher in areas underlain by the London Clay, although, for commercial reasons, detailed data are usually unavailable. Doornkamp (1995) offered an insight into how closely insurance premiums reflect geological reality.

To communicate the presence and severity of these hazards to a wide range of audiences, BGS has developed a National Geohazard Assessment: GeoSure. This GIS-based model provides an interpretation of the geological map that includes consideration of geotechnical data, geohazard data, published literature and expert judgement. Potential users of the data indicated that they wanted little or no geological information to be visible at point of use (though this is accessible to expert users). The dataset had to be compatible with a wide variety of GIS systems, paper-based systems and computer-driven decision support systems, usually operated automatically or by staff with little or no geological knowledge. In its simplest form, GeoSure provides a hazard assessment of the ground at any location on the mainland, describing hazard potential between A (very low) and E (very high).

Although superficially simple, the national model is based upon over 700 000 GIS components and 10 000 rock types, each of which was attributed. The system initially took over 5 years to assemble, and is updated every year, as our understanding of Earth systems improves and geological maps are updated.

For the shrink–swell model of Great Britain, use is made of the National Geotechnical Information Database, which contains information derived from over 1 000 000 downhole tests. Using a GIS system, the borehole data (alongside other information) are used to attribute each rock type in the country with a shrink–swell potential rating, with ratings correlated with volume change potential. The data are then modified by a further factor that takes into account the thickness of any superficial materials near the surface. Figure 9 shows the results of this modelling in the Hadleigh area, where a complex (from the perspective of the general public) geological sequence involving the

London Clay Formation, Claygate Gate Member and the Bagshot Formation are overlain by Head and a sequence of Quaternary gravels. The shrink–swell model of the area reflects how this succession influences the volume change capacity of the ground at near surface.

Similarly, for the Hadleigh area, Figure 10 shows the potential for slope instability. The diagram clearly shows slope instability to the south of Hadleigh, where slopes in the London Clay have been steepened by long-term erosion of the coast.

Setting policy. Within the UK, the overarching framework for land-use planning is to secure the most efficient and effective use of land in the public interest. With an increased emphasis on sustainable development, there has been pressure on local authorities to take a longer-term view of the likely impact that decisions involving the environment can have. To make the best decisions, planners are required to link science to policy (Culshaw *et al.* 2006). The UK government has promoted a range of e-government initiatives with the intention to increase the use of information technology and web-based services in planning (see www.planningportal.gov.uk).

In the above sections, the use of geoscientific data to inform decisions on groundwater management, foundation conditions, ground investigations and contamination issues has been discussed. Many of these can be used at both the site-specific and regional scale, resulting in the production of regional attributed geological models and regional groundwater management plans.

Another area of research has been the development of decision support tools such as the Environmental Information System for Planners (EISP) (Culshaw *et al.* 2006). The EISP is a Web-based system designed to support decision-making within the UK by making environmental issues more widely accessible. The system is configured to support three planning functions, pre-application advice, development control and strategic planning, which it does by linking together geoscientific information with best practice and planning guidelines.

Future developments

With changes in legislation increasing the importance of geo-environmental information, land-use planners are now required to consider the implications and impact that large-scale development will have on the environment. Land-use planners, although willing to use geoscientific data, have placed demands on geoscientists to make their data more accessible, reliable and understandable. The traditional geological map is no longer an appropriate medium by which to present geo-environmental information. Geoscientists have learnt that it is essential to understand

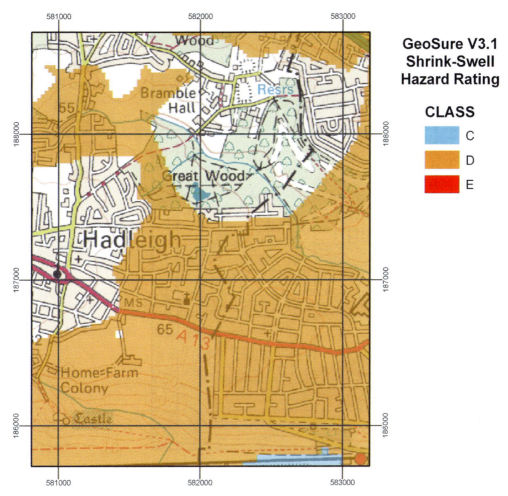

Fig. 9. Excerpt from BGS GeoSureV3.1 dataset showing the shrink–swell potential in the Hadleigh area. OS topography © Crown Copyright. All rights reserved. 100017897/2008.

their clients' needs to provide appropriate customized data outputs. It is only in this way that geoscientists within the urban environment can ensure that geoscientific data will be used within the planning process.

Advances in 3D modelling software and GIS techniques have resulted in a revolution in the way that geoscientific data can be displayed and interpreted. This has allowed urban geoscientists not only to provide raw geological data but also to produce integrated geoscientific information ideal for use within land-use planning. This information is provided within a 3D geological model, which is attributed with property data or a GIS system. The 3D attributed geological model can be used to predict not only the rock and soil type but also the variation in properties within any particular unit or formation. As a consequence, the new

modelling systems produce detailed and regional 3D models (Strange *et al.* 1998; Howland 2000), as well as models attributed with physical, chemical or hydrogeological property parameters, potentially at near site scale. As a result, these models can be used to provide solutions to many geo-environmental issues raised during the planning process. By using the 3D geological model in this manner, it has been demonstrated that geoscientists are now moving from conceptual ground models towards more realistic ground models based on actual ground investigation data (Culshaw 2005).

There are three main issues that will need to be resolved in the future. First, all users of digital geoscience data must understand the limitations of the data on which they base their assessments. This is becoming more critical as improvements in 3D modelling techniques are allowing

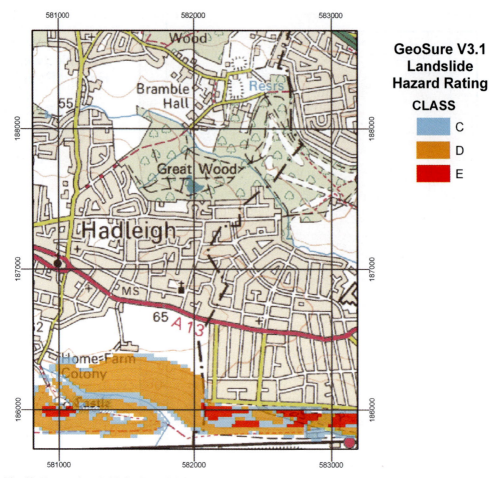

Fig. 10. Excerpt from BGS GeoSureV3.1 dataset showing the slope-instability potential in the Hadleigh area. OS topography © Crown Copyright. All rights reserved. 100017897/2008.

geoscientists to introduce a far greater level of realism to their models. It is essential, therefore, that planners can differentiate between observed and conjectural information. This is often referred to as the inherent uncertainty of a digital 3D model and the geoscientific datasets on which it is based. There are still difficulties in presentation and visualization of uncertainty calculations, making the resulting graphical representations difficult to interpret and use (Clarke 2004). Planners, ultimately, will need to be able to assess the risk associated with using these datasets and models so that sound judgements can be made.

The second issue is the ability to represent easily the variability within geological units. Currently, the attributed 3D geological models presented here display the bulk attributes of a particular unit. The level of resolution is limited by the amount of data available on which to model a particular geological formation or member. Lack of data can

therefore render some geological units nearly impossible to model, resulting in a significant loss of resolution to the model. Future work will have to focus on ways of representing property variation that is both realistic and understandable to land-use planners. These issues will need to be addressed if an uptake of digital geoscientific models and data is to be realized.

Finally, the key to the large-scale uptake of digital geoscientific data and 3D models within land-use planning is the efficient dissemination of these data, which will depend largely on the continued development of the Internet as a medium for the transfer of digital data and models. Already, Web-enabled platforms such as EISP are being developed, which will allow land-use planners to access geo-environmental information directly from the Internet. A future is imagined where a virtual site can be generated on a Web-based platform using a site's characteristics (e.g. its geology, geography, past land-use and data on existing developments), which will allow developers to visualize the impact of their proposed projects from the comfort of their desktop PC.

This paper is published with the permission of the Executive Director of the British Geological Survey (NERC).

References

ANONYMOUS 1995. *The Thames Gateway Planning Framework RPG9A*. HMSO, London.

BATES, M. R. 1998. Locating and evaluating archaeology below the alluvium: the role of sub-surface stratigraphic modeling. *Lithics*, **19**, 4–18.

BATES, M. R. & BATES, C. R. 2000. Multidisciplinary approaches to the geoarchaeological evaluation of deeply stratified sedimentary sequences: examples from Pleistocene and Holocene deposits in southern England, United Kingdom. *Journal of Archaeological Science*, **27**, 845–858.

BELL, F. G. & CULSHAW, M. G. 1998. Some geohazards caused by soil mineralogy, chemistry and microfabric: a review. *In*: MAUND, J. G. & EDDLESTON, M. (eds) *Geohazards in Engineering Geology*. Geological Society, London, Engineering Geology Special Publications, **15**, 427–441.

BERRY, F. G. 1979. Late Quaternary scour hollows and related features in central London. *Quarterly Journal of Engineering Geology*, **12**, 9–29.

BOBROWSKY, P. T. 2002. *Geoenvironmental mapping: methods, theory and practice*. Balkema, Rotterdam.

BOWIE, R. 2005. Creating a digital landslide. *Geoscientist*, **15**, 4–7.

BRISTOW, R., MORTIMORE, R. N. & WOOD, C. 1997. Lithostratigraphy for mapping the Chalk of southern England. *Proceedings of the Geologists' Association*, **109**, 293–315.

BRITISH STANDARDS INSTITUTION 1999. *British Standard Code of Practice for Site Investigations*. British Standards Institution, London.

BROOK, D. & MARKER, B. R. 1987. Thematic geological mapping as an essential tool in land use planning. *In*: CULSHAW, M. G., BELL, F. G., CRIPPS, J. C. & O'HARA, M. (eds) *Planning and Engineering Geology*. Geological Society, London, Special Publications, **4**, 211–214.

BRUNTLAND, G. 1987. *Our Common Future: World Commission on Environment and Development*. Oxford University Press, Oxford.

BURNETT, A. D. & FOOKES, P. G. 1974. A regional engineering geological study of the London Clay in the London and Hampshire Basins. *Quarterly Journal of Engineering Geology*, **1**, 257–296.

CANADIAN INSTITUTE OF PLANNERS 2000. What do planners do? About planning. Canadian Institute of Planners. World Wide Web Address: http://www.cip-icu.ca/English/aboutplan/what.htm.

CHANDLER, R. J. & APTED, J. P. 1988. The effect of weathering on the strength of London Clay. *Quarterly Journal of Engineering Geology*, **21**, 59–68.

CIRIA 2001. *Sustainable urban drainage systems—best practice manual*. Construction Industry Research and Information Association, London.

CLARKE, S. M. 2004. *Confidence in geological interpretation. A methodology for evaluating uncertainty in common two- and three-dimensional representations of subsurface geology*. British Geological Survey Internal Report, **IR/04/164**.

COMMUNITIES AND LOCAL GOVERNMENT 2006. *Planning Policy Statement 25: Development and Flood Risk. Full Regulatory Impact Assessment*. Communities and Local Government Publications, London.

CULSHAW, M. G. 2003. Bridging the gap between geoscience providers and the user community. *In*: ROSENBAUM, M. S. & TURNER, A. K. (eds) *New Paradigms in Subsurface Prediction*. Lecture Notes in Earth Sciences, **99**, 7–26.

CULSHAW, M. G. 2005. From concept towards reality: developing the attributed 3D model of the shallow subsurface. *Quarterly Journal of Engineering Geology and Hydrogeology*, **39**, 231–284.

CULSHAW, M. G. & ELLISON, R. A. 2002. Geological maps: their importance in a user-driven digital age. *In*: VAN ROONY, J. L. & JERMY, C. A. (eds) *Proceedings of the 9th International Association for Engineering Geology and the Environment Congress, Durban, 16–20 September 2002. Keynote Lectures and Extended Abstracts Volume*. South African Institute of Engineering and Environmental Geologists, Pretoria, 25–51.

CULSHAW, M. G., FORSTER, A. & NORTHMORE, K. J. 1994. Environmental geology maps for urban Britain—their relevance to less developed countries. *In*: WANG, S. & WANG, C. (eds) *Proceedings of LANDPLAN IV*. China Ocean Press, Beijing, 373–386.

CULSHAW, M. G., NATHANIAL, C. P. *ET AL*. 2006. The role of web-based environmental information in urban planning—the environmental information system for planners. *Science of the Total Environment*, **360**, 233–245.

DE MULDER, E. F. L. 1988. Thematic applied Quaternary maps—a profitable investment or expensive wallpaper? *In*: DE MULDER, E. F. L. & HAGEMAN, B. P. (eds) *Applied Quaternary Geology*. Balkema, Rotterdam, 105–117.

DEPARTMENT FOR COMMUNITIES AND LOCAL GOVERNMENT 2006. *Planning Policy Statement 9: Biodiversity and Geological Conservation. Final Regulatory Impact Assessment*. DCLG Publications, London.

DIMMOCK, P. S. & MAIR, R. J. 2007. Volume loss experienced on open-face London Clay tunnels. *Geotechnical Engineering*, **160**, 3–11.

DOCHARTAIGH, B. E., BALL, D. F., MACDONALD, A. M., LILLY, A., FITZSIMONS, V., DEL RIO, M. & AUTON, C. A. 2005. Mapping groundwater vulnerability in Scotland: a new approach for the Water Framework Directive. *Scottish Journal of Geology*, **41**, 21–30.

DOORNKAMP, J. C. 1995. Perception and reality in the provision of insurance against natural perils in the UK. *Transactions of the Institute of British Geographers*, **20**, 68–80.

ELLISON, R. A., ARRICK, A., STRANGE, P. J. & HENNESSEY, C. 1998. *Earth science information in support of major development initiatives*. British Geological Survey Technical Report, **WA/97/84**.

ELLISON, R. A., MCMILLAN, A. A. & LOTT, G. K. 2002. *Ground characterization of the urban environment: a guide to best practice*. British Geological Survey Internal Report, **IR/02/044**.

ELLISON, R. A., WOODS, M. A., ALLEN, D. J., FORSTER, A., PHAROAH, T. G. & KING, C. 2004. *Geology of London*. British Geological Survey, Keyworth.

FORSTER, A. 1999. *The engineering geology of the London area: 1:50 000 geological sheets 256, 257, 270 and 271*. British Geological Survey, Engineering Geology Series, Technical Report, **WN/97/27**.

HACK, R., ORLIC, B., OZMUTLU, S. & RENGERS, N. 2006. Three and more dimensional modelling in geo-engineering. *Bulletin of Engineering Geology and the Environment*, **65**, 143–153.

HIGHT, D. W. & JARDINE, R. J. 1993. Small strain stiffness and strength characteristics of hard London Tertiary clays. *Geotechnical Engineering of Hard Soils–Soft Rocks*, **1**, 533–552.

HINZE, C., SOBISCH, H.-G. & VOSS, H.-H. 1999. Spatial modelling in geology and its practical use. *Mathematische Geologie*, **4**, 51–60.

HOWLAND, A. F. 2000. The history of the development of procedure for the rapid assessment of environmental conditions to aid the urban regeneration process at London Docklands. *Engineering Geology*, **60**, 117–125.

HUTCHINSON, H. 1965. *A survey of the coastal landslides of Essex and South Suffolk*. Building Research Station Note, **EN/36/65**.

JACKSON, C. R. 2001. *The development and validation of the object-oriented quasi three-dimensional regional groundwater model ZOOMQ3D*. British Geological Survey Internal Report, **IR/01/144**.

JACKSON, I. 2004. Britain beneath our feet. *In*: British Geological Survey Occasional Publications, **4**, 114.

KAALBERG, F., HAASNOOT, J. & NETZEL, H. 2003. What are the end-user issues? Settlement risk management in underground construction. *In*: ROSENBAUM, M. S. & TURNER, A. K. (eds) *New Paradigms in Subsurface Prediction*. Lecture notes in Earth Sciences, **99**, 69–84.

KESSLER, H. & MATHERS, S. 2004. Maps to models. *Geoscientist*, **14**, 4–6.

LAWRENCE, D. J. D., ARKLEY, S. *ET AL*. 2007. *Northumberland National Park: Geodiversity Audit and Action Plan*. British Geological Survey Report, **CR/07/037N**.

LELLIOTT, M. R., BRIDGE, D. M., KESSLAR, H., PRICE, S. J. & SEYMOUR, K. J. 2006. The application of 3D geological modelling to aquifer recharge assessments in an urban environment. *Quarterly Journal of Engineering Geology and Hydrogeology*, **39**, 293–302.

MARKER, B. R. 1998. Incorporation of information on geohazards into the planning process. *In*: MAUND, J. G. & EDDLESTON, M. (eds) *Geohazards in Engineering Geology*. Geological Society, London, Engineering Geology Special Publications, **15**, 385–389.

MAYOR OF LONDON 2004. *The London Plan: Spatial Development Strategy for Greater London*. Greater London Authority, London.

MCKIRDY, A. P., THOMPSON, A. & POOLE, J. 1998. Dissemination of information on the earth sciences to planners and other decision-makers. *In*: BENNETT, M. R. & DOYLE, P. (eds) *Issues in Environmental Geology: a British Perspective*. Geological Society, London.

MCMILLAN, A. A., HEATHCOTE, J. A., KLINK, B. A., SHEPLEY, M. G., JACKSON, C. P. & DEGNAN, P. J. 2000. Hydrogeological characterisation of the onshore Quaternary sediments at Sellafield using the concept of domains. *Quarterly Journal of Engineering Geology and Hydrogeology*, **33**, 301–323.

NICKLESS, E. F. P. 1982. Environmental geology of the Glenrothes district, Fife region. Description of 1:25 000 sheet NO 20. *In*: Institute of Geological Sciences Reports, **82**, 15.

OFFICE OF THE DEPUTY PRIME MINISTER 2003. *Sustainable Communities: Building for the Future*. Office of the Deputy Prime Minister, London.

OFFICE OF THE DEPUTY PRIME MINISTER 2004. *Planning Policy Statement 23: Planning and Pollution Control*. HMSO, London.

OFFICE OF THE DEPUTY PRIME MINISTER & DEPARTMENT OF ENVIRONMENT, FOOD AND RURAL AFFAIRS 2004. *Creating Sustainable Communities: Greening the Gateway*. Office of the Deputy Prime Minister, London.

PAUL, T., CHOW, F. & KJEKSTAD, O. 2002. *Hidden Aspects of Urban Planning—Surface and Underground Development*. Thomas Telford, London.

ROYSE, K. R., PRICE, S., ENTWISLE, D., LELLIOTT, M. & TERRINGTON, R. 2005. *Thames Gateway Pilot Study, Results: Is there a need for Urban Geoscience in the Gateway?* British Geological Survey Report, **IR/05/063**, 34.

SITE INVESTIGATION STEERING GROUP 1993. Without site investigation ground is a hazard. *In*: *Site Investigation in Construction*. Thomas Telford, London, 56.

SMITH, A. & ELLISON, R. A. 1999. Applied geological maps for planning and development: a review of examples from England and Wales, 1983 to 1996. *Quaternary Journal of Engineering Geology*, **32**, S1–S44.

SOBISCH, H.-G. 2000. *Ein difitles raeumliches Modell des Quartaers der GK25 Blatt 3508 Nordhorn auf der Basis vernetzer Profilschnitte*. Shaker, Aachen.

STEADMAN, E. J., MITCHELL, P., HIGHLEY, D. E., HARRISON, D. J., LINLEY, K. A., MACFARLANE, M. & MCEVOY, F. M. 2004. *Strategic environmental assessment (sea) and future aggregate extraction: in the East Midlands region*. British Geological Survey Report, **CR/04/003N**.

STRANGE, P. J., BOOTH, S. J. & ELLISON, R. A. 1998. Development of 'rockhead' computer-generated geological models to assist geohazard prediction in London. *In*: MAUND, J. G. & EDDLESTON, M. (eds) *Geohazards in Engineering Geology*. Geological Society, London, Engineering Geology Special Publications, **15**, 409–414.

THOMPSON, A., HINE, P. D., GRIEF, J. R. & POOLE, J. S. 1998. *Environmental Geology in Land Use and Planning: Advice for Planners and Developers*. Report to the Department of the Environment.

TURNER, A. K. 2003. Putting the user first: implications for subsurface characterisation. *In*: ROSENBAUM, M. S. & TURNER, A. K. (eds) *New Paradigms in Subsurface Prediction*. Lecture Notes in Earth Sciences, **99**, 61–83.

TURNER, A. K. 2006. Challenges and trends for geological modelling and visualisation. *Bulletin of Engineering Geology and the Environment*, **65**, 109–127.

Communication in geology: a personal perspective and lessons from volcanic, mining, exploration, geotechnical, police and geoforensic investigations

LAURANCE J. DONNELLY

Halcrow Group Ltd, Deanway Technology Centre, Wilmslow Road, Handforth, Cheshire SK9 3FB, UK (e-mail: DonnellyLJ@Halcrow.com)

Abstract: Geologists are frequently required to convey the results, advice and recommendations from geological investigations to a variety of end users. Often, it is the communication of the information that is the most challenging and can be more difficult than the investigation itself. Most of these investigations use highly sophisticated scientific techniques and geological terminology. When combined with cultural and language barriers, and social, political, religious or economic constraints, this makes it difficult to convey the correct message, and for the recipient to understand the implications of the geological information. The failure to effectively and accurately communicate this message may reduce the usefulness of the information being provided. Communication must be considered part of a geological investigation because if the correct message is not conveyed properly, or is misunderstood, the consequences can be catastrophic. Communication is an ability that professional geologists must have to interact successfully with colleagues, other professionals and the public. It is a skill learnt by training and experience. Spoken communication relies on interpersonal skills and the ability to convey information effectively, confidently and consistently. This paper provides case studies and draws upon the experiences of the author.

For almost two decades, the author has participated in several geological projects around the world. These projects have included the monitoring and prediction of geological hazards (e.g. volcanoes and landslides), mining hazards (e.g. subsidence, fault reactivation, fissures and mine gas emissions), geotechnical ground investigations, mineral exploration, and the provision of geological expertise to support police searches and forensic investigations. Although many of these projects have been technically challenging, requiring geological judgements to be made, often with incomplete data and information, it is the communication of complex geological information that has been, and remains, the most challenging.

The results, advice and recommendations from geological investigations are subsequently conveyed to end users, clients, policy-makers, the public or the media. The recipient of this information may be other technical specialists or non-technical people, or both. Typical recipients of geological information range from school-children to specialists in their respective fields.

Geologists have not been (conventionally) trained in the skills of communication, so how do geologists convey the complex technical geological information to the decision- or policy-makers, and how do they overcome the physical, cultural, political, social, religious and interpersonal constraints that exist in different parts of the world during communication? The principal objectives of this paper are to raise awareness of the importance of communication, to outline some of the problems in communication, and to see how these have been overcome. It highlights some of the more basic fundamentals of communication, and it draws primarily on the experiences of the author with particular reference to communicating in sensitive and high-profile investigations.

Communication and geology

Communication may be considered the process by which geological information is conveyed (by a geologist) to another person, by means of verbal and non-verbal methods. This may also be considered as the sharing or exchange of geological knowledge. From the geologist's perspective, geological information is required to make the correct decision or judgement about 'the ground', or to assess the consequences and risks associated with a particular geohazard. The recipient requires the information to make decisions that could, for example, influence engineering design, determine the location of structures, roads and utilities, or could help to locate mineral resources, to find a grave, or to help save lives. Communication therefore consists of both the giving and receiving of information.

From: LIVERMAN, D. G. E., PEREIRA, C. P. G. & MARKER, B. (eds) *Communicating Environmental Geoscience*. Geological Society, London, Special Publications, **305**, 107–121.
DOI: 10.1144/SP305.11   0305-8719/08/$15.00 © The Geological Society of London 2008.

Professional geologists use technical language and this is as necessary as vocabulary when learning another language (Fookes 1997). Without technical language geology would not exist as a profession and scientific discipline. It is the responsibility of the geologist to judge the correct tone and technical content, and to make sure that jargon (unnecessary and extraneous use of technical terms) is not used when communicating with others. Levels of communication vary depending upon the education of the recipients; with specialists the communications can be highly technical, but with schoolchildren they must be in plain language. In mixed audiences using the correct level of technical content is difficult and needs to be considered carefully before engagement takes place.

Existing information and guidelines

There are relatively few reports available for geologists aimed specifically at communication. Publications that deal with communications usually refer to a variety of geological topics; for example, publications on geohazards and geological information include that by Forster & Freeborough (2006). Also, numerous websites now provide information on a range of geohazards (e.g. see the websites for the US Geological Survey, the Geological Society of London and the US Federal Emergency Management Agency). The material within these websites is useful for information on geohazards (landslides, mining, floods, tsunami, volcanoes and earthquakes).

Lyme Regis, on the south coast of England, and Ventnor, on the Isle of Wight, are areas with a high potential for landslides and have frequently experienced active landsliding. This has made the local councils aware of the need to communicate effectively with the public (including leaflets advising householders and the public) about the landslide hazards and what was being done to investigate and mitigate the effects of landslides (Cole & Davies 2002; Davis & Cole 2002; McInnes 2004).

In Britain, the shrinkage and swelling of clays during prolonged hot summer months frequently causes structural damage. Since the drought of 1976, the Institution of Civil Engineers and the Building Research Establishment have been proactive in raising awareness of the possibility for repairs that may be required as a result of subsidence damage (Freeman et al. 1994). The report by Freeman et al. (1994) provided information on the causes of subsidence, the distribution of clays susceptible to shrink–swell, what types of investigations to carry out and advice on how to make insurance claims. The increasing incidence of drought since 1976 and the greater awareness of the possibility of making claims for repairs

to houses damaged by subsidence created a need for more information about the hazard of shrinkable clay.

In Britain, the communication of landslide and subsidence hazards has been facilitated by the production of planning policy guidance, including publications by the Department of the Environment (1990, 1996), Department of Trade and Industry (1996, produced by the Office of the Deputy Prime Minister) and Department of the Environment, Transport and the Regions (2000). These guidelines provide information on the possible geological causes of potentially unstable land so that this may be considered during the early stages of the planning, redevelopment or rehabilitation of land.

The Coal Authority provides coal mine search services to inform home owners and developers of the potential mining hazards associated with the legacy of past coal mining and brine pumping in Britain (Law Society 1994). Published information on mining and other geohazards in Britain has been provided by, for example, Geomorphological Services Ltd (1987), Arup Geotechnics (1992) and Applied Geology Limited (1993). Similar information published in the USA includes work by Muton & Shimabukuro (1974), Marts et al. (1978), Nuhfer et al. (1993), Creath (1996), Noe et al. (1997), Holcombe et al. (2003) and Mileti et al. (2004).

Communication in other professions

Communication is recognized as being important in professions other than geology. In the medical profession, for instance, effective communication is crucial between doctors and their patients. Medical jargon is rarely used, and if it is, it is explained. Professional guidance notes to help doctors communicate effectively have been produced; these include publications by Dickson et al. (1989), Audit Commission (1993), Ong et al. (1995), Hind (1997), Royal College of Physicians of London (1997), Williams (1997), the NHS Confederation (1997) and the British Medical Association (1998). Although much of the information contained in these papers and reports is aimed, obviously, at the medical profession and at the doctor–patient relationship, there are some generic concepts that can potentially be applied to the geological professional. The medical profession has recognized the problems that arise when communication fails, between staff, different departments, and doctors and patients. These observations are similar to those in engineering geology, mining, geoforensics and geohazards investigations, especially where large teams are involved, with different personalities from different technical, social and cultural backgrounds.

Perhaps the solutions provided to the medical profession have application to the geosciences?

Types of communication

All geologists should be competent in both oral and written communication. Geologists need to communicate with all age groups, a wide range of other professions and across cultures. Competence in communication is therefore a critical part of geologists' training and capabilities. There are two main ways by which geologists conventionally communicate: (1) spoken (conferences, workshops, seminars, lectures and meetings); (2) written (reports, memoirs, maps, scientific papers, technical notes, letters, e-mail and computer data).

Spoken communication relies on interpersonal skills and the ability to convey information effectively, confidently and consistently (often, consciously or subconsciously relying on body language). These skills are important when geologists are providing information on an impending geohazard. Written communications, such as publications, reports and maps, allow geologists to communicate with each other, but are not necessarily the most effective form of communication when geological information needs to be conveyed to another (non-geological) professional or members of the pubic, who may not necessarily be familiar with complex geological language.

Communication skills

Communication may be learnt by training so that geologists can become better communicators; training and the continuation of professional development (CPD) may provide the necessary opportunity. The type of communication training needs to be planned and considered with respect to the geologist's background and professional role as a geologist (e.g. a forensic geologist v. a mining geologist v. an engineering geologist). Training courses therefore need to be properly designed and 'fit-for-purpose' to facilitate the requirements of the geologist (or group of geologists).

Geologists also communicate not just to convey information but to create and develop positive inter-professional relationships. Communication involves the interaction of individuals. It may be entered into voluntarily or non-voluntarily and sometimes involves emotive issues. Whereas many geological investigations rely on technical sophistication, innovation and fundamental science, interpersonal communication is the means by which geologists communicate their findings. There are many ways geologists may develop good interpersonal relationships, but there are very few guidelines or publications on how this may be achieved.

Circumstances will vary, but, in general, good relationships rely on some well-accepted characteristics (e.g. good manners, respect, laughing, compliments, friendliness and especially empathy, amongst many others). The good communicator must also be a good listener, using silence, reflecting, paraphrasing and non-verbal behaviour.

Geologists and communication with other professionals

Successful communication between fellow geologists is important to ensure that clients and other professionals do not receive conflicting, confusing or contradictory information. In civil engineering, for example, a structural engineer may be offered different advice from a geotechnical engineer or an engineering geologist, which is probably frustrating for the structural engineer. This situation may have arisen because it reflects the different training for the two disciplines; it may also be traced to the fact that many engineering geological decisions are based on judgement and interpretation. A co-ordinated and integral approach is therefore required in such circumstances for the outcome to be successful.

Geology is crucial to the civil engineer, who requires factual geological information on the ground in which he is working, the engineering characterization of the ground conditions, and information on groundwater and hydrogeology. The best services an engineering geologist can provide to a civil engineer are to get the geological characteristics of the site right (Fookes 1997). Once the geology is understood, this needs to be then clearly communicated to the engineer who will use the information to help make decisions.

Civil engineers, although technical subject matter experts, may not necessarily be familiar with the complex technical terminology used by engineering geologists. Too much geological terminology may potentially cause the engineer to become frustrated. Engineering geologists have the ability to make sound, rational decisions, based on partial and imperfect knowledge. Engineering geologists must reply on judgement and therefore this introduces a degree of uncertainty, as a result of 'gaps-in-knowledge'. These judgements are based on the geologists' training, observation and experience, and communication skills. Engineering geologists must therefore make accurate judgements and communicate the information to clients and engineers. Visual aids such as maps, cross-sections, photographs, drawings and 'back-of-an-envelope' sketches are often the solution during informal communications between the geologist and the engineer (Fig. 1).

Fig. 1. Communication with a range of other professionals and technical specialists. Top left, geologists discuss volcanic hazards during the inspection of lava flows, in the Valle del Bové, October 1992 eruption of Mt Etna, Sicily. Top right, discussions with mining engineers, surveyors and strata control experts at the adit entrance to a small mine in Kashmiri Pakistan in the Karakoram Himalayas. Bottom left, mining geologists, mining engineers and geologists from the Pakistan Geological Survey inspect maps during an exploration survey at high altitude in a remote part of the Karakoram–Himalayas. Bottom right, engineering geologists investigate a 4 m high, 4 km long, fault scarp in the South Wales Coalfield, discussing mining subsidence and fault reactivation mechanisms.

Forensic geologists, police officers and police search advisors who search the ground for murder victims' graves (Donnelly 2000a, b; Fenning & Donnelly 2004), may also find communication challenging (Fig. 2). This work involves teams of multidisciplinary experts such as geologists, anthropologists, botanists, victim recovery dog handlers, remote sensing aerial assets, behavioural profilers, clinical psychologists and military personnel. These searches are usually co-ordinated and managed by a Senior Investigating Officer (SIO). A conceptual geological model of the ground may be developed by the geologist to provide information about the target's age, size, geometry, expected depth of burial, time and duration of burial, and physical, chemical, hydrogeological and geotechnical variations compared with the surrounding ground. This information may then be used to determine the correct search strategy, the appropriate choice of instrumentation, and the optimum method of deployment. To successfully carry out such an operation, the main challenges are not necessarily technical but communication. The geologist conveys all of the above technical information to the SIO and other experts. The police officer may have already a team of multidisciplinary technical specialists. How does the geologist fit into this system? At what stage does the geologist approach

Fig. 2. Top, geologists and police officers inspecting the ground in the Midlands, following the discovery of human bones (later found to be a pauper grave). Bottom, geologists and police officers search the ground.

the crime scene, to reduce the risks of any cross contamination? How can the geologist begin to understand crime scene management and crime scene investigation, and the strict police protocols involved? The SIO, already possibly overloaded with a range of specialists, now finds that he or she has to deal with yet another specialist, the geologist (Fig. 3). This may potentially be problematic if the process is not carefully planned and communicated (Donnelly 2003, Harrison & Donnelly 2008).

There is clearly still the need to improve communication between geologists and other professionals. It is essential that good channels of clear communication are developed and maintained. The interface with geologists and other professionals may often take place on a one-to-one personal basis. For communication to be effective both the geologist and the other professional must be able and willing to give and receive information.

Geologists and communication in a multicultural world

Geologists, like other professionals, usually discuss and debate their findings, and consideration must be given to whether members of the public

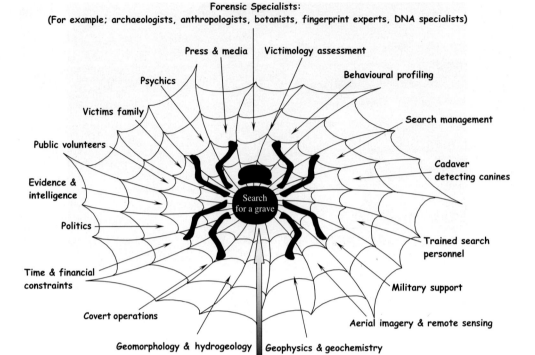

Fig. 3. The introduction of a forensic geologist to a complex, multi-disciplinary police search team must be carefully co-ordinated and properly managed. The geologist must be able to effectively communicate with the other subject matter experts, be aware of his/her limitations and understand the role and capabilities of the other experts (modified after Donnelly 2000*b*, in Harrison & Donnelly 2008).

(Anonymous 2002), or the client, should be part of those discussions. Often the recipient of geological information requires only a decision, and may not necessarily be concerned about the details of how that decision was determined. During the monitoring of a recent volcanic eruption, for example, some members of the public were present during scientists' debrief, discussions and debate. It was originally envisaged that this would strengthen and improve relationships between scientists and the public. However, it had the opposite effect, because the public considered the scientists' debates and discussions to represent uncertainty and inconsistency, which undermined some of the public's confidence. The communication of geological information to the public may be influenced by the following: (1) language barriers; (2) human influences, such as disinclination to ask (possibly because of embarrassment), anxiety, anger, forgetfulness, preconceptions, pride and age differences; (3) assumptions ('a little knowledge may be dangerous').

Each community, society and group of people has its own particular view of the natural environment and geohazards, although they may be subjected to the same events (Fig. 4). It is this view that needs to be very carefully considered before engaging with a community to discuss geohazards, consequences and risks. This will determine the type of language to use (technical or non-technical) and the manner in which to conduct the communication. Individual perception and public response is based on geohazards history, traditions, culture, religion, emotion, folklore, gossip, superstition, other non-scientific influences, knowledge about the risk, and experience. Individual judgement is based on previous personal experience of the geohazard rather than an objective, collective assessment of all the probabilities and consequences (Peltu 1991).

Effective communication is central, and this is particularly important when members of the public are being provided with information concerning potentially catastrophic geohazards.

Fig. 4. The communication of geological information to the public, multicultural and multiracial societies. Top left, evacuation camps established in Montserrat, during the eruption of the Soufrière Hills Volcano, Montserrat. Top right, local residents at a Montserrat evacuation camp displaced by volcanic hazards. Middle left, farmers in Singrauli, India, affected by mining hazards associated with large scale open cast and under ground coal mining operations. Middle right, terraced houses in Easington, County Durham, affected by mining subsidence. Bottom left and bottom right, children, women and unskilled men who scavenge coal from waste tips in Antioquia, Colombian Andes. These communities and environments, where geological and mining hazards have negatively affected lives require the clear and careful communication of geological information to the public and interpersonal skills.

Geologists who work in multicultural and multiracial societies should have an appreciation and understanding of the different types and levels of communication that may be required with the public and non-specialists. Particular attention should be paid to local customs, which it may be important to respect. Appropriate preparation and adequate provision of language interpreters and bilingual translators may be required to improve cross-cultural communication.

Communication is an interpersonal social skill, not a technical one, and as such requires an appreciation of the emotional dimension of the situation both before communicating and as a result of its impact. For communication to be effective the geologist must identify and understand the needs of the target audience. This includes an assessment of their state of knowledge, any gaps-in-knowledge, their appreciation of basic science, their language, cultural values, age profiles, and domestic, political and language constraints. Careful consideration must be given to the background of the particular audience. In any situation, effective communication, in the opinion of the author, may be achieved by face-to-face meetings to engage directly with the recipients, audiences and/or other professionals. Audiences of mixed ages, race, religions and scientific background are likely to have different understandings of geology and geohazards. In these circumstances, good visual aids facilitate effective communication (this may include, for instance, maps, photographs, animations and video footage).

Once the target audience has been engaged, the information may then be transferred by verbal, written, electronic or visual means. When the public, clients and professionals have been given information on geohazards they will then need to be informed on potential strategies on how to mitigate or avoid the hazard (Fig. 5).

Feedback is a critical part of communication. Many people may react adversely to an authoritarian stance and need to feel they are 'part of the process', and/or 'in control'. Continuity is important; a single meeting may not be sufficient, as geohazards do not simply cease. There is likely to be the need for a programme of regular meetings, and it is important that the same information, advice and recommendations are given in a calm, clear, non-ambiguous and consistent manner, making sure that, whenever possible, technical language is avoided or minimized (or if used, then explained).

Good communication is important during the monitoring and prediction of volcanic eruptions. There are several examples of successes and failures. For example, Nevado del Ruiz volcano is located in the Andean Cordillera of Colombia, approximately 100 km NW of Colombia's capital city, Sante Fe De Bogota. On 13 November 1985, a Plinian eruption generated a series of pyroclastic flows, which interacted with the snow and ice that formed the summit ice cap. The rapid transfer of heat from the eruption, combined with the seismic shaking, generated lahars (mud flows) and avalanches of saturated snow, ice, felled trees and rock debris. These flowed along drainage channels and within 4 h had travelled over 105 km, descending 5100 m, leaving a wake of catastrophic destruction and obliterating everything in their path. The town of Armero was buried beneath a blanket of mud. Approximately 24 740 people were killed or missing, 4420 injured and 5092 made homeless (Fig. 6).

Geohazard investigations were undertaken at Nevado del Ruiz, prior to the 1985 eruptions. Previous pyroclastic flow deposits and lahars were mapped and their extent was known, accurate reports of historical events were recorded and, following a period of monitoring the volcano, advice was made available from Colombian and international scientists who participated in the investigations. In the months prior to the eruption, communications were established between geologists and the government. The geologists attempted to explain the significance of the observed precursory activity, which included low-intensity earthquake swarms, a steam (phreatic) eruption, explosions, ash-fall deposits and small lahars within 30 km of the summit. Geological hazard maps were produced over a month before the fatal event. The Colombian officials issued alerts to prepare for mudflows, but unfortunately these reports were not properly disseminated. Pyroclastic flows and surges were generated, but it was not announced that these events were significant. Information on volcanic hazards was met with scepticism by the local authorities and the population. An evacuation of Armero was considered to be unnecessary by the authorities (this may also have been influenced by the fact that it was night with heavy rainfall). The violent lahars came in two surges, the first cold, the second hot, and these engulfed Armero for at least 2 h. The catastrophe at Nevado del Ruiz and Armero was exacerbated by failures in communications, cumulative human error, misjudgement, indecision and bureaucracy (Williams 1990a, b).

Montserrat is a British dependent island located in the West Indies. The Soufrière Hills Volcano, situated in the southern part of this island, has been in a state of almost continuous volcanic activity for the past 13 years, since 1995, after being dormant for about 400 years (Druitt & Kokelaar 2002). The Montserrat Volcano Observatory (MVO) was established soon after the occurrence of phreatic eruptions on 12 July 1995. The eruption of the Soufrière Hills Volcano was an event for which the local population was completely unprepared.

Pyroclastic surges and lahars have radiated from the volcano, travelling along river gullies towards the sea and engulfing numerous villages. This has resulted in the loss of use of a large part of the island, including the airport, main jetty and capital town, Plymouth (a new airport and jetty have now been built; Plymouth has been evacuated of all its residents and is currently buried beneath volcanic deposits), and there were some fatalities (Donnelly 2007).

During the early stages of the eruption some of the islanders and scientists were conscious of

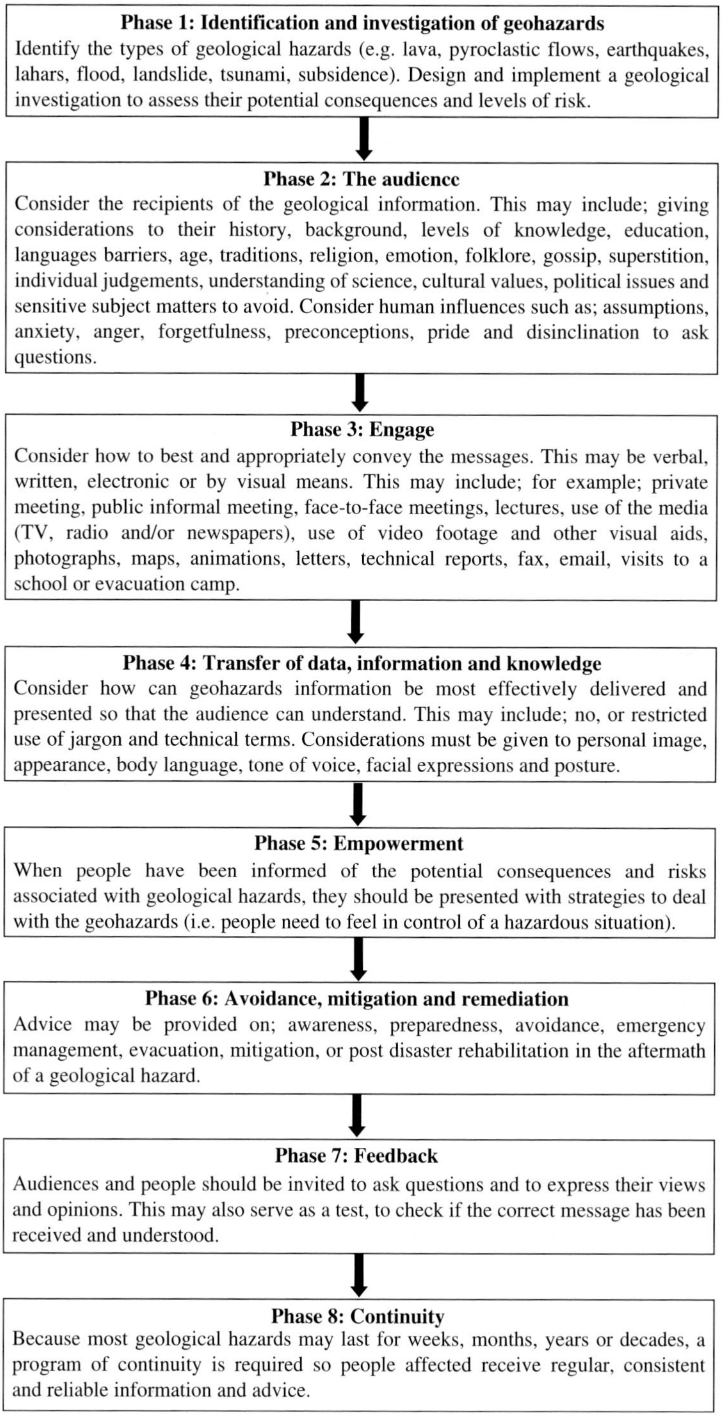

Phase 1: Identification and investigation of geohazards
Identify the types of geological hazards (e.g. lava, pyroclastic flows, earthquakes, lahars, flood, landslide, tsunami, subsidence). Design and implement a geological investigation to assess their potential consequences and levels of risk.

Phase 2: The audience
Consider the recipients of the geological information. This may include; giving considerations to their history, background, levels of knowledge, education, languages barriers, age, traditions, religion, emotion, folklore, gossip, superstition, individual judgements, understanding of science, cultural values, political issues and sensitive subject matters to avoid. Consider human influences such as; assumptions, anxiety, anger, forgetfulness, preconceptions, pride and disinclination to ask questions.

Phase 3: Engage
Consider how to best and appropriately convey the messages. This may be verbal, written, electronic or by visual means. This may include; for example; private meeting, public informal meeting, face-to-face meetings, lectures, use of the media (TV, radio and/or newspapers), use of video footage and other visual aids, photographs, maps, animations, letters, technical reports, fax, email, visits to a school or evacuation camp.

Phase 4: Transfer of data, information and knowledge
Consider how can geohazards information be most effectively delivered and presented so that the audience can understand. This may include; no, or restricted use of jargon and technical terms. Considerations must be given to personal image, appearance, body language, tone of voice, facial expressions and posture.

Phase 5: Empowerment
When people have been informed of the potential consequences and risks associated with geological hazards, they should be presented with strategies to deal with the geohazards (i.e. people need to feel in control of a hazardous situation).

Phase 6: Avoidance, mitigation and remediation
Advice may be provided on; awareness, preparedness, avoidance, emergency management, evacuation, mitigation, or post disaster rehabilitation in the aftermath of a geological hazard.

Phase 7: Feedback
Audiences and people should be invited to ask questions and to express their views and opinions. This may also serve as a test, to check if the correct message has been received and understood.

Phase 8: Continuity
Because most geological hazards may last for weeks, months, years or decades, a program of continuity is required so people affected receive regular, consistent and reliable information and advice.

Fig. 5. Conceptual flow chart to illustrate the main phases of communication during a geohazard investigation.

Fig. 6. Top left, the town of Manizales, Colombia, situated in the shadow of Nevado del Ruiz Volcano. Top right, view of the upper Lagunillas River valley, close the summit of Nevado del Ruiz. Bottom left, scoria, ash-rich pyroclastic flow deposits exposed on the upper reaches of Nevado del Ruiz. Bottom right, horizontally stratified ash, pyroclastic flow, pumiceous and mudflow (lahar) deposits on the walls of the Lagunillas River valley, exposed by erosion during the 1985 lahars that buried the town of Armero. Approximately 24 740 people were killed or missing, 4420 injured and 5092 made homeless. This was attributable, at least in part, to breakdown in communications between scientists and officials.

historical volcanic eruptions on neighbouring Caribbean islands. For instance, in 1909, the eruption of Mount Pelée on Martinique generated pyroclastic flows that killed at least 29 000 people. More recently, in 1976–1977, approximately 70 000 people on Guadeloupe were evacuated following a relatively small steam eruption on La Soufrière Volcano that lasted about 9 months. However, no major eruption followed and the evacuation was considered to have been unnecessary by many of the local people. Unfortunately, there was a breakdown in communications between the geologists, government and the public; no lives were lost but there was a significant negative economic impact on businesses and farms (Robertson 1995).

The move towards the evacuation of much of the population of Montserrat resulted in a situation where the communication of geohazards to the government and public was very important. In the early stage of the eruption on Montserrat different types of communications were established with the public. These included the daily issuing of statements via the media (TV and radio), regular meetings with community representatives and the issuing of newsletters (Fig. 7). During the early stages of the eruption the author experienced the benefits of personal engagement with the local community (Fig. 4). This supported more formal volcanic hazards announcements provided by the MVO, sometimes via the media and Government of Montserrat. An appreciation of interpersonal and social skills was necessary for creating an environment of trust within which a dialogue could be established to convey the necessary messages of the nature of volcanic eruptions and their implications for those threatened by them. This approach demonstrated the need for social and interpersonal skills as well as technical and scientific expertise, for the effective monitoring and communication of volcanic hazards.

During the eruptions of Mount Pinatubo, in the Philipines, in 1990 (where approximately 250,000 people were evacuated) and Rabaul in Paupa New Guinea in 1994, good communications between geologists, the authorities, and the population resulted in a positive response from the people affected by these volcanic eruptions. This is likely to have saved many thousands of lives (McGuire 1998).

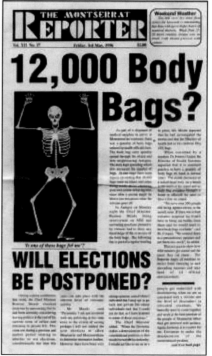

Fig. 7. Examples of leaflets and newsletters produced by the Government of Montserrat to help with the communication of information on volcanic hazards to the public. Reproduced by kind permission from the Government of Montserrat.

Fig. 8. Communication with the media. Top left, during the monitoring of the Soufrière Hills Volcano, Montserrat, for the production of an international TV documentary. Top right, and bottom left, journalists photograph a geologist working at a crime scene. Bottom right, local TV news crew interviewing a geologist describing mining hazards and their impact on the environment.

Geologists and communication with the media

Geologists sometimes have to communicate with the media (Fig. 8). Geologists are not conventionally trained to deal with journalists and so their responses should be carefully considered, so that the intended message is put across clearly, factually and without sensationalism (however, post-interview editing can change this). Failure to communicate the geologists' messages accurately may result in the media (and therefore the public) being given an erroneous estimation of a geohazard or misleading

information about a sensitive police investigation. If available, press officers or public relations specialists should be consulted prior to any interaction with the media, to obtain appropriate advice and to be made aware of any broader issues (Nield 2008).

Before geologists accept invitations by the media they should make sure they understand whether the interview may be recorded or live. Recorded interviews may give the opportunity to rehearse or review an interview before it is broadcast or reported (although this is not always the case). Live interviews do not give the opportunity for rehearsal prior to broadcasting or for the correction of mistakes. It is therefore essential that the geologist prepares for the interview, understands something about the usual programme, including its aims, objectives and target audience. This will allow answers to be prepared beforehand in the context of the interview. Geologists need to decide before the interview takes place exactly what the key points will be that they are trying to get across in the message. About three or four main points should be identified.

During interviews with the media and the public, geologists should come across as being confident and positive. The information given should be simple, clear and non-contentious, and ambiguity should be avoided. Jargon should not be used, but if geological and other scientific terms are used, then these should be explained in non-technical terms. During live interviews any mistakes made must be corrected during the interview. When being interviewed on television or for the production of a documentary, personal image, appearance, body language, tone of voice, facial expressions and posture are just as important as the verbal messages.

Speaking with the media (and public) gives geologists the opportunity to raise the profile of geology. During public speaking, it is always advisable to match the talk to the interests of the audience. The communication of geological information to the public, and the public promotion of science, can be entertaining and enjoyable. Magazine articles, newspapers, lectures and TV documentaries regularly focus on geology and in particular geological hazards. This enhances the public understanding of geology. What is more, geology as a profession depends on the next generation and constant flow of 'youngsters', and therefore professional geologists perhaps have a duty to participate in the public communication of geology (Donnelly 2002a). Working in such an interesting profession, it is not too difficult to supplement such talks and presentations with enthusiasm and impressive images of geohazards; always guaranteed to captivate audiences and the media. On occasions, some of these presentations have inspired tomorrow's generation of geologists. Further information on communicating with the media has been published by, for example, White et al. (1993) and the Royal Society (2000).

Summary

Communication of geological information is usually preceded by scientific (geological) investigations, the results of which are then conveyed by the geologist to the recipient. In many respects the communication of technically complex geological information is usually more challenging that the geological investigation itself. This is made more difficult where the socio-cultural background and language are markedly different from that of the communicator. The failure to effectively communicate geological information may blight land or have catastrophic consequences.

The geologist must make sure that the information is effectively and accurately communicated. Communication usually takes place by spoken or written means. A geologist relies on interpersonal skills, training and expertise to overcome any potential obstacles that may hinder good communication. Good geologists are not necessarily good natural communicators. The failure to effective and accurately communicate geological information, no matter how accurate and reliable the results of a geological investigation, may reduce the reliability of the information being provided.

Communication is a social skill, not a technical one, for the impersonal transfer of data and information. The most effective method of communication is the use of clear, simple, unambiguous, non-technical language. Visual material can facilitate effective communication, especially to a non-technical audience and other professionals with little or no knowledge of geology. The transfer of knowledge, to be wholly effective, needs to be done with confidence and consistency. The good communicator must also be a good listener, using silence, reflecting, paraphrasing and non-verbal behaviour. If possible, there should be feedback from the targeted audience (or individual).

During the monitoring and prediction of geohazards (e.g. volcanic activity), one of the important challenges is to understand the popular, public perception of the hazards and threat. The real challenges are to communicate the likelihood of an eruption and to call for an evacuation; this is often a very difficult decision, usually much more difficult that the science itself.

The accurate communication of information relating to geohazards by geologists to the public is critically important. Throughout history there are many examples where geologists got the science and communication right, got the science right but the communication wrong, or got both the science and communication wrong.

When working with the police, the forensic geologist must be aware of the limitations of his or her experiences and be confident to communicate with a multidisciplinary team of forensic investigators and police officers.

Communication with the media (and public) gives geologists the opportunity to raise the profile of geology. Media training and awareness is recommended before engaging with the media. Responses need to be carefully considered, so that the intended message is put across clearly and, factually, without sensationalism. Recorded interviews may give the opportunity to rehearse or review an interview before it is broadcast or reported. Live interviews do not give the opportunity for rehearsal prior to broadcasting and for the correction of mistakes. Information should be simple and non-contentious, and ambiguous jargon should not be used, but if geological and other scientific terms are used, then these should be explained in layman's terms. When addressing the public and media, personal image, appearance, body language, tone of voice, facial expressions, persona and posture are just as important as the verbal messages.

This paper has relied heavily on the author's professional experiences during the monitoring of volcanic hazards, mining hazards, exploration, geotechnical investigations and working with the police in many parts of the world. This paper has highlighted some key issues and has drawn attention to the importance of communication between geologists, and with other specialists, the public and the media. These experiences suggest that communication should be more formally taught, perhaps at undergraduate level with advanced (CPD) communication courses available to practising, professional geologists. It is throughout the geologist's career, however, and from experiences that the real skills of communication are tested and developed.

The author would like to acknowledge the support and assistance provided by the British Geological Survey, International Mining Consultants, Halcrow Group Ltd, Mr James White (Government of Montserrat) and Dr Richard Robertson (The Seismic Research Centre, The University of West Indies, Trinidad and Montserrat Volcano Observatory). The views expressed in this paper are those of the author and not necessarily the views of any of the organizations that have been mentioned in this paper.

References

ANONYMOUS 2002. *Dialogue with the Public: Practical Guidelines.* Research Councils UK. Developed for the Research Councils UK and the Office of Science and Technology by People Science & Policy Ltd & Taylor Nelson Sofres, London.

APPLIED GEOLOGY LIMITED 1993. *Review of Instability Due to Natural Underground Cavities in Great Britain. Summary Report.* Applied Geology Ltd, Royal Leamington Spa.

ARUP GEOTECHNICS 1992. *Review of Mining Instability in Great Britain. Summary Report.* Department of Environment, London.

AUDIT COMMISSION 1993. *What Seems to be the Matter: Communication between Hospitals and Patients?* HMSO, London.

BRITISH MEDICAL ASSOCIATION 1998. *Communicating Skills and Continuing Professional Development.* Board of Medical Education, British Medical Association, London.

COLE, K. & DAVIS, G. M. 2002. Landslide warning and emergency planning systems in West Dorset. England. *In*: MCINNES, R. & JAKEWAYS, J. (eds) *Slope Instability—Planning and Management.* Thomas Telford, London, 463–470.

CREATH, W. B. 1996. *Home Buyers' Guide to Geologic Hazards.* American Institute of Professional Geologists, Arvada, CO.

DAVIS, G. M. & COLE, K. 2002. Working with the community—public liaison in instability management at Lyme Regis, Dorset, England. *In*: MCINNES, R. & JAKEWAYS, J. (eds) *Slope Instability—Planning and Management.* Thomas Telford, London, 695–700.

DEPARTMENT OF THE ENVIRONMENT 1990. *Planning Policy Guidance Note 14: Development on Unstable Land.* HMSO, London.

DEPARTMENT OF THE ENVIRONMENT 1996. *Planning Policy Guidance Note 14: Development on Unstable Land. Annex 1: Landslides and Planning.* HMSO, London.

DEPARTMENT OF THE ENVIRONMENT, TRANSPORT AND THE REGIONS 2000. *Planning Policy Guidance Note 14: Development on Unstable Land. Annex 2: Subsidence and Planning.* DETR, London.

DEPARTMENT OF TRADE AND INDUSTRY 1996. *Going Public, an Introduction to Communicating Science, Engineering and Technology.* Department of Trade and Industry, London.

DICKSON, D. A., HARGIE, O. & MORROW, N. C. 1989. *Communication Skills Training for Health Professionals. An Instructors' Handbook.* Chapman & Hall, London.

DONNELLY, L. J. 2002a. Finding the silent witness. How forensic geology helps solve crimes. All-Party Parliamentary Group for Earth Science. *Geoscientist*, **12**, 16–17, 24.

DONNELLY, L. J. 2002b. Finding the silent witness. *In*: DONNELLY, L. J. (ed.) *Record of presentation on Forensic Geology and The Moors Murders to the House of Commons, Westminster Palace, on 12th March 2002, with contributions from J. R. Hunter and B. Simpson.* British Geological Survey & International Mining Consultants.

DONNELLY, L. J. 2003. The applications of forensic geology to help the police solve crimes. *European Geologist–Journal of the European Federation of Geologists*, **16**, 8–12.

DONNELLY, L. J. 2007. Engineering geology of landslides on the volcanic island of Montserrat, West Indies. *Quarterly Journal of Engineering Geology & Hydrogeology*, **4**, 267–292.

DRUITT, T. H. & KOKELAAR, B. P. (eds) 2002. *The Eruption of the Soufrière Hills Volcano, Montserrat, from 1995 to 1999.* Geological Society, London, Memoirs, **21**.

FENNING, P. J. & DONNELLY, L. J. 2004. Geophysical techniques for forensic investigations. *In*: PYE, K. & CROFT, D. J. (eds) *Forensic Geoscience. Principles, Techniques and Applications.* Geological Society, London, Special Publications **232**, 11–20.

FOOKES, P. G. 1997. The First Glossop Lecture. *Quarterly Journal of Engineering Geology*, **30**, 293–424.

FORSTER, A. & FREEBOROUGH, K. 2006. *A Guide to the Communication of Geohazards Information to the Public*. British Geological Survey, Urban Geoscience and Geohazards Programme, **IR/06/0009**.

FREEMAN, T. J., LITTLEJOHN, G. S. & DRISCOLL, R. M. C. 1994. *Has Your House Got Cracks? A Guide to Subsidence and Heave of Buildings on Clay*. Institution of Civil Engineers and the Building Research Establishment, London.

GEOMORPHOLOGICAL SERVICES LTD 1987. *Review of Research into Landsliding in Great Britain*. Department of the Environment Open File Reports, Report No. 14.

HARRISON, M. & DONNELLY, L. J. 2008. Locating concealed homicide victims; developing the role of Geoforensics. *In*: RITZ, K., DAWSON, L. & MILLER, D. (eds) *Criminal and Environmental Soil Forensics*. Soil Forensics International, Edinburgh Conference Centre, 30 October–1 November 2008, Springer (in press).

HIND, C. 1997. *Communication Skills in Medicine*, British Medical Journal, London.

HOLCOMBE, E. A., ELLIS, D., TOOBY, J. & ANDERSON, M. G. 2003. *Public Awareness Documentation to Improve Slope Stability Conditions*. Poverty Reduction Fund, St Lucia, MoSSaiC Management Report, **3**.

Law Society 1994. *Coal Mining Searches. Law Society's Guidance Notes and Directory*. The Law Society's Stationery Society Limited, London.

MARTS, M. E., HODGE, D. C., SHARP, V. L., SHERIDAN, F. E., MACGREGOR, J. M. & CULLEN, J. M. 1978. *Social Implications of Volcano Hazard: Case Studies in the Washington Cascades and Hawaii*. Department of Geography, University of Washington, Seattle.

MCGUIRE, W. J. 1978. Volcanic hazards and their mitigation. *In*: MAUND, J. G. & EDDLESTON, M. (eds) *Geohazards in Engineering Geology*. Geological Society, London, Special Publications **15**, 79–95.

MCINNES, R. 2004. Instability management from policy to practice. *In*: GLADE, T., ANDERSON, M. & CROZIER, M. J. (eds) *Landslide and Risk*. Wiley, Chichester, 401–428.

MILETI, D., NATHE, S., GORI, P., GREENE, M. & LEMERSAL, E. 2004. *Public Hazards Communication and Education: The State of the Art*. Update of Nathe, S., Gori, P., Greene, M., Lemersal, E. & Mileti, D. 1999. *Public Education for Earthquake Hazards*. Natural Hazards Informer, 2. Natural Hazards Research and Applications Information Centre, Institute of Behavioural Science, University of Colorado at Boulder.

MUTON, B. J. & SHIMABUKURO, S. 1974. Human adjustment to volcanic hazards in Puna District, Hawaii. *In*: WHITE, G. F. (ed) *Natural Hazards: Local, National and Global*. Oxford University Press, New York, 151–159.

NHS CONFEDERATION 1997. *Better Guide. Better Communications for the NHS Trusts*. NHS Confederation, Birmingham.

NIELD, T. 2008. Altered priorities ahead; or how to develop fruitful relationships with the media. *In*: LIVERMAN, D., PEREIRA, C. P. G. & MARKER, B. (eds) *Communicating Environment Geoscience*. Geological Society, London, Special Publications, **305**, 5–10.

NOE, D. C., JOCHIM, C. L. & ROGERS, W. P. 1997. *A Guide to Swelling Soils for Colorado Homebuyers and Homeowners*. Colorado Geological Survey, Special Publication, **43**.

NUHFER, E. B., PROCTOR, R. J. & MOSER, P. H. 1993. *The Citizen's Guide to Geologic Hazards*. American Institute of Professional Geologists, Arvada, CO.

ONG, L. M., DEHAES, J. & LAMMES, F. B. 1995. Doctor–patient communication; a review of the literature. *Social Science and Medicine*, **40**, 903–918.

PELTU, M. 1991. Risk perception in the real world. *New Scientist*, 17, August, p. 4.

ROBERTSON, R. E. A. 1995. An assessment of the risk from future eruption on the Soufrière Volcano of St. Vincent, West Indies. *Natural Hazards*, **11**, 163–191.

ROYAL COLLEGE OF PHYSICIANS OF LONDON 1997. *Improving Communication between Doctors and Patients*. RCP, London.

ROYAL SOCIETY 2000. *Scientists and the Media: Guidelines for Scientists Working with the Media and Comments on a Press Code of Practice*. Royal Society, London.

WHITE, S., EVANS, P., MIHILL, C. & TYSOE, M. 1993. *Hitting the Headlines, a practical guide to the media*. British Psychological Society, Leicester.

WILLIAMS, D. 1997. *Communications Skills in Practice: A General Guide for Health Professionals*. Jessica Kingsley, London.

WILLIAMS, S. N. (ed.) 1990a. Nevado del Ruiz Volcano, Colombia, I. *Journal of Volcanology and Geothermal Research*, Special Issue, **41**, 379 pp.

WILLIAMS, S. N. (ed.) 1990b. Nevado del Ruiz Volcano, Colombia, II. *Journal of Volcanology and Geothermal Research*, Special Issue, **42**, 224 pp.

Hazard and vulnerability assessment and adaptive planning: mutual and multilateral community–researcher communication, Arctic Canada

NORM R. CATTO & KATHLEEN PAREWICK

Department of Geography, Memorial University, St. John's, NL, A1B 3X9, Canada
(e-mail: ncatto@mun.ca)

Abstract: Communities in Arctic Canada are faced with natural geological and environmental hazards. Successful adaptation requires assessment of hazards from a physical science perspective, and appropriate communication with the communities. Transforming a hazard assessment exercise into an effective plan for adaptation requires an intimate cultural understanding. Hazard assessment involving substantial input from all research, administrative, socio-economic and cultural communities will lead to more appropriate and valuable analyses of risk, sensitivity and vulnerability. Residents and communities can contribute greatly to the identification and assessment of natural hazards. Community-driven communication is essential for meaningful risk analysis, adaptive planning and vulnerability assessment. Developing relationships with local media can be extremely beneficial. Using the practices of participatory community planning allows local environmental changes to be assessed and responded to by the people affected. Establishing effective working partnerships is essential for a true vulnerability assessment. The particularly sensitive nature of hazard assessments indicating increasing risk and vulnerability, and the continuing socio-economic changes in some communities, in the work described here, required consideration of the most appropriate methods of communication for each instance. The relationships that have emerged through the course of work in the communities have differed markedly from those originally envisioned, and also exhibit significant differences between communities.

Successful adaptation requires assessment of hazards from a physical science perspective, and appropriate communication with affected communities. Increasingly, a multi-hazard approach is being taken in the process of identifying and quantifying vulnerabilities (commonly referred to as vulnerability assessment or risk analysis; ITC 2006). Comprehensive studies can span several years and engage numerous researchers. When geoscientists later complain that their careful assessments have not been taken into account in subsequent community decision-making, the manner in which their findings were communicated can be a very significant factor (Blanchard-Boehm 1996; Alexander 2007; Pasquarè & Pozzetti 2007). Appropriate communications require that the communicator takes account of a variety of considerations that will influence the clarity, persistence and retention of the message, and the receptivity of the audience (e.g. Heyd 2007). Although many adaptations are logically addressed through local planning processes, care must be taken to find the right times and places to introduce geoscientific materials. This paper examines continuing climate-change hazards assessment and adaptive planning efforts in three Canadian Arctic communities, to address the recurring questions of what works and what does not in communication efforts concerning geohazards.

The geoscience perspective

Geoscientists who desire to effectively communicate geoscience commonly perceive the problem as a two-component system: assembling the necessary information, and presenting it in a clear manner. The guiding assumption is that, if the information can be clearly presented, the community will 'become educated' or 'geologically literate', and will respond in a manner that a professional geoscientist would deem appropriate.

The issue of communication is particularly significant for hazard and vulnerability assessment. If there are no people involved, or if an event occurs without negatively affecting or inconveniencing humans, then there is no hazard. Exposure that results from voluntary choices theoretically can be reduced or eliminated if human behaviour more closely mirrors geological understanding. Exposure that is involuntary, as a result of the climate and/or geology of a region, can be recognized, and the knowledge used to reduce vulnerability.

When hazards adversely affect communities to an excessive degree, either a lack of knowledge (geoscientific or environmental) or a wilful disregard of existing knowledge may be assumed by the geoscientist. Education in this context can be taken to mean either a basic introduction to physical

From: LIVERMAN, D. G. E., PEREIRA, C. P. G. & MARKER, B. (eds) *Communicating Environmental Geoscience*. Geological Society, London, Special Publications, **305**, 123–140.
DOI: 10.1144/SP305.12   0305-8719/08/$15.00 © The Geological Society of London 2008.

principles, or a stern warning as to the consequences of the disregard of the known principles, or both. If the geoscientist provides a clear assessment of the conditions and hazards, then the community should respond. The emphasis behind this approach is that the geoscientist's primary objective is clear presentation of sound geoscience.

Geoscientists can only present concepts in which they have confidence. Unconsolidated coastal bluffs or floodplains are natural hazards to the geoscientist, and will eventually cause problems for any human residents. From this perspective, any structure built on a coastal bluff or floodplain can be considered to be at risk. However, because the exact time of the next major flood or coastal storm cannot be specified, and because erosion seldom progresses in a strictly linear fashion, quantitative or temporally definitive statements can be geologically untenable. Assessment of a quantitative degree of risk is complicated by the uncertainties surrounding the exact nature and magnitude of future climate change and variation, regardless of cause.

Qualitative statements are preferred to semi-quantitative estimates in these circumstances. To people without geoscience training, however, such statements commonly appear imprecise, vague and unreliable. Geoscientists can be reluctant to make qualitative or relative statements concerning risk, leaving administrators, communities and residents without guidance or input. Unless the natural hazard is linked to the consequences for a community in tangible form, the efforts involved in identification and assessment may be largely futile, and fail to influence decision-making or planning in the vulnerable community.

The difficulties of translating geoscientific language into the language and terminology used by the intended audience to garner an effective response have been addressed by several researchers (e.g. Blanchard-Boehm 1996; Huntington 2000; Alexander 2007). However, efforts that are strictly confined to avoiding terminology and choosing simple wording, without considering the socio-economic and cultural perspectives of the audience, are unlikely to be truly successful. A study that was conducted from primarily a scientific viewpoint, with limited or no input concerning socio-economic aspects, cannot be presented in only those terms. Simple presentation of the geotechnical facts in isolation from community context may not be effective in communicating volcanic hazards that potentially necessitate evacuation (Chester 1993).

Residents of small communities throughout Canada have a close connection to the landscape. Most residents of northern Canada are engaged in either primary resource occupations or tourism. Many families have lived in the same communities for generations. In the process of living in and looking at their environments, they have observed much. In Arctic Canada, where all communities are coastal and dominantly ethnically Inuit, knowledge of the land remains widespread, particularly among community elders. Residents have acquired a large volume of geological and environmental knowledge, albeit unrecognized, uncategorized and unquantified.

In endeavouring to communicate with these communities, geoscientists potentially have advantages. Residents have knowledge, and geoscientists could discuss matters in non-technical fashion with people who already have acquired information. Residents can see the consequences of geological and environmental processes directly, without the technological buffers that exist in urban North America. Despite these advantages, however, communication of geoscience requires more than assessing the hazard and delivering the message. Transforming a hazard assessment exercise into an effective plan for adaptation requires an intimate understanding of the culture of the people and communities involved, extending across a variety of spatial scales, socio-economic groups, and all levels of governance. Hazard assessment involving substantial input from all research, administrative, socio-economic and cultural communities will lead to more appropriate and valuable analyses of risk, sensitivity and vulnerability.

Multi-hazard assessment

Geoscientists play a key role in larger multi-hazard risk assessments, identifying baseline physical risk factors in the environment and evaluating how they may respond to further change, human-induced or otherwise. Risk assessments (ITC 2006) generally characterize: (1) event probability and magnitude; (2) the exposure and sensitivity of aspects of the human community (i.e. population, infrastructure, communications, economic and other activities) in relation to various magnitudes of event; (3) cost projections (potential losses) following from the above.

Hazard risk assessments are multidisciplinary exercises wherein geoscientists typically find themselves members of larger teams concerned with emergency preparedness, disaster management and development planning outcomes. Other team members will probably include professional staff, bureaucrats, first responders, community leaders and business representatives. Internal communications can present challenges in these settings, let alone communication with the greater public. However, learning to communicate across disciplines and cultures is a critical first step in addressing acknowledged risks.

Simply communicating the potential of a given hazard to do harm is not sufficient to change potentially adverse behaviour. In case after case, communities that have had not only warnings but actual prior experience of a given hazard impact will exhibit what to an outsider appears to be a wilful negligence of predictable consequences. Hazard assessments must be understood and applied by the affected community at large. In the instance of low-frequency events, memory can be an issue: a local population often tends to collectively 'forget' or downplay a problem the further removed they are from its last manifestation.

Many communities have accepted proactive response to identified hazards in the short term, enthusiastically putting the means in place to avoid serious consequences, only to fail later by not implementing it rigorously enough. All too frequent examples occur where communities located on the banks of a periodically flooding river or at the foot of steep slopes allow development in the recognized flood or landslide zones. An appropriate hazard avoidance strategy may have been brought into force, typically in the form of a land-use policy that defines 'no build' areas or otherwise assigns special development requirements on a geographical basis. Does a lack of compliance in this case signal a simple failure of political will? Perhaps, but community interests and history can also weave a dense web that can snare even the best-intentioned actors for change.

Community resilience and adaptation

Communities are complex adaptive systems. Scientists in a variety of disciplines have been studying complex systems to better understand and model the world. Early study of transformational processes in ecosystems (Holling 1986) has been built upon in recent years by a multidisciplinary group of collaborators known as the Resilience Alliance (http://www.resalliance.org). Resilience is defined as the capacity of a system to absorb, accommodate or respond to disturbance. Adaptation in a resilient system is considered to be cyclical. Holling (1986) introduced the use of a stylized Mobius strip (the infinity symbol; Fig. 1), to illustrate the adaptive cycle. The successive phases that an adapting system goes through include growth (or exploitation), conservation, release ('creative destruction' or collapse), and reorganization (Holling 1986; Gunderson & Holling 2002).

Another useful framework for viewing community adaptation can be found in the applied domain of community economic development.

Communities are considered to be resilient if they take intentional actions to increase the ability of citizens and institutions to respond and adapt (Centre for Community Enterprise 2000). Resilience changes over time in response to changes in knowledge, and in socio-economic and political conditions.

Human communities exhibit unique composites of dynamic traits and social–ecological linkages on a number of scales (Berkes 1999; Berkes *et al.* 2003). Interpreting Holling's (1986) adaptive cycle, a window of opportunity occurs during the uncertain backloop of a given system's response to disturbance, when novelty and experimentation are favoured. An adaptive window might be seen as opening in response to increasingly apparent climate change as communities pursue practical solutions to emerging local problems. These adaptations may be conditioned by everything from day-to-day responses of single residents to the much slower moving developments in policies and programmes administered by various levels of government.

This interacting set of adaptive cycles and responses at different spatial and temporal scales is an example of 'panarchy' (see Holling 1986). The diverse responses to challenges at different levels may appear to represent anarchy, especially during periods of release (or 'collapse'). However, although the situation may appear anarchic to an observer with a fixed view or reference point, adaptation by communities continues, either consciously or unconsciously (e.g. Catto & Catto 2004; Hassan 2007). A 'collapse' in this sense is in the eye of the beholder: changes are continuing at numerous spatial and temporal levels.

'Revolt' and 'remember' are two key behavioural responses within panarchy (Gunderson & Holling 2002). Both exert fundamental influences on adaptive capacity. The 'revolt' connection can cause changes in one social–ecological cycle to destabilize a larger and slower one. The 'remember' connection aids renewal by drawing down the accumulated knowledge residing in a larger, slower cycle. Envisioning a community in these terms, local governance and institutions reside at a level intermediate to cycles of individual, familial and operational knowledge and adaptation, and those of the prevailing world-view and a host of external agents.

The importance of these organizations as economic, social and political actors supporting local development is perhaps obvious enough, so what does the concept of panarchy add to an understanding of community adaptation? Besides being a useful way to shift thinking from the mechanics of cause and effect to instead consider interacting change processes at various scales, it highlights

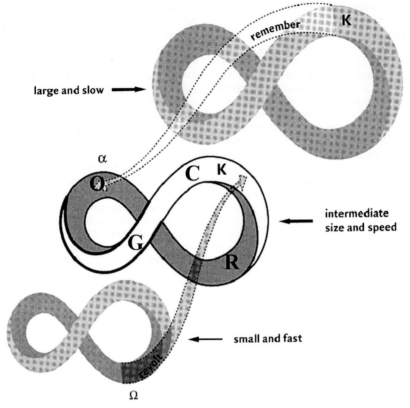

Fig. 1. The adaptive cycle and panarchical connections. Each adaptive cycle passes through phases of growth (G), conservation (C), release (R), and reorganization (O). Multiple adaptive cycles exist on different spatial and temporal levels, ranging from rapidly occurring cycles with limited spatial scales ('small and fast') to cycles that progress slowly but influence broad areas ('large and slow'). Interjection of a 'revolt' behavioural response (Ω) from a smaller scale cycle into a larger one can initiate an interaction (K), which can destabilize the larger cycle and trigger a release. Conversely, interjection of a 'remember' behavioural response from a larger, slower-acting cycle can aid in re-organization (α), accelerating the transition from the reorganization to the growth phase. After Gunderson & Holling (2002) and Berkes *et al.* (2003).

integral creative, cultural and communications functions that contribute to adaptation (Heyd 2007).

Planning for adaptation

Planning is an attempt to manage change. It brings together what is known in the present with scenarios for what is likely to happen in the future, to make decisions in the best interests of the parties at hand. It repeatedly asks 'what if?': What if that area floods? What if that shoreline continues to erode? Geoscience can aid community planning by clarifying how and where various physical processes will proceed and over what time frames. Answering the 'what ifs' suggests a variety of adaptations, physical, operational, political and otherwise. In turn, geoscientists can also offer

invaluable insights into the likely consequences of many adaptations, thus aiding in the identification of the best of many alternatives.

A distinction must be made between 'adaptation planning' and 'adaptive planning'. Adaptation planning is planning undertaken with the specific goal of addressing hazards to the population over time. Adaptive planning, however, qualifies the planning process itself as a platform subject to mid-stream adjustments to achieve desired ends. Adaptive planning addresses itself to 'the problem' of projects with unclear end results, as opposed to those undertakings with clear objectives suited to 'predictive planning' strategies (IDEA 2007). In large measure, it entails having alternative or contingency plan(s) for every element of the planning process. Adaptive planning is well suited to adaptation planning efforts.

Planning for adaptation is a place-based activity. Although it may draw on very sophisticated computer modelling to illustrate possible futures, any 'virtual' world used is very much grounded in the real world. At the community level, hazards response and adaptation entails both individual and collective actions and may also call upon outside resources. Information about how the community operates and what it has to work with are best collected first hand. Establishing effective working partnerships at the local level is essential for any planning effort.

Transforming a hazard assessment exercise (especially those that indicate increasing risk and vulnerability) into an effective plan for adaptation must involve a significant communication effort on the part of the scientists. Community decision-makers must believe that a hazard message they are to implement is one that is significant, well researched and accurate. They need to feel confident that it is sufficiently well understood by the population they represent to justify sacrifices that may have to be made in the short term to avoid more serious consequences later. Recognizing from the start that community leaders may not be themselves entirely comfortable interpreting or conveying scientific information, researcher(s) should be prepared to become partners in a continuing hazards education process, offering support as required.

Arctic Canada: communities and hazards

Communities in Arctic Canada face a variety of natural hazards. Extreme cold, protracted periods of darkness, and inter-annual variability in climatic conditions have influenced every aspect of Arctic life, including the movements of terrestrial species across an ice-dominated land-and-seascape that extends across seasonal ice into productive marine areas for much of the year. Northern peoples, along with the animals and plants that sustained them, have all adapted to the harsh climatic conditions, responding to many challenges to survival through changes in their distribution and behaviour. Adaptive lessons learned over generations of human occupation are manifest in the distinct cultures that have evolved in the region.

The last two centuries of human history in the Arctic have marked a phase of particularly rapid social, technological and economic change for indigenous populations. These changes have spawned further adaptations, many of which are still continuing. Since the 1950s, there has also been a transition from small, highly mobile and kinship-structured human communities to heterogeneous populations of a more spatially defined and settled nature with growing complements of permanent infrastructure. Adaptation by relocation is no longer as easily accomplished for the human inhabitants of the Canadian Arctic. Many features of the modern north (e.g. industrial development, institutional and wage-based economic attachments, land claims and legal tenure systems, and harvesting regulations) have acted to constrain the former variety of options made available by mobility. Vulnerability has increased in consequence.

Since 1970, changing and varying climate added to the challenges facing Arctic communities. Significant climate warming has occurred in the north over this period and particularly in the western Arctic, with attendant sea ice reduction, permafrost and ground ice degradation, slope instability, and new coastal hazards (Johannessen et al. 1999, 2004; Johnson et al. 2003; ACIA 2004; Nichols et al. 2004). Human-induced climate change is expected to be most pronounced at high latitudes (ACIA 2004). Human communities are experiencing a variety of consequences, ranging from costly infrastructure damage associated with changing ground conditions, to dangerous travel conditions attributed to less predictable weather (Furgal et al. 2002; ACIA 2004).

The changes in the environment have not gone unnoticed by Inuit residents. Extensive documentation of both traditional Inuit knowledge and recent observations of climate change and variation has been conducted (Fox 2000, 2002; Thorpe et al. 2001, 2002; Furgal et al. 2002; Jolly et al. 2002; Nickels et al. 2002; Nichols et al. 2004).

Hazards accentuated by changing climate may be pushing Arctic communities towards the limits of their capacity for adaptation. How much change and uncertainty can they cope with? More generally, what distinguishes the community that bounces back from hard knocks and the one that comes apart at the seams? Perspectives vary among community development workers, health staff, economic development officers, and local and national politicians. Disaster management practitioners are also increasingly pursuing these themes as they look beyond crises to recovery and mitigation.

The physical science perspective on successful human adaptation to climate change holds that both a rigorous assessment of hazards and their appropriate communication to the communities they may affect are needed. The transformation of geohazards information into demonstrable adaptation, however, requires that the assessment process be expanded to engage local knowledge and cultural perspectives, and to take account of socio-economic factors, governance mechanisms, and the variety of levels at which all of these elements interact. This calls for an integrated physical and social science approach, and also requires consideration of each community as a distinct entity.

Addressing community challenges (economic, environmental, social or health-related) at the local level has long been a job for community members active or employed in local government, community services, law enforcement, and a host of related non-governmental organizations. In our continuing research, we have been exploring community planning and development functions to determine how they might better serve to build community resilience and support local climate change adaptation.

Community-based work was organized around the collaborative production of local climate change adaptation plans. This was accomplished using open and participatory community planning processes. For each community, the research has proceeded in the following sequence: (1) preliminary familiarization visits and local pre-planning; (2) environmental change and community data compilation; (3) local planning consultations; (4) adaptation plan preparation with stakeholder review and editing.

Three communities were studied: Tuktoyaktuk, Sachs Harbour and Gjoa Haven. The communities differ in the nature and severity of geological and environmental hazards, in their socio-economic and cultural milieux, and in their vulnerability to natural hazards and environmental change; factors that have had to be considered in all researcher–community communications.

Tuktoyaktuk

Tuktoyaktuk (69°25′N, 133°00′W), Northwest Territories, is located on the south shore of the Beaufort Sea, 140 km north of Inuvik (Figs 2 and 3). It grew from being a traditional home to a few families to a permanent settlement for over 300 people by the 1950s. Growth was accentuated when the community was selected to serve as a base for petroleum exploration operations in the Beaufort Sea and Mackenzie Delta. Tuktoyaktuk is accessible year-round by air, by river barges throughout summer, and by an ice road from early January to April. It is the most northerly point in the Canadian Arctic accessible by road and the largest coastal settlement in the western Canadian Arctic. The community lies within the Inuvialuit Settlement Region. The population (2006) of 870 is predominantly Inuvialuit (western Arctic Inuit), but includes some Dene and Métis residents. Non-aboriginal residents account for less than 10% of the population (Statistics Canada 2006).

Tuktoyaktuk has a tundra climate (modified Köppen-Geiger Et). Daily mean temperatures in January and July are $-27\,°C$ and $11\,°C$, respectively (Environment Canada 2007). Mean annual precipitation in the region is 170 mm, of which 56% falls as snow. The modal snow pack depth is 40 cm, and snow cover typically persists for 210–230 days. Tuktoyaktuk is underlain by continuous permafrost, with a maximum thickness of c. 300 m. Thermokarst lakes and patterned ground are widespread.

The Beaufort Sea has been steadily rising for at least the past 30 000 years. Sea level is currently rising in this region at c. 3.5 mm a^{-1}, the combined result of glacio-isostatic response and change in global sea level (Manson et al. 2005). The combination of rising sea level, increased storm and wave activity, and unlithified ice-rich coastal sediments make the coastline highly susceptible to erosion. The coastline was intensively studied because of concern for the potential damage to infrastructure resulting from coastal erosion (e.g. Hequette et al. 1995; Hill & Solomon 1999; Forbes et al. 2004; Manson et al. 2005; Solomon 2005). Average rates of recession approximate 1 m a^{-1}, with maximum rates reaching 10 m a^{-1}. Coastal protection measures have been employed, including concrete slabs, rip-rap, sandbags and beach nourishment, but have proved ineffective under current storm conditions (Fig. 3).

Continuing climate change in Tuktoyaktuk is predicted to result in flooding, increased thermal and mechanical erosion rates, beach migration, increased rates of freshwater lake breaching, and destabilization of sediments in the coastal zone. Some areas of Tuktoyaktuk are predicted to suffer complete inundation during future storm events. This research has sparked debate in the community as to whether to erect more coastal protection along the peninsula, or to redevelop the community in nearby areas of higher ground, abandoning the low-lying areas of the peninsula.

Several of the conclusions of the scientific research, including the necessity of extreme care when excavating permafrost or placing structures on it, and the ineffectiveness of shoreline protection structures over the long term, match observations by the community elders and other residents, based on their experience. The similarity between these sets of observations indicates the value of mutual collaboration.

The design of much of the 'permanent' community infrastructure (such as roads and the airport) has assumed the continued presence of permafrost, but not the accelerated thermokarst observed in recent years. Consequently, Tuktoyaktuk has already implemented many adaptation strategies, including the development of new technologies for building foundation construction, placing insulation under buildings, increasing fill thickness, snow clearance in sensitive areas to allow active

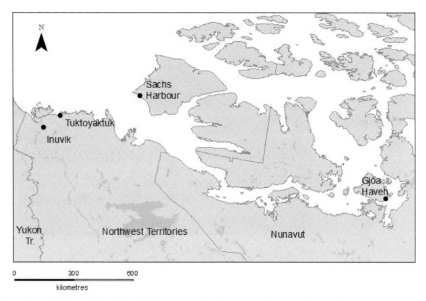

Fig. 2. Locations of Tuktoyakuk, Sachs Harbour and Gjoa Haven, northwestern Arctic Canada.

layer thickening, and avoiding ice-rich terrain for new developments (Smith *et al.* 1998).

In geotechnical terms, Tuktoyaktuk faces both the most severe and the most obvious natural hazards of the three communities discussed here. The population of the community also has the greatest direct and site-specific knowledge of the hazards, and a keen perception that changes are under way. Potential ability to adapt to the hazards is strengthened by the high visibility of coastal erosion and permafrost ablation within the community. Importantly, it is also highly visible to outsiders, including the responsible government agencies, in part because of the community's accessibility to geoscientists, and in part because of the effectiveness of these geoscientists in communicating to outside audiences. Despite the effectiveness of geoscience communication, many residents of Tuktoyaktuk remark that many scientists come and go, but they and their results are never heard from again.

Sachs Harbour

Sachs Harbour (71°59′N, 125°14′W) is located on the southwestern coast of Banks Island, Northwest Territories, 523 km NE of Inuvik (Figs 2 and 4). It is the only permanent community on Banks Island. Established as a trading post in the 1920s, Sachs Harbour did not grow in population until the 1960s, when government efforts were made to encourage permanent Inuvialuit communities. Although the community has experienced significant out-migration in recent years because of a relative lack of local economic opportunities, the latest population count recorded 122 residents (Statistics Canada 2006). The community is predominantly Inuvialuit, with the only non-Inuvialuit residents being teachers. All residents are involved in traditional activities.

Sachs Harbour has a Mid-Arctic climate, with a mean January temperature of -29 °C and a mean July temperature of 7 °C (Environment Canada 2007). Total precipitation is 128 mm a^{-1}, with *c.* 60% as snow. Snowpack depths seldom exceed 30 cm. Sachs Harbour is underlain by continuous permafrost, with thermokarst features and patterned ground common in silt-dominated sediments (French 1976; French & Harry 1990; Belliveau 2007). The coastal bluffs consist of unconsolidated ice-rich silt-dominated glacial deposits, with segregated ice lenses locally composing more than 50% of the surface areas of bluff faces.

At Sachs Harbour, sea level is rising at *c.* 3 mm a^{-1}. However, the hazard posed by coastal erosion is less severe than at Tuktoyaktuk, although some buildings in Sachs Harbour are at risk of failure because of undercutting and thermal ablation (Belliveau 2007). The restricted marine fetch and more northerly latitude allow offshore ice to persist longer at Sachs Harbour, reducing wave energy. Much of the bluff erosion is due to thermokarst degradation of segregated ice lenses, rather than due to wave impacts. The result is to produce a pattern of bluff retreat, with reduced slopes, coupled with shoreline progradation as disturbed

Fig. 3. Tuktoyaktuk. (**a**) Tuktoyaktuk is currently undergoing coastal erosion, as a result of rising sea level and permafrost ablation. (**b**) Efforts to reduce erosion by installing shoreline protection have had limited effect.

Fig. 4. Sachs Harbour. (**a**) Sachs Harbour is built on silty and sandy glacial deposits. (**b**) Continuing permafrost ablation and coastal erosion pose hazards to the community.

sediment accumulates at the seaward edges of the bluffs (Manson *et al.* 2005). Within Sachs Harbour, although slopes have both shown gullying and thermal erosion, most bluffs have not shown measurable retreat since detailed surveys began in 2002 (Belliveau 2007). To the west of the community, more exposed coastal bluffs are retreating at rates up to 3 m a^{-1}, resulting from melting of segregated ice and subsequent slumps and flows.

At present, thermokarst and wave erosion are not major concerns for community infrastructure. However, rising sea level, decreased sea ice and the increased effectiveness of storm events (Johannessen *et al.* 2004; Nichols *et al.* 2004) are predicted for the future, leading to increased thermal and mechanical erosion along coastal bluffs. Increased precipitation since 1956 has led to increased runoff and erosion along slopes within the community (Belliveau 2007). Increased summer and autumn precipitation will also increase coastal thermal erosion.

Sachs Harbour has seen less dramatic infrastructure damage to date than has Tuktoyaktuk. As it is also much smaller, there is limited infrastructure to be subject to potential impacts. None the less, several housing sites along the shoreline experienced erosion serious enough to warrant removal or relocation of structures. Several properties elsewhere in the community experienced significant damage as a result of apparent permafrost degradation, often exacerbated by poor drainage systems. With rising temperatures and increased precipitation, this will continue to pose a problem for infrastructure.

Geoscience research at Sachs Harbour has been less extensive than at Tuktoyaktuk, with relatively little work conducted between *c.* 1988 and 2000. Sachs Harbour is accessible only by air, except for a short summer period when barge traffic is possible, and the small population limits the demand for air service. Consequently, the community of Sachs Harbour has been somewhat isolated from the community of geoscientific researchers. The population is less than at Tuktoyaktuk, and there is a relative lack of economic opportunities. Geoscience researchers arriving at Sachs Harbour should thus expect to work with people who have not been as intensely exposed to previous research efforts, although they still possess much local knowledge. Arctic climate change at Sachs Harbour, however, was the subject of one of the most extensively documented early research efforts respecting indigenous observations by social scientists (IISD 2005).

Gjoa Haven

Gjoa Haven (68°37'N, 95°53'W), Nunavut, is located in on the SE coast of King William Island, 1500 km east of Inuvik and 1100 km SE of Sachs Harbour (Figs 2 and 5). It is the only permanent community on King William Island. Although frequently visited by Inuit hunters, permanent settlement at the site did not occur until the 1950s. Subsequently, however, Gjoa Haven grew rapidly. The population of 1064 in 2006 represented an increase in excess of 10% since 2001, and almost 20% since 1996. This consistent and rapid community growth presents a striking contrast to the relatively stagnant population at Sachs Harbour and the decreasing numbers at Tuktoyaktuk, and has resulted in continuing pressure for new residential development. More than 96% of Gjoa Haven's residents are Inuit. The community position along a key section of the Northwest Passage provides opportunities for economic growth from shipping and tourism, but also carries risk of potential damage from petroleum spillage (Catto & Papadimitriou 2006; Papadimitriou 2007).

Gjoa Haven has an arctic (Köppen-Geiger Et) climate, with a January mean of -34 °C in January and a July mean of 8 °C (Environment Canada 2007). Temperature rises are apparent since 1984 for all months, but most notably in June and September, with means currently exceeding 0 °C. The number of days per year when temperatures are high enough to thaw permafrost is thus rising, intensifying the extent of permafrost thaw in Gjoa Haven. Mean annual precipitation has also increased since 1983, with a current mean of 200 mm a^{-1} (60% snow).

Gjoa Haven is currently undergoing glacioisostatic emergence at *c.* 1 mm a^{-1}. The community is built on a succession of raised gravel and sand beaches developed on glaciofluvial and glaciomarine gravel, forming a continuous series of low terraces from the highest point to the shoreline. There are no wave-cut bluffs in excess of 1 m in height. Continuous permafrost underlies the community, but segregated ice lenses are rare. Thermokarst features are present only in areas of anthropogenic disturbance, and are very shallow. Surface gullying is evident along the river valleys, and on sandy slopes (Papadimitriou 2007).

Previous geoscientific investigations concentrated on the identification of sediments and geomorphological features. In contrast to Tuktoyaktuk and Sachs Harbour, no detailed assessment of natural hazards related to climate change and variation was undertaken in the community prior to 2006 (Papadimitriou 2007). Thus, the observations of environmental change made by the residents of Gjoa Haven prior to that time were completely independent of the geoscience research community.

Fig. 5. Gjoa Haven. (**a**) Gjoa Haven is built on a succession of raised gravel and sand beaches. (**b**) Gullying has locally exposed pipelines, creating a potential hazard.

Summary

The selected communities offer a range of hazards profiles and adaptation scenarios. Tuktoyaktuk is facing the most immediate and serious hazards of the three, given its low-lying and submergent character and rapidly progressing coastal erosion. It is a relatively large and politically influential Inuvialuit community that maintains economically important regional port infrastructure. Although it is already experiencing significant infrastructure impacts as a result of environmental change, it is a community that has had significant capacity to cope with changes to date and is thereby finding it difficult to come to terms with the longer-term prospects of relocation suggested by local flood risk projections.

This contrasts sharply with Sachs Harbour, a small and isolated Inuvialuit community. Although it faces less severe or immediate environmental changes than does Tuktoyaktuk, Sachs Harbour faces serious challenges. It is economically and politically dependent on outside agencies and has suffered from dwindling population and services for many years. Adaptation to existing environmental changes is thereby made more difficult as local capacity is already suffering.

Gjoa Haven affords the scenario of an Inuit community that, although conscious of subtle and continuing environmental changes, has not encountered serious local consequences to date. The community is isolated but well resourced and managed. It is also rapidly growing, so erosion does present some challenges to land administrators tasked with identifying suitable areas for additional housing and other new development. Another concern that residents have is in relation to potential impacts associated with increased ship traffic in the region as warming conditions reduce ice hazards in the Northwest Passage.

Multi-scale communication challenges

Communicating hazard and adaptation messages requires an intimate understanding of the culture of the people and communities involved, extending across a variety of spatial scales, socio-economic groups, and all levels of governance. This is where project partnerships show their worth: some will be productive, whereas others may prove disappointingly superficial. Although most researchers will quickly come to terms with key cultural and socio-economic realities, the particular challenges associated with communications at different scales may be forgotten.

Mutual researcher–community communications, or the direct interchange between geoscientists and the population involved in their research undertakings, will take many forms throughout the life of a project. In the Canadian Arctic, these communications are often negotiated by researchers with community representatives to a significant extent through the research licensing and ethics approvals process required before any research project can commence. In both Northwest Territories and Nunavut, prospective researchers are required to apply for licences for any type of geoscience research. Approval of the communities involved is required for the licence to be granted.

Geoscientists should keep in mind that every community and project will be different. Thus, these proposals for communications should include not only a variety of means, but some contingency plans in the event that things do not proceed as originally planned. For example, geoscientists should be prepared to distribute community-specific materials to a stakeholder group for review in the event that a key public consultation fails to attract satisfactory attendance.

When considering the panarchical connections operating between various scales of activity, researchers need to identify the means by which they can facilitate necessary flows of information up ('revolt', or creative action) and down ('remember'). Lack of or failing institutional memory can present problems: staff turnover and poor record-keeping can quickly bury useful information. Key messages will need regular reinforcement over time. Creativity must be exercised in documenting them in ways that will encourage continuing reference and use. Visual documentation (posters, photographs) can be extremely effective.

Multilateral researcher–community communications refers to the direct and indirect interchange throughout the larger network of individuals and organizations that have an interest in the research undertaking, even if they are not active partners in it. Benefits can certainly flow from unanticipated coincidence of interest. However, the passage of project information from party to party in this realm can also be fraught with potential for miscommunication. People will talk to each other: many interpersonal exchanges occur without the knowledge of either the geoscientist or the primary project partners. As a result, incorrect messages may be extensively propagated before a problem is identified. Where researchers cannot hope to respond to every episode of poorly transmitted or incomplete information, they must take a proactive approach, preparing clear and concise information for general distribution at regular intervals throughout their project period. Rather than leaving it to chance or previous efforts, researchers should ensure that their distribution list is up to date and be on a constant watch for prospective interested parties outside the community. Materials prepared should also be designed both to encourage the reader to pass them along to others in their circle and to make it simple to do so.

Building relationships

Effective community relationships generally require some time to develop. Geoscientists must not be discouraged when difficulties emerge in a hazards assessment project. Early issues illuminate sensitive topics, formative experiences and other factors that have contributed to current circumstances and attitudes. These need to be thought of as the exercise that builds stronger partnerships, so partners-in-the-making need to be on the lookout for them. To this end, it is useful to keep the following questions in mind throughout the hazards assessment and adaptation process.

What else is going on?

It is likely that are your project is not the only one the community is engaged in and, consequently, regardless of how compelling it may be, it cannot attract all of the attention, all of the time. Rather than adding to the workload of already busy community organizations, hazards assessment and adaptation efforts need to be seen as integrating readily with existing functions and activities.

Who is available?

With the benefit of knowing what other activities the community is engaged in, it should become easier to identify those individuals and organizations in the best position to contribute to the process. Capitalizing on those with more resources must be balanced by accommodations for those with limited capacity.

When is the best time?

One more way to gain perspective on a given community is to study the commonalities of its residents, including their schedules. It is important to be aware of the seasons and the associated activities (hunting, fishing, holidays, community events) that are important to the local population and that will thereby compete for their attention. Perfect timing for hazards communications may not be attainable, and should be less of an objective than the constancy of the message and community relations over time.

Notwithstanding extensive pre-project consultation efforts and permitting-period agreements, the relationships that actually emerged through the course of work in these three Arctic communities differed markedly from those originally envisioned. In some cases, a key staff member of a project partner was unavailable or left their position during the course of the project. In other instances, an initial agreement to be a project partner turned out to be difficult to realize once the work began. Limited organizational resources and rising demands on the time and energies of community leaders are both important constraints. The original model of a small group of committed and respected local residents serving the functions of both the project steering committee and the 'community editors' for the documents to be produced has survived, albeit more as a series of people to consult individually rather than a co-operating independent unit.

Clearly, communities not only differ from one another, they also experience internal changes through time that can undermine the best-laid plans and intentions. Such was the case for all three of the Arctic communities studied here. Adaptive planning to address these difficulties when and where they arise is therefore necessary; both to ensure the integrity of the overall project, and to preserve important relationships that may falter or otherwise not meet earlier expectations for whatever reason during the course of the effort.

Participatory practices

Effective communication is vital for results. However, many residents of Arctic Canada are reluctant to participate in one-way exercises in communication. Increasingly, providing information to scientific communities that is not returned to the communities, or passively receiving a lecture outlining one or more hazards (or risk, sensitivity and vulnerability), is of limited interest. In other spheres concerned with managing change, and particularly those such as community planning and economic development that are exercised at a local scale, the last few decades have seen a steady trend towards increasing public participation. A 'ladder' of citizen participation (Arnstein 1969; Fig. 6) has become a standard reference and measure by which engagement in public process is evaluated. People confined to the lower tiers tend to be less willing participants. The objective should be to strive for participation at the uppermost rungs, facilitating citizen power-sharing.

Co-management is one example of the logical application of this hierarchy to public process. Entrenched today in many Canadian Arctic land- and resource-use management frameworks, this power-sharing mechanism combines traditional and scientific knowledge bases (and decision-makers)

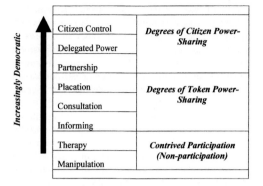

Fig. 6. Ladder of Citizen Participation (Arnstein 1969). In successful communication, efforts must be made to endow communities with real power. Ideally, providing geoscience information allows citizens to assume control of the response to natural hazards. Geoscientists should provide information and indicate consequences of geological phenomena, but should not confine their efforts to simply 'informing' the population of the problem, or engaging in 'consultation' or efforts to placate the population, without any sincere intention of modifying the proposed solution.

to make decisions about conservation, land-use planning and other development. As the new standard, it has created higher expectations in communities for the access and authority they should exercise with respect to outside researchers and scientific information gathered from their community.

Hazard assessment involving substantial input from all research, administrative, socio-economic and cultural communities leads to more appropriate and valuable analyses of risk, sensitivity and vulnerability. Understanding the complex interactions of the community with the environment, including both biophysical and human components, means that more perspectives need to be included in its decision-making processes. Participatory research practices empower the community at the centre of the hazard assessment. Residents and communities can and do contribute greatly to the identification and assessment of natural hazards. Participatory action research, however, entails processes where geoscientists (often engaged as consultants) undertake the projects with the express requirement of training local people to such a level as will allow them to manage the same work in future. New capacity is thereby built within the community to maintain key data gathering processes and determine how the resulting information is to be used.

Community-based research efforts of this nature may be seen in a more favourable light by a population that has reasons to doubt the findings of outsiders. This does not mean that they will be altogether free of bias. The perspective they reflect, however, will be a local one that other local observers should be better equipped to interpret and reinterpret as necessary. The process emphasizes attitudes (such as openness, pride and optimism) and values (such as primacy of education, diversity, and planning) that align with a functionally democratic world-view.

In much the same way as the practices of participatory community planning generally encourage assessment of local environmental changes by the people affected, community-driven communications should be acknowledged as an essential part of mutual researcher–community relationships. Risk analysis, vulnerability assessment and adaptation planning all have the potential to engender interaction among community members. The community will tend to make and protect a space where concerns can be aired away from outside ears. Researchers entering a community that is not their own should therefore be prepared to respect private critical comment and discussion outside the research framework. It is important to resist the urge to respond with explanations or corrections in every instance. As ever, being a good listener is an important relationship-building skill.

Participatory planning

Community planning is a cyclical function. It is a vehicle for regularly revisiting collective circumstances in a public sphere to guide development-related decision-making. A participatory approach emphasizes learning and the enhancement of system resilience. The strategy comprises a series of safe-to-fail experiments at the community level towards the development of an evolving model of planning that will better account for factors contributing to community resilience. This entails co-management: use of traditional and scientific knowledge bases and decision-makers to make decisions in concert about conservation, land-use planning and other development.

Communities are complex and dynamic entities. Conceiving of adaptation in a community context involves an inventory of the constituent elements of a typical settlement (its infrastructure, economic base and population) from which a framework for analysis can then be constructed. Adaptations at various spheres and scales can be used to derive a composite adaptation profile, but the maxim of the whole being more than the sum of its parts also applies. The fundamental interrelations that characterize any community certainly represent the most challenging element of the adaptive process to capture, as they are not only many and various, they are also in constant flux. A bewildering array of activities and behaviours, politics and players can make it difficult to find a way into a constructive community–researcher partnership at the best of times. In the particular circumstance of geoscientific research that addresses themes of risk, change and an uncertain future of a given community, heightened sensitivity should be anticipated even if it does not necessarily manifest itself in the manner desired. The many variables at play mean that the researcher cannot simply work from a shopping list of adaptations to change.

Planning and community development practice is generally conceived as an exercise in social co-operation wherein no single stakeholder has penultimate insight or absolute control. The common goal of fostering a strong community presumably brings everyone to a table where stock is taken, differences are aired and alternative scenarios weighed. The ideal to strive for is a model of power-sharing.

Communication strategy

Hazard assessment involving substantial input from all research, administrative, socio-economic and cultural communities will lead to more appropriate and valuable analyses of risk, sensitivity and vulnerability. Effective reciprocal community–researcher communications must be established to produce meaningful results, especially in cross-cultural settings. Increasingly, community members expect true interaction and information-sharing on the part of outside researchers.

This community planning effort was designed with this concern in mind. In particular, visits to Tuktoyaktuk were meant to provide a means of giving residents an update regarding the research completed by other geoscientists. Developing a longer-term relationship with researchers can be difficult for a community, as many scientists are limited by their project terms and funding, and thereby do not have an easy way to return; as much as they might like to. Most geoscientists are only too happy to stay in touch in other ways and to answer questions that the community may have that relate to their research. It is important, therefore, to have a way of remembering who does what and how they can be reached.

In this research, a number of communications tools were put to work to convey hazards information and assessment findings, and to facilitate adaptation planning. The following summarizes the lessons learned.

Language

Keep it simple. Plain language reporting does not necessarily come easily. Find yourself a community editor (or two or three!). Geoscientific terminology can be exclusive, but inclusivity is essential in community communications. There are many rules of thumb (i.e. avoiding long sentences and paragraphs; paying attention to formatting so pages are not overloaded with text; using photos wherever possible, etc.) but, in general, 'less is more'.

Appropriate translation and interpretation. Simply using English may not be enough. Even in communities with a substantial number of bilingual residents, never underestimate the impact of translated materials and provision of interpreter(s) at gatherings. Besides being mandatory in some contexts (many government-administered processes), taking the time and trouble to look after these matters will signal to the other-language community that you are placing a high value on the relationship with them. In the Inuvialuit and Inuit communities, it was also the only way to engage a significant number of the most respected and experienced members of the community.

Format

Formal documentation. Accountability requirements in an institutional, contractual or community-based project setting mean that reports that are long on content but somewhat lacking in style will remain for years to come. Final project documentation remains an area where some creativity would be appreciated, as everyone is familiar with references to long-forgotten documents gathering dust in so many offices. Hazards communications generally merit a more energetic, action-oriented format and need to be designed with an eye to making them useful tools for community administrators, decision-makers and organizers. Including useful reference materials (especially maps, photos, chronologies, overviews and case studies), action lists and contact information will enhance the chances of the hazards document staying in arms-reach of the people who most need the message regularly and positively reinforced. Computing technologies afford researchers more options (CD-ROMs, DVDs, video, websites) to effectively record and report project activities and outcomes. Serially edited computer-generated slide presentations were used in each Arctic community planning process forum to record participant input and other data. This material not only eventually documented the final consensus, but allowed for easy review and confirmation of stated opinions and facts at every stage of the consultation process.

Formal gatherings. The convention of public meetings to address matters of public interest will also be with us for some time to come. They continue to offer a necessary platform for the direct presentation of key information with opportunities for those attending to ask questions and offer opinions or concerns in the presence of decision-makers. Participatory practices tend to engender more interesting and interactive gatherings, but even so the meetings have one unavoidable downside: they happen when and where they happen. There is a lot of competition for people's time. Assuming that sufficient interest has been generated through advertising, word-of-mouth and other means to attract participants, other circumstances may prevent them actually getting there. Recognizing this, organizers of important meetings schedule their event to avoid other activities of importance to the community (i.e. regularly scheduled organizational or recreational functions including church, Council meetings, bingo, etc.) and to take place outside normal business hours. Special accommodations can be made to overcome some of the potential remaining problems (e.g. on-site childcare to allow parents to attend), but scheduling conflicts will remain. Where possible, holding an open house during the day preceding or following a major public meeting can afford another opportunity for interested parties to be included. Similarly, scheduling a series of small-group sessions can often produce comparable results.

Continuing informal communications. Accountability to the community at large merits equal time and effort to that given to formal communication vehicles. Maintaining a contact distribution list with which to disseminate periodic project updates and other concise materials should be a cornerstone of a larger communications plan. Less formal communications also include mechanisms that passively present key information to the general public. The poster is a particularly versatile tool in this regard. With a suitable public display location and an attractive design, it can build awareness of project aims and outcomes for years at a time. Computing technology has brought graphically sophisticated presentation within the reach of geoscientists. As poster presentations are a common means of conveying scientific work to other scientists, researchers should be able to provide community-specific hazards information and adaptation-oriented exhibits with limited expense. Certainly, translation should be undertaken as required for poster text but it will certainly be a less costly and time-consuming exercise than doing an entire report, and it is likely to be read by more people!

Acknowledgements. Besides the usual thanks to project funders and scientific associates, researches should never forget that the primary partners in these efforts are the communities: they are front-and-centre in any and all acknowledgements. As space allows, plenty of photographs of local participants should be included, used with their permission.

Media

Radio. Even in 2007, local radio remains the most important medium in the Canadian Arctic. It offers significant versatility to the hazards communication effort. Community radio stations are a primary vehicle for sharing community news and views. Besides broadcasting public service announcements on upcoming meetings and interviews on continuing projects, community radio can be used interactively. The phone-in can have regionally specific protocols (southern hosts tending to keep the talk going no matter what, whereas Arctic hosts will simply put on some music between calls) but is a wonderful ice-breaker. It may also allow people who are not able to attend public meetings to participate.

Internet. Computer access is rapidly increasing in the north. Web-mounted materials are well worth the effort to compile, translate and maintain. Again, plain language and plenty of explanatory images from the community should be used to aid comprehension. By including relevant links to scientific background materials and comparable community-based projects elsewhere, this platform can be used to support the growth of a larger community of interest.

Conclusion

Geoscience is too important to be left strictly to geoscientists. Canadian Arctic residents already contribute greatly to the scientific identification and assessment of natural hazards in their regions. Applying participatory planning practices to adaptation planning processes is a logical extension of this communication, allowing local environmental changes to be assessed and responded to by the people affected.

This continuing research aims to assess municipal planning practice as a means of enhancing community resilience; to support municipal decision-making on pressing infrastructure issues; to facilitate mutually beneficial interdisciplinary and inter-community communication; and to identify practical applications of hazard assessment in a community context. Engaging community members in timely information-sharing, discussion, analysis and planning respecting their continuing adaptation is an immediate objective of this project, with the longer-term goal being the fostering of social learning and institutional 'memory' in support of a more sustainable community future. Establishing an effective working partnership in each community has been an essential precursor to the effective pursuit of this project.

Adaptation is a continuing process. Geoscientists and others attempting to support adaptation in Arctic communities must recognize the primacy of longer-term relationships with local people and organizations in all their dealings there.

Relationships contribute to understanding and trust, which in turn will enhance community receptivity to hazard messages. This is particularly important in cases of hazard assessments that reveal increasing risk and vulnerability. Developing relationships at the community level does take time, but, in so doing, the researcher will benefit from other important lessons that serve the ultimate project ends by highlighting potential stumbling blocks early on in the process.

The relationships that have emerged through the course of our work in three communities have differed markedly from those originally envisioned, exhibiting both the significant differences between communities and the need for adaptive approaches to community-based geohazard assessment and subsequent planning.

Partners in this project include the communities of Tuktoyaktuk, Sachs Harbour and Gjoa Haven; Natural Resources Canada; and Memorial University of Newfoundland. Research support has been provided by ArcticNet, Natural Resources Canada, Infrastructure Canada, Aurora Research Institute, and the Nunavut Research Institute. We thank T. Bell and M. Petterson for their reviews, which improved the final manuscript. Many thanks go as well to the Centre for Community Enterprise, Ecology North, the Municipal and Community Affairs Department of the Government of the Northwest Territories and the RCMP for the input of their staff, and the use of their materials and/or premises. In Tuktoyaktuk, we especially thank Sarah McKay and family, Peter Nagosak and David Nasogaluak; in Sachs Harbour, the Haogak, Kudlak and Carpenter families; in Gjoa Haven, Gideon Qitsualik, Simon Okpakok, Ben Kogvik, Sarah Wade, Raymond Kamookak and Michael Anguttitauruq, Sr; and so many others who have given generously of their time, insight and good humour along the way.

References

ACIA 2004. *Impacts of a Warming Arctic: Arctic Climate Impact Assessment.* Cambridge University Press, Cambridge. World Wide Web Address: http://www.acia.uaf.edu.

ALEXANDER, D. 2007. Making research on geological hazards relevant to stakeholders' needs. *Quaternary International*, **171–172**, 186–192.

ARNSTEIN, S. 1969. A ladder of citizen participation. *Journal of the American Institute of Planners*, **35**, 216–224.

BELLIVEAU, K. 2007. *Coastal geomorphology of southwest Banks Island, NWT: historical and recent shoreline changes and implications for the future.* MSc thesis, Memorial University, St. John's, NL.

BERKES, F. 1999. *Sacred Ecology: Traditional Ecological Knowledge and Resource Management.* Taylor & Francis, London.

BERKES, F., COLDING, J. & FOLKE, C. 2003. *Navigating Social–Ecological Systems: Building Resilience for Complexity and Change.* Cambridge University Press, Cambridge.

BLANCHARD-BOEHM, R. D. 1996. When scientists and emergency managers warn, does an at-risk public hear and respond? *In*: AMIN, S. G. & FULLERTON, S. (eds) *International Business Practices, Contemporary Readings*, 1996 edn. Academy of Business Administration, Cumberland, MD, 523–529.

CATTO, N. R. & CATTO, G. 2004. Climate change, communities, and civilizations: driving force, supporting player, or background noise? *Quaternary International*, **123–125**, 7–10.

CATTO, N. R. & PAPADIMITRIOU, S. 2006. Sensitivity, exposure, and vulnerability to petroleum pollution, Gjoa Haven coastline, NU. abstract, ArcticNet Annual Meeting, Victoria, BC. World Wide Web Address: http://www.mun.ca/geog/research/catto_petroleum.ppt

Centre for Community Enterprise 2000. The Community Resilience Manual: A Resource for Rural Recovery and Renewal. World Wide Web Address: www.cedworks.com.

CHESTER, D. 1993. *Volcanoes and Society.* Edward Arnold, London.

Environment Canada 2007. Climate data, temperature and precipitation. World Wide Web Address: http://www.climate.weatheroffice.ec.gc.ca.

FORBES, D. L., CRAYMER, M., SOLOMON, S. M. & MANSON, G. K. 2004. Defining submergence and erosion hazards in the Canadian Arctic. (Arctic Coastal Dynamics: Report of the 4th International Workshop, St. Petersburg, Russia, November 2003.) *Berichte zur Polar und Meeresforschung*, **482**, 196–202.

FOX, S. L. 2000. Arctic climate change: observations from the Inuvialuit Settlement Region. *In*: FETTERER, F. & RADIONOV, V. (eds) *Arctic Climatology Project, Environmental Working Group Arctic Meteorology and Climate Atlas.* National Snow and Ice Data Centre, Boulder, CO. World Wide Web Address: http://www.aari.nw.ru/projects/Atlas/Meteorology/HTML/PRIMER/OOINTRO/inuit_knowledge_of_climate.pdf

FOX, S. 2002. These are things that are really happening: Inuit perspectives on the evidence and impacts of climate change in Nunavut. *In*: KRUPNIK, I. & JOLLY, D. (eds) *The Earth is Faster Now: Indigenous Observations of Arctic Environmental Change.* Arctic Research Consortium of the United States, Fairbanks, AK, 12–53.

FRENCH, H. M. 1976. Geomorphological processes and terrain disturbance studies, Banks Island, District of Franklin. Geological Survey of Canada, Current Research, **76–1A**, 289–292.

FRENCH, H. M. & HARRY, D. G. 1990. Observations on buried glacier ice and massive segregated ice, western Arctic Coast, Canada. *Permafrost and Periglacial Processes*, **1**, 31–43.

FURGAL, C., MARTIN, D. & GOSSELIN, P. 2002. Climate change and health in Nunavik and Labrador: lessons from Inuit knowledge. *In*: KRUPNIK, I. & JOLLY, D. (eds) *The Earth is Faster Now: Indigenous Observations of Arctic Environmental Change*. Arctic Research Consortium of the United States, Fairbanks, AK, 266–300.

GUNDERSON, L. & HOLLING, C. S. 2002. *Panarchy: Understanding Transformations in Human and Natural Systems*. Island Press, Washington, DC.

HASSAN, F. 2007. Extreme Nile floods and famines in medieval Egypt (AD 930–1500) and their climatic implications. *Quaternary International*, **173–174**, 101–112.

HEQUETTE, A., RUZ, M.-H. & HILL, P. R. 1995. The effects of the Holocene sea level rise on the evolution of the southeastern coast of the Canadian Beaufort Sea. *Journal of Coastal Research*, **11**, 494–507.

HEYD, T. 2007. Rapid natural changes: a perspective from environmental philosophy. *Quaternary International*, **173–174**, 161–165.

HILL, P. R. & SOLOMON, S. M. 1999. Geomorphic and sedimentary evolution of a transgressive thermokarst coast, Mackenzie Delta Region, Canadian Beaufort Sea. *Journal of Coastal Research*, **15**, 1011–1029.

HOLLING, C. S. 1986. The resilience of terrestrial ecosystems: local surprise and global change. *In*: CLARK, W. C. & MUNN, R. E. (eds) *Sustainable Development of the Biosphere*. Cambridge University Press, Cambridge, 292–317.

HUNTINGTON, H. P. 2000. Using traditional ecological knowledge in science: methods and applications. *Ecological Applications*, **10**, 1270–1274.

IDEA (Institute for Dynamic Educational Advancement) 2007. Adaptive vs. predictive: Is the end clear? World Wide Web Address: www.i-d-e-a.org/adaptive.html.

IISD (International Institute for Sustainable Development) 2005. *Sila Alungotok: Inuit Observations on Climate Change*. Video. International Institute for Sustainable Development, Winnipeg, Manitoba. World Wide Web Address: www.iiisd.org.

ITC (International Institute for Geo-Information Science and Earth Observation) 2006. *Education*. World Wide Web Address: http://www.itc.nl/education/courses/short_courses/2007/0763.asp.

JOHANNESSEN, O. M., SHALINA, E. V. & MILES, M. W. 1999. Satellite evidence for an Arctic sea ice coverage in transformation. *Science*, **286**, 1937–1939.

JOHANNESSEN, O., BENGTSSON, L. *ET AL*. 2004. Arctic climate change: observed and modelled temperature and sea-ice variability. *Tellus*, **46**, 328–341.

JOHNSON, K., SOLOMON, S., BERRY, D. & GRAHAM, P. 2003. Erosion progression and adaptation strategy in a northern coastal community. *In*: PHILLIPS, M., SPRINGMAN, S. M. & ARENSON, L. U. (eds) *Proceedings—8th International Conference on Permafrost, Zurich, Switzerland, July 20–25, 2003.*

International Permafrost Association, Zurich, **8**, 489–494.

JOLLY, D., BERKES, F., CASTLEDEN, J. & NICHOLS, T. & THE COMMUNITY OF SACHS HARBOUR 2002. We can't predict the weather like we used to: Inuvialuit observations of climate change, Sachs Harbour, Western Canadian Arctic. *In*: KRUPNIK, I. & JOLLY, D. (eds) *The Earth is Faster Now: Indigenous Observations of Arctic Environmental Change*. Arctic Research Consortium of the United States, Fairbanks, AK, 92–125.

MANSON, G. K., SOLOMON, S. M., FORBES, D. L., ATKINSON, D. E. & CRAYMER, M. 2005. Spatial variability of factors influencing coastal change in the Western Canadian Arctic. *Geo-Marine Letters*, **25**, 138–145.

NICHOLS, T., BERKES, F., JOLLY, D. & SNOW, N. & THE COMMUNITY OF SACHS HARBOUR 2004. Climate change and sea ice: local observations from the Western Canadian Arctic. *Arctic*, **57**, 1.

NICKELS, S., FURGAL, C. *ET AL*. 2002. Putting the human face on climate change through community workshops: Inuit knowledge, partnerships, and research. *In*: KRUPNIK, I. & JOLLY, D. (eds) *The Earth is Faster Now: Indigenous Observations of Arctic Environmental Change*. Arctic Research Consortium of the United States, Fairbanks, AK, 300–333.

PAPADIMITRIOU, S. 2007. Climate-related hazards and risks to community infrastructure: Gjoa Haven, Nunavut. Unpublished research report, Masters of Environmental Science, Memorial University of Newfoundland, St. John's, NL.

PASQUARÈ, F. & POZZETTI, M. 2007. Geological hazards, disasters, and the media: the italian case study. *Quaternary International*, **173–174**, 166–171.

SMITH, J. B., HULME, M., JAAGUS, J., KEEVALLIK, S., MEKONNEN, A. & HAILEMARIAM, K. 1998. Climate change scenarios. *In*: FEENSTRA, J. F., BURTON, I., SMITH, J. & TOL, R. S. J. (eds) *Handbook on Methods for Climate Change Impact Assessment and Adaptation Strategies, Version 2.0*. United Nations Environment Programme and Institute for Environmental Studies. Vrije Universiteit, Amsterdam, 3-1–3-40.

SOLOMON, S. M. 2005. Spatial and temporal variability of shoreline change in the Beaufort–Mackenzie Region, Northwest Territories, Canada. *Geo-Marine Letters*, **25**, 127–137.

Statistics Canada 2006. Community profiles, 2006 Census. World Wide Web Address: http://www.statcan.ca/english/census06/data/profiles/community/Index.cfm.

THORPE, N., HAKONGAK, N. & EYEGETOK, S. & THE KITIKMEOT ELDERS 2001. *Thunder on the Tundra: Inuit Qaujumajatuqangit of the Bathurst Caribou*. Generation Printing, Vancouver, BC.

THORPE, N., EYEGETOK, S. & HAKONGAK, N. & THE KITIKMEOT ELDERS 2002. Nowadays it is not the same: Inuit Qaujimajatuqangit, climate and Caribou in the Kitikmeot Region of Nunavut, Canada. *In*: KRUPNIK, I. & JOLLY, D. (eds) *The Earth is Faster Now: Indigenous Observations of Arctic Environmental Change*. Arctic Research Consortium of the United States, Fairbanks, AK, 198–239.

Communicating geoscience to indigenous people: examples from the Solomon Islands

M. G. PETTERSON[1], D. TOLIA[2], S. J. CRONIN[3] & R. ADDISON[1]

[1]*British Geological Survey, Keyworth, Nottingham NG12 5GG, UK (e-mail: mgp@bgs.ac.uk)*

[2]*Ministry of Natural Resources, PO Box G35, Honiara, Solomon Islands*

[3]*Institute of Natural Resources, Massey University, Private Bag 11 222, Palmerston North, New Zealand*

Abstract: This paper examines communicating geoscience to indigenous peoples using a communication model that closely follows geological models for pollution issues. Although geoscientists will expend large amounts of energy in understanding a scientific process, relatively little energy is often expended in the analogous communication model. Reasons for this include a narrow focus on pure science, lack of confidence in engaging in communication and negative perceptions of communication ideas. Indigenous peoples are defined as 'first occupiers' of regions or nations relatively untouched by the predominant 'Western–Asian' technological-oriented culture. Few indigenous peoples are totally 'untouched' by the dominant world culture. Four cases studies from the Solomon Islands explore communication strategies relating to land access, a live volcanic event, the setting up of a gold mine, and raising awareness of volcanic hazards. Generic best practice advice offered includes the following: understanding of indigenous culture, customs, values, taboos and political–governance structures; involvement of indigenous people at every level of the communication process; identifying and including all stakeholders; a clear message, method and outcome focus; usage wherever possible of face-to-face communication and pictures as well as words; involvement of the community in practical exercises; a thorough follow-up and evaluation process; and sufficient time to allow the process to be effective.

Communication between humans should be instinctive and come with ease. Humans evolved to communicate and share ideas and knowledge and yet there is abundant evidence throughout the world of the negative impacts of inappropriate, unclear, incomplete or aggressive communication.

Scientists can struggle with communication. They may be so enthusiastic to share their knowledge that they fail to follow some basic rules, invalidating the very messages they wish to convey. So what are the basic rules? In many ways the rules are similar to the scientific analysis of movement of chemical species through the Earth's near-surface. To analyse this issue the scientist uses the source–pathway–receptor scientific paradigm. A chemical species has to have a source. If the chemical entity moves it must move along a certain path and when it stops moving it acquires a new 'home' within a receptor host. Geoscientists model these processes deeply and in considerable detail, examining how a chemical species is bonded to its source, how likely it is to be freed from its source, through what medium or range of media it will move, the environmental conditions of the pathway in terms of pH, Eh, temperature, salinity, pressure, composition, etc., and then what

environmental conditions must apply to bind the chemical species to a new source.

So, at first sight it seems surprising that geoscientists can get communication so wrong. Communication, in essence, originates from a communicator, is transmitted through one medium or another, and is received by a receiving audience. The communication process, therefore, closely follows the source–pathway–receptor scientific paradigm many geoscientists live their professional lives by. But possibly because geoscientists do not always give the same care, attention and forethought to the communication process as they may to the source–pathway–receptor model, their communication may fail to make the desired impact. At best the message may be ignored, at worst it is misunderstood, misconstrued and then has negative impacts. Some areas of science are aware of this disconnect in communication between scientists and their audience. Two current examples of this phenomenon in the greater scientific world are medical and climate-change science. UK medical science has become so worried about stories in the media making false claims for new treatments or drugs and/or incorrect interpretations of new scientific thinking that cause general alarm

From: LIVERMAN, D. G. E., PEREIRA, C. P. G. & MARKER, B. (eds) *Communicating Environmental Geoscience*. Geological Society, London, Special Publications, **305**, 141–161.
DOI: 10.1144/SP305.13   0305-8719/08/$15.00 © The Geological Society of London 2008.

that it has set up a professional communication body to counteract this trend through careful cultivation of the 'real message' by highly qualified medical scientists. Similarly, in the high-profile climate-change debate those scientists who consider themselves to expound the 'real current thinking' as opposed to 'sensationalist charlatans' are making concerted efforts to get their message across in an appropriately understandable manner, thus identifying more outlandish or extreme or non-mainstream scientists by exposing them for what they possibly are: lone voices with unusual interpretations of a pre-selected dataset, separated from the majority of professional climate-change scientists and thinkers.

So what happens with the geo-communication process that can go so badly wrong when in essence geoscientists should be comfortable with the communicator–message transmission–audience receiver model? The answer is more complex than first appears but probably involves an inability of some geoscientists to appreciate, or even their derision of, what may be considered a 'touchy-feely social science' approach to communication; a lack of devotion of quality thought and time (something the same people would not do for their latest *Nature* manuscript that they lovingly nurture through to publication); and a lack of appreciation of the key elements of communication; that is, the actual message(s), which method is most appropriate and how to get inside the head of the target audience or range of audiences. In the modern world communication is actually a difficult minefield that needs considerable thought and planning to cross successfully.

The pitfalls of communication are varied and numerous. First we must consider the message. Exactly what is the message or series of messages the geoscientist wishes to communicate? What is the motivation for the communication? What is the desired impact of the communication? Is the motivation appropriate for the desired impact? How is the message to be communicated? Through the written word? E-mail? Internet publication? Paper communication? TV? Radio? Face to face? The range of communication transmission media in the modern world is the most varied ever in the history of humanity, and they all have differing impacts. Who is the intended audience? How do they vary? How do they think? What message and message transmission method is most appropriate? Politicians are only too aware of the pitfalls of communication and employ a variety of communication gurus and spin doctors to enable them to communicate effectively. Even so, we are all familiar with examples of inappropriate communication by politicians. This is somewhat alarming. If the politician who eats, drinks and sleeps communication gets things wrong, what chance does a poor old

geoscientist whose prime concern is their science have in succeeding?

Despair is of course pointless. Geoscientists can and do communicate effectively. There are many good examples. However, few geoscientists would come to the conclusion that there is little else the geoscientific community could do to improve effective communication. Geoscientists can learn from others about best practice in communication, customize other thinking for their own benefit and add to the body of knowledge in this area.

This paper focuses on communicating geoscience to a very different audience and culture from the 'comfort zone' audience of most geoscientists. Like any experiment or philosophical or scientific analysis, consideration of an extreme end-member can be very helpful. In some ways, such consideration of a very different culture is particularly instructive, as the reasons for different communication approaches are obvious. What is more difficult to perceive is that within a geoscientist's host community or region or country there may be a wide range of sub-cultures that have not been taken into account. So we can all learn, apply and customize lessons learned from communities that have very different cultures from our own because whether we like it or not we have been forced to consciously consider carefully crafted communication strategies. We have to do this because if we ignore it our whole project or area of scientific research, or livelihood, or even personal security may be threatened.

Communicating with indigenous people

Indigenous people are hereby defined as the 'first arrived' people within a region or country, who may hold a set of cultural and development values that are very different from those of twenty-first century society in Europe, North America, Australasia and many parts of Asia and South America. There are many examples of indigenous peoples, from the North and South American Indians, Amerindians and Inuit, to the Aborigines and Maoris of Australia and New Zealand, and the tribal peoples of Darjeeling, Burma and Indonesia. This paper focuses on the Melanesian people of Solomon Islands in the SW Pacific region.

What characterizes indigenous people and what are the specific challenges in communicating with indigenous people?

The characteristics of indigenous people are really the subject of expertise of an experienced anthropologist rather than a geologist. Every situation, tribe, area, region, country, family and individual is different, and it is hard not to fall into the traps of stereotyping and generalizing.

However, the authors offer insights, thoughts and examples from their own experience of working amongst and with Melanesian people for a long time, and in one case being a Melanesian! We leave it to the reader to decide whether or not these observations are of any value.

Melanesian people share a range of high-level cultural and historical characteristics with other indigenous people. They have a long history of isolation and lack of exposure to other human societies, especially those very different from their own. They possess close links of attachment to the land and environment they live on and in. These feelings are particularly acute, perhaps, for small island populations. Strong familial and tribal attachment and bonding expresses itself as a series of complex human relationship interactions, governance hierarchies, an acceptance of the way things are, a willingness to share labour and wealth amongst the family or tribe, and a strong sense of belonging. There is also a well-defined sense of 'us and them', with a strongly developed wariness of 'them' and a tendency to remain, as far as possible, within the host community and limit interaction with other tribal groups to a minimum. Melanesia, with a cumulative population of around 6 million across Papua New Guinea and Papua, Solomon Islands, Vanuatu, Fiji and New Caledonia, contains around one-third of the world's spoken languages, reflecting a long history of tribal isolationism, intertribal warfare, head-hunting and cannibalism. There is no tradition of written history. Tribal shared history and tradition is passed on through oral transmission or oral history. In Melanesia this is referred to as 'kastom' history or 'kastom' stories. Melanesian people have a shared set of cultural and spiritual values normally based on direct experience of the immediate environment in which the people exist. This will encompass a religious and philosophical set of beliefs and tenets. In Melanesia this whole area of shared custom and belief goes under the shorthand title of 'kastom'.

Well-defined roles for male and female exist with set boundaries that are normally impossible to cross. The economic system is closely allied to a hunter–gatherer way of life with or without agriculture. There will be a service economy and limited manufacturing (undertaken only for the immediate needs of the tribe). Usually the economy is a non-cash economy.

The above characteristics are particularly true for those indigenous peoples who have not been exposed to the outside world in any meaningful way. Of course, examples of these people are becoming fewer and fewer as the world becomes ever more populated. Perhaps the best modern examples of relatively untouched indigenous people include the tribes of deepest Amazonia, Papua New Guinea and Indonesia. Most indigenous people have had to make some sort of accommodation with the dominant world culture of the moment and the levels of accommodation vary enormously. The indigenous people of North America and Australia are examples of people who have become overwhelmed by subsequent immigrant populations and struggle to maintain their original way of life. Melanesia is an example of a region of the world in which the original people are still by far the most numerous and they struggle to meet the challenges of balancing their kastom society with the ever-increasing demands and intrusiveness of the 'modern' world.

Geography of Solomon Islands

Solomon Islands is situated east of Papua New Guinea and NE of the Queensland coastline of Australia (Fig. 1). The country is an island archipelago nation situated between longitudes 156° and 170°E and latitudes 5° and 12°S. Most of the population of 400 000 people live on the larger islands, which form a double chain in the western part of the archipelago; namely, Makira, Malaita, Guadalcanal, Santa Isabel, Choiseul and New Georgia. Solomon Islands became an independent nation in 1978 after having been a Protectorate Nation of the UK for over a century. Honiara, the capital of Solomon Islands, is situated within Guadalcanal: Guadalcanal and Malaita are the two most populous islands. The main economy of Solomon Islands is based on copra, cocoa, palm oil, timber and fisheries, with mining beginning to make a significant contribution (for example, the Gold Ridge mine, Central Guadalcanal, contributed an estimated 30% to the gross domestic product in 1988–1989).

Cultural aspects of Solomon Islands that affect communication

As with any communication process it is important to understand as much as possible about the target audience: how they think; their attitudes, opinions and values; and how they may respond to messages delivered in different ways.

Solomon Islands is inhabited predominantly by Melanesians (the dominant ethnic group) who have inhabited the islands for at least 50 000 years. Other ethnic groups residing in Solomon Islands include Polynesians, Micronesians, Chinese and Europeans. The Melanesian population of the Solomon Islands retain traditional dance, song and story telling, along with traditional healing, sorcery, totems and taboos. The culture involves respect for Bigmen (men who through deeds, strength, wealth or

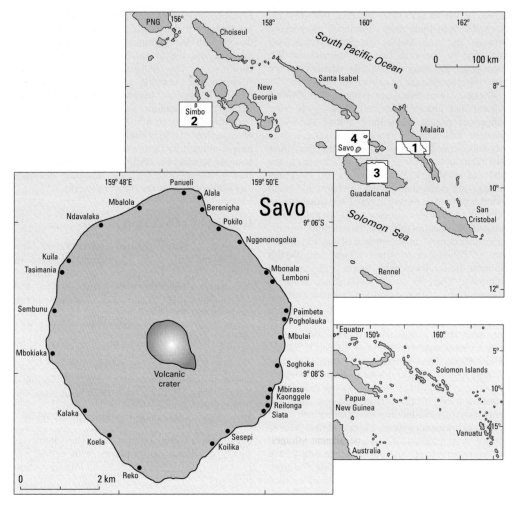

Fig. 1. Location of Solomon Islands, showing main islands of the archipelago nation. Boxes indicate the case study area: 1, Kwaio, Malaita; 2, Simbo, Western Province; 3, Gold Ridge, Central Guadalcanal; 4, Savo, 35 km NW of Honiara. Insets show location of Solomon Islands relative to Australia and give the distribution of villages on Savo as an example of rural population patterns in Solomon Islands (most are now situated adjacent to the coast) (adapted from Cronin *et al.* (2004) with acknowledgements to Kluwer Academic Publishers).

intelligence gain prominence) and these Bigmen or chiefs play an important role in settling disputes, maintaining relations within tribes, overseeing justice and enforcing cultural traditional practices. In addition to Bigmen, elders are also highly regarded, and children and young people are obliged to remain quiet when elders or Bigmen speak. In traditional society, women have little chance for voice in public debates or decisions; young people are also marginalized in decision-making processes. Alongside traditional beliefs, the dominant religion is Christianity, with the Church of Melanesia sitting alongside a range of Christian sects. The only major non-Christian

religion present in Solomon Islands is the Bahai religion. Religion, religious festivals, and religious rituals and events can play a strong role in Solomon Islands and are important for communication. Traditional religion and beliefs remain a strong influence at most levels of society.

Traditional governance at a local and regional level is both hierarchical and relatively democratic. Unlike Polynesian governance systems that focus largely on monarchical or feudal inherited position systems, Melanesia has a strong tradition in selecting chiefs and tribal elders by merit. Chiefs attain their status through developing a record of wise decision-making and provision of high-quality advice as well as demonstrating high-level rhetorical and negotiation skills. Chiefs can lose their status if they do not perform at a high enough standard. Women are not usually major players in traditional governance: chiefs are all men. There are various levels of chief from village elder or headman to paramount chief, the latter having responsibility for a region or number of villages. There are regular meetings of paramount chiefs where whole-island or whole-region issues are discussed and debated. These events are also for inter-communal discourse. Meetings are held at a range of levels at regular intervals, from the village and village church level upwards to the paramount chief level. Through these meetings most of the male population is consulted with, and women can and do influence debates.

Alongside the traditional governance model runs the official governance model run on UK parliamentary democratic lines. The Queen's representative in Solomon Islands is the Governor General and there are elected members of parliaments including the Prime Minister, members of the national and regional parliaments, and ministers of state. In most cases the two governance systems work well together and each relies upon the other for effective governance, though there are times of friction (for example, between an elected regional member of parliament and a paramount chief).

In most parts of the Solomon Islands the original population was low but grew quickly, leading to the development of permanent villages. Island interior regions in more recent times have become depopulated as people moved to the coast to take advantage of developing economic, educational, health and transport infrastructure (Fig. 1 shows an example of this population pattern). To this day, island interiors in most islands are undeveloped, mainly comprising dense, pristine primary or secondary rainforest. Solomon Islands remains a largely rural country with the village being the most fundamental unit of habitation and rural cultural values being highly respected. Many houses are of the traditional leaf design using traditional rainforest materials, although wood and sheet metal houses are gradually taking over. Urbanization is now rapid, with around 25% of the current population residing in towns such as Honiara, Auki and Gizo. Many urban dwellers retain very close ties with their village.

Education is, in theory, universal throughout the country. In practice, access to education is variable and depends on supply, particularly the availability of trained teachers. Primary school is more accessible than secondary school. Most children undertake some level of education and study. Literacy rates vary but are probably at around the 60% level.

Locally produced newspapers (such as the *Solomon Star*) are avidly and widely read.

There are a range of health issues in Solomon Islands, particularly respiratory infections, malaria and diarrhoea, resulting from poor water supplies, sanitation facilities and health infrastructure. Malaria has been a particularly debilitating issue, with malaria rates amongst the highest in the world. There are a range of hospitals and rural health centres distributed throughout the country, although health care is at a basic level in the more remote areas. Water supplies are generally gravity-fed, rain-tank, or wells with or without pumps.

The main economic activities on Solomon Islands include the harvesting of coconut plantations, fishing and slash-and-burn agriculture to exploit the fertile tropical soils for subsistence and sale of excess produce in local markets. Coconuts are generally harvested near the coast, whereas inland plantations include sweet potato, cassava, taro, yam, banana and occasionally rice. Other food sources include pigs and chickens, along with marine products.

Communications in Solomon Islands remain rudimentary in most areas. There are no railways, few metalled roads and a variable network of unmetalled roads. Inter-island transport occurs through regular sea and air services. Many areas of rural Solomon Islands remain isolated to the present day. There is a national radio station, and TV and satellite TV is becoming increasingly important, although there are many rural households that will not access TV, the Internet, etc. The Internet is slowly arriving at more places, with e-mail and Internet surfing starting to make an impact even in rural areas.

Melanesians place a very high value on land in recognition of the special interdependence of human society and land that is essential to environmental management and survival within traditional socio-economic systems. This high cultural value placed on land results in the prevalent strongly held view that the land must be honoured, respected and cared for responsibly to ensure that future generations can likewise enjoy and be sustained by the land. Land is a highly prized capital asset with deep social significance. At times, land acts as a religious 'store' or 'bank'. This view is, perhaps, a real example of the essence of the 'sustainable development' paradigm enunciated by Brundtland (1987) whereby every generation ensures that the most fundamental economic and social asset society possesses (the land) is cared for and passed on in an enhanced or equivalent state to the next generation. It is no accident that the most important word in the Pijin language is 'blong' (meaning belong, to be part of), which emphasizes strong land, language and tribal roots. Melanesians are mainly subsistence crop and livestock (pigs and chickens) farmers, as well as being hunter–gatherers.

Land is held almost exclusively in customary ownership, passed down in a matrilineal or patrilineal system, depending on the local tribal kastom. As most of this land is not documented in legal terms, land disputes are common. Landless people are particularly vulnerable, as status, wealth and subsistence agriculture are closely interrelated. Landless people tend to drift to towns and urban areas. Land ownership is a complex concept in detail in Solomon Islands. Property rights over land are communally owned by kinship or clans. Social and cultural values of land (a value that may exceed 'commercial value' in a Western context) affect controlling customary land ownership attitudes, are flexible, and may change over time. Ownership patterns are complex and undocumented except through oral history. Land boundaries are poorly defined. Some societies within the Solomon Islands are matrilineal. An example of land inheritance from Central Guadalcanal is given to illustrate some of these issues. The area is dominated by the Mbahomea tribe, whose traditional social structure is matrilineal with land entitlement inherited from the female line. The legendary origins of the people are from two genealogical descents and subsequent clans. There are at least 17 clans with customary land title and rights in this area. The identification of clan land ownership is not an easy process. Land ownership has to be defined through a range of criteria that include a detailed clan knowledge of sites of archaeological, historical, religious and cultural importance and value. These sites hold particular significance to each clan or a single group (Naitoro 1995). A detailed knowledge of the location and significance of such sites builds up the credibility of clan claims over land ownership.

Communication insights

The section above that briefly describes the political, cultural, geographical, societal and technological aspects of Melanesian society in Solomon Islands throws up a number of key points that must be considered by any geoscientist who may wish to work in the country, especially if they are involved in communication.

It is important to involve local people at all levels of communication. Governance, clan, tribal and chieftain systems are complex. Melanesians pride themselves on consensual debate and decision-making, particularly amongst the men. Any communication strategy must include these elements of traditional decision-making and debate.

The strong familial and tribal affiliation must be taken into account in any communication strategy. Melanesian culture is underpinned by the 'wantok system' (one-language). In a part of the world where there are so many different languages, association with others who speak your language defines a tribe or extended family to a large degree. Tribal or family members will refer to others in their tribe as 'my wantoks'. In many parts of Solomon Islands men and women may lead very different lives. Communication with women must be done in a sensitive manner that takes into account local values.

As so much of geoscience affects, to some degree, land and sea issues, communication must take account of the strong attachment to land (including the offshore reef). This affects many aspects of geoscience, such as access to field and study areas and the perceptions local people may develop in response to survey, research and exploration activities.

A range of communication techniques should be developed that acknowledge the fact that Melanesians are largely from an oral tradition of communication. Face-to-face meetings at a range of levels will be important, as will the need to be as inclusive as possible. The radio is a powerful medium and is widely listened to. The Internet and TV may be of use but their impact will be limited, especially in rural areas. Visual materials are always appreciated and help with the message. Melanesia is full of local languages. Most people speak Pijin and this will be the most important language for discourse and writing, although it is even better if messages can also be translated in local languages. English is widely spoken in Honiara, although even there people appreciate part of the discourse in Pijin.

Communities are widely dispersed and travel may be difficult. Any serious attempt at communication will be time consuming, and this should be factored into the planning of activities.

The remaining part of the paper will focus on real events from a communication viewpoint with an analysis of lessons learned.

Example 1: land access in Central–West Malaita (Kwaiio)

As part of its core role the Solomon Islands Geological Survey (SIGS) must access as much land as it can to undertake geological surveying and mineral reconnaissance (Fig. 2). This immediately brings into light the issue of land ownership, land attachment, ill-defined land boundaries and the potential to become unwittingly involved in land disputes.

SIGS therefore developed sophisticated methods of communicating with local people, particularly

Fig. 2. Mapping in Solomon Islands is largely confined to geotraverses along rivers that cut through the rainforest and produce rock outcrop. Kwaio in Malaita, like other areas, required a great deal of care in ensuring mapping parties had gained the permission of landowners to survey their ground.

landowners, prior to undertaking any surveying mission. Radio transmissions advising local people of a forthcoming survey in their area are transmitted from around 6 weeks prior to any proposed field visit. One month before any field work a forward access and logistics party is sent out to hold a series of village meetings in the proposed field area. These meetings aim to include all landowners and any other interested parties from the communities that live in the field area.

The main message is that the Solomon Islands Government is about to hold a survey and is asking permission to enter the land of a range of landowners and seek assistance for logistical and field support. The second message is to convey the purpose of the mission and explain as fully as possible why geological surveys are important and the benefits to the Solomon Islands of geological mapping. This is a vital message to convey, as there is always a degree of suspicion about geological activities. Some people confuse geological surveying and exploration with mining and think that any activity may result in landowners being robbed of valuable material that is rightfully theirs. Special efforts are made to explain why rock and stream sediments are taken, what will happen to the samples, and how the results will be interpreted and presented. In particular, it is emphasized that these samples are not valuable in monetary terms.

The only real method of communication transmission apart from radio use is face-to-face

meetings. Maps and visual materials support oral delivery of the message. In the majority of cases this method of communication proved to be ideally suited to the purpose. Most landowners are willing and happy to allow access and provide paid local workers to assist with the survey and offer local logistical support where they can. If landowners object, the SIGS will not access their land, although this rarely happens.

One incident occurred, however, that underlined the great importance of undertaking a comprehensive communication campaign, particularly for a long-term mapping mission. The incident in question occurred on the island of Malaita, the second largest island in Solomon Islands after Guadalcanal. Malaita was one of the last large islands to be mapped partly because it is densely populated and landowner sensitivities have always been high. A previous attempt to map northern Malaita in the 1970s was aborted after local opposition. One particularly sensitive tribe was thought to be the Kwaio tribe of central Malaita, and particularly careful consultations were set up to agree access to field areas during the 1990s field campaign. In most cases, the mapping of Kwaio went very well and the local people were very accommodating. However, in one area things went badly wrong. The SIGS workers first began to get nervous when they were following one particular river (in the rainforest-covered Solomon Islands the only decent geological exposures are in river exposures) and the local field assistants insisted on 'downing tools' and holding meetings every kilometre or so. This was highly unusual. The concerns of the field assistants were varied but largely focused on doubts as to whether or not the field party had genuine permission to access the land in the upper parts of the river course. After the fourth such meeting it was decided reluctantly to abandon the trip and re-discuss land access issues with landowners and chiefs.

The field party (which comprised some 15 SIGS officers) retreated to the main road and headed northwards back to base camp in three Land Rovers together with field equipment and geological samples. As the field party proceeded north their progress was blocked by a road block and the Land Rovers were quickly surrounded by over 100 machete-wielding Kwaio people, some of whom were a little the worse for alcohol, and many of whom were angry and noisy. The leader of the group approached the SIGS leader and accused SIGS of failing to notify and seek permission for access for this particular area of Kwaio. If true, this alleged land trespass was a serious offence by kastom standards and would have to be punished; compensation would be sought. The situation was very delicate and people's safety and possibly lives could have been at stake. The Group Leader wanted to hold a number of SIGS officers captive as ransom and was urging the group to burst LandRover tyres, etc. This proposal was not acceptable to the SIGS officers, who carefully negotiated with the Group Leader and suggested that instead of people, he could hold geological samples as 'ransom'. The Group Leader reluctantly agreed to this suggestion and finally allowed the field party to leave; the SIGS team drove away with a heavy sigh of relief.

This incident was unacceptable to SIGS as representatives of the Solomon Islands Government. Many discussions were held with a range of regional Kwaio Leaders and a Council of Paramount Chiefs was called. At this council evidence was heard from both SIGS and the Group Leader who had caused the road block and geological field party stoppage incident to occur. SIGS was asked to explain why it was holding the survey, and SIGS officers stressed, with collaboratory evidence and witnesses, that they had done all they possibly could to consult with local landowners and follow kastom with respect to land access. The Group Leader stated that, in his view, he had been excluded from any prior land consultations, that he was suspicious of the purposes of the geological survey and initially he was asking for high levels of compensation. The Paramount Chiefs duly considered all evidence and stated they were impressed with the consultation efforts of SIGS

and stated that as forward-looking tribal elders they understood that national geological surveys were undertaken for the good of the country and the benefit of communities. They asked the Group Leader (gently) if he had any serious objections to allowing SIGS back onto the area in question and he finally agreed after hearing the support of the Paramount Chiefs for the continuation of the survey. The survey was allowed to continue.

Example 1: lessons learned

SIGS already knew from work in many parts of the Solomon Islands that the communication technique was appropriate and correct for geological surveying land access. SIGS knew that Kwaio was a sensitive area and put extra effort into consulting with a wide range of local people prior to any surveying. What had not been picked up were local political rivalries and leadership rivalries, which led to a lack of communication with one particular leader who wished to make an incident of this affair. So there was a lack of identification of a key stakeholder and target audience that could have led to rather dire consequences. Luckily, the tense situation was defused quickly. The Paramount Chiefs held the highest levels of power in the local area and they were impressed with the amount of energy and effort SIGS had expended with respect to consultation. Because of these efforts they came down on the side of SIGS. If SIGS had not planned the communication and consultation process as professionally as it had done, the incident described above would have become much more serious, would have jeopardized the future of the survey on Malaita, and could have compromised the lives of SIGS officers.

Example 2: volcanic crisis on Simbo

Simbo is situated some 300 km NW of Honiara. The island is part of the Western Province of Solomon islands, being one of the more southerly islands of the New Georgia island archipelago. The island contains one of the four subaerial volcanoes within Solomon Islands, although there are no historical records of eruptions from this volcano, e.g. Pettersen *et al.* 1999. In 1993 the central volcanic crater of Ove on Simbo began to emit larger volumes of sulphurous gases than normal, causing alarm to the local population. This report highlights this event from a communication of geoscience standpoint. In this example the communication was very different from the long-term, well-planned land-access seeking communication exercise as described in example 1. This is an example of reactive and responsive communication as part of crisis management. The example throws up a range of lessons learned, particularly in the area of inappropriate communication style and then managing a way out of what had become a rather negative communication situation.

Background

Simbo (Fig. 3) is an island of some 14 km^2, approximately $7\frac{1}{2}$ km from north to south with a maximum width of about $2\frac{1}{2}$ km. It comprises two areas of high ground, up to about 330 m high, linked by a low-lying isthmus of raised coral reef. The hill masses, both north and south, are composed of old volcanic cones of andesite lava and tuff, which exhibit various degrees of activity and freshness of preservation of volcanic features. The northern half of the island is most subdued in topography and contains few obvious signs of recent volcanic activity. The southern half of the island has a more rugged topography and is the site of a number of active fumaroles and hot springs. One such centre of fumarolic activity is centred on Ove crater and Ove Lake at the southwestern tip of the island. It was there that villagers noted unusual activity on the afternoon of Thursday, 11 February.

First notification of activity and assessment

On 11 February 1993 at 19:40 h a radio–telephone message was received from the Honourable Lilo (a Simbo Chief and Member of Parliament) in Simbo by Dr. R. Addison (R.A.), the then Director of Geology, advising him of the onset of volcanic activity at Ove crater at the southern end of the island of Simbo. The report described activity commencing at 15:00 h with volumes of black smoke, a strong smell of sulphur, explosions and fire.

The Director notified the Permanent Secretary of Natural Resources, the Chief Administrative Officer (CAO) of the National Disaster Council and the Senior Geologist of the Geology Division.

Following that, R.A. went to the Solomon Telekom Headquarters to obtain a better reception

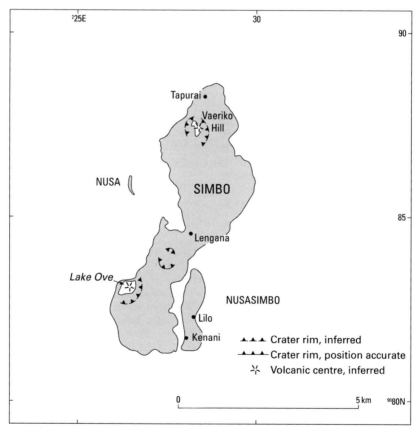

Fig. 3. Map of Simbo, showing locations of the main volcanic area and key centres of population. Margin grid numbers refer to topographic grid, UTM zone 57, Mercator projection.

of the communication and thereby a better understanding of the events of eruption. Reception at Solomon Telekom Headquarters was no better but sufficient information was obtained to determine that an eruption could be under way and to advise the villagers to attempt to move away from the volcano, avoiding gas or ash clouds that might drift down-wind from the crater. The Director advised the villagers through the Honourable Lilo to move to the north of the island, believing that the effects of the eruption would be less severe in that area.

Following this communication the Director contacted the Solomon Islands National Disaster Council (NDC) and subsequently joined the team now assembled at the NDC Headquarters, by which time the NDC had established communications link with the island and had confirmed that a eruption appeared to be in progress. The Director of Geology briefed the NDC as to the report received by him and the likely effects and time scale of an eruption should the incident be confirmed and an eruption have commenced.

The Director's advice was that events and phenomena reported by villagers were consistent with the onset of an eruption and that Simbo was regarded as dormant but still potentially active and dangerous. He advised that gas clouds emanating from a volcanic eruption, even at an early stage, are potentially life-threatening. His further advice was that a visual inspection of the eruption was essential in evaluating the immediate risk to the inhabitants of the island and in assessing the need to evacuate the population from all or part of the island. The CAO (NDC) suggested that if the Director would be willing to visit the island, a helicopter could be arranged to leave Honiara at 05.00 on the following day, 12 February. The Director agreed that he and the then Senior Mapping Geologist of the Geology Division (Mike Petterson, referred to henceforth as M.G.P.) would be prepared to carry out an inspection of the volcano, and the arrangements for the visit were finalized.

It was also decided that the Director of Geology and the NDC should broadcast advice to the islanders of Simbo via radio through the Solomon Islands Broadcasting Corporation (SIBC).

Response to the Simbo alarm

At 21.15 h arrangements were made to broadcast advice and instructions to the villagers of Simbo using the SIBC. This broadcast was issued at 21.30–22.00 h; a transcript of the advice given by the Director of Geology is given below.

Text of radio broadcast by the Director of Geology, Solomon Islands Broadcasting Corporation, 11 February 1993

'Having received notification of the possibility of the initiation of an eruption of Ove volcano on the island of Simbo, I would like to advise on appropriate action that they should take.

'My advice is that villagers living close to the crater, in settlements such as Ove, Kenana and Lilo should prepare to move northwards away from the eruption. For the time being areas to the north should be safe, especially if sheltered by high ground.

'If the present style of activity intensifies during the next few hours, villagers should attempt to leave the area of the eruption. Seek shelter in the lee of hills, cliffs, or caves; houses will provide no protection. Any river valleys that drain directly from the crater should be avoided; the valleys could channel lava, ash flows or gas flows and could be extremely dangerous.

'If activity becomes explosive, ash and volcanic bombs will be carried down-wind from the crater. Safer areas will lie up-wind of the eruption.

'It is expected that the eruption may become more intense but this is most likely to happen over a period of one or two days. Even if the eruption weakens the villagers should remain prepared to evacuate the whole island.'

Following the broadcast the Director of Geology returned home to prepare for the visit to Simbo. At 23.00 h R.A. received a further message from the NDC advising him that villagers were complaining through radio messages of increased smoke and fumes causing nausea, chest pains and stinging eyes. The ground was reported to have been shaken by seismic shocks. R.A. advised that the villagers should move northwards away from the crater, avoiding passing through the clouds of smoke, and should use wet cloths as masks to prevent inhalation of the gas and smoke.

At 04:40 h, Friday, 12 February, NDC transport collected the Director and M.G.P. from their homes at Naha, Honiara and conveyed them to Honiara Airport. The flight to Simbo took off from Henderson Field (Honiara Airport) at 06:00 h carrying R. Addison, Director of Geology, J. Hasiau, Chief Administrative Officer of the National Disaster Council, M. Petterson, Senior Geologist of the Ministry of Natural Resources and G. Siapu, Information Officer for the National Disaster Council. The flight reached Simbo at 09:00 h.

The flight over the volcano consisted of a number of circuits during which video film and still photographs were taken and observations and notes were made. Following the circuits of the volcano the helicopter landed at Nusa Simbo and later at Lengana to interview villagers about the events of the previous few days and to give them advice on the likely process of events associated with a volcanic eruption and the steps that they should take to minimize the risks to themselves and their families. The interviews and briefing sessions ended at 12:00 h, at which stage the pilot of the helicopter requested that the return to Honiara should be made to avoid being caught in storm conditions that he had been advised of on the route back to Henderson Field. Although the events at this time are understandable in the sense that this was a response to an emergency, a serious communication error was made at this point. From the viewpoint of the Simbo residents, who are island-bound and close to what was perceived to be significantly increased volcanic activity, the sight of a number of non-Simbo people, some even obviously non-Solomon Islander, landing in a helicopter, issuing some words of reassurance and then taking off in a helicopter away from the 'danger zone' was nothing short of a public relations disaster. In hindsight, one or two members of the party should have remained behind with the Simbo community to demonstrate commitment, and to take time to discuss and further assess the situation on the ground. This communication mistake came back to 'bite' very quickly.

Volcanological report

During the approach to the island no smoke or ash cloud could be discerned, even at a relatively close distance. Only as the helicopter crossed the ridge between the two peaks on the southern half of the island could smoke or steam be seen emanating from the crater at Ove. The circuits of the crater revealed it to be lined with bleached broken rocks and to have a number of small active fumarolic vents (fissures between rocks) from which steam and smoke were issuing to be carried in low billows downwind in a northeasterly direction. The area from which most of the smoke or steam appeared to be issuing was black, as if discoloured by volcanogenic sublimates. Other vents were spaced around the circumference of the crater, below the rim. A finely dispersed cloud of smoke hung in a haze over the hill NE of Ove Lake. A moderately strong smell of sulphur dioxide was detected from within the helicopter. No suitable landing spot was seen, therefore no request to land at the crater was made.

Following the stops at Nusa Simbo and Lengana, a second series of circuits of the crater were made, during which the smoke was perceived to have thickened in consistency and to be flowing over the crater rim, down the slope of the cone, to be carried away as a ground-hugging cloud across the ridge NE of Ove Lake. At no time on either of the inspections were any flames, magma, pyroclastic debris or 'true' volcanic vent observed.

Accounts of Simbo inhabitants of the events of 11 February

Communication is, by its nature, a two-way process. It is important, not only from a scientific viewpoint, but also from a communications viewpoint, that the audience or the stakeholders are genuinely listened to. This involves active and passive listening skills. In a tradition that relies on oral rather than written history and records analysis of recent events through oral reporting and a study of kastom stories, this is not only best practice in terms of communication, but is also an excellent scientific approach, as vital information about phenomena is recorded, albeit in an unconventional manner (e.g. see below, and Petterson *et al.* (2003) for the case study relating to the the eruption history of Savo).

Account of Joseph Sione, Area Constable, Nusa Simbo. A party of tourists from Gizo visited the crater early in the day and later, a villager visiting the crater at 15:00 h, to make the daily collection of megapode eggs, reported changes in the activity. Fire was seen in the centre of the crater and the smoke had a bad smell, but no increase in the size of the crater was noticed. No ash fall was seen but a hissing noise was heard from the crater and ground tremors were felt around the village from about 18:00 h. Later the smoke and bad smell over the village made breathing difficult and painful and caused eyes to sting. All the villages on the island were affected by smoke, including Lengana, and Tapurai. This was unusual because previously no smoke had ever been seen coming from Ove crater, nor were there any kastom stories of eruptions of the volcano.

Account of the Hon Lilo, Lengana. At 15:00 h people noticed smoke and a bad smell close to the crater and at 16:00 h thick smoke had developed and the bad smell had spread across the island by 18:00 h. Mr. Lilo approached to within 200 m of the crater at 21:00 h and saw large amounts of thick smoke rising in pulsing clouds from the crater to a height of 40 to 50 m, and being carried away to the northeast by the wind. He reported a white glow around the vent. In the village he reported that it was difficult and painful to breathe and that the smoke caused eyes to sting. There had been little wind all night long. Rumbling noises had been heard in the night and these had been heard also some days previously. As a result of the reaction of the villagers to the gas and smoke, it had been decided to bring the people from the outlying villages to Lengana and prepare the canoes for an evacuation of the island. On being questioned, the Hon Lilo reported that there had been no change in the size of the crater or in the temperature of the ground, although this was apparently higher than earlier this century since people who had lived near the crater around 1900 had moved away as the ground temperature had increased. The Hon Lilo reported a kastom story of a snake that came out of the crater and crawled down to the sea.

Scientific assessment of the activity reported and witnessed on Simbo between 11 and 12 February

The appearance of the smoke and steam seen around the crater on 12 February are consistent with an increase in fumarolic type of volcanic activity. This might or might not develop further into a full eruption, with the potential to damage or destroy the island, its vegetation, fauna, villages or inhabitants. However, a number of features reported are inconsistent with the inference of an incipient eruption. If fire was seen then an open vent would have been expected to be present and pyroclastic debris would have been ejected from the vent. Neither of these phenomena were seen. A red rather than a white glow, as reported, would be expected from a low-temperature eruption. Assuming, however, that these features had been inaccurately reported, and relying on the phenomena observed during the over-flight, it was concluded that an eruption could be commencing but that it was still in an early phase, and that steps should be taken to prepare the villagers in the event that eruption would proceed into a destructive phase.

Advice to villagers given on 12 February and follow-up communications during the days after 12 February

In both villages similar advice was given, to the following effect.

(1) The activity noted on 11 and 12 February could proceed to a full volcanic eruption or alternatively it could decline to the earlier level.

(2) If the activity continues to a full eruption it will do so gradually, probably over a period of 3–5 days, and significant stages in the development of the eruption would warn villagers with sufficient time for emergency procedures to be implemented.

(3) The steps taken on the previous evening had been entirely correct.

(4) As activity seemed to be lower now than on the previous night, villagers should return to their homes but remain on stand-by. They should prepare a few belongings and supplies of food and water for a possible evacuation, and ensure that the whereabouts of family members were known at all times.

(5) In the event of a return to heightened activity, villagers should again gather at Lengana to await further developments and instruction on evacuation.

Villagers were advised on the phenomena that would be seen or heard in the event of an eruption commencing and that regular observation of the crater and surrounding area should be made and changes in the activity noted and reported to the NDC and the SIGS. The indications of an eruption include: (1) renewed smell of sulphurous gas in the atmosphere around the villages; (2) rise in ground temperature around the crater; (3) rise in the temperature of hot springs and fumaroles, or change in their appearance or smells; (4) increase in ground tremors, particularly if repeated and periodic; (5) noticeable noise, rumbling or explosions from the crater; (6) changes in the level of the water or the shoreline of Ove Lake. On detecting any of these signs villagers should prepare to congregate at Lengana. If conditions worsen then they should gather at Lengana and await evacuation.

Phenomena that normally appear later in the process of an eruption and that if detected, would prompt immediate gathering at Lengana in preparation for evacuation include: (1) any fire or red glow issuing from the crater; (2) any eruption of volcanic ash or debris from the vent; (3) any eruption of lava from the old or new vents; (4) any very dramatic increase in the precursor signs of an eruption mentioned above.

Villagers were advised of the importance of prompt action. The villagers had already experienced the spread of a gas cloud over the island and the danger of such an occurrence was emphasized. They were advised that domestic and wild animals would show early signs of being affected by gas clouds, and that they should be observed if renewed activity was suspected. In moving about the island during an eruption they were advised of the dangers of travelling below the path of a smoke or gas cloud that would be carried in the direction of the prevailing wind. An attempt should be made to leave the area by other routes.

In evacuation they were advised to restrict the number of possessions that they should attempt to carry. If in doubt about the steps they should take they were advised to err on the side of caution. In the event of the occurrence of conditions that caused them grave concern they were advised that they were at full liberty to evacuate themselves to any island where they might expect the provision of shelter and food from wantoks, prior to an official NDC evacuation.

Following the provision of this advice the NDC–MNR team boarded the helicopter and returned to Honiara.

In response to villagers' requests (following the perceived unnecessarily rapid leaving of the visiting party from Honiara by helicopter on 12 February) Simbo residents were assured that an SIGS observer would be sent to the island as soon as possible and that a seismometer would be installed to monitor volcano–seismic activity, provided that a spare instrument was available.

Actions of 13 and 14 February

At 08:30 h M.G.P. received a telephone call notifying him of increased activity at Ove crater, Simbo. The activity included loud noises from the crater and ash eruptions. He was advised that the people of the island had again gathered at Lengana in preparation for an evacuation. M.G.P. and R.A. met with the NDC in Honiara. Office records of the communications from Simbo were examined, in which it was indicated that the crater of the volcano had opened and that clouds of black smoke were being emitted. In view of the renewal of activity and the increased concerns of Simbo residents and regional community leaders, R.A. and M.G.P. offered to revisit the island with a seismologist, A. K. Papabatu, to carry out an inspection of the volcano and instal a seismometer. NDC agreed to arrange seats on the scheduled flight to Gizo and passages by military patrol boat to Simbo. The team left Honiara for Gizo at 14:30 h.

The party arrived at Gizo at 17:00 h and attended a briefing of the Western Province Disaster Committee (WPDC). Later the party boarded the patrol boat *Savo* for the trip to Simbo, arriving there at around 20:00 h, after nightfall. At that time it was just discernible that activity at the crater was less intense than on the previous visit. Being unable to make any further observations the party instructed the boat to proceed to the jetty at Lengana for the night. A trip ashore confirmed that no noxious gases could be detected and that wildlife around the village appeared to be unaffected. The party spent the night on board the patrol boat *Savo*, as no accommodation could be provided in the village because of the need for accommodation of the villagers from Nusa Simbo.

On Sunday, 14 February, seismologist A. Papabatu installed the seismometer in the school store at Lengana and commenced the recording of the seismic activity of the island. Examination of the early recordings revealed no signs of volcano–seismic activity. At about 09:00 h a party including Geological Survey staff and representatives of the Western Province Disaster Committee, led by L. Wickham, boarded the motor vessel *Heliboe* to sail around the headland to the Ove area, where they transferred to a small boat to land at the northern end of Ove Lake.

Volcanological account of the inspection of Ove crater and its environs

On the approach to the crater along the lakeside, villagers indicated areas of forest on the eastern shore and ridge that had been discoloured. The discoloration appeared to be a burning caused by heat or acids dissolved in steam, as it was restricted to the area of forest beneath the path of the plume of smoke and gas observed during the flight on 11 February. Similar discoloration was later seen on leaves of trees and plants around the crater. Trees in that area were shedding dead leaves in large numbers. These effects indicate the extent and harmful nature of the clouds of gas, steam and smoke. Wildlife in the area of the lake and crater did not appear to have been affected. Measurements were taken of the temperature of hot springs and fumaroles at the southern end of Ove Lake and beside the sea at the foot of the volcanic cone; the temperature in both localities was 102 °C, similar to the temperature recorded by Geological Survey staff in 1955. Activity at the crater was very much reduced from that witnessed on the helicopter flight, so that an approach to the top of the crater was not judged to be hazardous.

From the rim of the crater it was observed that the dimensions of the crater were, as far as could be judged, similar to those recorded in earlier years, 40 m by 50 m in plan and 40 m deep. A number of small steam fumaroles (at least five) were still active but these did not pose a threat to the observers. The temperature recorded at an upper fumarole, close to the crater rim, was 100 °C. The walls and floor of the crater consisted of bleached and fractured rock and rock debris, altered by hydrothermal activity and coated, thickly in places, by sulphur deposits of varying colours (yellow, red and black). The fumaroles were being emitted from narrow fissures through and between the broken rocks.

A large area of the crater wall on the north side of the rim, estimated at about 20 m high by about 15 m wide, appeared to be blackened and altered. In this area the sulphur appeared to have been burnt and melted. Patches and pools of black and yellow sulphur appear to have flowed and solidified in small pools and lobate flows in hollows of the wall (Fig. 4). Other areas exhibited an etched and eroded karstic appearance, as if dissolved or melted. In overhanging areas of the wall the sulphur had formed small stalactites. Small patches of black sulphur appeared to have been thrown through the air to spatter on the rocks below and trickle downwards until cool enough to solidify. The activity that generated these effects seemed to have been most intense near the middle to upper parts of the north wall of the crater; material cooled and solidified as it flowed down to the base of the crater. Clearly, the conditions that generated the phenomena noted on the crater wall no longer pertained. All of the material observed was cool and solidified. The cause of the melting

Fig. 4. Remobilization of sulphur deposits within Ove crater, Simbo. Remobilization and burning of sulphur deposits within the crater was the most likely cause of the volcanic incident in 1993.

and burning is not known, However, the events at the crater almost certainly were the cause of the clouds of steam and smoke that burnt the vegetation around the crater and caused the distress and alarm among the villagers. The description of the symptoms felt by villagers is consistent with the inhalation of sulphur dioxide gas. One observation of particular note is that the volcanic activity died down after heavy rainfall.

During the following days Mr. Papabatu continued to monitor the seismometer, and on 16 and 18 February he visited the crater to make further observations of activity and measure the temperatures of fumaroles. The only seismic activity recorded during that period was tectonic in origin, and temperatures of fumaroles and hot springs were normal at around 100–102 °C.

Scientific conclusions

During the days of 11 and 12 February a significant event occurred at Ove crater, which on first inspection by helicopter and investigation appeared to be an increase in fumarolic activity that could be the precursor to a volcanic eruption of some size. The event resulted in the passage of a cloud of gas-charged steam and smoke over the villages to the north and west, carried by the prevailing west or SW wind. The event was relatively short-lived and by 14 February had ceased, the level of the activity at the volcano then being normal. It was concluded that this should allow the villagers to return to their homes and a stand-down of emergency and relief operations.

The true nature of the event is difficult to determine. Certain evidence of villagers is inconsistent with an increase in fumarolic activity; the report of flames and sparks, the report of a white light. These would be consistent with a full volcanic eruption, of which there is no geological evidence at the crater. Alternatively, the melting of the sulphur might have been caused by high-temperature fumarolic activity but some continued high temperatures would have been expected to be evident in the area of the crater. This was not the case.

Some villagers enquired as to the possibility that a fire lit by tourists could have caused a volcanic eruption and this suggestion was further investigated. Simple experiments carried out at the Ministry of Natural Resources indicate that the sulphur deposits from Ove crater could be ignited by a flame, producing a yellow or red melt that would flow like oil or wax and carry the flame with it; at higher temperatures (*c.* 200 °C) the liquid sulphur becomes black and extremely fluid, and retains its colour when cooled. Such an ignition by fire on the crater rim could spread quickly by the melting of the sulphur and flow of the burning melt down the wall of the crater. Such a scenario would be consistent with the flames and the white glow seen by the villagers (sulphur burns with a blue flame). This would also be consistent with the rapid end of the event in the rains of 12 and 13 February, the lack of a temperature rise in the hot springs and the lack of heating of the rocks of the crater. It is therefore concluded that a small fire lit on the top of the crater rim could have ignited a sizeable sulphur fire and that this resulted in the clouds of gas, steam and smoke. The only unexplained phenomena are the ground shakes and the rumbling noises reported by the villagers.

As a precautionary measure a seismologist was stationed temporarily on the island to instal and maintain a seismometer and train villagers in the maintenance of the equipment. No volcanic related seismicity was recorded.

Advice was given to representatives of the village communities with regard to the continuation of their own monitoring activities, and is presented below.

'It is important that the people of Simbo are aware of the signs from the volcano that activity is increasing. Such signs should be reported to the Solomon Islands Geological Survey. These features are:

'Any increase in the temperature of the ground around the crater or elsewhere or increase in the temperature of the fumaroles or hot springs.

'Any dramatic change in the water level of Lake Ove or apparent tilting of the shoreline.

'Any increase in the amount of steam, smoke or gas such as was experienced over the last few days. In reporting these features islanders should attempt to describe the height and density of the clouds and if any forceful lateral blasting of steam or smoke was visible.

'Islanders should be aware that gas could be emitted from the crater silently and they should always observe the behaviour of wild and domestic animals, particularly captive or domestic birds, that will show serious effects of gassing much earlier than human beings.

'Any continuous or repeated high frequency earthquakes, any explosions or rumbling noises.

'Any widespread discoloration or burning of vegetation around the crater.

'Any fall of dust or ash from clouds over the volcano.

'Any red glow or red flames from the crater should be noted and reported.

'If these continue, preparations should be made to evacuate outlying villages and assemble at appointed spots. Early activity is more likely to be gentle at first and to intensify over a period of a few days before becoming a serious threat to life. As the eruption intensifies the level of the alert will increase and assisted evacuation will be carried out only on the instruction of the National Disaster Council. Any villagers who prefer to leave the island temporarily during earlier stages of an eruption would of course be free to do so.'

Example 2: lessons learned

Key scientific messages were conveyed to the Government of Solomon Islands, the Government of the Western Province, the Minister for Natural Resources and community leaders. They included the following main points.

(1) In view of the recognition that, although the present incident was not likely to have been related to an increase in volcanic activity nevertheless the potential existed for some future eruption, it was recommended that further evaluation and long-term monitoring of the volcano be instituted by the Ministry of Natural Resources. This should include a quarterly examination of activity at the crater and the installation of a permanent seismic monitoring station at Lengana.

(2) Quarterly reports of activity should be provided to NDC, Western Provincial Government, and Simbo Community Representatives.

(3) A volcanic hazard and risk assessment should be carried out for Simbo and this should be integrated into an evacuation plan that it was recommended should be prepared by the National Disaster Council.

(4) Copies of the hazard and risk assessment should be provided to Western Provincial Government and Simbo Community Representatives.

(5) Public awareness of the potential risks involved in a volcanic eruption should be improved by further broadcasts on SIBC and by audio-visual presentations to communities on the island. This should also be carried out on the island of Savo.

Some of these messages were heard and others were not. There has been no progress with respect to a volcanic hazard assessment of Simbo, few reports of activity were ever written, and no permanent seismic station was ever installed. The one area that has received some attention is in raising public awareness and improving education in relation to geohazards. (One example of this, in the case of Savo, Solomon Islands, is given briefly below but has also been described in detail by Cronin *et al.* (2004).) The April 2007 tsunami event hit the Western Province including Simbo and relatively few lives (around 50) were lost because people were prepared with respect to the advance warning signs of tsunamis approaching (particularly after the devastating Indian Ocean tsunami of Boxing Day 2004) and most headed for higher ground.

Overall the 1993 volcanic incident on Simbo was well handled in terms of communication. The most important messages were communicated by radio, through community leaders and directly at public meetings involving as many Simbo residents as could be reached (Fig. 5). The feedback from the residents was very positive. The National Disaster Council were well prepared at a national and regional level, and once the event was labelled as 'significant' it triggered a series of pre-arranged communication and operational activities. Local community representatives were involved at every level; this reflects the strength of Melanesian society and the manner in which it is structured: people have to be consulted and leaders leave people out at their peril. The one major error (with the benefit of hindsight) was the rapid deployment of an 'expert team' by helicopter with only a brief consultation period allowed between 'experts' and the local community. The whole timbre of this style of communication ('outsider',

Fig. 5. Community meeting on Simbo with local residents attempting to explain, as fully as possible, likely scenarios with respect to the volcano and future activity. The local community was discontented that the geologists arrived and left by helicopter, and insisted they returned to spend more time with the community.

'experts' arriving to speak to rural village residents using a helicopter as a means of transport) was rather incongruent and ineffective in terms of communication. The hidden message could have been interpreted as 'bigmen arriving from outside through hi-tech transport and discharging only their statutory duties'. In contrast, the follow-up visit whereby people arrived by boat and spent days with the local community in a range of public and private meetings, with one scientist remaining behind with a seismometer for a further 4 weeks, proved to be very effective and appreciated all round. The latter form of communication took account particularly of the key stakeholders (the Simbo residents) and the style of communication they appreciate the most (several open public meetings, allowing many people to contribute and allowing a considerable amount of time for debate).

Example 3: Gold Ridge mine, Central Guadalcanal

This example is discussed briefly here from a communication viewpoint. (Readers are directed to Tolia & Petterson (2005) for further details. Some of the account below is abridged from that paper.) The Gold Ridge mine represents the largest single private investment ever in the country. It remains the only medium-scale mine in Solomon Islands and is a spearhead for mining investment. The Government of Solomon Islands had to get the communication strategy right. Many things were dependent on effective two-way communication. The strong attachment to land culture becomes particularly strong in cases where new money is derived from some form of new land use, in this case mineral extraction. Key issues include identification of land ownership, land compensation rights, royalties, resettlement and rehousing, provision of new social welfare facilities and infrastructure, employment and training or education opportunities, etc.

Communication stakeholders included the national government, the regional government of Guadalcanal, the mining company, landowners, and community representatives. A number of tribes were involved from the community side and it was imperative that all were included. The Solomon Islands Government set up a special Gold Ridge task force whose mission was to attract this major investment consensually and fairly. A sustainable minerals approach was adopted in the sense that all key factors of sustainable development were taken into account: sustainability, the economy, politics, environmental protection, social factors, and identification of lasting benefits to a wide range of stakeholders.

The various communities were encouraged to set up representative groups and leaders. The Government acted as the 'go-between' between the mining company and the affected communities in an effort to ensure fair play. The optimal solution was fair, reasonable and transparent compensation for landowners and affected communities, and an equitable deal with the mining company that allowed the company to make a reasonable profit whilst the Solomon Islands exchequer also benefited. This was a tough challenge and involved many hours, days and weeks of painstaking public meetings at a range of levels, negotiations with key decision-makers on all sides, public education and awareness campaigns, numerous radio broadcasts and one-to-one meetings.

The Solomon Islands Government strongly encouraged the company to be patient and not to move too quickly. Perhaps more than any other factor this helped the success of the communication process. The end goal was the attraction of the mine but only if consensual agreement could be reached with the local tribes and safeguards were in place for resettlement, compensation, continuing royalty or production payments, and environmental protection.

Gold Ridge, Central Highlands, Guadalcanal, Solomon Islands

Gold Ridge is situated in the geographical centre of Guadalcanal. Alluvial gold was first discovered in placer beach deposits by European adventurers, who first set foot on the island in 1568 (Guppy 1887) and subsequently named the islands Solomon Islands after the proverbial wealth of the Biblical King Solomon. It was not until the earlier part of the twentieth century that geologists began to unravel the hard rock epithermal gold source of the placer gold, although serious exploration began only in the 1970s and 1980s. It was not until 1994, however, that a mining company seriously moved the exploration target forwards to a viable mining proposition, with Saracen Minerals and then Ross Mining taking the deposit forwards to a full-scale mine, which poured its first gold in August 1997. This became Solomon Islands' first medium-scale mine and a landmark in the development of this young, independent country.

Both Saracen Minerals and Ross Mining adopted highly creditable approaches to community interaction and negotiation prior to mine development. The companies recognized the strong sense of land ownership and land attachment present in traditional Solomon Island culture. From some perspectives traditional Melanesian lifestyles are reasonably true examples of 'sustainable development', with human lifestyles being in harmony with the delicate rainforest, coast, and coral reef and lagoon environment. Melanesian people have safeguarded these environments for at least 50 000 years.

The Mines and Minerals Department and in particular the Director of Geology (D. Tolia) closely advised Saracen Minerals and Ross Mining at every development step that led to the final mine. In particular, there were protracted negotiations between company, government and landowners over a 3 year period. Even establishing who the rightful landowners were was a difficult exercise, as nothing is written down in traditional Solomon Islands custom. Establishing land ownership became closely linked to the strong oral history tradition (embedded in kastom stories) of the islanders and their precise knowledge of the location of historical sites of cultural significance (e.g. 'Tambu' sites of high religious, historical and cultural significance). Once landowners were identified, tripartite landowner– or community–government–company negotiations and communication strategies ensued. There were many complex issues that required resolution, some of which are highlighted above, and it is beyond the scope of this paper to discuss every issue (see Tolia & Petterson 2005, for further details). It is instructive, however, to consider a few key issues.

Perhaps the biggest issue was arriving at a consensual way forwards for mining to go ahead. Many factors were considered, including royalty payments and compensation, rehousing of families located within the mining area, and minimizing environmental and community impacts. Royalty payments and compensation were the most difficult issue to resolve and are always the source of continuing discussion. Melanesians have a particularly sensitized consciousness relating to compensation, and a failure to arrive at consensual agreement in this area can result in mining plans being totally abandoned. Compensation is paid to exchange 'capital' tied up in land (e.g. land ownership and land rental) and land-based economic activities (such as farming, fishing, etc.) for an agreed monetary figure. This is particularly difficult with mining, as it is almost inevitable that some areas will not be remediated after mining to the point where there is a net zero impact on the land and its ecosystem.

The local Guadalcanal inhabitants had to be compensated for the loss of their traditional land rights (land ownership, hunting, access to 'Tambu' sites, etc.), their traditional houses and villages (this case involved dealing with Highland bush villages, which are becoming more of a rarity in Solomon Islands as most people move to the coast), their traditional way of making a living (largely through subsistence agriculture) and a particularly sensitive subject involved small-scale mining (the villagers have panned the rivers that drain the Gold Ridge deposit for gold). Remarkably, consensual deals were struck and fair and realistic levels of compensation were achieved. Local small-scale miners agreed to give up their rights to river-panning within an agreed area. Villagers affected by mining were rehoused in custom-designed new villages some 20 km further west and on the plains adjacent to the coast. The villagers were closely consulted in house and village design, with community suggestions being acted upon by company-contracted architects and builders. The objective was to reproduce the villagers' original lifestyle and community structure as far as possible. There were perceived 'improvements' such as improved quality of housing, and ready access to health, religious and education facilities (purpose-built schools, churches and health centres were built to service the villagers), although there were also perceived losses that included resettlement in the lowlands (much hotter than the Highlands of Central Guadalcanal) and the need to mix with tribes that the Gold Ridge communities were not used to mixing with. It would be difficult to deny that, in material terms at least the villagers had benefited as a result of mining becoming a part of their way of life. However, it was a big challenge for the relocated communities to settle into the Low-lands adjacent to the coast and the radical change in lifestyle. The sustainability test would be addressed only after a number of years of living in new communities that have developed a new economic base (thus manifesting capital transfer from their original land-based economy and mineral wealth to a different but lasting economy). Unfortunately, ethnic unrest between 2000 and 2003 (unrelated to the mine) caused the mine to close and the resettlement village to be destroyed, leaving the specific sustainability question open.

Royalty payments included not only landowners but also government. In the case of Solomon Islands and Gold Ridge this involved both National Government and Provincial Government. Negotiations included the Central Province (which has jurisdiction over Guadalcanal) and the national Solomon Islands Government. It was in the interests of the company to ensure that both government parties signed up to an agreement that distributed royalty payments in a fair and equitable manner. Subsequent rancour between the Central Province and National Governments could be a threat to the mine. Solomon Islands is a poor but highly democratic country with decision-making often devolved to very local levels. This reflects traditional tribal customs, which value highly the decision-making powers of single tribes and language groups. Thus there is a healthy respect between National and Provincial Government and between the traditional tribal methods of government and more recent 'Western-style' political structures. However, this healthy respect cannot always be matched in terms of funding, as provincial devolved

government can be an expensive exercise and in the Solomon Islands there is precious little money to be shared within government circles. In spite of this, a consensual agreement was finally struck and the mine went forwards with agreed proportions of royalty divided between Provincial and National Governments.

Other key issues revolved around environmental impact. The Gold Ridge mine is situated within a pristine world-class tropical island rainforest environment. It is a region of high relief, steep slopes, high rainfall, occasional cyclones, and high levels of seismicity and landslip-induced geo-hazards (Hackman 1980). Both Saracen Minerals and Ross Mining engaged in a variety of complex baseline studies, which provided an inventory of the natural pre-mining environment. These studies focused on a wide range of phenomena including baseline geochemistry, aquatic and terrestrial fauna and flora, anthropogenic and archaeological heritage, and community lifestyles. Ross Mining took over responsibility for mine development and finalized a plan that involved a number of high-specification tailing dams and lagoons with the objective of capturing and redeveloping all mine tailings and minimizing output to the local rivers. Stringent monitoring programmes were designed to measure impact, and the local community was involved in regular discussions. Ross Mining devised a range of options for post-mine land reme-diation and redevelopment, although these respon-sibilities passed over to a third company (Delta) when Ross sold the Gold Ridge mine in 1999.

In conclusion, it can be argued that the pre-mine and early mining stage (1994–1999) of the devel-opment of Gold Ridge is an example of best prac-tice in terms of key stakeholder dialogue and involvement, and the achievement of consensual agreements. Unfortunately, a period of civil and ethnic unrest within Solomon Islands (problems that were external to mining activities) closed the mine in 2000: the mine remains closed at the time of writing, although the Solomon Islands Govern-ment is currently working hard to reopen the mine.

Example 3: lessons learned

This whole communication process was largely very successful by any performance measurement. It was ambitious, to say the least, to begin mining in a remote rainforest location involving commu-nities totally unaware of mining and its impact. It is true that mining has become common in Solomon Islands' neighbouring country, Papua New Guinea, but to the tribes of Central Guadalcanal the Papua New Guinea mines could almost be in another universe.

There were a number of keys to the 'winning' of this communication strategy. Solomon Islanders with a deep understanding of Central Guadalcanal culture designed the whole process in close consultation with the incoming 'foreign' culture (i.e. the mining company). It would have been much more difficult for the mining company on its own, even with the best will in the world, to successfully discharge this ambitious communication feat. The recognition of land ownership issues and compensation issues being fundamental to the success of the communication strategy was another 'win'. Patient attempts to create and/or encourage representative stakeholder groups from all quarters (community, government and company) were vital. An open, even-handed, transparent and fair process with clear and well-explained rules was a fundamental imperative. Finally, patience was a very important factor; years were spent in communicating and negotiating.

Example 4: raising awareness of volcanic hazards, Savo

This example is an abridged version (with a communication focus) of Cronin et al. (2004). Readers are directed to this paper for further details.

Savo is an andesitic to dacitic stratovolcano situated 35 km NW of Honiara. It is an approximately circular volcano measuring some 6 km in diameter. Recent eruptions have been dominated by crater-centred block and ash flows and lahars. All the c. 3000 population of Savo live on coastal plains formed by the accumulation of block and ash flow and lahar deposits, and are vulnerable to future volcanic activity. Eruptions on Savo could also affect other islands and tsunamis could be a significant geohazard. As the country's capital town of Honiara (containing a high percentage of the nation's vital infrastructure and population) is close to, and in direct line of sight of Savo, it is at a significant risk from eruptions and volcanic-induced tsunami hazards. During previous eruption episodes Honiara did not exist.

Two of the authors (M.G.P. and S.J.C.) have worked on Savo since 1992 and have visited and studied the island many times. Readers are directed to Petterson et al. (2003) for further reading with respect to the geology and volcanology of Savo. Scientific studies of Savo have incorporated a range of communication study methodols in recognition that kastom history and wisdom captures information about previous eruptions that are unrecorded elsewhere (Toba 1993; Petterson et al. 2003). Communication with the people of Savo has thus been central to all activities on Savo.

Education of the local people with respect to potential geohazards has occurred over the past few decades, but only in a rather ad hoc fashion. This perceived knowledge and awareness gap led to the design and implementation of a week-long workshop, funded by SOPAC in Honiara and on Savo in 1999. Readers are directed to Cronin et al. (2004) for a full account of the thinking and philosophy, as well as the outcomes of this workshop. The experience is reported in abridged form here with a focus on the communication techniques used, the activities undertaken, the key stakeholders that were communicated with, and the outcomes.

The workshop week was designed along the educational model of 'participatory rural appraisal' (Chambers 1994, 1997; Bar-On & Prinsen 1999), which aims to actively involve all key stakeholders with respect to a particular issue through a range of pedagogical techniques (teaching sessions; practical sessions; scenario modelling; mapping of key 'value holdings' such as water supply, land, houses, etc.; estimations of value; activities to determine priorities; assessments of risk, vulnerability and mitigation, etc.). The aim is to involve in particular those members of the community who usually do not have a voice, in this case the women. This has to be done sensitively, as it is not always possible to involve, for example, women in every activity as it goes against kastom. However, the workshop facilitators tried to involve women wherever possible.

The workshop was divided into two halves: a 3 day session in a motel in Honiara followed by a 3 day session on-island in Savo. The Honiara sessions were all-male affairs (Fig. 6), but the on-island sessions involved female participants, as much as possible. Representative stakeholders with respect to the volcanic hazard theme of the workshop included: Savo Chiefs; members of the Savo Provincial Government; Central Province planners and administrators; National Government planners; National Disaster Council officials; a health–water quality officer; a representative of the Red Cross; a representative of the Church of Melanesia; Solomon Island Geological Survey officers; and interaction with around 40% of the population of Savo in one form or another. The Honiara sessions were classroom based: largely a mixture of presentations and practical 'what if scenarios' and 'hazard, asset, risk and mitigation assessments'. On-island sessions involved field work focusing on risk, hazard, assets and mitigation, and community-wide workshops that involved teaching sessions, listening sessions and practical sessions. The practical sessions divided the community along gender lines in sensitivity to local kastom but also as a way of directly involving the women and recording their 'mind maps' and thoughts on

Fig. 6. The Honiara-based initial sessions for the 1999 Savo volcanic hazards workshop.

a range of issues, which are very different from the mens' 'mind maps'. Workshops were held at three geographical centres on the island. At each centre all surrounding villages were invited to attend. We estimated we reached something like 40% of the population of Savo through these activities.

Key pedagogical aims of the workshop were: (1) to raise awareness, educate and inform; (2) to gather information, opinion, and facts and figures; (3) to encourage community-led and community-participation methods, dialogue and solutions; (4) to end with a series of recommendations that would embed a community-focused programme of activities with respect to volcanic hazard awareness on Savo, in Honiara and beyond.

Key tangible results of the workshop included the involvement of a large number of people and all essential stakeholder groups. It allowed market testing of hazard assessment maps of Savo in terms of understanding by the general population. It generated a set of highly valuable data, facts and figures relating to: resource vulnerability; risk mitigation strategies; volcanic monitoring (involving the local population and geologists); emergency and hazard mitigation tasks and responsibility identification should an eruption occur; volcano-related kastom knowledge; mapping of resources essential to village livelihoods from a female and male perspective; community-based hazard mitigation operational plans. It also produced recommendations for maturing ideas presented at the workshop.

Example 4: lessons learned

The Savo example is a good case study with respect to involving ideas and thinking from rural development education experts. The focus is on community involvement and community-led education as opposed to 'expert'- or 'teacher'-led education programmes. Key stakeholders are identified, as are under-represented parts of the community (e.g. women in this case). Strategies are developed to involve all members of the community and give them equal weight. Respect for local knowledge and wisdom as well as custom is paramount to success. Overall the workshops were a success. The programmes were not as community-led as they could have been, as there was not enough time set aside to win over the population and reduce levels of shyness and self-consciousness, particularly amongst the women. There was insufficient time set aside for the exercise; ideally the whole process should probably take 3–4 weeks for the workshops, with a number of follow-up sessions in the following year or so. Recommendations from the workshop were not followed up, as it was unfortunate that widespread ethnic tension affected Solomon Islands after the workshop. However, the workshop is a possible model for future community communication engagement and the fact it that this approach has been formally published (Cronin *et al.* 2004) may help others to make progress in this vital area of communicating geoscience to indigenous communities.

Conclusions

This paper documents four case studies from Solomon Islands with respect to communicating geoscience to indigenous peoples. The main lessons learned from this analysis of the case studies in the context of Solomon Islands and Melanesia are as follows.

(1) Involve local people in any communication strategy.

(2) Get to know the indigenous people you are to communicate with as well as you can in terms of culture, customs, value systems, language and politics.

(3) Involve indigenous people at every level of the communication, from earliest planning to post-communication evaluation; ensure stakeholders and representatives are correctly identified and be as inclusive as possible.

(4) Clearly define the aims and objectives of the communication, the key messages to be conveyed and the desired outcome.

(5) Design evaluation criteria to assess success or failure and effectiveness; give the process sufficient time (very important).

(6) Where possible, design and implement follow-up communication programmes; share knowledge and results and engage with other workers in the field so that communication processes can become ever more appropriate, customized and relevant.

The authors respectfully acknowledge the help and support of Solomon Islanders throughout the country. This work is a summary of many experiences across the country that would have been impossible without the help, interest and generosity of local people.

References

BAR-ON, A. A. & PRINSEN, G. 1999. Planning, communities and empowerment. An introduction to participatory rural appraisal. *International Social Work*, **42**, 277–294.

BRUNDTLAND, G. (ed.) 1987. *Our Common Future*. The World Commission on Environmnet and Development. Oxford University Press, Oxford.

CHAMBERS, R. 1994. Participatory rural appraisal (PRA): analysis of experience. *World Development*, **22**, 953–969.

CHAMBERS, R. 1997. *Whose Reality Counts? Putting the First Last*. IT Publications, London.

CRONIN, S. J., PETTERSON, M. G., TAYLOR, P. W. & BILIKI, R. 2004. Maximising multi-stakeholder participation and community volcanic hazard management programs; A case study from Savo, Solomon Islands. *Natural Hazards*, **33**, 105–136.

GUPPY, H. B. 1887. *The Solomon Islands—Their Geology, General Features and Suitability for Colonisation*. Swann, Sonnenschein, London.

HACKMAN, B. D. 1980. *The Geology of Guadalcanal, Solomon Islands*. Overseas Memoirs of the Institute of Geological Science, **6**.

NAITORO, J. H. 1995. *Report of the social, environmental study of Gold Ridge, Central Guadalcanal, Solomon Islands*. Solomon Islands Government Publications, Honiara.

PETTERSON, M. G., NEAL, C. R. *ET AL.* 1999. Geological and tectonic framework of Solomon Islands, SW Pacific: Crustal accretion and growth within an intra-oceanic setting. *Tectonophysics*, **301**, 35–60.

PETTERSON, M. G., CRONIN, S. J., TAYLOR, P. W., TOLIA, D., PAPABATU, A., TOBA, T. & QOPOTO, C. 2003. The eruptive history and volcanic hazards of Savo, Solomon Islands. *Bulletin of Volcanology*, **65**, 165–181.

TOBA, T. 1993. *Analysis of Savo* kastom *stories on the eruption of Savo volcano*. Seismological Unit, Water and Mineral Resources Division, Ministry of Energy Water and Mineral Resources, Honiara, Technical Report, **TR 4/93**.

TOLIA, D. & PETTERSON, M. G. 2005. The Gold Ridge Mine, Guadalcanal, Solomon Island's first gold mine: A case study in stakeholder consultation. *In*: MARKER, B., PETTERSON, M. G., McEVOY, F. & STEPHENSON, M. H. (eds) *Sustainable Mineral Operations*. Geological Society, London, Special Publications, **250**, 149–160.

Framing volcanic risk communication within disaster risk reduction: finding ways for the social and physical sciences to work together

JENNI BARCLAY[1], KATHARINE HAYNES[2,3], TOM MITCHELL[4],
CARMEN SOLANA[5], RICHARD TEEUW[6], AMII DARNELL[1], H. SIAN CROSWELLER[1],
PAUL COLE[6], DAVID PYLE[7], CATHERINE LOWE[8], CARINA FEARNLEY[9] &
ILAN KELMAN[10]

[1]*School of Environmental Sciences, University of East Anglia, Norwich NR4 7TJ, UK*
(e-mail: J.Barclay@uea.ac.uk)

[2]*Risk Frontiers, Macquarie University, Sydney, N.S.W. 2109, Australia*

[3]*Centre for Risk and Community Safety, RMIT, Melbourne, Vic. 3001, Australia*

[4]*Institute for Development Studies, University of Sussex, Brighton BN1 9RE, UK*

[5]*School of Earth and Environmental Sciences, University of Portsmouth, Portsmouth PO1 3QL, UK*

[6]*Department of Geography, Environment and Disaster Management, Coventry University,*
Coventry CV1 5FB, UK

[7]*Department of Earth Sciences, University of Oxford, Oxford OX1 3PR, UK*

[8]*Department of Geography, University College London, London WC1E 6BT, UK*

[9]*Department of Earth Sciences, University College London, London WC1E 6BT, UK*

[10]*Centre for International Climate and Environmental Research, Oslo, N-0318, Norway*

Abstract: Sixteen years have passed since the last global volcanic event and more than 25 since a volcanic catastrophe that killed tens of thousands. In this time, volcanology has seen major advances in understanding, modelling and predicting volcanic hazards and, recently, an interest in techniques for reducing and mitigating volcanic risk. This paper provides a synthesis of literature relating to this last aspect, specifically the communication of volcanic risk, with a view to highlighting areas of future research into encouraging risk-reducing behaviour. Evidence suggests that the current 'multidisciplinary' approach within physical science needs a broader scope to include sociological knowledge and techniques. Key areas where this approach might be applied are: (1) the understanding of the incentives that make governments and communities act to reduce volcanic risk; (2) improving the communication of volcanic uncertainties in volcanic emergency management and long-term planning and development. To be successful, volcanic risk reduction programmes will need to be placed within the context of other other risk-related phenomena (e.g. other natural hazards, climate change) and aim to develop an all-risks reduction culture. We suggest that the greatest potential for achieving these two aims comes from deliberative inclusive processes and geographic information systems.

Volcanoes are an integral part of our natural environment with over 1000 potentially active volcanoes worldwide. Around 60 eruptions occur annually (Simkin 1993; Simkin & Siebert 2000) with over 500 million people living in volcanic risk zones (Thouret 1999). Volcanic activity is as variable as it is common, with eruptions ranging from the passive effusion of lava to violent explosions that affect global climate. Eruption longevity also ranges from a few seconds to, for example, the 2500 year continuing eruption of Stromboli in Italy. The most recent examples of wide impact eruptions were those of Mt. Pinatubo in 1991, which perturbed the global climate system; and Nevado del Ruiz in 1985, where more than 23 000 lives were lost.

The area affected by the associated volcanic phenomena varies with eruption style and intensity but is typically of the order of tens to hundreds of square kilometres (Blong 1996). This rises by several orders of magnitude when ash fall and secondary impacts (such as volcanically induced tsunami or drinking water contamination) from larger eruptions are considered. Conversely, many

From: LIVERMAN, D. G. E., PEREIRA, C. P. G. & MARKER, B. (eds) *Communicating Environmental Geoscience*. Geological Society, London, Special Publications, **305**, 163–177.
DOI: 10.1144/SP305.14   0305-8719/08/$15.00 © The Geological Society of London 2008.

volcanoes that are potentially active can remain in a state of inactivity for hundreds or even thousands of years, lowering awareness of their threat.

Although the potential impact of volcanic eruptions on the population around them is clear, considerable challenges exist in communicating those risks: it is desirable to be aware of potential activity and the threats it poses before a volcanic crisis emerges; it is desirable to know the pattern of likely activity and how and when it might change during the course of an eruption; and, of course, it is highly desirable to know when an eruption has ceased altogether. Unfortunately, even with the best possible scientific monitoring these questions are difficult to answer with a strong degree of certainty. The absence of certainty is at the heart of the difficulties involved in framing and quantifying risk in both the social and physical sciences (Stirling 2003).

Communication pathways and development of policies inherent to encouraging risk-reducing behaviour are extremely important. Repeating complex information in differing, simpler ways does not substitute for understanding why and how the message failed to have an impact. For example, in many cases the dangers may well be known to the vulnerable population, who fail to act because of other life pressures, not because of a knowledge deficit. Often also, scientific information is available but becomes distorted, misrepresented or misunderstood during its translation from scientist to local community or decision-makers. This may be because of difficulties in comprehension, but may also be related to a mismatch between the information gathered or available and the information actually needed by the population; or because of the way the information is communicated by physical scientists (volcanologists). (In this paper we refer throughout to those responsible for the gathering and interpretation of monitoring and physical science information related to the eruptive phenomena collectively as volcanologists. Volcanologists may be based close to a volcano or range of volcanoes (e.g. in a volcano observatory) but may also be academic scientists (from research institutes or university settings) from any country. Currently, volcanologists rarely have any formal training or grounding in science methodologies and epistemologies other than the traditional physical sciences (geology, physics, chemistry, mathematics, biology).

This paper summarizes some of the key findings from work that has a bearing on volcanic risk communication and embodies some of the discussion that has arisen as the result of a UK ESRC–NERC funded network (ESRC (Economic and Social Research Council) and NERC (Natural Environment Research Council) SPIDER Network (Science and Policy Interfaces for DisastER Reduction: www.spidernetwork.org)) to explore the interface between physical and social science approaches to managing disaster risk and uncertainty. The paper also analyses the methods and practices best suited to using volcanic risk communication as a tool to encouraging risk-reducing behaviour and actions before, during and after volcanic eruptions. We conclude that there is a need to mesh technical scientific information (where the focus must be on providing increasingly accurate, timely information) with appropriate communication techniques (so information is suited to the audience). This might involve more participatory social science methods designed to validate this scientific knowledge with policy-makers and local communities so as to build trust and engender ownership. This can be done most effectively when a strong network of highly motivated individuals drawn from a variety of stakeholder groups has been established before an ensuing volcanic crisis. Realistically, this requires that the risk from volcanic eruptions is viewed not as an isolated phenomenon but within the broader contexts of other (natural and man-made) risks and decisions about economic and social development.

Hazard assessment and communication

Summary of methods

Like most natural phenomena, the processes that cause and control volcanic eruptions are only partially understood and monitored. In the absence of robust physical models capturing the full range of behaviours, volcanologists rely on a range of data to determine the likely trends in activity (e.g. seismicity, deformation and gas emissions; Fischer *et al.* 1994; Cornelius & Voight 1996; Daag *et al.* 1996; Watson *et al.* 2000). The resultant data can be grouped into three sets of predictive information (Newhall 2000; Newhall & Hoblitt 2002): long-term forecasts of behaviour (e.g. when or how often is the volcano likely to erupt?); medium-term forecasts of behaviour (e.g. when it does erupt what is the likely pattern of behaviour?); and short-term forecasts of behaviour (e.g. what is likely to happen tomorrow given its activity today?). The absolute accuracy of these forecasts tends to increase as the length of forecast made becomes shorter (Newhall & Hoblitt 2002).

Much information relating to long-term probabilities is derived from empirical data relating to past activity and its impact, or data from carefully chosen analogue volcanoes. As assessment moves towards the shorter-term behaviours and changes (more commonly used during a crisis itself), there is a stronger reliance on monitoring data, where interpretation can be a mixture of empirical observation based on past activity or patterns of behaviour, or using existing theory to interpet data in terms of the underlying physical process. Inevitably these datasets, like our understanding of the physical process, are incomplete and the resulting uncertainty requires a strong subjective element of judgement in the output information.

The most usual repository for long-term forecasts of behaviour is the volcanic hazard map. A hazard map is usually a spatial representation in two dimensions of regions likely to be inundated by a variety of volcanic hazards. Traditionally, volcanic risk maps incorporate the potential extent of volcanic materials (hazard map) together with likely levels of public exposure to these hazards. More recent hazard maps represent inundation in probabilistic or semi-probabilistic terms. They have not, as yet, begun to incorporate more complex data pertaining to people's capacities to cope and adapt to volcanic impacts, with a recent paper by Marzocchi & Woo (2007) possibly the only exception. During, or in anticipation of, the short- and medium-term changes during a volcanic eruption, hazard maps are turned into risk maps and can be revised and updated as activity progresses, and may be commonly linked to an alert level (Newhall 2000). During developing crises new scientific information is often given in the form of factual statements, which can feed into a judgement by volcanologists of an accompanying alert level.

Although much of the final interpetation can be qualitative and subjective in nature, recent advances, both technological and in our understanding of physical process, are allowing volcanologists to take a more quantitative approach to warning statements (Sparks 2003). Some argue strongly for taking a more formalized approach to the process of expert judgement, a path that is currently being taken at many volcano observatories (see Newhall & Hoblitt 2002). These include the construction of event trees for use during volcanic crises (Newhall & Hoblitt 2002), the use of weighted expert elicitation (Aspinall & Cooke 1998) or Bayesian Belief Networks (Aspinall et al. 2003, 2006). These are largely used to formalize the process of collating empirical and modelled evidence, and are particularly helpful in tackling the issue of presenting insufficient and/or uncertain data. There remains, however, a considerable degree of subjectivity in most volcanic hazard assessment.

Current role of volcanologists in hazard assessment and communication

The clearest purpose of this volcanic hazard assessment is to inform the civil authorities and the public of the likelihood of a volcanic eruption and what

phenomena to expect should one occur (Sparks 2003). However, it is less clear to what extent these messages are designed to go beyond informing the civil authorities and the public into the arena of encouraging risk-reducing behaviour, particularly over long time scales. However, in his compilation of information relating to volcano warnings, Newhall (2000) summarized six criteria by which the success of a volcano warning might be evaluated: accuracy; clarity; timeliness; degree of dissemination; credibility; and degree of catalysis (for action to reduce risk). The International Association for Volcanology and Chemistry of the Earth's Interior (IAVCEI) Sub-committee for Crisis Protocols (1999) also recognized the problem of separating out the purpose of this information in their advice to 'ask civil defense and other officials whether they wish only factual information and forecasts or also suggestions of possible mitigation measures'. Many researchers (e.g. Aspinall et al. 2003; McGuire et al. 2008; Solana et al. 2008) have acknowledged that volcanologists are often asked to make immediate recommendations that have an impact on public safety in crisis situations. Taking this principle even further, Peterson (1996) advocated strongly that volcanologists need to take some responsibility for developing plans for protecting and caring for people.

In practice, the primary purpose of this information is usually some combination of education and motivation to mitigate or reduce risk. However, the extent to which volcanologists should move towards the more interventionary stance advocated by Peterson has not been debated in the literature and is an issue that we attempt to address further in this paper.

Volcanologists on communication before, during and after volcanic crises: insights from retrospective accounts of volcanic activity

In part owing to the impact that volcanoes have on local populations and the involvement of scientists, there is a good tradition of detailed commentary on communication processes during past crises by the volcanologists. These can be used to explore some of the central themes discussed above. Generally these crises can be split into two categories: those where few or no long-, medium- or short-range forecasts of potential activity were made (e.g. El Chichon 1982; Pinatubo 1991); and those where some prior knowledge was available (e.g. Mount St. Helens 1980; Montserrat 1995).

All retrospective accounts discuss the need for short- and preferably medium-range forecasts in advance of any unrest or volcanic activity. For example, in an analysis of the 1980 Mount St. Helens and 1991 Mount Pinatubo eruptions, Newhall & Punongbayan (1996) advocated the existence of 'baseline geologic and monitoring information' to give scientists an extremely valuable headstart in the process of hazard assessment. In his analysis of the communication differences during the Guadeloupe (1976) and St. Vincent (1979) crises, Fiske (1984) also concluded that improved geological and geophysical information would have enhanced communication on Guadeloupe. Once such baseline data have been obtained it is less clear how or where they should be disseminated to maximize their potential. For example, maps or information were collated and made available prior to the climactic eruption of Mount St. Helens (Crandell & Mullineaux, cited by Newhall & Punongbayan 1996); and also prior to the continuing crisis of the Soufrière Hills Volcano, Montserrat (Wadge & Isaacs 1988). However, the information was not used in any planning activities. Most retrospective accounts advocate some kind of co-operative partnership between scientists and the authorities to ensure that relevant information is presented in a meaningful way and acted upon. For example, visual media (videos, television broadcasts) have been seen to be valuable in communicating information relating to volcanic hazards (e.g. Punongbayan *et al.* 1996; Loughlin *et al.* 2002; Haynes *et al.* 2008*a*), particularly where there is little or no prior awareness of volcanic activity. However, the analysis of communication is usually to increase the potential for clear education in a crisis, and it is less clear how and when such strategies can be used for planning or to persuade people to change behaviour and thus encourage risk-reducing actions.

Inclusion of the local community in the communication process also is strongly advocated. Most researchers acknowledge that in crises volcanologists have an obligation to ensure that their information is understood and that they involve trusted members of the local society both to make decisions and to act upon the information they convey, as well as, in some instances, conveying the information itself. For example, a local order of nuns was used to convey information to the Aeta Indians on the slopes of Pinatubo (Newhall & Punongbayan 1996). Loughlin *et al.* (2002) advocated the use of local clerics in galvanizing the Monserratian population).

There are a few counter-examples where volcanic crises have not involved co-operative relations between scientists and administrators or there was no attempt to involve the broader local population in risk management. For example, during the eruption of Vesuvius during the Allied Occupation of Italy in 1944 (Chester *et al.* 2007) military decisions were taken about evacuation. In 1999 there was an enforced evacuation of Baños on the slopes of Tungurahua, Ecuador. However, this latter case was of limited success as the local population reoccupied the town by force $2\frac{1}{2}$ months later (Lane *et al.* 2004), suggesting that such a strong-armed approach may be of limited use, particularly in long-lived crises. When Tristan da Cunha's volcano erupted in 1961, the entire population self-evacuated, but despite the best efforts of the UK government to keep the evacuees in England, almost all returned in 1963 (de Boer & Sanders 2002).

Perhaps as a consequence of the well-publicized conflict between scientists during the Guadeloupe eruptive crisis in 1976 (Fiske 1984), researchers agree that information should come from one common source and that disagreements between scientists should not be aired beyond scientists themselves (Voight 1990, 1996; Aspinall *et al.* 2003). These problems still exist, as a similar situation recently occurred in Tenerife (Solana & Spiller 2007). The IAVCEI protocol for the conduct of scientists during volcanic crises (IAVCEI 1999) dedicates many paragraphs to this issue, summarized in the abstract as 'speak publicly with a single scientific voice, especially when forecasts, warnings, or scientific disagreements are involved'. The consequences of not doing so are a perceived threat of confusion, loss of credibility and trust, and the erosion of confidence by lay public and stakeholders, as uncertainty and differences of opinion among scientists may be interpreted as a sign of incompetence (IAVCEI 1999; Solana & Spiller 2007).

However, on Guadeloupe the very nature of the activity, with its slow build-up and lingering threat, was the real cause of the problems for the scientists and authorities. In contrast, the uncertainty on St. Vincent was claimed by Fiske (1984) to be minimized by the excellent baseline monitoring and the good communication efforts of the scientists with each other, and towards the public and authorities. St. Vincent had experienced volcanic eruptions with a very similar pattern of activity in the recent past, making both the public and authorities well rehearsed in their actions. Although comparisons can be made between the ways in which the Guadeloupe and St. Vincent events were managed, the nature of the volcanic activity and the problems with uncertainty also influenced the outcome. The volcanic disaster at Nevado del Ruiz in 1985 was due, in large part, to public confusion caused by the lack of a co-ordinated message and straightforward advice. Colombian and foreign scientists failed to communicate efficiently with each other and ultimately with the authorities, who in turn grossly underestimated the situation (Voight 1990). In contrast, the volcanologists involved at Mt. Pinatubo were successful in predicting the eruption and its associated risks, and in the communication of these to a large, sceptical and varied target group. This was due to the timely and appropriate education of all concerned (i.e. the public, authorities, media and scientists). However, again, there was an element of luck attached, in the classic precursory activity generated by the volcano, which erupted on cue without a long run-up time that could have perhaps motivated evacuees to drift home. As Newhall & Punongbayan (1996) noted, although the risks were successfully mitigated, the outcome could easily have been very different.

There is some evidence that long-lived volcanic crises pose a particular challenge. In some instances, these may be the well-documented cases where volcanic unrest (abnormal activity such as earthquakes or unusual geothermal activity that is not an eruption in itself) does not result in a magmatic eruption (Long Valley, Hill 2006; Campei Flegrei, Barberi & Carapezza 1996; Yellowstone, Lowenstern *et al.* 2006; Tenerife, Solana & Spiller 2007), or longer episodes of volcanic activity such as that witnessed at the Soufrière Hills Volcano, Montserrat (1995–present) and the continued threat from lahars at Pinatubo (Newhall & Punongbayan1996). In these instances, the short-term forecasting of sudden and hazardous changes in activity becomes considerably easier than the long-term forecasting of the integrated outcome of this activity. Long-term forecasting must connect with planning decisions related to the impact of all the activity (e.g. When will it stop? When can I reoccupy this area? How tall does this bridge need to be?) and necessarily involves the communication of considerable uncertainty. There is also the danger that communication processes conducted over extended periods can lead to breakdowns in relationships between stakeholder groups when trust and credibility may be lost (e.g. Montserrat, Pattullo 2000; Fergus 2004, Vesuvius, Solana *et al.* 2008).

The effective management of uncertain hazards requires a tentative balance between precaution, reassurance and a large element of trust in the risk management team. Dealing with uncertainty by means of a protective attitude and evacuations can undermine the credibility of the risk management team through a public perception of false alarms. On the other hand, managers pressured to maintain a more relaxed management policy or give precise predictions may unintentionally neglect the implications of this uncertainty (e.g. Montserrat, Pattullo 2000; Haynes *et al.* 2008*b*). Different goals (for example, between scientists, emergency managers and government officials) can often lead to

differences in characterizing uncertainty and risk, differences that can compromise effective communication and ultimately management. Although longer time periods allow for the collection of more baseline data, they also allow these differing goals, attitudes and responsibilities to simmer and compound an increasingly volatile situation. In this environment, successes are hard won and mistakes long remembered (see Haynes *et al.* 2008*b*).

There is an implicit tension in these writings between the need to present a concerted singular scientific voice relating to volcanic information, and the empirical finding that volcanic risk communication works best as an inclusive process. Perhaps as a consequence of this tension, no volcanologists working in volcanic regions advocate involving key decision-makers and the general public in the process of 'expert' judgement, even though it is conceded that volcanic warnings can take the form of both educational statements and a discussion of how these hazards may be mitigated or will affect public safety. It would seem that the concept of inclusivity does not yet give a formalized voice to non-scientific opinion when forecasting the impact of volcanic hazards.

Social science based approaches and their commentary on the volcanic risk communication process

Difficulties in the communication of uncertainty are common to almost all fields of risk communication. The accounts above demonstrated how the outcome of a volcanic situation is largely governed by the management and communication of the uncertainty. It is helpful to frame these findings within the wider literature on risk communication, particularly the development of the risk communication process (Pidgeon *et al.* 1992; Fischhoff 1995; Bier 2001*a, b*).

Early approaches assumed an 'objective risk' and an 'ignorant public', whose knowledge 'deficit' (compared with that of the experts) required that they be provided with simple information. This has now progressed to a more mature and detailed view of risk communication. Fischoff (1995) showed how each risk communication stage builds on its predecessor by an accumulation of psychological, social, cultural, economic and political factors (see Fig. 1). Much volcanic hazard assessment work fits into the 'earlier' categories of 'getting the numbers right' and 'conveying the meaning of the numbers in a clear and concise way'. This is clearly an essential component of the whole process but only a partially successful strategy even when the purpose is just to educate. For example, a sole focus on producing the

Information flow

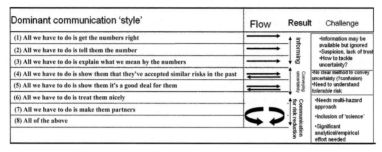

Fig. 1. Consequences and challenges of differing or evolving styles of risk communication relative to volcanic hazards (modified from Fischoff 1995).

correct numbers can raise suspicions in uncertain situations (Bier 2001*b*): an early lack of dialogue can be interpreted as an admission of confusion or a lack of understanding by the scientists themselves. This is recognized in IAVCEI's determination to have scientists speaking with 'one voice' and perhaps reflected in the problems observed during long-term volcanic eruptions or crises. Equally, when messages are supplied for the purpose of education alone (without dialogue) this can fuel a sense of being wrongly treated (Bier 2001*b*) and the strongest motivation for listening comes from the need to use and interpret information to fuel prejudices. Examples of this include the long-lived crisis on Montserrat (Haynes *et al.* 2008*b*, *c*) and the recent Tenerife crisis (Solana & Spiller 2007). The knowledge can also become politicized to achieve political or developmental aims (e.g. Montagne Pelée, Martinique, 1902, where an election was impending; Tanguy 1994). Many of the retrospective accounts documented above give further examples of this problem.

It is now understood that increased hazard awareness and knowledge do not necessarily lead to risk reduction activities (Sims & Baumann 1983; Handmer 2000; Kirschenbaum 2005). This has significant implications for rethinking how we communicate and reduce risks. Judgements of risk have been shown to be heavily influenced by a trade-off between risk and benefits. Therefore in the planning stages, before an emergency arises, communications need to focus more on the development of a mutual understanding of an acceptable or tolerable risk framed within a wider discussion to tackle the socio-economic causes of vulnerability and create sustainable livelihoods. In the summary shown in Fig. 1 this requires

moving from stages 1–3, through stages 4–6 (where something of the needs and social and political context of the audience is considered) to the situation where the various stakeholders become actively involved in the risk assessment process themselves.

Social science based approaches to the risk communication process have consequently been formulated in response to this crisis in confidence in the success of 'top-down' science-driven communication models that may alienate their target audience. On a more fundamental level, social scientists such as Wynne (1992, p. 115) have suggested there has been an 'institutionalised exaggeration of the scope and power of science knowledge and this has created a vacuum in which should exist a vital social discourse about the conditions and boundaries of scientific knowledge in relations to moral and social knowledge'.

The rejection of science-driven communication models has trickled down to literature on disaster management (Wilbanks & Kates 1999) and to the UN International Strategy for Disaster Reduction (ISDR), the body that oversees implementation of disaster reduction through the UN system and member governments: 'Efficient disaster reduction requires interaction among scientists, decision-makers and informed citizens. However, the limitation of science and technology in responding to the problems of people and political processes identifying and managing risks needs to be carefully considered. An over concentration on technical abilities that compose the economic, social and political dimensions of societies will provide disappointing results in sustained commitments to risk reduction. In particular circumstances, science and technology can be misapplied sometimes, provoking or aggravating risks to society' (UN-ISDR 2004, p. 9).

Thus the challenge to the value of science under conditions of uncertainty has been answered by the social science and development community with a heavy investment in community-based disaster risk management (CBDRM). CBDRM places greater value on local knowledge, local ownership, vulnerability and capacity assessments, and on participatory methods (see, for example, ProVention Consortium: www.proventionconsortium.org). CBDRM allows calculations about risk and uncertainty to be left to communities, who are expected to make choices about risk management decisions based on their own knowledge of the environment in which they live and the livelihood options available to them.

Within a volcanic risk management sphere, research in this tradition is in its infancy but there are a few studies that provide some evidence for the value of these approaches. For example, studies on communications in the volcanic Caribbean (Solana 2001; Haynes et al. 2008c; McGuire et al. 2008) showed that failures in understanding scientific messages derived mainly from inexperience (reflected by the use of jargon and not using familiar examples in the area to explain uncertainty) and lack of trust (scientists not verifying that the message had been understood correctly and decision-makers not asking questions). Taking it further, the work by Cronin et al. (2004a, b) on mental mapping through a Participatory Rural Appraisal approach, and by Haynes et al. (2008a) on cultural understandings of volcanic hazard maps, drew on social science perspectives but did not reflect the action orientation of many CBDRM projects. Tobin & Whiteford (2002) and Gaillard (2006) both examined the resilience of traditional communities to volcanic hazards in Ecuador and the Philippines respectively, but again employed retrospective analysis. Institutionally, the UN Development Program's (UNDP 2004) case study of volcanic risk reduction in Goma is among the most advanced, calling on UN agencies to develop and apply integrated risk management tools, increase the participation of local authorities and civil society, and use public education to strengthen the active adoption of disaster reduction concerns at the community level.

Although more research in a CBDRM tradition is expected in volcanic regions, criticisms have been made that the vast majority of participatory techniques employed by the social sciences still reflect the development practitioner–community linkages described above, with co-operative work between researchers and community members focused around resolving problems and democratizing research. The question of how to scale up to include a wider range of stakeholders, including

scientists, is rarely considered in the disaster literature (Haynes et al. 2005). Although participation in this field is often seen as curative, bottom-up and a way of pressurizing governments to reduce vulnerability, this remains difficult when also placed in the context of scientific uncertainty about the behaviour of volcanic systems.

Enriching these processes with scientific hazard assessments is thus problematic. For volcanologists this involves new ways of thinking about the concepts of risk and uncertainty: volcanic risk must sit in a broader, more dynamic framework that incorporates a wider range of approaches and practitioners to include these other factors that contribute to risk reduction. Equally, many researchers (e.g. Wynne 1992; Fischer 2000) have discussed the need to make both key decision-makers and the general public aware of the degree of uncertainty with which information is conveyed; yet, while participatory decision-making processes are becoming more popular in addressing the challenges posed by disaster risk (e.g. Wood et al. 2002; Mercer et al. 2007), opening highly technical discussions about the quantification of uncertainty to such processes may not help with transparency and inclusion of involved decision-makers (Bier 2001a; see Fig. 1). The statistical approaches described above go some way to help volcanologists clarify 'the value of knowing how little you know' (Morgan & Henrion 1990) but the literature does not provide any clear indication of how best and when to convey this information.

Getting to the stage where the message is not only delivered clearly but where the communicator understands something of the audience (see Fig. 1) also requires significant analytical and empirical effort (Fischhoff 1995) as it is an iterative process, but the benefits in terms of risk-reducing behaviour are greater.

The incentives for governments and communities to act to reduce volcanic risk, even with successful communication with scientists, are still untested. If hazard assessment works best where baseline data have been gathered then researchers and knowledge intermediaries must understand how to tailor the communication of this scientific knowledge about volcanic risk and uncertainty to motivate risk-reducing development in times of quiescence. It is likely that this process will be markedly different from issuing warnings in times of crisis when authorities and the public are more motivated to listen. A long-term approach to building trust between scientists, authorities, the media and the public is vital, but a stand-alone process centred on the dangers posed by a dormant volcano is unlikely to be successful in reducing risk unless it is situated within a continuing multi-hazard approach to disaster risk reduction.

At the moment, there is a lack of insight as to the best strategy for this style of communication, but it should be emphasized that there is a very clear role for scientific information in the communication circuit necessary for disaster risk reduction. For example, the ideal situation is where a set of beliefs about volcanic activity is resilient or adaptable to changes in circumstance (in this instance, most usually brought about by changes in volcanic behaviour or the impact of the eruption itself). A clear understanding of the likely range of volcanic behaviour, the degree of uncertainty in predicting change, and trust in those who determine this are very important in establishing this adaptive and resilient state (Fischhoff 1995; Solana 2001; Haynes 2006; Haynes 2008*b*, *c*; Solana *et al.* 2008). Therefore, it is imperative that robust methods are developed involving the public, key decision-makers and volcanologists to develop a mutual understanding of an acceptable or tolerable risk.

Discussion

Like most natural hazards, the risk associated with volcanic eruptions is inadequately quantified, intermittent and the response of the public to risk messages is embedded within the framework of their own lives and concerns. As conveying uncertain information is notoriously difficult, the following discussion focuses on finding a pathway that may enable volcanologists to work with decision-makers and the public to develop a mutual understanding of acceptable or tolerable risks and how to reduce risk to this level. This needs to answer some of the tensions implicit in communicating volcanic risks to encourage risk-reducing behaviour.

The broader context of volcanic risk reduction

The communication of volcanic hazards and the management of the population affected by these phenomena are inextricably linked. Effective volcanic risk communication will address the socio-economic causes and consequences of people's exposure to volcanic hazards rather than simply discussing the hazards themselves. The empirical and descriptive findings to date place a strong emphasis on the need for a pro-active policy of social research and CBDRM. Although research within the traditions outlined above has aimed to reduce casualties in volcanic disasters and has attempted to improve relationships between stakeholders in volcanic regions, few approaches have exhibited qualities akin to the holistic risk reduction approach articulated in the Hyogo Framework for

Action (UN-ISDR 2005). Exceptions would probably include Dibben & Chester's (1999) Azores-based study of human vulnerability in volcanic environments, which allowed the 'identification of points where intervention may be successful in reducing the likelihoods of suffering in a society' (Dibben & Chester 1999).

Ideally, volcanologists should become more aware of their role in Disaster Risk Reduction (DRR) and treat pre-crisis risk communication, planning and education with the same importance as gathering 'baseline data'. Scientists must reassess their roles to be effective, and in many cases this may already happen in an informal capacity. So, such processes must go much further than the production of reports and maps delivered to appropriate government institutions and include meaningful participation of scientific representatives at all levels, accompanied by effective evaluation of that process. Building trust and understanding is a key component of DRR and also of an effectively managed crisis. Thus, the relationships between all groups (scientists, media, authorities and the public) must be developed in advance of a crisis.

Most scientists working on volcanoes would probably consider their greatest obstacle is finding enough resources to enable them to collect sufficient data to test hypotheses (Mackinson & Nottestad 1998; Mercer *et al.* 2007). A lack of training and awareness of social science research methods means that physical scientists (in this context, volcanologists) can be unable and unwilling to accept local knowledge as data (Mackinson & Nottestad 1998). They should not be blamed for this, given the compartmentalization of research training and the professional pressure to publish in scientific journals. Few social scientists are well versed in scientific data collection methods, but often use their understanding of local knowledge to expose weaknesses in the use of scientific knowledge for disaster prevention. However, splitting knowledge into two camps, scientific and local, oversimplifies the dynamics within volcanic regions. Studies on decision-making in volcanic crises have often pointed to the key roles played by policy bodies and disaster management units (Mitchell 2006). The significance of these bodies and the bureaucratic knowledge that resides with their employees is magnified within a DRR context, considering their need to develop and implement precautionary policies and allocate resources. By further complicating the knowledge mix, the value of people who have the ability to move between multiple knowledge traditions is magnified (Pelling & High 2005). Educational and professional training institutions should perhaps train DRR generalists rather than specialists; and research teams should include members who are able to work across multiple disciplines (Haynes *et al.* 2005).

The first outcome of this process should be to create flexible, knowledgeable and participatory disaster management regimes, able to adapt to rapid changes in the availability of environmental and social assets. Debate remains over whether efforts to build resilience should foster institutions that are able to remain unchanged despite the impact of high-magnitude, low-frequency events, or whether it is more helpful to promote flexible institutions that are able to continuously and rapidly adapt and realign to social and environmental situations (Dovers & Handmer 1992; Holling 2001). In practice, little work has been conducted on creating flexibility within disaster management regimes, although Pelling & High (2005) considered the role of learning, issue champions and shadow systems (communications within organizations that are not officially recognized) for engendering adaptability. This could form a component of a new research agenda for volcanic disaster reduction. Particular attention may also be given to how different forms of disaster governance either thrive or struggle in different institutional and governmental environments.

Implicit in this interdisciplinary 'disaster reduction' approach is the desire to view volcanic hazards within the broader context of all naturally occurring hazards, including the challenges posed by climate change. In practice, this is a tall order requiring an integrated approach to hazard assessment involving physical scientists well beyond the sphere of volcanology, the long-term interest of established practitioners of disaster risk reduction, and an engaged local management community. This is likely to happen only if the benefits of this approach become quickly apparent, and at the moment there are few successful examples or even experiments to draw on.

There is an urgent need for longitudinal studies of this process to refine methods and provide examples of best practice in differing contexts, and we have perhaps have much to learn from other natural disasters, although this is beyond the scope of the current paper.

In tandem with this approach there must be a real attempt to permanently diversify or protect the livelihoods of those living in areas threatened by volcanic hazards (see Gaillard 2006; Kelman 2006). The intention is for these people to become less dependent on the ecological assets associated with living close to a volcano. In practice, permanent livelihood diversification may be difficult and costly, and the process must be complemented with social welfare or diversification mechanisms that temporarily compensate for loss of earnings. Research should be focused on developing inventories of vulnerable livelihoods, developing policy options for protecting or diversifying these (Mitchell 2006), and compiling economic cases that justify such policy options.

The distinct role of volcanologists within the context of disaster risk reduction

It is recognized that the communication of risks associated with each volcano is made unique by the conditions of the volcano itself, the social and economic conditions around the volcano, and the pre-existing knowledge base of both of these factors. As described above, the development of more inclusive processes of communication and management as visualized in the Hyogo Framework have often involved the marginalization of scientific information. There is an important role for scientific information to play, particularly in aiming to address the provision of reliable technical information in a format understandable and relevant to the audience

Our knowledge of volcanic processes continues to increase and our ability to forecast the impact of volcanic activity subsequently improves across the long-, mid- and short-range time scales outlined above. None the less, particular challenges still exist in communicating both what is understood about a volcano and its likely behaviour and what is not. Flexible disaster management regimes need to be able to accommodate changes in the range and quality of volcanic hazard information following any formalized assessment (and before an actual crisis) and during any volcanic crisis. Such a flexible approach requires local and international decision-makers to develop a good understanding of the strengths and weaknesses of the information but also a real effort from volcanologists to listen, learn and then tailor and adapt their hazard-related messages to the needs of the affected community, with the constant monitoring of how those messages are consumed by target audiences.

The development of this flexibility also requires something of an improvement in the scope and frequency of formalized studies of hazard communication across a variety of volcanic examples. Robust methods need to be developed for allowing dialogue between the community, authorities and the scientists at a number of levels to address risk reduction effectively. In particular, a concerted effort to find and deliberate on the best methods for conveying and dealing with scientific uncertainty would be welcome. For example, volcanologists could make more effort to distinguish between outcome uncertainty and assessment uncertainty (Bier 2001*a*). Significant assessment uncertainty can be reduced as the 'baseline' information becomes improved and diversified with increased monitoring, but outcome uncertainty may not be improved as it relates to the intrinsically chaotic behaviour of some volcanic systems, where small changes in subsurface conditions can result in large changes in eruptive behaviour at the surface (e.g. Melnik & Sparks 1999; Sparks 2003).

Finally, to engage fully with volcanic disaster reduction strategies there are some very difficult questions that must be asked and debated among volcanologists and within existing risk communication frameworks.

(1) At what point should we engage with 'non-specialists' during the hazard (or risk) assessment process? How do we incorporate their views and opinions into the process of hazard assessment, and do we aid the translation into risk assessment?

(2) During the process of risk communication to what extent can we separate the process of education from the encouragement of risk-reducing behaviour? From whom should we seek guidance about what types of information needs to be communicated: the public or the decision-makers?

(3) How do we make decisions about conveying uncertainty and how do we do it? Are there certain audiences that should be apprised of the intricacies of the technical judgements and those where dwelling on uncertainty is needlessly confusing? How do we deal with dynamic and changing uncertainty without losing credibility and trust?

(4) To what extent should engagement with volcanic disaster reduction be modified in a crisis with little prior baseline information, both about volcanic behaviour and social and economic factors?

Without at least addressing these complex questions, the possibility of true integration of social and physical science-based research strategies may be considerably lessened. Perhaps a useful repository for inclusive processes could be the formalization of this input into Volcano Early Warning Systems (Fearnley *et al.* 2007).

Tools for volcanic disaster reduction

This is not intended to be an exhaustive overview of methods, but rather a brief outline of those that might have most impact in volcanic disaster reduction over the coming years. In the demanding context of volcanic risk reduction the prime need is for methods that can be used flexibly and assist in the iteration of communication to all stakeholders.

Geographic information systems (GIS). A GIS is not just a mapping tool, it can be used to integrate and explore diverse datasets, as well as for knowledge transfer (e.g. Rosenbaum & Culshaw 2003; Toyos *et al.* 2007). For volcanic risk management a GIS can be used to: compile hazard and risk maps; to allow eventual minimization of risk (with the integration of land-use and hazard information); develop evacuation plans; deal with an impending or current eruption (e.g. model the opening of a new vent); and provide a record of buildings, economic resources, people, etc. (Pareschi *et al.* 2000). Importantly, a computer-based technology can be suitable for real-time management of volcanic crises if fundamental information is updated and adapted (Gomez-Fernandez 2000). Furthermore, a GIS can be used to incorporate the challenge of scientific uncertainty. Zerger (2002) found that such an inclusion was superior to binary risk mapping as it led to more informed emergency management decision-making.

A critical barrier to the use of GIS in disaster risk reduction, particularly in developing countries, is the lack of available map data, computing resources, and trained personnel (Coppock 1995). Fortunately, images from space satellites, notably Landsat, and elevation data from the Space Shuttle Radar Topography Mission (SRTM), can be freely downloaded from the Internet. GIS processing of these free satellite datasets can produce 1:50 000 to 1:250 000 scale maps of population distribution and terrain; key information for disaster risk reduction in poorly mapped volcanic regions (Teeuw *et al.* 2008).

Public participation GIS (PPGIS), through the interaction of community interests and GIS technology, develops a richer database. The public will bring with them a diversity of experiences and local knowledge that can contribute to academic and scientific knowledge. In return, the public will receive participation in the processes affecting their lives. However, participatory research inherently involves an element of blending the seemingly incompatible (see Williams & Dunn 2003; Cronin *et al.* 2004b). Disaster response has recently been assisted by 'virtual globes', such as Google Earth, which allow community-derived information, such as disaster damage reports and GPS location coordinates, to be uploaded and viewed by disaster managers.

Juxtaposing 'official', spatially referenced data with local knowledge provides meaningful geographical understandings (Williams & Dunn 2003) but raises important questions about interpretation of accuracy. Participatory Rural Appraisal or PPGIS maps are not spatially accurate in a geometric sense, although relative locations (and topological relations) are preserved. It is important to thus focus on the purpose of the communication tool; for example, for scientific exploration of data or for public understanding.

Deliberative processes. Deliberative and inclusive processes (DIPs) are increasingly used worldwide to give the historically excluded a voice in decisions (Pimbert 2001); and to bring together a variety of stakeholders with different forms of knowledge to work together. Accordingly, DIPs are an attempt to re-engage with the core foundation of democracy and involve diverse voices in the process of making policy. Researchers have listed many different participatory processes that can be considered as DIPs (see Pimbert 2001), but Wakeford (2001) listed four categories: deliberative focus groups, consensus conferences, citizens' juries and scenario workshops. The examples he gave for each of these are almost exclusively from a developed world context, simply because a good range of examples from developing nations are lacking. As Pimbert & Wakeford (2001) found, until the last 2 or 3 years it was very difficult to find examples from developing countries that are more than elaborate participatory rural appraisal (PRA) processes.

Scientists have a key role to play in DIPs, but what makes DIPs different is that scientific knowledge is openly deliberated upon and sometimes challenged by citizens who have more decision-making control. This changes the traditional role of scientists, who need to shift their frame of reference from being implementers and deliverers to facilitating the analysis, planning and action of local people (Pimbert 2001): 'Professionals from science, health, planning, engineering have specialist knowledge that can usefully feed into citizen deliberations, and a place at the table must be reserved for such actors to ensure inclusive forms of participation' (Pimbert 2001, p. 81).

Often in developing countries, the lack of a representative democracy and of trust between policy actors increases the need for NGOs and donor organizations alike to find ways to ensure citizens' voices are heard in decision-making processes. However, poor and vulnerable people often cannot access decision-making forums, because of adverse power relations, illiteracy and their inability to leave their livelihoods. This means that, if poor and vulnerable people are to participate in decision-making, their involvement needs to be carefully planned and resourced. As yet, donors, NGOs and governments in developing countries have been unwilling to pay for the involvement of traditionally marginalized people, although they are often willing to pay *per diems* to elected officials. These issues resonate strongly with volcanic risk reduction, where a high proportion of volcanoes are in developing countries and where scientists, government officials, media and local people need to work together to decide policies and approaches. In this context and taking account of the challenges, DIPs can help volcanic risk reduction efforts by increasing trust, by encouraging open deliberations of scientific uncertainty by those likely to be most effective, and by drawing attention to the issues by organizing such events.

Unlike GIS, where some studies are beginning to prove its worth in volcanic risk reduction, DIPs are relatively untested in this field beyond a single Caribbean example (Mitchell 2004, 2006; Mitchell & Haynes 2007), and there are also considerable gaps and theoretical challenges that need to be addressed. Holmes & Scoones (2001) have identified three key areas, all relevant to volcanic risk reduction.

(1) How do DIPs fit into broader policy processes and wider policy networks? In particular, for volcanic risk reduction this would relate to placing it into the context of other challenging risks.

(2) More clarity is needed on whom to include and exclude.

(3) The subverting influence that the need for power can have on DIPs needs to be considered (i.e. the influence of conflicting and competing needs on this process).

More generally, few DIPs have been conducted in a disaster risk reduction context but those few have enjoyed some success. For example, researchers have found that hazard mitigation plans or products that include stakeholders in their design were more effective at communicating risk information (Carroll 1995), and more in tune with the community concerns and resource limitations (Simpson 1992). However, no research has been conducted in the disasters field on what learning and experience people take away from these processes (Yosie & Herbst 1998; Adler *et al.* 2000). Furthermore, the task of understanding how communities interact and participate with scientific information beyond managed deliberative or analytical processes is under-researched. Scott (1985, 1990) found that people without the resources to do anything more substantive refer to science and technology in a satirical way, making jokes about the information. This fits with research conducted in Montserrat looking at cultural expressions of crisis, where poetry, song, art and street theatre formed the basis of social commentary about daily scientific bulletins on the local radio about the volcanic risk (Mitchell 2002). However, other forms of citizen engagement with science appear to contradict the characterization of Western science as unhelpful or damaging, as is often considered by participatory rural appraisal processes that foreground local knowledge and ignore expert knowledge. A study by Thompson *et al.* (1998) looked at access to information related to the 1997 El Niño event and found that farmers in Sub-Saharan Africa were accessing regional and local climate forecasts through the Internet, as the weather patterns they were facing were unfamiliar and they wanted to know which planting and harvesting decisions to make.

These examples show that using DIPs for volcanic risk reduction shows promise, but the evidence base has yet to be created. There is much scope for the building and testing of action-oriented research on DIPs, but this will require supportive interdisciplinary networks, where scientists and social scientists are willing to work together to expose their disciplines to volcanic risk assessment and mitigation processes shaped and led by vulnerable communities.

Conclusions

The review of the state of knowledge in volcanic risk communication, both from the perspective of volcanologists and social scientists, has led to a better definition of objectives and highlighted important areas of research opportunities. The objective of volcanic risk communication is both to educate and to encourage risk-reducing behaviour. To promote risk-reducing behaviour inextricably links volcanic risk communication to risk management strategies and encourages a more inclusive approach involving many stakeholders. Robust methods must be developed for allowing dialogue between the community, authorities and the scientists at a number of levels to address risk reduction effectively. This conclusion is reinforced by observations from analyses of previous volcanic crises.

The increasing recognition in risk management of the utility of techniques such as community-based disaster risk management (CBDRM) will necessitate a reassessment of the roles of hazard specialists, who will need to alter from deliverers to a role that involves 'real' participation and an agreement to consider and incorporate the analysis, planning and wishes of local people. An all-hazards approach, or indeed an 'all-vulnerabilities' approach, will need a current investment in DRR generalists who can work across multiple disciplines.

Despite advances in our understanding of volcanic processes, hazard assessments still involve some degree of subjectivity and therefore uncertainty. The outcome of many previous volcanic situations has been determined by the management of the different degrees of uncertainty. Therefore, critical avenues of further research in this field include: (1) effectively conveying uncertain information; (2) methods for making decisions in uncertain situations; (3) methods for dealing with dynamic and changing uncertainty without losing credibility and trust. Ultimately, all these new techniques need to be put to the test, with the challenge of saving lives and livelihoods during a volcanic crisis as the most significant incentive for change.

This paper was written as the result of discussions facilitated by the UK Economic and Social Research Council (ESRC)–National Environmental Research Council (NERC) funded SPIDER (Science and Policy Interfaces for Disaster Reduction) Network, of whom many authors are members. We thank D. Liverman for allowing us to produce this paper at short notice and D. Chester for his helpful review. C. Hickson, R. Herd and J. Burgess are thanked for their informal reviews, which provided us with much food for thought. S. Crosweller, A. Darnell and C. Fearnley are in receipt of UK ESRC–NERC Interdisciplinary PhD studentships, and C. Lowe holds a UK ESRC studentship.

References

ADLER, P. S., BARRETT, R. C., BEAN, M. C., BIRKHOFF, J. E., OZAWA, C. P. & RUDIN, E. B. 2000. *Managing Scientific and Technical Information in Environmental Cases: Principles and Practices for Mediators and Facilitators.* Report for US Institute for Conflict Resolution, RESOLVE and the Western Justice Foundation.

ASPINALL, W. & COOKE, R. M. 1998. Expert judgement and the Montserrat Volcano eruption. *In*: MOSLEH, A. & BARI, R. A. (eds) *Proceedings of the 4th International Conference on Probabilistic Safety Assessment and Management PSAM4, 13–18 September 1998, New York City, USA.* Springer, New York, 2113–2118.

ASPINALL, W. P., WOO, G., VOIGHT, B. & BAXTER, P. J. 2003. Evidence-based volcanology: application to eruption crises. *Journal of Volcanology and Geothermal Research*, **128**, 273–285.

ASPINALL, W. P., CARNIEL, R., JAQUET, O., WOO, G. & HINCKS, T. 2006. Using hidden multi-state Markov models with multi-parameter volcanic data to provide empirical evidence for alert level decision-support. *Journal of Volcanology and Geothermal Research*, **153**, 112–124.

BARBERI, F. & CARAPEZZA, M. L. 1996. The problem of volcanic unrest: The Campi Flegrei case history. *In*: SCARPA, R. & TILLING, R. I. (eds) *Monitoring and Mitigation of Volcanic Hazards.* Springer, Berlin, 771–786.

BIER, V. M. 2001a. On the state of the art: Risk communication to decision-makers. *Reliability Engineering and System Safety*, **71**, 151–157.

BIER, V. M. 2001b. On the state of the art: Risk communication to the public. *Reliability Engineering and System Safety*, **71**, 139–150.

BLONG, R. J. 1996. Volcanic hazards risk assessment. *In*: SCARPA, R. & TILLING, R. I. (eds) *Monitoring and Mitigation of Volcanic Hazards.* Springer, Berlin, 675–698.

CARROLL, J. C. 1995. *Anticipated disaster relief, community participation, and the adoption of hazard mitigation strategies: The experience of four California counties.* PhD thesis, University of Oregon, Eugene.

CHESTER, D. K., DUNCAN, A. M., WETTON, P. & WETTON, R. 2007. Responses of the Anglo-American military authorities to the eruption of Vesuvius, March 1944. *Journal of Historical Geography*, **33**, 168–196.

COPPOCK, J. T. 1995. GIS and natural hazards: an overview from a GIS perspective. *In*: CARRARA, A. & GUZZETTI, F. (eds) *Geographical Information Systems in Assessing Natural Hazards*. Kluwer, Dordrecht, 21–34.

CORNELIUS, R. R. & VOIGHT, B. 1996. Real-time seismic amplitude measurement (RSAM) and seismic spectral amplitude measurement (SSAM) analyses with the materials failure forecast method (FFM), June 1991 explosive eruption at Mount Pinatubo. *In*: NEWHALL, C. G. & PUNONGBAYAN, R. S. (eds) *Fire and Mud: Eruptions and Lahars of Mount Pinatubo, Philippines*. University of Washington Press, Seattle, WA, 249–268.

CRONIN, S. J., GAYLORD, D. R., CHARLEY, D., ALLOWAY, B. V., WALLEZ, S. & ESAU, J. W. 2004a. Participatory methods of incorporating scientific with traditional knowledge for volcanic hazard management on Ambae Island, Vanuatu. *Bulletin of Volcanology*, **66**, 652–668.

CRONIN, S. J., PETTERSON, M. G., TAYLOR, P. W. & BILIKI, R. 2004b. Maximising multi-stakeholder participation in government and community volcanic hazard management programs: A case study from Savo, Solomon Islands. *Natural Hazards*, **33**, 105–136.

DAAG, A. S., TUBIANOSA, B. S., NEWHALL, C. G. ET AL. 1996. Monitoring sulphur dioxide emission at Mount Pinatubo. *In*: NEWHALL, C. G. & PUNONGBAYAN, R. S. (eds) *Fire and Mud: Eruptions and Lahars of Mount Pinatubo, Philippines*. University of Washington Press, Seattle, WA, 409–414.

DE BOER, J. Z. & SANDERS, D. T. 2002. *Volcanoes in Human History*. Princeton University Press, Princeton, NJ.

DIBBEN, C. J. L. & CHESTER, D. K. 1999. Human vulnerability in volcanic environments: The case of Furnas, São Miguel, Azores. *Journal of Volcanology and Geothermal Research*, **92**, 133–150.

DOVERS, S. W. & HANDMER, J. W. 1992. Uncertainty, sustainability and change. *Global Environmental Change*, **2**, 262–276.

FEARNLEY, C., DAVIES, G., MCGUIRE, W. & TWIGG, J. 2007. Developing an alternative methodological and conceptual approach to interpreting and utilising volcanic forecasting with early warning systems. *Cities on Volcanoes, 5 Conference*, Shimbahara, Japan, November 19–23, 2007.

FERGUS, H. A. 2004. *Montserrat. History of a Caribbean colony*, 2nd edn. Macmillan, London.

FISCHER, F. 2000. *Citizens, Experts, and the Environment: The Politics of Local Knowledge*. Duke University Press, Durham, NC.

FISCHER, T. P., MORRISEY, M. M., CALVACHE, M. L., DIEGO GOMEZ, M., TORRES, R., STIX, J. & WILLIAMS, S. N. 1994. Correlations between SO_2 flux and long period seismicity at Galeras volcano. *Nature*, **368**, 135–137.

FISCHHOFF, B. 1995. Risk perception and communication unplugged: Twenty years of process. *Risk Analysis*, **15**, 137–145.

FISKE, R. S. 1984. Volcanologists, journalists, and the concerned local public: A tale of two crises in the Eastern Caribbean. *In*: Geophysics Study Committee (ed.) *Explosive Volcanism: Interception, Evolution, and Hazard*. National Academy Press, Washington, DC, 170–176.

GAILLARD, J.-C. 2006. Traditional communities in the face of natural hazards: The 1991 Mount Pinatubo eruption and the Aetas of the Philippines. *International Journal of Mass Emergencies and Disasters*, **24**, 5–43.

GOMEZ-FERNANDEZ, F. 2000. Contribution of Geographical Information Systems to the management of volcanic crises. *Natural Hazards*, **21**, 347–360.

HANDMER, J. 2000. Are flood warnings futile?: Risk communication in emergencies. *Australasian Journal of Disaster and Trauma Studies*, **2**. World Wide Web Address: http://www.massey.ac.nz/~trauma/issues/2000–2002/handmer.htm.

HAYNES, K. 2006. Volcanic island in crisis: Investigating environmental uncertainty and the complexity it brings. *Australian Journal of Emergency Management*, **21**, 21–28.

HAYNES, K., KELMAN, I. & MITCHELL, T. 2005. Early Participatory Intervention for Catastrophe to reduce island vulnerability (EPIC). *International Journal of Island Affairs*, **14**, 56–59.

HAYNES, K., BARCLAY, J. & PIDGEON, N. 2008a. Volcanic hazard communication using maps: an evaluation of their effectiveness. *Bulletin of Volcanology* **70**, 123–38.

HAYNES, K., BARCLAY, J. & PIDGEON, N. 2008b. The issue of trust and its influence on risk communication during a volcanic crisis. *Bulletin of Volcanology* **70**, 605–21.

HAYNES, K., BARCLAY, J. & PIDGEON, N. F. 2008c. Whose reality counts? Factors affecting the perception of volcanic risk. *Journal of Volcanology and Geothermal Research* **172**, 259–72.

HILL, D. P. 2006. Unrest in Long Valley Caldera, California, 1978–2004. *In*: DENATALE, G., TROISE, C. & KILBURN, C. R. J. (eds) *Mechanisms of Activity and Unrest at Large Calderas*. Geological Society, London, Special Publications, **269**, 1–24.

HOLLING, C. S. 2001. Understanding the complexity of economic, ecological and social systems. *Ecosystems*, **4**, 390–405.

HOLMES, T. & SCOONES, I. 2001. Participatory environmental policy processes: experiences from north and south. *PLA Notes*, **40**, 76–78.

IAVCEI Sub-committee for Crisis Protocols 1999. Professional conduct of scientists during volcanic crises. *Bulletin of Volcanology*, **60**, 323–334.

KELMAN, I. 2006. Island security and disaster diplomacy in the context of climate change. *Les Cahiers de la Sécurité*, **63**, 61–94.

KIRSCHENBAUM, A. 2005. Preparing for the inevitable: environmental risk perception and disaster preparedness. *International Journal of Mass Emergencies and Disasters*, **23**, 97–127.

LANE, L. R., TOBIN, G. A. & WHITEFORD, L. M. 2004. Volcanic hazard or economic destitution: Hard choices in Baños, Ecuador. *Global Environmental Change*, **5**, 23–34.

LOUGHLIN, S., BAXTER, P. J., ASPINALL, W. A., DARROUX, B. & MILLER, A. D. 2002. Eyewitness accounts of the 25 June 1997 pyroclastic flows and surges at Soufrière Hills volcano, Montserrat and implications for disaster mitigation. *In*: DRUITT, T. & KOKELAAR, P. (eds) *The Eruption of Soufrière Hills Volcano, Montserrat, from 1995 to 1999.* Geological Society, London, Memoirs, **21**, 211–230.

LOWENSTERN, J. B., SMITH, R. B. & HILL, D. P. 2006. Monitoring super-volcanoes: Geophysical and geochemical signals at Yellowstone and other large caldera systems. *Philosophical Transactions of the Royal Society, Series A*, **364**, 2055–2072.

MACKINSON, S. & NOTTESTAD, L. 1998. Combining local and scientific knowledge. *Reviews in Fish Biology and Fisheries*, **8**, 481–490.

MARZOCCHI, W. & WOO, G. 2007. Probabilistic eruption forecasting and the call for an evacuation. *Geophysical Research Letters*, doi:10.1029/2007GL031922.

MCGUIRE, W., SOLANA, M. C., KILBURN, C. R. J. & SANDERSON, D. 2008. Improving communication during volcanic crises on small, vulnerable islands. *Journal of Volcanology and Geothermal Research* (in press).

MELNIK, O. & SPARKS, R. S. J. 1999. Non-linear dynamics of lava extrusion. *Nature*, **402**, 37–41.

MERCER, J., DOMINEY-HOWES, D., KELMAN, I. & LLOYD, K. 2007. The potential for combining indigenous and western knowledge in reducing vulnerability to environmental hazards in small island developing states. *Environmental Hazards*, **7**, 245–56.

MITCHELL, T. 2004. Mainstreaming disaster risk reduction: a trial of 'future search' on St. Kitts, West Indies. *In*: MALZAHN, D. & PLAPP, T. (eds) *Disasters and Society from Hazard Assessment to Risk Reduction.* Logos-Verlag, Berlin. 123–29.

MITCHELL, T. 2006. *Building a disaster resilient future: lessons from participatory research in St. Kitts and Montserrat.* PhD thesis, University of London.

MITCHELL, T. C. 2002. *A new method for evaluating community sensivity to risk information combining creative expression with a rapid evaluation approach: case study of Montserrat.* Masters Thesis, Rutgers, The State University of New Jersey, USA.

MITCHELL, T. & HAYNES, K. 2007. Routes to Island Disaster Resilience ID21 Insights 70, November 2007. World Wide Web Address: http://www.id21.org/insights/insights70/art06.html.

MORGAN, M. G. & HENRION, M. 1990. *Uncertainty: A Guide to Dealing with Uncertainty in Quantitative Risk and Policy Analysis.* Cambridge University Press, Cambridge.

NEWHALL, C. G. 2000. Volcano warnings. *In*: SIGURDSSON, H., HOUGHTON, B., MCNUTT, S., RYMER, H. & STIX, J. (eds) *Encyclopaedia of Volcanoes.* Academic Press, New York, 1185–1197.

NEWHALL, C. G. & HOBLITT, R. P. 2002. Constructing event trees for volcanic crises. *Bulletin of Volcanology*, **64**, 3–20.

NEWHALL, C. G. & PUNONGBAYAN, R. S. 1996. The narrow margin of successful volcanic-risk mitigation. *In*: SCARPA, R. & TILLING, R. I. (eds) *Monitoring and Mitigation of Volcano Hazards.* Springer, Berlin, 807–838.

PARESCHI, M. T., CAVARRA, L., FAVAVLLI, M., GIANNINI, F. & MERIGGI, A. 2000. GIS and volcanic risk management. *Natural Hazards*, **21**, 361–379.

PATTULLO, P. 2000. *Fire from the Mountain: The Story of the Montserrat Volcano.* Constable & Robinson, London.

PELLING, M. & HIGH, C. 2005. Understanding adaptation: what can social capital offer assessments of adaptive capacity? *Global Environmental Change A*, **15**, 308–319.

PETERSON, D. W. 1996. Mitigation measures and preparedness plans for volcanic emergencies. *In*: SCARPA, R. & TILLING, R. I. (eds) *Monitoring and Mitigation of Volcano Hazards.* Springer, Berlin, 701–718.

PIDGEON, N., HOOD, C., JONES, D., TURNER, B. & GIBSON, R. 1992. Risk perception. *In*: ROYAL SOCIETY STUDY GROUP (ed.) *Risk Analysis, Perception and Management.* Royal Society, London, 89–134.

PIMBERT, M. 2001. Reclaiming our right to power: some conditions for deliberative democracy. *Participatory Learning and Action*, **40**, 81–84.

PIMBERT, M & WAKEFORD, T. 2001. Overview—deliberative democracy and citizen empowerment. *Participatory Learning and Action*, **40**, 23–28.

PUNONGBAYAN, R. S., NEWHALL, C. G., BAUTISTA, M. L. P. *ET AL.* 1996. Eruption hazard assessments and warnings. *In*: NEWHALL, C. G. & PUNONGBAYAN, R. S. (eds) *Fire and Mud: Eruptions and Lahars of Mount Pinatubo, Philippines.* Seattle, University of Washington Press, 67–85.

ROSENBAUM, M. S. & CULSHAW, M. G. 2003. Communicating the risks arising from geohazards. *Journal of the Royal Statistical Society, A*, **166**, 261–270.

SCOTT, J. 1985. *Weapons of the Weak: Everyday Forms of Peasant Resistance.* Yale University Press, New Haven, CT.

SCOTT, J. 1990. *Domination and the Arts of Resistance: Hidden Transcripts.* Yale University Press, New Haven, CT.

SIMKIN, T. 1993. Terrestrial volcanism in space and time. *Annual Review of Earth and Planetary Sciences*, **21**, 427–452.

SIMKIN, T. & SIEBERT, L. 2000. Earth's volcanoes and eruptions: An overview. *In*: SIGURDSSON, H., HOUGHTON, B., MCNUTT, S., RYMER, H. & STIX, J. (eds) *Encyclopaedia of Volcanoes.* Academic Press, New York, 249–261.

SIMPSON, D. 1992. Risk and disaster: Arguments for a community-based planning approach. *Berkeley Planning Journal*, **7**, 98–120.

SIMS, J. H. & BAUMANN, D. D. 1983. Education programs and human response to natural hazards. *Environmental Behaviour*, **15**, 165–189.

SOLANA, M. C. 2001. Communications during volcanic emergencies. A handbook for the Caribbean. Benfield Greig Hazard Research Centre. World Wide Web Address: http://www.benfieldhrc.org/disaster_studies/projects/Carib.2003.pdf.

SOLANA, M. C. & SPILLER, C. L. 2007. Communication between professionals during volcanic emergencies. *Eos Transactions, American Geophysical Union*, **88**, 288–288.

SOLANA, M. C., KILBURN, C. R. J. & ROLANDI, G. 2008. Communicating eruption and hazard forecasts on Vesuvius, Southern Italy. *Journal of Volcanology and Geothermal Research*, **172**, 308–14.

SPARKS, R. S. J. 2003. Forecasting volcanic eruptions. *Earth and Planetary Science Letters*, **210**, 1–15.

STIRLING, A. 2003. Risk, uncertainty and precaution: some instrumental implications from the social sciences. *In*: BERKHOUT, F., LEACH, M. & SCOONES, I. (eds) *Negotiating Environmental Change: New Perspectives from Social Science*. Edward Elgar, Cheltenham, 33–77.

TANGUY, J. C. 1994. The 1902–1905 eruptions of Montagne Pelée, Martinique: Anatomy and retrospection. *Journal of Volcanology and Geothermal Research*, **60**, 87–107.

TEEUW, R. M., APLIN, P., KERVYN, M., ERNST, G., MCWILLIAM, N. & WICKS, T. 2008. Hazards and disaster management. *In*: *Handbook of Remote Sensing*. Sage, New York (in press).

THOMPSON, A., JENDEN, P. & CLAY, E. 1998. *Information, Risk and Disaster Preparedness: Responses to the 1997 El Niño Event*. SOS Sahel International, London.

THOURET, J. C. 1999. Urban hazards and risks: Consequences of earthquakes and volcanic eruptions: An introduction. *GeoJournal*, **49**, 131–135.

TOBIN, G. A. & WHITEFORD, L. M. 2002. Community resilience and volcano hazard: The eruption of Tungurahua and evacuation of the Faldas in Ecuador. *Disasters*, **26**, 28–48.

TOYOS, G. P., COLE, P. D., FELPETO, A. & MARTI, J. 2007. A GIS-based methodology for hazard mapping of small volume pyroclastic density currents. *Natural Hazards*, **41**, 99–112.

UNDP 2004. *Reducing Disaster Risk: a Challenge for Development*. UNDP, Geneva.

UN-ISDR 2004. Living with risk—a global review of disaster reduction initiatives. World Wide Web Address: www.unisdr.org.

VOIGHT, B. 1990. The 1985 Nevado del Ruiz volcano catastrophe: Anatomy and retrospection. *Journal of Volcanology and Geothermal Research*, **44**, 349–386.

VOIGHT, B. 1996. The management of volcano emergencies: Nevado del Ruiz. *In*: SCARPA, R. & TILLING, R. I. (eds) *Monitoring and Mitigation of Volcano Hazards*. Springer, Berlin, 719–769.

WADGE, G. & ISAACS, M. C. 1988. Mapping the volcanic hazards from Soufrière Hills Volcano, Montserrat, West Indies using an image-processor. *Journal of the Geological Society, London*, **145**, 541–552.

WAKEFORD, T. 2001. A selection of methods used in deliberative and inclusionary processes. *Participatory Learning and Action*, **40**, 29–31.

WATSON, I. M., OPPENHEIMER, C., VOIGHT, B. ET AL. 2000. The relationship between degassing and deformation at Soufrière Hills Volcano, Montserrat. *Journal of Volcanology and Geothermal Research*, **98**, 117–126.

WILBANKS, T. J. & KATES, R. W. 1999. Global change in local places. *Climatic Change*, **43**, 601–628.

WILLIAMS, C. & DUNN, C. E. 2003. GIS in participatory research: Assessing the impact of landmines on communities in North-west Cambodia. *Transactions in Geographical Information Systems*, **7**, 393–410.

WOOD, N. J., GOOD, J. W. & GOODWIN, R. F. 2002. Vulnerability assessment of a port and habor community to earthquake and tsunami hazards: Integrating technical expert and stakeholder input. *Natural Hazards Review*, **3**, 148–157.

WYNNE, B. 1992. Uncertainty and environmental learning: Reconceiving science and policy in the preventative paradigm. *Global Environmental Change*, **2**, 111–127.

YOSIE, T. F. & HERBST, T. D. 1998. *Using Stakeholder Processes in Environmental Decision Making: An Evaluation of Lessons Learned, Key Issues and Future Challenges*. Report for American Industrial Health Council.

ZERGER, A. 2002. Examining GIS decision utility for natural hazard risk modelling. *Environmental Modelling & Software*, **17**, 287–294.

Communicating environmental geoscience;
Australian communication pathways

COLIN J. SIMPSON

*IUGS Commission on Geoscience for Environmental Management (GEM), 73 Beasley Street,
Torrens, A.C.T. 2607, Australia (e-mail: simpsons@grapevine.com.au)*

Abstract: Effectively communicating the role of geoscience in environmental, sustainable development, and sustainable resource management issues is not a straightforward process; it requires different approaches that depend upon the audience being addressed. These audiences are broadly differentiated into three groups: scientists, governments and the general public. The communication process is complicated further by the difficulty that geoscientists can have in identifying the appropriate communication pathways to use if their endeavours are to be successful. Such pathways are not generally taught during formal scientific education and, as a consequence, it may require considerable experience for individuals to understand the processes involved. The World Wide Web now makes that process much easier. As an example of the types of understanding required, this paper outlines the geoscience communication pathways that exist at present in Australia, with an emphasis on government pathways, for the communication of geoscience, both nationally and internationally. It is hoped that this Australian example may stimulate geoscientists in other countries to record and publish (in simplified formats) the appropriate pathways required for effective environmental geoscience communication in their country.

Effectively communicating the role of geoscience in environmental, sustainable development, and sustainable resource management issues is not a straightforward process. Scientists are generally good at communicating with fellow scientists and particularly with scientists in the same discipline because they 'speak the same language'. However, when it comes to communicating with non-scientists, or with scientists in non-geoscience disciplines, it can often be a very difficult task. This is especially so, when geoscientists try to communicate with people about environmental matters when the audience consists of non-scientists, and with people who have no understanding of the relationship between geoscience and environmental matters.

Effective communication may require different approaches depending upon the educational background of the audience being addressed. These audiences can be broadly classed as scientists, government administrators and the general public. The communication process is complicated further by the difficulty that geoscientists can have in identifying the appropriate communication pathways to use if their endeavours are to be successful. It raises questions of exactly who they should talk with, and whether one organization can open better communication opportunities than another.

Within all science disciplines, including geoscience and its related disciplines, it is likely that there are already established pathways that can be used effectively to communicate with other scientists and non-scientists. The existence of formal links between different scientific and non-scientific organizations may also have established considerable influence and recognition between the organizations involved. The existence of such pathways is not generally taught or explained during formal scientific education and, as a consequence, it may require considerable experience for individuals to understand the processes involved. The Internet can often allow such pathways to be readily identified. However, some pathways may not be formally defined and it is up to the scientist to select the appropriate pathway to communicate effectively with the intended audience.

The use of established pathways for better communication is essentially a 'political' process involving the identification and selection of the most appropriate organization or people to contact to try and influence them to promote, through their established linkages, the information provided to them. The decision on which pathway to use may depend on whether additional benefits can be identified from the influence that some organizations or people in the pathway can provide to assist the process of getting important information to the right endpoint. Such pathways are referred to herein as 'influence' pathways.

In many countries there are growing numbers of scientists being employed to address environmental issues. In Australia, such 'environmental' scientists

From: LIVERMAN, D. G. E., PEREIRA, C. P. G. & MARKER, B. (eds) *Communicating Environmental
Geoscience*. Geological Society, London, Special Publications, **305**, 179–184.
DOI: 10.1144/SP305.15   0305-8719/08/$15.00 © The Geological Society of London 2008.

are generally unlikely to have any significant geoscience background or training. This paper outlines the established geoscience communication 'influence pathways' that exist for communicating geoscience to scientists and/or government personnel both within Australia and internationally. The first part of this paper deals with the influence pathways that can be used to communicate with scientists.

Scientific influence pathways

In Australia a prime link in the scientific communications network is the Australian Academy of Science (http://www.science.org.au/). The objectives of the Academy are to promote science through a range of activities. It has defined four major programme areas: education and public awareness, science policy, international relations, and recognition of outstanding contributions to science. The Academy acts as a focal point for contact between government, scientific experts, community leaders, educators and industry. It has 20 National Committees that are widely representative of its scientific disciplines. The role of the National Committees is to foster a designated branch of natural science in Australia, and to serve as a link between Australian scientists and overseas scientists in the same field. They are frequently called on to advise on science policy matters.

Because of the multidisciplinary nature of environmental science the Academy does not have a specific National Committee addressing environmental issues. The Academy's activities

in sustainability are carried out by the Joint Academies Committee on Sustainability (JACS), with membership from the four Australian learned academies (Australian Academy of Science, Australian Academy of Technological Sciences and Engineering, Academy of the Social Sciences in Australia, and Australian Academy of the Humanities).

Figure 1 shows the geoscience linkages into the various National Committees of the Academy. Of the 20 Committees currently established by the Academy, the nine shown have, to a greater or lesser extent, direct involvement with geoscience topics. Each of the National Committees shown has linkages with geoscience-related societies, institutes or associations, which means that geoscientists who belong to these professional bodies will already have, via their professional body's committee, access to an established communications pathway into the National Committee.

Figure 2 shows the linkages that the Academy's National Committee for Earth Sciences (one of the nine listed in Fig. 1) has established in both the national domain and the international sphere. These types of linkages are typical of linkages developed by the various National Committees shown in Figure 1.

Figure 3 shows the established international linkages into the International Council for Science (ICS) (http://www.icsu.org) (formerly known as the International Council of Scientific Unions; ICSU). The Australian Academy of Science is the formal adhering body representing Australia on the International Council for Science. The ICS is a non-governmental

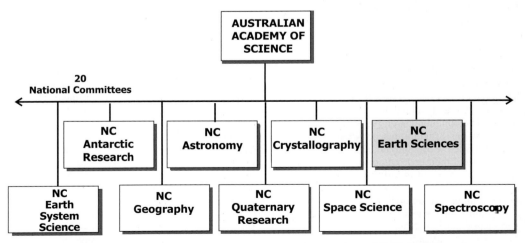

Fig. 1. Australian Academy of Science National Committees related to geoscience. NC, National Committee.

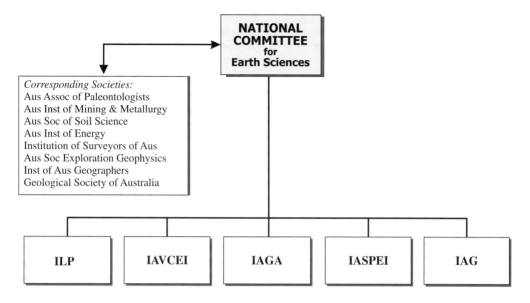

ILP   **International Lithosphere Program**
IAVCEI **International Association of Volcanology and Chemistry of the Earth's Interior**
IAGA   **International Association of Geomagnetism and Aeronomy**
IASPEI **International Association of Seismology and Physics of the Earth's Interior**
IAG   **International Association of Geomorphologists**

Fig. 2. National and International linkages of the National Committee for Earth Sciences.

organization and is the peak world body for all science disciplines, and has a global membership that includes both national scientific bodies (107 members) and international scientific unions (29 members). The ICS is the prime organization that represents science, including geoscience, and environmental issues, to the United Nations.

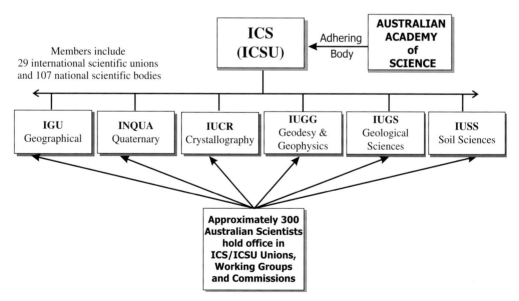

Fig. 3. Geoscience links into the International Council for Science.

Government-linked influence pathways

Australia's system of government is based on the British Westminster system. A Federal government administers national governance. Each State has its own government to administer internal government of the State, and at the local (shire) level government is administered by local governments. All levels of government undertake environmental management within their respective legislation. At the local government level, geoscience is not commonly used and geoscientists are not routinely employed except on a contract basis. Communication at that level is normally on a direct person-to-person basis.

Each State government has either a geological survey or the equivalent of a Department of Mines or Resources, as well as one or more departments that administer environmental policy. The Australian Government has both a national geological survey (Geoscience Australia; which is also responsible for offshore marine geoscience within Australia territorial waters) and a Department of Environment and Water Resources (DEWR), which develops and implements national policy, programmes and legislation to protect and conserve Australia's natural environment and cultural heritage. Several other government departments also have related environmental mandates and some of them are listed on the DEWR website (http://www.environment.gov.au/about/library/govtdepts.html).

Communication linkages between the State organizations equivalent to geological surveys or mines departments and Geoscience Australia is on a one-to-one basis and collaborative research projects between State–State and/or State–Federal organizations are established as required. Each year there is a combined meeting (the Chief Government Geologists meeting) of all directors of State geological surveys and the Director of Geoscience Australia; these meetings also include New Zealand (GNS Science).

Internally, the State and Federal government departments have the normal linkage pathways between their organizations and their ministerial offices, and other departments. Such pathways are not necessarily available to external, non-government agencies or individuals.

However, within these systems, the Australian Academy of Science also plays a significant role that involves maintaining linkages between government organizations, ministerial departments and the scientific community. The prime activity of such communication is undertaken by the Prime Minister's Science, Engineering and Innovation Council (PMSEIC).

The PMSEIC is the Australian Government's principal source of independent advice on issues in science, engineering, innovation, technology, and relevant aspects of education and training, and their contribution to the economic and social development of Australia. To underpin its advisory role, the Council has resources to examine Australia's science and engineering capabilities and the effectiveness of their organization and utilization. The PMSEIC has three types of members as shown in Fig. 4: Ministerial members, a Standing Committee of non-ministerial Ex-officio members, and Appointed Scientist members chosen in a personal capacity. The Council meets in full

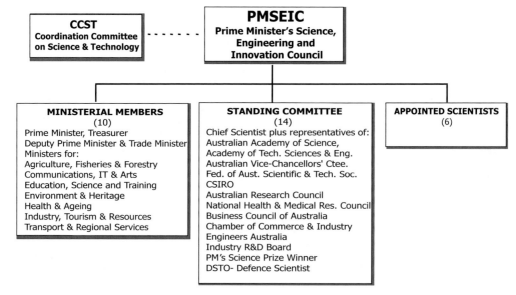

Fig. 4. Scientific links into the Prime Minister's Science, Engineering and Innovation Council (PMSEIC) (2006).

session twice a year. Current information can be found at: http://www.dest.gov.au/sectors/science_innovation/science_agencies_committees/prime_ministers_science_engineering_innovation_council/.

At present, the 10 Ministerial members of the PMSEIC include the Prime Minister, the Deputy Prime Minister and Minister for Trade, the Treasurer, and the Ministers of portfolios involved with elements of PMSEIC focus (Fig. 4). The 14 non-ministerial Ex-officio members who constitute the Standing Committee of the Council represent major science agencies, and science and industry groups. The role of the Standing Committee is to oversee and contribute to studies and research aimed at improving understanding of major, science, engineering and innovation issues. The Standing Committee meets four times a year (including two full meetings of the Council) and much of its work is undertaken through working groups comprising members, and those co-opted from industry, universities, science agencies and government departments. The Standing Committee responds to issues referred by Government or by meetings of PMSEIC; and also identifies and develops a range of issues to be considered by PMSEIC.

Informally linking into, and complementing the work of, the PMSEIC is the Coordination Committee on Science and Technology (CCST) (http://www.dest.gov.au/sectors/science_innovation/science_agencies_committees/coordination_committee_on_science_and_technology.htm), which brings together Deputy Secretaries and heads of Australian Government departments and agencies with an interest in science and technology. Membership of CCST is currently: the Chief Scientist of the Australian Government; nine government departments; six government agencies; five research funding agencies or committees, and four research performing agencies. The CCST facilitates networking, exchange of information, strategic thinking and coordination of activities in areas of science and technology. Several members sit on both the PMSEIC and the CCST. The four major Public Funded Research Agencies (PFRAS) (CSIRO, DSTO, ANSTO and AIMS) also have links into CCST. The outcome of CCST meetings is primarily an up-to-date and broad information base for providing well-coordinated advice to Government on science and technology matters. There is also scope in CCST for initiating co-operation between departments and agencies on specific science and technology issues, problems or identified opportunities.

These two major committees (the PMSEIC and the CCST) that involve Federal Government representatives for science, research, environment, resources and agriculture, and that link externally to industry, can operate as national and international hubs with very significant influence pathways between all members. They also provide the additional external pathway linkages via bodies such as the Academy of Science, and the PFRAS, and to their links to other national and international organizations. Organizations such as the PMSEIC and CSST can provide very important advice to a government that normally does not contain any elected politicians with a university science education.

This paper cannot cover all the influence pathways that exist but it identifies major ones to give some insight into how such pathways and linkages can operate. Within the Australian Government, for example, there are a number of additional councils and committees under the Council of Australian Governments (COAG) (http://www.coag.gov.au/) that relate to environmental and resource issues. Similarly, the Natural Resource Management Ministerial Council (NRMMC) (http://www.mincos.gov.au/), the Primary Industries Ministerial Council (PIMC) (http://www.mincos.gov.au/) and the Environment Protection and Heritage Council (EPHC) (http://www.ephc.gov.au/) are all potential influence pathways. Other government operations, such as the National Land and Water Resources Audit (NLWRA) (http://www.environment.gov.au/land/nlwra/index.html), have a number of National Committees that report to Ministerial Councils via the NLWRA.

Although this paper has focused on the government pathways and linkages, similar pathways also exist in non-government professional associations, institutions and societies, etc. The advent of the World Wide Web now provides an unprecedented means of more readily identifying such links and influence pathways. In many instances, websites may identify the executive body, chair, and sometimes all the members of a committee or organization. Such information can indicate the potential linkages for organizations or individuals (such as scientists in private practice) to establish communication. Such linkages can allow for a wider range of views to be considered from a more diverse range of people involved in environmental geoscience issues than if such influence pathways did not exist. There may also be scope for private sector organizations that specialize in providing improved communication practice, etc., to develop effective influence pathways to assist their clientele to communicate into major applications areas both nationally and internationally to assist in the transfer of knowledge, technology and best practice relating to environmental geoscience.

Conclusion

Both nationally and internationally significant influence pathways already exist to allow environmental geoscience information to be promoted into relevant areas. However, identifying such pathways is not necessarily an easy task. The World Wide Web now provides an unprecedented means of more readily identifying relevant influence pathways and associated links. The descriptions and the associated diagrams herein give a brief overview of some of the various influence pathways that operate across governance, geoscience, environment and other science disciplines in Australia, and between Australian organizations and the international scientific community. Ultimately it is the personal decision of scientists to select the pathway that they believe will be the most useful communications linkage to their intended audience.

iugs-gem.org) has an International Working Group on Communicating Environmental Geoscience (CEG) (www.mun.ca/canqua/ceg/). CEG is keen to assist in promoting better understanding of the various geoscience pathways to be followed within countries to achieve successful communication. It is hoped that this Australian example may stimulate geoscientists in other countries to record and publish (in simplified formats) the appropriate pathways linking similar governance, geoscience and environment, and associated scientific activities in their country.

Endnote

The International Union of Geological Sciences (IUGS) Commission on Geoscience for Environmental Management (GEM) (http://www.

The author gratefully acknowledges the assistance of P. McFadden, Chief Scientist of Geoscience Australia, and Fellow of the Australian Academy of Science, whose extensive knowledge of the major scientific linkages within Australia and internationally provided the basis for this paper.

Communication of geoscience information in public administration: UK experiences

BRIAN MARKER OBE

40 Kingsdown Avenue, London W13 9PT, UK (e-mail: brian@amarker.freeserve.co.uk)

Abstract: This paper is intended to provoke thought and discussion rather than to set out any 'right way' to communicate geoscience information. Public administration is complex, operating at several levels. It involves a wide variety of people, many of whom have little or no geoscience knowledge. It is important for geoscientists to understand administrative procedures so that results can be provided in the right form at the optimum time. There should also be a good understanding of the views, requirements and capacities of each potential target audience. This is best achieved through direct consultation and discussion. Consultation also helps to build trust and to guide the design of specific products. Results need to be presented logically, clearly and in straightforward language supported by good illustrations. These need to be tailored to fit the needs of each target audience; a single output will seldom meet the specific needs of all. The focus should be on the matters that are of importance to each audience, rather than on the research as such. Good dissemination of results is crucial and may require continuing efforts rather than just taking place at the end of the study. Consultation, presentation for non-specialists, and dissemination are time consuming. There needs to be adequate provision of staff time and money to support these. This may require a change in attitudes of some funding organizations. It is wise to plan consultation, presentation and dissemination from the commencement of work, revising plans as a fuller understanding of systems and audience requirements is gained.

This contribution is based on observations made during over 30 years of personal experience as an official in a central government department charged with: preparing and advising on legislation, policy and guidance on minerals, waste management and responses to geological hazards; and specifying and managing research in support of those tasks. Additional experience came from teaching adult education classes on applied geoscience topics. The paper is pitched at the general rather than the site-specific level, although some comments might apply to both. It is unwise to over-generalize from specific experiences, so this paper is intended to provoke thought and discussion rather than to set out opinions on any 'right way' to undertake communication. Readers who would prefer a review of international attempts at communication of geohazards information, rather than a personal view, are encouraged to refer to Forster & Freeborough (2006).

A key point is that sound science is of little practical value if no one pays attention to it. In the interests of sustainable development, it is wise to be proactive in identifying geoscience issues and problems, but all too often research takes place after problems have occurred. This reflects a generally low appreciation at the administrative level of the significance and importance of geological and geomorphological issues that, ultimately, requires good communication and education. Authorities need to be convinced that the benefits of investment will outweigh subsequent costs and are affordable.

Good communication is not just a matter of expressing results clearly and accessibly. It requires careful consideration of many different things. This paper commences with a brief description of the administrative context in the UK so that those engaged in other systems can assess the relevance of the stated views to their own circumstances. It goes on to consider audiences for information, consultation, presentation, dissemination and constraints, before drawing some conclusions.

The administrative context

The UK is part of the European Union, therefore legislation and regulation comes from European, as well as domestic, sources. Administrative arrangements in the UK operate at national, country (i.e. England, Northern Ireland, Wales and Scotland), regional and local levels. England is divided into a number of regions with their own administrations. Within these, a large number of local authorities are responsible for local areas, including implementation of the planning system. Therefore there are several levels of interaction between tiers of government, and with the general public, that have to be co-ordinated.

Within administrations, elected members are responsible for making decisions whereas unelected

From: LIVERMAN, D. G. E., PEREIRA, C. P. G. & MARKER, B. (eds) *Communicating Environmental Geoscience*. Geological Society, London, Special Publications, **305**, 185–196.
DOI: 10.1144/SP305.16   0305-8719/08/$15.00 © The Geological Society of London 2008.

officials develop, give advice on, and implement policies and procedures. Members take account of, but are not bound to follow, the advice of officials. Officials are organized into units that have distinctive responsibilities but these are reorganized from time to time, often with staff changes and, sometimes, consequent loss of continuity, documentation and corporate memory. Although officials implement decisions taken by elected members, there is also a need for liaison between officials within and across the tiers of administration to make sure that all relevant matters are taken into account and potential problems, conflicts and mismatches in policies are identified, discussed and resolved at an early stage. Within administrations, there is recognition of the need for a sound evidence base for policy but sometimes a lack of appreciation that this should include geological information.

Availability of expertise is very variable. Some authorities may specifically employ geologically trained staff for work on obviously relevant topics, such as minerals or waste management. Others do not. Staff dealing with topics such as built development and conservation infrequently have a geoscience background. If geoscience issues arise in the absence of specific expertise, advice may be sought elsewhere within the authority. For instance, planning units faced with geological hazards may consult building control departments. But many building control officers, although they have an understanding of foundation issues, are structural engineers, rather than civil engineers or geologists, so the extent of that help may be limited. Alternatively, advice may be sought externally, by contract, from commercial consultancies, the British Geological Survey (BGS), or academic departments, although this is usually kept to an essential minimum for reasons of costs.

Only exceptionally is geological expertise available amongst elected members or senior officials. However, it is unwise to assume that they are wholly unaware of geological issues. They often have to deal with concerns of the public over minerals or waste management proposals, or events such as floods, subsidence, contamination, pollution and landslides. However, they may not overtly recognize these as coming within the ambit of geosciences or the need for sound geological investigation to address such matters at an early stage.

In addition, executive agencies are responsible for specific regulatory matters. Thus, the Environment Agency in England and Wales, or the Scottish Environment Protection Agency, are responsible for safeguarding the environment in those countries. Similarly there are agencies responsible, for example, for nature conservation or for protection of the national heritage. All have their own expert advisers, but only some employ geoscientists. However, there is a much greater appreciation of the need to understand technical issues amongst these bodies than in administrations. This is partly because they are charged with advising Government on the topics for which they are specifically responsible, and are statutory consultees required to be consulted on development plans and planning applications. Also, they may need to commission works. For instance, the Environment Agency has responsibilities for flood defence.

Some relevant parties are not, because of their status, statutory consultees. For instance, the BGS is not funded for that purpose because it is a research institute, yet it is a key source of expertise and advice. However, some advice published by Government to explain good practices in planning does draw the attention of planners and developers to BGS information holdings and advice (e.g. Office of the Deputy Prime Minister (ODPM) 2003).

In the UK, many functions have been privatized including, for example, the water utilities, which, of course, employ hydrogeologists as a matter of course. However, in general, the private sector uses commercial consultancies for geological advice and it is mainly those consultancies that draw on the expertise and information held by the BGS, other research institutes, and academic institutions.

The general public becomes involved in administrative processes in two main ways: during public consultations and when specific issues arise. Consultation is required during the development of policies and guidance at the national tier of government; spatial and sustainable development strategies at the regional level; and planning and management strategies and plans at the local level. Although there are strong opportunities for democratic input, responses can be very variable depending on awareness and understanding of the issues, and are often limited by lack of time and resources. Securing involvement of people from lower income and minority groups can be particularly difficult. Specific issues such as single planning applications often lead to public opposition, and hazardous events lead to lobbying for action to be taken. Sometimes lobbyists are well informed, but often they are not.

Plans and programmes are subject to Sustainability Appraisal, which includes strategic environmental assessment (ODPM 2003). In addition, development proposals that may cause significant environmental effects are subject to environmental impact assessment (Department for the Environment, Transport and the Regions (DETR) 2000). It is open to all parties to comment on the resulting documents before any decision is taken. Both types of document are required to have summaries that are aimed at the wider public, but geoscience matters are only part of these overall assessments. There is a necessary interface between these and other sciences as well as social and economic information. Therefore these documents are generally prepared by multidisciplinary teams. Monitoring of plans, and mandatory reviews of them at 5 year intervals provide key opportunities for the input of new findings.

This is a complicated system that requires close liaison between all relevant parties, at a number of levels, within the availability of staff resources, encouraged partly through legal requirements to consult statutory consultees and the public on development plans and planning applications. Unfortunately, overall, geological understanding is variable, and often weak. The evidence base of geoscience information is used to a varying degree in preparation of development plans and environmental appraisal depending on accessibility of data and the form in which it exists. Therefore geoscientists need to present data in the right way, appreciate administrative procedures, and understand when information needs to be provided if effective advice is to be given. Similar comments are likely to apply to many other administrative structures.

Audiences

Likely audiences for results include subject specialists, experts in other disciplines, or people untrained in any sciences at all. These may include ministers and other elected members, officials, developers, landowners, financial institutions, planners, non-governmental organizations and the general public.

Wider audiences vary greatly in level of education, cultural and social diversity, and personal interests. Interests within mixed communities are not homogeneous. Therefore it is important to assess the range of interests, opinions and understanding. Language barriers may also have to be taken into account. All audiences have distinctive viewpoints and capacities to deal with issues, even if the issue in question is common to everyone. There can be particular problems in dealing with 'single issue' lobbying groups because these may take a narrow view of what should be done when a wide range of potentially conflicting matters actually need to be taken into account in the interests of sustainable development. However, geoscientists should be aware that they themselves may also be regarded as a potentially self-serving, single issue lobby by administrations and communities. Substantial interactions between scientists and potential audiences are needed to overcome such attitudes.

In general, geoscience information is not a key interest of many people who may need to become engaged, unless minds are concentrated by events such as a major development initiative or a natural disaster. Rather, a wide range of economic and social issues including health, employment, housing, crime levels and education understandably take precedence and absorb most attention and funds. Indeed, it can be difficult to convince stakeholders of the need to take geoscience issues seriously when many do not even appreciate what the geosciences involve, commonly confusing these with archaeology or simply the study of past life. Those who have a general awareness of geology sometimes think that, because it deals with events on a geological time scale, it is not very relevant to the present except, perhaps, in respect of earthquakes, volcanic eruptions and tsunamis. This is partly a result of a basic education system that may touch lightly on those topics, plate tectonics, the fossil record and pollution, but is less likely to refer to matters such as subsidence, landslides, contamination and general foundation conditions until more advanced levels.

Moreover, it cannot be assumed that advice, however well founded, will be gladly received. For instance, the writer has encountered instances where local residents did not wish to hear about subsidence hazards because they feared a fall in value of, or difficulties in selling, properties if this were to become widely known. In another place, elected members opposed the publication of a hazard map because they feared that it would damage investment in their area, until it was pointed out that neighbouring authorities that lacked such maps had similar problems but were not able to give developers any assurance of where problems might exist. Complacency can also be a factor. For example, people living close to a volcano that has not erupted for several hundred years may assume it to be either extinct or unlikely to cause problems within their lifetimes. It can be difficult to dissuade them of this until volcanic activity becomes very apparent. Even then, people may be reluctant to accept warnings of the need to leave, as was seen in the 1980 Mount St. Helens eruption. Even if authorities appear to accept recommendations, these will not necessarily be acted upon, as was shown, for example, in the destructive 1985 lahar event at Armero, Colombia (Donnelly 2008). The hazard was understood but, in the event, no warning was given. Communities may also be suspicious of advice from people from different cultural or social backgrounds for instance; understandably, when citizens of former colonial territories are advised by people from the previously occupying nation, or where people on low incomes harbour suspicions of those they regard as being from privileged backgrounds. Dealing with scepticism and building trust and confidence are crucial and best done through close liaison and working with administrations and communities prior to, and during, research rather than afterwards. Scientists sometimes see this as a burden delaying the real, important, work, but it is often essential.

Consultation

Consultation is a key aspect of many procedural systems and is mandatory in respect of environmental and sustainability assessments. However, consultation is also valuable for: seeking relevant information; gaining an understanding of issues, audiences and administrative systems; and building confidence amongst stakeholders. It is therefore needed both before and during research. The use of research steering groups drawn from key stakeholders and augmented, if necessary, with independent experts can be very valuable in guiding research and, importantly, commenting on the suitability of presentation of results. Proper consultation can be complicated, time consuming and sometimes frustrating, and is often not fully budgeted into work costs and timetables. It is prudent to carefully plan consultation, supported by adequate resources, before work commences, and to revise plans, as necessary, as work proceeds.

It is wise to plan consultations at the outset and to update the approaches, as necessary, during the work. Some matters that need to be considered are the following.

(1) What is the administrative context?
(2) How will results be incorporated and used?
(3) Who are the relevant groups?
(4) Where are they located?
(5) What are their levels of understanding?
(6) What is the best way of engaging with each?
(7) What information should they be provided with?
(8) What information might they be able to provide?

Key principles of consultation include inclusiveness, transparency, openness and clarity, independence (e.g. if necessary, using a neutral convener), commitment, accessibility, accountability, productivity and adequate resources. Approaches include workshops, focus groups, standing liaison groups, public meetings, exhibitions and Internet communications (Environment Council 2004). It is important to clarify the purpose of the consultation, choose appropriate methods of engagement, demonstrably use the results, distil any lessons for future engagement, and revise techniques to secure involvement of any groups that have not been properly engaged. It is generally good practice to sound out, and

listen carefully to, audience concerns and attitudes first rather than commencing by telling them what it is felt that they should be doing.

Presentation

Geoscientists are trained to prepare scientific papers. That often carries through, consciously or unconsciously, to the preparation of many other types of document. Scientific papers tend to commence with a review of previous research, to state what activities have been undertaken, to express the geological context and only then discuss the applied implications and set out conclusions. An abstract, in technical language, is presented that covers the whole of the content of the paper. That approach is unlikely to fit well with the requirements of many non-scientists, who require a summary that focuses on the essentials of those findings that are relevant to them. If the audience is geoscientifically inexperienced, that requires careful editing, simplification and explanation. It would be beneficial if more geoscientists were introduced to writing for non-technical audiences during their training.

Many potential audiences for geoscience information lack knowledge of basic concepts. In work intended for dissemination to these, the aim is to convey a basic understanding of the relevant issues and consequences, rather than teaching them geology.

Common sources of misunderstanding

Amongst many non-scientists there is a generally weak appreciation of scientific method, including a failure to distinguish between hypothesis, theory and fact. Confusion between these can lead to perverse responses including under- or over-reactions to findings, leading to unnecessarily restrictive or excessively lax policies, misplaced investment or failure to react. Therefore conclusions need to be carefully framed. Dissemination of information needs to be carefully planned and handled. Some particular matters that may be poorly understood are the following.

Hazard. The identification of a hazard may give rise to excessive concern even when the likelihood of adverse impacts is low. Conversely, if areas are attributed with a low level of hazard that is often read as meaning that nothing adverse will occur. Hazard studies commonly classify land into high, medium or low hazard zones in the area being considered. As 'high' in one area may be 'moderate' in another, this can be misleading to those who have no comparative reference standard. It is therefore important to convey a realistic idea of the relative scale and frequency of likely impacts. Also, there is a low level of public awareness that many hazards can be dealt with. There needs to be a greater understanding that development can, in most circumstances, still take place although the costs of mitigation can sometimes be so high as to make specific developments uneconomic. Although major hazardous events may be widely regarded as 'acts of god', victims often look for someone to blame, perhaps in the hope that a failure of responsibility might lead to liability and, thus, to potential compensation. There can sometimes, therefore, be significant resistance to objective evaluations and explanations. Conclusions can seldom be precise and definitive but there is likely to be a serious loss of confidence if any assessment or prediction, no matter how guarded, appears to the audience to be incorrect.

Vulnerability and risk. These terms have specific technical meanings that are not widely known. In particular, there is often uncertainty about the threshold level of risk that should stimulate action by public authorities, whether expressed in terms of life, health or financial loss. People tend to fear and exaggerate things that they are unfamiliar with (e.g. landslides in areas where these occur only rarely) but may be much more tolerant of familiar factors (e.g. road traffic accidents) that are far more likely to affect them. This can lead to under- or over-reactions to research findings. A key question is 'What is acceptable risk?' Answering this is essentially a political decision to be taken after a public debate. It is important, therefore, to put these issues into context.

Uncertainty and probability. The expression of uncertainty can be a difficult issue because of a tendency on the part of many people to equate uncertainty with unreliability. Expressing these in terms of confidence levels is not widely understood. For general audiences, it can be better to use the more widely understood 'language of gambling' such as a one in 10 chance of an event taking place. The writer has encountered instances where individuals have refused to accept statistically tested data because they seem to them 'unreliable' whereas they have been willing to use data that have not been statistically tested at all because they seems to them to be 'more precise'. Also, there is limited awareness of the real significance of averages, means, and ranges.

Return periods, for events such as flooding. A 100 year return period for a specific size of event may often be perceived as meaning 'we are safe for 100 years, so why worry?' When a '100 year flood' occurs a few years later, there can be a mistaken perception that advice was wrong and a loss of confidence in research findings.

Defence against hazards. There is often a perception that engineering measures can eliminate risk whereas these generally reduce risk to a perceived acceptable level. The writer once asked planners in a specific area how they took account of flood hazard when identifying areas for new development. The response was, worryingly, that they did not need to because protective embankments had been in place for over a century. There can also be unrealistic demands for action to be taken even when there is little or no prospect of a satisfactory long-term solution. This occurs because of a lack of awareness about how hazards can be reduced and managed through well-planned investigation, mitigation, monitoring and remedial work, and of the constraints on what can be realistically achieved.

Relevance of change. Most research is required to end by a specific date. Commissioning bodies then tend to think of results as complete. However, all areas are subject to social, economic and environmental changes. These can lead, for instance, to changes in Earth processes, hazard and resource potential, land use and management practices, and, with urbanization, increased levels of risk. New administrative structures, procedures and guidance can lead to past advice lapsing. Personnel may retire or move away, leading to a loss of familiarity with, or expertise on, specific issues and of 'corporate memory'. Therefore research results and recommendations may need to be reviewed at intervals but funding organizations may be reluctant to 'repeat' work even though the original results may become increasingly misleading as time passes.

Limitations. Great care is needed in how limitations on findings are expressed because it is very easy to give non-specialists the impression that findings are too vague to be believed.

Careful explanations are needed.

Text

There is a major difference between fully describing research and findings and communicating essential issues to specific audiences. To meet the needs of wider audiences, results generally need to be explained in relatively simple terms, logically structured, and in straightforward language. The writer has sometimes encountered researchers who regard widely understandable outputs as something that can be prepared quickly, almost as an afterthought. Simplification while retaining the essentials of any findings is actually a difficult and time-consuming task that requires significant effort because audiences may be very diverse in education, cultural backgrounds, attitudes and aspirations. It is necessary to take time to know and understand the target audience(s) and to identify what is important to them. That is an iterative consultative process.

Caution is needed because some audiences are better informed. It is very easy to sound condescending or patronizing when the target person or audience actually knows more about the issues than one thinks they do. That can cause irritation. Therefore it is wise to establish levels of understanding within different sectors of the intended audiences early on.

Following a major environmental geology mapping initiative in the UK, a well-illustrated guide to environmental geology for planners and developers was prepared by both planners and geoscientists (Thompson *et al.* 1998). This used straightforward language, was structured in terms of issues of direct interest to planners (e.g. minerals, waste management, hazards, and supporting information technology). It was well received by the intended audience, but might not have met the specific needs of others, such as the general public, because they are often interested in only one or two local issues rather than the whole text.

Public authorities generally wish to have advice that is consistent with their existing or emerging plans, policies and programmes. There are real difficulties in trying to influence a change of direction in these, particularly if the change might, for example, be closer to the proposed policies of a rival political party. It is important, therefore, to gain a clear understanding of the policy context by listening to officials and approaching issues from their point of view and, as far as possible, to link results into the existing policy framework. This requires special communication skills, so the best outputs may be those prepared by teams including experts in both science and communication.

Elected members, whether at national, regional or local level, face many priorities that are actually, or seem to them to be, more important than geoscience issues. The capacity to understand and react to these is as varied as it is amongst the wider public. Arguments need to be clear, strong and brief to change the perception of priorities, although sometimes events will themselves alter imperatives. Ministers, other elected members, and senior administrators have limited time to devote to any one issue so it is often a matter of dealing with an issue on only one or two pages. An approach to setting out the issues (given as an example, not a template) is to: (1) clearly state the issue(s); (2) summarize the recommendation(s) or options, together with reasons, in a few lines; (3) summarize the environmental, economic and social implications of each (as appropriate); (4) set out essential discussion, stating any key limitations on findings, but leaving supporting material to annexes; (5) state the conclusions (which should be supported by clear evidence and lead logically into the recommendations or options); (6) set out essential supporting material only, in annexes, limited to that which develops or constrains the conclusions and recommendations.

A key test is whether or not each sentence is essential. This approach can be difficult for scientists trained to describe all aspects of a research project for their peers. A common reaction amongst geoscientists is that it is impossible to do justice to a difficult and complicated subject within such a short document. However, it is possible to do so effectively if one has to. It also needs to be kept in mind that it is often an official who prepares and submits this material, rather than the geoscientist, so careful discussion may be needed before the document is prepared and discussion of drafts is important.

It is often desirable to state as clearly and concisely as possible the costs and benefits of each option, how long each would take to be implemented, and how present and recommended actions might constrain future decisions. An approach to considering ground conditions that could be adapted for use in this way has been provided by Hounjet & Ngan-Tillard (2007). They examined ground conditions and assessed the suitability of trial areas for development of various types. They then used the nature of foundations that would be required in different parts to assess relative development costs.

Some costs and benefits can be fairly readily estimated, in financial or human terms, such as risks in terms of possible financial losses or numbers of people who might be harmed over a given period. Others can only be approached subjectively; for instance, impacts on landscapes. Economists have a number of techniques for developing proxy financial estimates for such costs that are often familiar to officials and elected members in other contexts, and may be taken by them as persuasive in respect of policies and decisions, even though some of these rest primarily on public opinion (e.g. contingent valuation, which assesses willingness to pay to avoid a particular outcome, or willingness to accept an outcome if compensated in some way). The findings of such methods do not always fit well with the principles of sustainable development, as they rest on public perceptions rather than objective evidence. Careful dialogue with economists is needed if the commissioning organization feels the need for such methods of evaluation.

It can also be psychologically useful to present results positively, in terms of opportunities for use, and suitability of, land, rather than constraints and limitations, even though these are 'two sides of the same coin'.

Planning guidance needs to be expressed in terms that can be appreciated by planners and developers, as well as other interests that might support or oppose planning proposals. Little more than a statement of policies might be needed if these audiences are well versed in the issues, but if these are unfamiliar then guidance also needs to perform an educational function (see, for example, DETR 2002). That is especially so where, for instance, ground problems occur only intermittently and therefore local experience of these is limited. It is particularly important to draw attention to examples of good practices adopted in similar circumstances elsewhere.

Decision support systems, if well designed, may help to guide users through a necessary logic chain. For instance, the BGS has developed a prototype environmental information system for planners. This is based on a logic tree that reflects the various stages of the planning system (preparation of regional spatial strategy, preparation of the development plan, pre-application enquiries, and planning application). This provides summary information at the right level of detail to the user but also indicates key information and advice that is needed, and where it can be sought (if not included within the system), at the various stages for which it will be needed. Although this provides the necessary supporting information, it does not attempt to replace the users' responsibility for making recommendations on policy or planning applications (Alker 2002).

The wider public is likely to focus on the implications, positive or negative, that findings are likely to have for them and how they should react to these. It is useful to keep in mind that, in many cases, recipients of advice do not actually feel the need for detailed information, leaving that to the experts. Rather, they usually require a straightforward description of the issue and to be told what to do about it, who to ask questions of, what to ask, how advisers can be contacted, and when to ask. It is prudent to clarify these matters when results are published.

For good reasons, geoscientists normally use a great deal of technical terminology amongst themselves that is not widely understood, and is likely to dissuade inexperienced readers. This should be avoided or, if absolutely essential, should be explained in the text. Glossaries are useful for some audiences but often not for the general reader, who may be put off by the text before ever reaching the glossary.

There is value in using non-geoscientists, whether other staff or, for instance, steering or focus groups, to test the proposed presentation of the key messages.

Maps and models

Much geoscience information is communicated by means of maps, whether traditional or electronic. That has advantages with some audiences (for instance, planners use maps regularly), but only if these are presented in the right way. Line work needs to be as clear and simple as possible. Legends need to be modified and simplified to concentrate on the essentials required by the specific audience, the purpose of the map, and, especially, how the map should be used. Aspects of appropriate use are commonly covered in disclaimers, whereas it is often better, for a general audience, to explain how to use the map in more positive terms.

An initiative was undertaken in the UK to develop and apply techniques of environmental geology mapping for land-use planning. Over 50 areas were mapped, mainly by the BGS (Smith & Ellison 1999). Initially, results were prepared in traditional geological and thematic maps and were little used by planners. However, it took a step in which separate technical and summary (non-specialist) reports and maps specifically giving planning advice were prepared to make real progress (see, for instance, Bunton *et al.* (1996), prepared by both planners and geoscientists).

The use of a geographic information system (GIS), 3D ground maps, and explanatory or predictive models is increasing. GIS is often persuasive because outputs look professional, but non-geologists are unlikely to appreciate that these outputs are only as reliable as the data on which they are based. The geoscientist is able to evaluate the limitations of a dataset or system at the outset, but others are unlikely, and often unable, to do so. The writer has encountered some geoscientists who seem to feel that GIS displays and 3D models are automatically more comprehensible to non-technical users of information than traditional media, but that is not generally so. These outputs are subject to the same requirements for simplification and explanation as any other geological representations if they are to be properly appreciated. There is also a danger that GIS specialists who do not possess geoscience training might manipulate layers inappropriately. Sound design of the legend or description, informed by an understanding of the intended audience, is essential. Moreover, a digital model may be regarded with suspicion as a 'black box' that produces results in ways that a general audience cannot understand. Careful explanation of and building of confidence in these becomes even more important.

Illustrations

Well-selected diagrams and photographs are usually essential when communicating ideas, but images need to be carefully and sparingly selected so that the reader does not become lost in detail. Geoscientists often underestimate the complexity of many diagrams that they present because of deep familiarity with their subject. Diagrams for non-specialists need to be clear and simple. Much depends on the conciseness and clarity of captions. It can be useful to look at examples prepared to communicate health issues, because that sector has generally progressed further than the geosciences in communicating issues to the public. Diagrams after the style of a 'strip cartoon' can be valuable in demonstrating processes and impacts. Video presentation can also be useful but use has been limited in the past by costs. Short sequences are now often included on websites and DVDs, and are valuable if selected carefully.

There is also value in using carefully selected formats and illustrations to improve the visual and professional appearance of results. These are more likely to be read if they look inviting, but are often more convincing to specific audiences if local examples and case studies are provided.

Collaboration between experts

Because many tasks involve a call on more than one science and, increasingly often, on social and economic expertise, there is a strong need for communication between experts in different disciplines. This is not a minor matter. There are sometimes subtle differences in approaches, concepts and use of language that need to be resolved during collaboration. That is best done if all disciplines form a cohesive team that works together throughout. It is important to resolve communications within the team before results can be communicated effectively with the target audiences.

Dissemination

Particular problems are access to, and availability of, results. If these are confined to the scientific literature then they will be known only to a relatively small circle of experts and are unlikely to be acted upon. Thorough, well-directed dissemination is therefore essential to success. A single output aimed at a wider audience is unlikely to fit the requirements of all because of the diversity of organizations and individuals that need to become involved. Dissemination to wider audiences requires customized outputs. Provision of information, whether through printed documents, electronic media or face-to-face contacts, depends on the capacities of specific audiences. Good analysis of potential audiences is required if results are to be made fully accessible.

The initiative, mentioned above, undertaken in the UK to develop and apply techniques of environmental geology mapping for land-use planning covered over 50 areas, mainly urban. Initially, results were prepared in traditional geological formats and were little used by planners. Steering groups, drawn from key local organizations, were introduced to guide subsequent projects, and this helped greatly in securing more relevant results. It took a step in which separate technical and summary (non-specialist) reports were prepared to make real progress. The local authorities and steering groups played a major part in disseminating results and seminars were held on completion of the work. The review of the use of these products undertaken later (Smith & Ellison 1999) found that, of 50 studies, about 20% were little used and only about 10% had fairly high use, with the remainder having moderate use. In some cases, their existence has since been forgotten. Unsurprisingly, most of those that scored highly were prepared late in the initiative when specific planning and land suitability maps were included.

The guide to environmental geology for planners (Thompson et al. 1998) was well received at dissemination seminars. A large number of copies were distributed at relevant events. Case studies were mounted on a website. Otherwise the report was available from the consultancy that undertook the work. This probably limited the subsequent success of the work because the report was not available from any major publishing house or in bookshops and quickly went out of print.

Work undertaken on landsliding at Ventnor, Isle of Wight, as part of the same overall research programme, has probably led to the most successful geoscience communication initiative, to date, in the UK. The initial research was assisted enthusiastically by the local authority. Results were disseminated through separate seminars for elected members, insurance interests and a wider audience. Press and media briefings were provided. A leaflet summarizing the findings was delivered to all households and businesses in the area and later updated (McInnes 2002). A shop was rented in central Ventor for several months, at which the public could meet researchers, ask questions and discuss concerns.

The local authority subsequently supported extensive additional monitoring and research, published revised and additional reports (e.g. McInnes

2003), circulated new leaflets at intervals, and set up a Centre for the Coastal Environment to promote longer-term awareness and education on coastal issues, including landslides. The authority undertook a survey of public awareness of the issue and reactions to the report that had been provided. This proved a high level of awareness. In addition, all respondents considered that the report was either very informative or informative. Moreover, initially there had been problems in securing insurance cover in the area but 76% of respondents confirmed that they had obtained full insurance cover. This confirmed that dissemination to the insurance companies had also been effective (McInnes 2007). The initiative was then extended, under European Union funding, to other member states to develop and disseminate good practice, resulting in some outputs that are models of their kind (e.g. Fairbank & Jakeways 2006). The strong success of this initiative rests on continuing enthusiasm and commitment within the local authority, the preparation of readily available well-directed products, and careful attention to continuing dissemination.

A further example that can be cited is work undertaken for the Union des Associations Techniques Internationales, World Federation of Engineering Organizations and the UK Overseas Development Agency as part of the International Decade of Natural Disaster Reduction (Institution of Civil Engineers 1995). It is a comprehensive and well-written source of advice on the nature of, and responses to, disasters that deserves to be widely read. The ambitious aim was to provide an overview, practical guidance and an *aide-mémoire* for public administrators, staff of agencies involved in development programmes, managers of public utilities and commercial and industrial enterprises, educators, community and voluntary workers in non-governmental organizations, members of professional groups, and property developers, owners and occupiers, particularly in urban areas. However, it was published by a specialist publisher of engineering texts, was relatively long, and was not aimed at specific audiences amongst those listed. This may have limited the extent to which it has been read by those outside the engineering profession.

More generally, printed documents, even if these are published by public authorities, commonly have small print runs and limited advertising, which seriously limits success. For instance, the writer has experienced circumstances in which only a few dozen copies of reports were printed. Copies were sent to relevant authorities and interest groups. Yet awareness remained low because, although these were received by relevant authorities, they were not necessarily sent to the right people in those organizations. Some were returned to the sender, occasionally with a note complaining at the waste of government money in providing them in the first place. Other organizations, not on the mailing lists, remained unaware of the material, or became aware later, only to find that the material was out of print. It is important, therefore, that awareness is raised before material is dispatched, that it should be directed to the right people, and that sufficient copies should be produced to satisfy the whole of the intended 'market'. Also, results may be useful over a long period but the initial initiative soon fades from memory, so repeated dissemination may be required.

This is a matter of 'market penetration'. Advertisers develop a strategy by scoping the market, identifying the key messages and the media to be used, and allocating significant resources to the initiative. Following an initial intensive campaign, there are usually less intensive reminders at appropriate intervals, followed by subsequent larger campaigns, if necessary, to re-establish the 'brand'. Geoscientists might learn from that approach.

Leaflets may be of value in reaching wide audiences if these are clear, concise, and well and attractively designed, but it is important to identify the best outlets at which to make these available (e.g. schools, public libraries, municipal offices) and to secure the co-operation of those who might distribute them. In some cases, especially in respect of concerns over, and responses to, geohazards, it can be best to distribute these to every household and business, if necessary taking account of language diversity. Where literacy is limited, of course, leaflets are of limited value and visual aids and/or direct presentations are essential.

Parallel publication on the Internet and on CD has made many results more widely available, but only for those audiences that use information technology. Some socio-economic groups are unlikely, at present, to have access to such sites or IT skills. Even those who do, including some who may have geoscience backgrounds, may be too busy to search for material. It is important to consider who may be missed out, and how to reach them, and, again, to raise awareness that the material exists through carefully focused prior announcements.

Care is required in handling the public and the media. Fear of misrepresentation by journalists may make researchers reluctant to connect with the media. However, reluctance to engage can be interpreted by the media as 'having something to hide' so transparency is sensible, although not without risk. Journalists are by no means always hostile and negative. They often report information fairly if it is explained carefully to them, ideally through direct contacts, or alternatively through carefully drafted press statements. Brief press announcements with short notes to editors can be very useful in drawing attention to issues but must be very concise or they will be edited by journalists who may have limited understanding of the issues. This can result in misleading or unbalanced messages in the published article. It is prudent to also make such statements more widely available so that any misunderstandings can be more easily rectified. The time taken is an investment, rather than a burden. It can save time correcting problems that arise later.

Public presentations, accompanied by visual material, are often essential. Seminars are frequently held at the end of work. Even if aimed at specific groups of stakeholders, these are likely to attract only a small number of participants, often those who are already aware of the issues, and do not spread results as widely as they deserve. The advertising of such events, the choice of location and the time of day can all be crucial. Several events may be needed. In general, it is better to go to the chosen audience(s) than to expect them to come to the researchers.

Radio and television are possible vehicles for communication but it is often difficult to secure more than a few minutes of air time, which is seldom enough to present all that needs to be said. Even a short item can be valuable in drawing attention to research initiatives, publications, websites and dissemination events. If an opportunity does arise, then careful preparation of short sentences on the most important issues only is needed if the time is to be used effectively.

It can be useful to draw on good practices already in use elsewhere to demonstrate the effectiveness of proposed approaches. For instance, in England there is an initiative to identify 'beacon authorities' that can be commended to, and assist, other local authorities on particular issues. This can be particularly important for areas where ground problems occur only intermittently and local experience of these is sparse.

Education should not be overlooked. Preparing course material for teachers can help to alert the next generation; also, importantly, things that pupils learn can feed back to their parents.

It is important, therefore, to identify the best means of reaching all relevant audiences and the best means of doing so. The formulation of a dissemination plan should be carried out well before the end of the study. Results may have been prepared in the necessary presentational forms but will be used effectively only if all relevant audiences are aware of their existence and significance.

In summary, awareness of results can be stimulated through direct contacts such as seminars and public meetings, press statements, radio or television interviews and websites. Careful selection of the appropriate approaches and careful

preparation are needed. Publication on the Internet or on CD is useful but will not reach those who are not IT literate. Usually at least some paper reports, summaries or leaflets are needed. It can also be useful to provide specific material for teachers to use in local schools. It is often useful to draw on examples of good practices used successfully in other areas that experience similar issues. The numbers of copies must be sufficient to serve the whole of market both initially and for the time that results will remain in use.

It is prudent to plan dissemination early on and to update the strategy as work, including consultations, progresses. Some matters that might be considered are as follows:

(1) What, and how large, are the target audiences?

(2) Where are they located and how dispersed are they?

(3) What are their levels of understanding?

(4) What are the key messages for each?

(5) What media should be used? (e.g. website, seminar, leaflets, reports, meetings, press announcements, etc.)

(6) How should outputs be designed?

(7) How many copies should be produced?

(8) What are the best strategies for drawing attention to results?

(9) Is initial dissemination only sufficient, or should follow-up events take place at intervals?

Constraints

There will always be constraints on the presentation and communication of geoscience information, both at the general and site-specific levels. Ideally, budgets would be adequate to secure all of the necessary information but the process of research commonly identifies as many new questions as it does answers. The statement that 'we need to undertake further research before we can give advice' is almost invariably an unwelcome one. It may be true, but can be perceived as self-seeking, for additional funds, on the part of researchers. Also, decisions must often be taken quickly based on the best available information at the time.

General (strategic) assessments of issues are generally funded through either research grants or specific contract commissions. Research grants have the advantage of providing reasonable academic freedom to pursue investigations but with the risk that the required answers may not be available at the necessary level of detail for application at the right time. Academic research is increasingly driven, however, by the need for peer-reviewed papers in prestigious journals, and subsequent citations, but those journals are less likely to be consulted by, or understood by, many of the people who need to take account of findings. The present author is aware of a few instances where grants have included, in the description of the intended work, the preparation of additional outputs for non-scientists, but when these studies have approached conclusion, the researchers have declined to prepare those outputs because allocated money and time were running short and the researchers did not see these products as contributing to their career objectives. That is short-sighted and can limit the success of valuable work that has been completed. Encouragingly, there are now strong initiatives from eminent organizations to promote better communication of science (for instance, the Royal Society 2006).

Contract commissions, such as those from government, are generally closely specified at the outset. That may be seen as inhibiting scientific freedom but, on the other hand, may be more likely to secure strict relevance to customer requirements if the initial specification of work is sound and comprehensive, costed realistically and closely managed. Most meet the objectives within the resources allocated, but the writer has often observed that time and money allocated to preparing results for non-scientists is significantly underestimated in tenders.

'Closed-ended' research projects may give rise to problems because of the likely subsequent need to revisit results and to maintain and update databases for future use. Ideally, administrations would secure those tasks, but funds are often not allocated for the purpose, or decline as time passes. Also, research teams move on to other tasks on the completion of the work in hand. Attention needs to be given to whether monitoring and review are essential or simply desirable. Review of results is most likely to be accepted, or funded, if it is linked to specific stages in the administrative system; for instance, where there is a requirement for periodical reviews of policy initiatives or development plans.

Conclusions

This paper is essentially a review of some personal experiences in the UK intended to provoke discussion rather than to provide a 'right way' to communicate. Some aspects are likely to be relevant more widely, but the variety of social, economic and environmental circumstances is such that it is difficult to generalize about approaches. Some central issues for communication of geoscience information in public administration are as follows.

(1) It is necessary to understand the complexity of administrative structures and procedures, interactions between different levels of administration and with the wider public, and when and how best to engage with these.

(2) There is a generally low level of appreciation and understanding of the nature and relevance of, and relatively low priority often given to, geoscience information at many levels, requiring an educational aspect to some outputs such as leaflets for the public and planning policy guidance;

(3) It has to be accepted that geoscience issues are not key concerns of most politicians, administrators or the public, unless specific damaging events occur; this may lead to difficulties in engaging with the right people and in securing adequate proactive funding.

(4) The nature of applied geoscience work and educational and social diversity, and varied personal interests amongst potential audiences, may require researchers to work closely with, for instance, sociologists, economists and professional communicators.

(5) It is important to think about matters from the point of view of the audience and to listen carefully to audience concerns and attitudes first rather than commencing by telling the audience what it is felt that it should be doing.

(6) Information is not necessarily received gladly, particularly if it raises concerns about hazards and possible associated costs and impacts, so results need to be prepared and disseminated with care and sensitivity.

(7) It is necessary to devote adequate funds and time throughout to consultation, presentation and dissemination, and not to regard these as after-thoughts.

(8) Because of the diversity of potential audiences, a single output is unlikely to suffice. Material needs to be distilled and simplified to the essential minimum, and framed in terms of issues that the target audience is interested in.

(9) It is often wise to adopt a positive tone in presenting results, emphasizing opportunities for, rather than constraints on, use of land.

(10) Communication is a practical skill in itself, and experts in communication may be needed to help.

(11) Results can be used effectively only if all relevant audiences are aware of their existence and significance. Careful selection of the appropriate approaches and careful preparation are needed.

(12) Consultation, presentation for non-scientists and dissemination are essential activities that take significant time and resources. Commissioning bodies need to be more aware of this.

(13) Because of economic, social and environmental changes, results may need to be reviewed and revised at intervals. That needs to be more widely understood.

Because this paper is based largely on personal experience, it is, even more than usual, a reflection only of the author's views. However, I have benefited from working, and discussing these matters, over the years, with many people, particularly D. Brook OBE, M. Culshaw, A. Forster, R. McInnes OBE, D. Jarvis, M. Pettersen, A. Thompson, J. Poole and P. Hine.

References

ALKER, S. 2002. Integration of environmental information into a decision support tool for urban planning—an environmental information system for planners (EISP). *In: Proceedings of 23rd Urban Data Management Conference (Prague)*, 103–110.

BUNTON, S., WATERS, C. N., PRINCE, G. & NORTHMORE, K. 1996. *A geological background for planning and development in the City of Bradford Metropolitan District. Vol. 1. A guide to the use of earth science information in planning*. BGS Technical Report, **WA/96/1**.

Department of the Environment, Transport and the Regions (DETR) 2000. *EIA—a guide to procedures*. Thomas Telford, London.

Department of the Environment, Transport and the Regions (DETR) 2002. *Planning Policy Guidance Note 14. Development on unstable land. Annex 2. Subsidence and planning*. The Stationery Office, London.

DONNELLY, L. J. 2008. Communication in geology: a personal perspective and lessons from volcanic, mining, exploration, geotechnical, police and geoforensic investigations. *In:* LIVERMAN, D., PEREIRA, C. P. G. & MARKER, B. (eds) *Communicating Environmental Geoscience*. Geological Society, London, Special Publications, **305**, 101–121.

ENVIRONMENT COUNCIL 2004. *Good practice for stakeholder engagement in the aggregates sector*. Environment Council, London.

FAIRBANK, H. & JAKEWAYS, J. 2006. *Mapping coastal evolution and risks in a changing climate—a training pack*. Centre for the Coastal Environment, Ventnor.

FORSTER, A. & FREEBOROUGH, K. 2006. *A guide to the communication of geohazards information to the public*. British Geological Survey Urban Science and Geohazards Programme Internal Report, **IR/06/009**.

HOUNJET, M. W. A. & NGAN-TILLARD, D. J. M. 2007. Urban planning combining soil data and urban structure characteristics in GIS. *In:* CULSHAW, M. G., REEVES, H. J., JEFFERSON, I. & SPINK, T. (eds) *The 10th IAEG International Congress: Engineering Geology for Tomorrow's Cities*. Pre-Congress Proceedings CD. Geological Society, London.

INSTITUTION OF CIVIL ENGINEERS 1995. *Megacities: Reducing Vulnerability to Natural Disasters*. Thomas Telford, London.

MCINNES, R. G. 2002. *Advice to homeowners—managing ground instability on the Isle of Wight*. Isle of Wight Centre for Coastal Management, Ventnor.

MCINNES, R. G. 2003. *Coastal defence: a non-technical guide*. Standing Conference on Problems Associated with the Coastline. Cross Publishing, Chale.

MCINNES, R. G. 2007. Landslide management in a changing climate—coordinating the community response. *In:* MCINNES, R. G., JAKEWAYS, J., FAIRBANK, H. & MATHIE, E. (eds) *Landslides and Climate Change—Challenges and Solutions*. Taylor & Francis, London, 505–512.

OFFICE OF THE DEPUTY PRIME MINISTER (ODPM) 2003. *The Strategic Environmental Assessment Directive: guidance for planning authorities*. Office of the Deputy Prime Minister, London.

ROYAL SOCIETY 2006. *Science in the public interest: communicating results of new science research to the public*. Royal Society, London.

SMITH, A. & ELLISON, R. A. 1999. Applied geological maps for planning and development: a review of examples from England and Wales. *Quarterly Journal of Engineering Geology*, **32**(supplment), S1–S44.

THOMPSON, A., HINE, P. D., POOLE, J. & GREIG, J. R. 1998. *Environmental geology in land use planning—a guide to good practices*. Symonds Group, East Grinstead.

Environmental geoscience; communication challenges

DAVID G. E. LIVERMAN

Geological Survey of Newfoundland & Labrador, Department of Natural Resources, Government of Newfoundland & Labrador, PO Box 8700, St. John's, NL A1B 4J6, Canada (e-mail: dliverman@gov.nl.ca)

Abstract: Geologists whose research deals with environmental problems such as landslides, floods, earthquakes and other natural hazards that affect people's health and safety must communicate their results effectively to the public, policy-makers and politicians. There are many examples of geological studies being ignored in policy and public action; this is in due in part to geoscientists being poor communicators. Scientists often use complicated and difficult to understand language, talk mostly to other scientists, and are not trained to work with the media. They generally are not encouraged by their employers and funding agencies to communicate to nonscientists. Environmental geoscientists must make their research publications more accessible to the public by including plain-language summaries. They should work with media and communications professionals, and seek training in how to communicate better. They need to understand the different approaches that will work with different audiences. Universities, employers and funding agencies should encourage environmental geoscientists to improve communication skills, and to reward attempts to explain their research to non-scientists.

The effectiveness and impact of scientific research often is compromised by the difficulty of communicating results to those who might make best use of its conclusions. Environmental geoscience has direct and important application in policy- and decision-making. There are numerous examples of where scientific work has clearly indicated a direction in planning and policy, yet this was ignored. These examples ranges from the global scale, where some countries resist scientific advice on climate change; to the local, where people live in places that are very vulnerable to landslide, earthquake, flood or other hazards. Policy-makers frequently ignore the natural variation in Earth systems when making decisions, and lack the long-term perspective that palaeoenvironmental research can offer.

This paper explores the issues surrounding communication in the sciences in general, and more specifically as they pertain to the field of environmental geoscience. There is an extensive body of work dealing with science and communication, science and public policy, communication of risk, and public perception of natural hazards. Many practising geoscientists, however, are unaware of these areas of study. This paper attempts to provide some direction to such research, and a general introduction to the concepts covered.

There is a widening gulf between scientists and those who could be using science in planning and decision-making. The British novelist and writer C. P. Snow outlined the 'two cultures' of science and humanities (Snow 1993). Although Snow's argument was aimed at delineating the lack of mutual comprehension between scientists and those with an arts and humanities background, increasing specialization has made the divide between scientists and who might use their science wider. Scientists now frequently cannot understand the work being done in other scientific disciplines, or even by specialists within their own general discipline. The general public, policy-makers and politicians may have some science background, but this is inadequate when science is presented without consideration for its audience. Hartz & Chappell (1998) in their report aptly entitled 'Worlds Apart', suggested that the 'two cultures' have evolved into 'two separate and unequal societies ... those who are scientifically literate (and reasonably well-informed), and those who are not'. They suggested that improved communications between scientists and the media is essential to secure the long-term future of science in the USA.

Cavazza & Sassi (2004), writing on behalf of the organizing committee of the International Geological Congress in 2004, stated the following as part of their 'strategic vision for the Earth Sciences': 'skepticism as well as outright hostility towards modern science and/or its technological applications have been expressed recently by a wide range of groups ... It is therefore vital that geoscientists communicate effectively their knowledge to the public and to policymakers in order to increase the understanding of science, to inform policy decisions, and to make new findings accessible to those who might need them.'

From: LIVERMAN, D. G. E., PEREIRA, C. P. G. & MARKER, B. (eds) *Communicating Environmental Geoscience*. Geological Society, London, Special Publications, **305**, 197–209.
DOI: 10.1144/SP305.17   0305-8719/08/$15.00 © The Geological Society of London 2008.

McCloskey (2007) discussed scientific response to the 2004 tsunami disaster and wrote: 'We are failing in a big way to have our voices heard . . . . It seems to me that we have a lot to learn from our colleagues in the climate sciences. Their science is just as full of uncertainty as [that of] earthquake or tsunami scientists. They have, however, been more active in making sure that their concerns are voiced in the right places and at the right volume.'

Both Cavazza & Sassi (2004) and McCloskey (2007) called for scientists to increase their involvement and activity so as to influence both policy and public response, yet, as it will be argued below, environmental geoscientists frequently lack the tools to do this effectively. The need to improve skills in this area is critical; the results of research in environmental geosciences have direct implications for the health, safety and well-being of much of the Earth's population. Scientific research can be well funded, carried out superbly, and show clear direction to future policy. If it is not communicated effectively to those affected by it, it might just as well not have been done at all. As Hartz & Chappell (1998) indicated, if science is not seen to be playing an important role in decision-making, then the funding to conduct such research may be questioned.

Environmental geoscience; specific communication challenges

In this paper the term 'environmental geoscience' is used in the most general way, encompassing such fields as natural hazards, environmental geochemistry, engineering geology, hydrogeology, medical geology and any other means by which geoscience can assist in solving those problems affecting society that are derived from natural and human-induced hazards and pollution.

The issue of communication of scientific research spreads far wider than that of the environmental geosciences. Problems common to all sciences include the use of complex technical language, publication of results in inaccessible media, difficulty of explaining scientific uncertainty, and lack of training in media and communication skills (Hartz & Chappell 1998).

Environmental geoscience faces particular challenges within the geosciences. When considering the geosciences as a whole, the 'target' audience for scientific communication is varied. Much of geoscience research is directed towards resource development: the mining and energy industry. The challenges of communicating complex concepts certainly still exist in those fields, and the communication of risk and uncertainty is important. The audience, however, is likely to have some background in the geosciences, and the implications of misinterpretation of communication are mostly economic. There is thus perhaps an obligation on the part of the audience to inform and educate themselves on the geosciences, as they are choosing to make financial decisions based on scientific advice. It is rare for scientific research in the resource development area to have direct implications for human health and safety (apart from when examining the environmental impact of such activities). As Handmer (2000) pointed out, a failure to adequately communicate risk in the environmental geosciences can directly result in immediate deaths, and thus intense critical scrutiny of the communication process.

Thus communication challenges in environmental geosciences differ from those in the geosciences as a whole in that the scientific input provided into policy- and decision-making reflects not just on economic aspects, but also on health and safety issues. The focus on risk and probability matches that in the field of medical research, where it is vital that informed decisions on health and well-being be made based on scientific research. Given the similar challenges it is important to note that geosciences and other historical sciences differ markedly from the experimental sciences (Cleland 2001). Researchers in the medical field define risk and probability based on controlled experiments. The nature of the Earth sciences means that often such experiments are impossible to devise. When, for instance, the probability of an earthquake striking a given area is estimated, the basic method is to review knowledge of past occurrences. The record of past events is incomplete, and fragmentary. In a controlled experiment, error bounds can be reduced by increasing the number of trials or the sample size. This is not possible when looking at the variation through time of natural processes. Thus the level of uncertainty in conclusions may be greater, and hard to reduce with further research, increasing the difficulty in communicating such results.

Examples of failures in communication in environmental geosciences

Most researchers in environmental geoscience know of examples where they are puzzled by planning or policy decisions that apparently fly in the face of scientific advice. The cause often lies in communication: policy-makers lack the scientific background and skills to understand what scientists are telling them, and scientists lack the ability to present their science in a form that is comprehensible. The public frequently has difficulty understanding scientific assessments of environmental problems. The solution to many environmental problems is often thought to be more scientific research, or to fund more detailed scientific studies. In many examples, however, adequate science exists, yet does not seem to be taken into account in decision-making; this points to failures in communication. Some recent highly selective examples ranging from local to global in scope are outlined below.

In Newfoundland, Canada, floods cause considerable economic loss that has to be borne by a comparatively small population. The flood in Badger in 2003 is estimated to have caused $(Canadian) 12 million damage, a significant economic impact on a province with a population of approximately 500 000 people. Floods in Stephenville, in 2005, are estimated to have caused close to $20 million damage. Flood hazard mapping was undertaken in the 1980s and 1990s, covering many communities in the province, including Badger and Stephenville. Analysis of these flood disasters indicates that development continued in high-risk flood zones after the publication of the hazard maps, increasing the impact of the subsequent flooding events (Liverman 2007). This suggests problems not in the science, but in its communication.

The 2005 flooding associated with Hurricane Katrina in the USA was predicted with remarkable accuracy by research well in advance of its occurrence (Fischetti 2001; Travis 2005). The research was well documented in articles in the popular science press, including detailed descriptions of the likely impact of a major hurricane on the Gulf Coast. For example, the following appeared in *Scientific American*: 'A major hurricane could swamp New Orleans under 20 feet of water, killing thousands. Human activities along the Mississippi River have dramatically increased the risk, and now only massive reengineering of southeastern Louisiana can save the city' (Fischetti 2001). However, when Katrina struck the Gulf Coast, the lack of preparation both in infrastructure and planning did little to mitigate the effects of the hurricane. The reasons for this are complex and subject to considerable investigation and research, but scientists were ultimately unsuccessful in provoking an appropriate policy and planning response to their conclusions (Laska 2005). The success in communicating these same conclusions to the popular science media makes this case even more puzzling.

On 26 December 2004, the margins of the Indian Ocean were struck by a tsunami, a natural disaster of enormous proportions with a staggering loss of human life. Although Indian Ocean tsunamis were known to be unusual events they were by no means unprecedented, and the lack of preparation may have been due, in part, to a failure of scientists to communicate the importance of rare but high-impact events (Alverson 2005; McCloskey 2007). Tsunamis had affected wide areas on the margins of the Indian Ocean. In 1883, the Krakatoa explosion caused a devastating tsunami in Java and Sumatra (36 000 estimated fatalities), but limited effects also were seen in Sri Lanka and India, mostly in areas affected severely in 2004 (Choi *et al.* 2003). The absence of a tsunami warning system, and the lack of preparedness for such an event, contrasts to the tsunami warning system set up in the Pacific Ocean. The Pacific is subject to much more frequent tsunamis than the Indian Ocean. The frequency and severity of these events provided sufficient impetus to fund and maintain a warning system. The intervals between tsunamis in the Indian Ocean were much greater, and only the Krakatoa event caused major loss of life.

On the global stage, it can be argued that the failure of several major first-world countries to take prompt action on carbon dioxide emissions since scientific consensus on anthropogenically induced climate change emerged well over a decade ago is, in part, a failure of communication. Shackley & Wynne (1996), for instance, argued that discussion of uncertainty in climate model predictions, an accepted part of scientific discourse, has led to undermining of scientific authority when applied to policy. Boykoff & Boykoff (2004) ascribed the reluctance of the US Government to address climate change issues in part to disjuncture between a scientific community that deals in a language of uncertainty and probability and a political culture that requires certainty before action. Etkins & Ho (2007) discussed the large gap between the scientific community and the general public in terms of their understanding, awareness and perception of risks associated with climate change. Climate change offers further challenges in communication, as the process of change is slow by human time scales; in general, it is harder to initiate responses to hazards that develop over long time scales as opposed to rapid-onset events. Effective action on climate change required major changes in policy with serious political implications. As such, even when scientists effectively communicated their results to policy-makers, political considerations made taking action difficult until such action gained broad support within the community at large.

The longer-term perspective provided by palaeoenvironmental research needs to influence policy development. Agricultural management on the Canadian prairies is based, in part, on what is considered 'normal' levels of rainfall. 'Normal' was defined mostly based on the records of the last century or so, the period of European occupation and exploitation of the resources, and more specifically by the period covered by instrumented observations of weather. Sauchyn *et al.* (2002) showed that the initial development of agriculture on the Canadian prairies took place at a time of anomalously wet years. The climate of the 20th century was unusual in that there were no periods of prolonged drought, and the 1960–1990 period was the most benign in nearly 1000 years. Long-term palaeoenvironmental records show that drought was a frequent occurrence over the past few thousand years, and that perhaps prairie agriculture has flourished under atypical weather conditions. Understanding the long-term variations in climate is thus essential in planning development and management of this vital industry. It is thus important to ensure that the results of such research are effectively communicated to policy-makers.

Pereira (2006) analysed the effectiveness of national geological surveys in influencing policy by examining the policy areas in which the surveys thought they should have inputs, and comparing them with the acknowledgement of the geosciences in government focal point reports. There was a clear disparity between the potential input of the government geological agencies and the demonstrated output in government publications. This can be ascribed to ineffective communication between environmental geoscientists and policy-makers.

Obstacles to effective communication of environmental geoscience

Medium and audience

Most scientific communication takes places to an audience of peers; a group of fellow scientists who are familiar with the concepts and language used. The standard medium of communication is the scientific paper, published in a refereed journal, or a presentation at a scientific meeting; all using language that has become increasingly specialized. Scientific journals are rarely read by anyone other than scientists, and with the proliferation of specialized publications, it is unlikely that most journal papers are seen by anyone other than other specialists in the particular field of science. Scientists are trained to write for this audience, and thus face difficulties when trying to adapt their writing or presentation skills to other means of communication: the media, reports written for public consumption, and documents designed for policy-makers. They also face challenges in determining the appropriate audience for their information. Often efforts are focused on the 'general public', which, in many

cases, are less effective than focusing on those who might be able to use scientific results to influence and change policy; and making information available to those affected by the impacts of environmental problems.

Measures of effectiveness

The only means to gauge whether efforts in communication are achieving their objectives is to provide some means of measuring their effectiveness, yet this is rarely done. For example, the IUGS COGEOENVIRONMENT commission that existed from 1990 to 2004 had as one of its major tasks 'increasing awareness of the essential contribution of geological processes to sound planning and management of the environment' (COGEO website, http://www.sgu.se/hotell/cogeo/). As part of that effort, the commission produced a 12 page brochure *Planning and Managing the Human Environment: The Essential Role of the Geosciences* (COGEOENVIRONMENT 1995). This used specific examples and short case histories to explain to planners, government authorities and the general public what Earth sciences can contribute to environmental management. The brochure was translated into six languages, and distributed widely, primarily through Earth sciences organizations. Over 10 000 copies were produced, but Tony Berger, one of the leaders of this initiative, suggested that the distribution was not linked to a clearly defined target audience. There was also no means of measuring how effective the brochure was in achieving its objectives, and thus this effort may in fact have had little influence with planners and managers (A. R. Berger, pers. comm.).

Language

A major obstacle to communication simply is the language used by scientists to outline their findings to their peers in the forum of choice, the scientific paper. The conventions of scientific writing include extensive use of a convoluted impersonal writing style combined with extensive use of technical terms. Findings or conclusions are usually given with appropriate acknowledgement of uncertainty, and alternative hypotheses. The extensive use of citations and referencing of other work to clearly acknowledge sources and provide support for conclusions is also unfamiliar to readers outside the academic community.

There are good reasons for the adoption of this style and method of writing. Scientists go to great lengths to try and write with precision, and qualify their statements with assumptions and uncertainty clearly stated. This is the best method of clearly showing that the scientific method has been followed in the research. In addition, to some extent, the use of technical terminology is essential; scientists observe objects and phenomena for which no words exist in 'plain' English. The degree of specialization in scientific research, however, has made much scientific writing incomprehensible not just to non-scientists, but also to scientists themselves. Glanz (1997) discussed efforts within the physics community to develop guidelines for improving the clarity of writing, where the problem has become so serious that one physicist is quoted as suggesting that recent colloquia in his own department were so hard to understand that he was reluctant to encourage students to attend in case they were 'turned off from physics'.

Hartz & Chappell (1998) presented the results of a poll of 1400 scientists and journalists; 62% of journalists agreed with the statement that 'most scientists are so intellectual and immersed in their own jargon that they can't communicate with journalists or the public'. The extent to which this problem is acknowledged amongst scientists is shown by the fact that 50% of scientists agreed with them.

Risk and uncertainty

There are two related areas of science in particular that can cause problems in communication: risk and uncertainty. These problems span the sciences but are critical in the field of environmental geosciences, perhaps more so than they are in the geosciences in general.

The scientific method when applied to prediction of future events always results in a degree of uncertainty regarding outcomes. It is good scientific practice to consider alternative hypotheses and to reach tentative conclusions with an appropriate degree of caution. However, such uncertainty can be misinterpreted when communicated to non-scientists. Bernkopf et al. (2006) found that 'the uncertainty regarding the interpretation of the science inputs can influence the development and implementation of natural hazard management policies'. As indicated above, uncertainty as expressed in climate prediction has been used as a reason to discount studies (Shackley & Wynne 1996).

Many non-scientists expect certainty when presenting the results of scientific research. A poll conducted in the UK (MORI/Science Media Centre 2002) showed that 71% of those polled 'looked to scientists to give an "agreed view" about science issues'; 61% expected science 'to provide 100% guarantees about the safety of medicines'. Scientists, understandably, are reluctant to provide such certainty in the presentation of results. Hartz & Chappell (1998) documented that 63% of journalists and 82% of scientists surveyed

agreed that 'most members of the news media do not understand probability and statistics well enough to explain the results of scientific research'.

This difficulty is prominent in risk and hazard mapping, where geoscientists assign probability to the occurrence of hazardous events. Hazard zones are often defined on the basis of probability of recurrence. The one in 100 year (1%) flood zone is in common usage, yet this means of communication often results in misconceptions. Rather than the correct interpretation of a 0.01 probability of a flood occurring in any given year, many people believe that this designation means that the area will flood periodically with 100 years between floods (Ogle 2004). Mileti et al. (2004) pointed out that scientists expend much effort in defining and refining the probabilities of future hazardous events occurring, but the public interest can be expressed much more simply: will the event occur or not, and if it does will it affect me?

The communication of risk is fraught with difficulty, with a fine line needing to be drawn between downplaying real danger and eliciting a response that may be inappropriate. Probability estimates of the occurrence of an event lead to unpredictable, and sometimes surprising reactions. An internal guide to communicating risk in public health stated 'public reaction to risk sometimes seems bizarre, at least when compared with scientific estimates .... the suggestion that a hazard poses an annual risk of death of "one chance in x" may cause near-panic or virtual indifference' (Department of Health 1997).

Most attention in the natural hazards literature is focused on failures in communication, which result in disasters causing more damage than anticipated because of lack of response to warnings from those affected. As argued above, the disasters at Badger, Stephenville and New Orleans might have been mitigated if the response to risk and hazard mapping had been more effective. The health field can call on many examples of inappropriate responses of another kind; for instance, identification of risks associated with vaccination can cause a decrease in usage, and thus a much greater risk of illness or death caused by the illness being vaccinated against. In these examples, over-emphasizing the danger results in actions that overall increase risk.

Such inappropriate response also may occur in the environmental geosciences, particularly in the area of environmental geochemistry, where the results of scientific studies have direct implications for health. Di Giulio et al. (2008) have documented negative effects on a community caused by difficulties in communication of results of an environmental geochemistry study. Publication of results without consideration of public reaction caused severe economic and social problems for the affected community. The level of concern regarding lead in the environment led not only to communities being unable to sell agricultural produce, but also to residents having difficulty finding alternative employment. The relationship between researchers and the community was, in consequence, severely compromised.

In Bangladesh, concern over the health consequences of arsenic in groundwater led to recommendations to transfer to surface supplies for drinking water. Such supplies are frequently a source of water-borne disease and may overall carry a greater health risk than that of the high-arsenic groundwater (Caldwell *et al.* 2003; Lokuge *et al.* 2004). The very serious health effects of arsenic in groundwater had to be balanced against the overall health effects of the response proposed.

Dealing with the media

One main medium for distributing scientific information to the public is the mainstream media: newspapers, magazines, television and radio. The relationship between science and the media was explored by Hartz & Chappell (1998), and their report identified numerous concerns that scientists have when dealing with journalists. A common concern of scientists dealing with the media is that findings will be portrayed in an inaccurate or misleading manner. Only 11% of scientists surveyed by Hartz & Chappell (1998) had great confidence in the press, and similar responses were interpreted as showing that scientists in general were not comfortable with media coverage of scientific research. This is perhaps due to the fact that 73% of those surveyed in a Royal Society survey in the UK had no training whatsoever in engaging with the public or media (Royal Society 2006).

The lack of media training means that scientists are unaware of the way in which journalists work, and what they are looking for. Journalists need to provide editors with an interesting story, and thus will look for angles that provide such interest. Thus stories will concentrate on human interest, drama and controversy. Journalists also will attempt to present a balanced view of any scientific controversy, even if the consensus scientific view strongly favours one side (Boykoff & Boykoff 2004).

Scientists, on the other hand, look for media coverage to educate the public about their work (over 40% cited this as an important reason for engagement with the media in the Royal Society Survey), yet misunderstand the nature of media coverage. Nield (2008) has cogently outlined common misconceptions of the way the media operate.

Scientific culture

A major disincentive to scientists interested in communicating to non-scientists is the lack of encouragement and reward to do so, from their peers, their employers and their funding agency. In addition, a reluctance to engage the public lies within the scientific community itself.

A prime obstacle cited by those interviewed by Hartz & Chappell (1998) is a loss of status amongst their peers. There is a perception amongst scientists that scientists with a high media profile are no longer doing worthwhile research themselves, and thus turn to public engagement as being in some way less demanding. A UK survey found that 20% of scientists agreed with the statement that scientists who engaged with the public were less well regarded by their peers. In qualitative interviews several scientists expressed the opinion that public engagement would be detrimental to their careers (Royal Society 2006).

A second reason is the lack of reward and incentive provided by institutions and funding agencies. The measures used in defining career advancement for researchers in academic organizations are generally based on grant money sourced, academic publications and support of graduate students. Thus a major reason for not engaging with the non-scientific community is the need to spend more time on research (64% of respondents, Royal Society 2006).

The surveys of Hartz & Chappell (1998) and the Royal Society (2006) showed that comparatively few scientists engage with the public and media. Of those surveyed by Hartz & Chappell (1998), 25% had never talked to a member of the media, or had their research described in the media.

Discussion

Who should do the communicating?

The difficulties in communicating science to non-scientists have resulted in new areas of specialization: the profession of scientific communicator. Degrees in technical and scientific communication are offered at many institutions and emphasize technical writing skills. With the rise of specialist scientific communicators, should the scientist take a secondary role in communication? If this is the case, the scientist still needs to be able to communicate well with the communications specialist, as the process of 'translation' of scientific results into a format considered to be appropriate for public distribution may still result in misinterpretations and misunderstanding.

However, there is a strong argument that the scientist has a responsibility to learn how to communicate their findings effectively to a variety of audiences. Surveys in the UK have shown that scientists are by and large trusted by the public, particularly if they work at a university (Corrado & Duthie 2006; Table 1). Information conveyed directly by scientists carries more weight with the public than when it is interpreted by the media or governing bodies. Thus if a scientist has the skills to communicate directly there are considerable advantages in doing so, first, in ensuring accuracy of the information, and second, in levels of trust.

If it is accepted that scientists should take responsibility for communicating their work outside the scientific community then it is useful to look at means of improving the effectiveness of such communication.

Education and training

Discussions on geoscience education generally focus on raising the level of geological literacy amongst the general public. There are many local, national and international initiatives that aim to improve geoscience education. There is no doubt that communication of scientific concepts is much easier if the audience is scientifically literate, and, with communication being dependent on both

Table 1. *Trust in professions, UK, 2006*

	Trusted to tell the truth (%)
Doctors	92
Teachers	88
Professors	80
Judges	75
Clergyman/priests	75
Scientists	72
Television news readers	66
The police	61
The ordinary man/woman in the street	56
Pollsters	51
Civil servants	48
Trade union officials	41
Business leaders	31
Government ministers	22
Politicians generally	20
Journalists	19

Responses to the following question were tabulated by Ipsos MORI: 'Now I will read you a list of different types of people. For each would you tell me if you generally trust them to tell the truth, or not?' (Corrado & Duthie 2006).

communicator and audience, these efforts benefit scientific communication. The benefits of such efforts mostly are seen in the long term.

Environmental geoscientists are often faced with issues of immediate concern and need to be able to communicate their science directly to those without formal education in the geosciences, or the sciences. It is unrealistic to expect that politicians and policy-makers have either the time to be educated in the geosciences, or the interest in being educated when an issue arises. Community groups in developing countries may have little or no education at all in terms of the common definition of the developed world (although such communities may have a very strong understanding of the natural environment through their own experiences and culture). Thus environmental geoscientists must learn to communicate with a range of audiences.

There is little effort made to educate the geoscientist in techniques and methods of effective communication outside their peer group. Courses in communication often are part of undergraduate geoscience education. The focus of such courses, however, tends to be on communicating with scientific peers: technical writing, preparation of posters and presentations. These skills are, of course, important, and are used in the majority of communication that graduates will use in their professional life. It is hard to find, however, an undergraduate geoscience course that emphasizes communication outside the scientific community. There is a similar dearth of training at the graduate or professional level. In Canada, where most provinces require geoscientists to be professionally registered, the standard curriculum defining the basic education for a geoscientist does not include any component of communication with the public, and professional development opportunities are similarly sparse.

Scientists in general, and environmental geoscientists in particular, are not inherently poor communicators. As in any group, there are different levels of ability and competence in communication. The ability to communicate, however, like any skill, is learned through training and experience. Hartz & Chappell (1998) found that 81% of the scientists surveyed were willing to undertake training in improving communication skills, and thus it is important that such training opportunities be provided.

Useful research in the health disciplines has been done in the general area of communication of risk. Natural hazards have been a major focus of study in geography, particularly in understanding response and perception, and how this affects planning. The results of much research in the social sciences are highly relevant to communication of environmental geoscience. However, the relatively narrow focus in training of most geoscientists, and the scarcity of true interdisciplinary conferences, meetings and scientific publications, means that environmental geoscientists are not as aware of such studies as they might be. Mileti *et al.* (2004) distilled much social science research into a simple and direct guide for communicating natural hazards information. They emphasized that, to communicate effectively, it is essential to have a sound understanding of how people react to and perceive hazards.

In their conclusions and recommendations the Royal Society (2006) highlighted concerns that scientists mostly see their role as educating the public, not to 'debate, listen and learn as part of a genuine dialogue'. They suggested that younger researchers needed to be encouraged to engage with the public, and that such work should be seen as a positive factor in career development and advancement. In the right setting, and entering into discussion with the right attitude, scientists can learn much from the public. This will assist them in understanding their audience, and improving their ability to communicate with them.

Medium of communication

For scientific research to be at its most effective in providing the information required for informed decisions to be made, other outlets for communicating results need to be explored, with appropriate language and illustrations, and aimed at particular audiences. The first stage in effective communication is recognizing that methods other than those generally used by the scientific community (peer-reviewed papers and reports, presentations at scientific conferences) are required. Understanding the target audience is vital: a presentation made to the public at large should be very different from one made to politicians or policy-makers, which again should be drastically different from the standard scientific paper. Traditional means of scientific communication can be made more accessible, however. For example, the annual meeting of the European Geoscience Unions makes a strong effort to integrate the media with the meeting, with specific presentations that might be of media interest highlighted, excellent facilities for the press, daily press conferences and more. This is generally results in more exposure for the meeting in the media, and distribution of major results to the public. Similar efforts are made by other organizations, notably the American Geophysical Union, and the Geological Society of America at their annual meetings.

The Royal Society (2006) recommended that along with a standard scientific abstract, papers should also include a short summary of the results of the paper, plus an evaluation of the significance of the results, written at a non-scientific level. This was supported by Hartz & Chappell (1998) who stated 'conventional means of scientific communication need to be adapted to improve accessibility', i.e. publishers of scientific papers should require authors to include summaries of their findings—written in plain English—that put the work in perspective and explain its relevance and importance'. This assumes that papers published in scientific journals will be read by any other than the scientists working in that specific field of endeavour. Similar efforts are often seen in government and company reports, with an executive summary preceding the details.

Non-traditional means of publication of results offer greater opportunity, however. Such publications require standard methods of scientific writing to be adapted, or abandoned, to make the product understandable by the target audience. A Canadian example of such an initiative is the GeoScape project, a series of community-focused products designed to provide residents with important information on hazards, and other local geological features (Turner *et al.* 2002). This series of posters and accompanying websites are aimed at general geoscience education, with a strong environmental geology emphasis. Each poster focuses on a specific community, and they are developed through consultation with geoscientists, educators and others based in that community.

The advent of the widespread use of the Internet means that information easily can be provided in a variety of formats, designed for a range of audiences. Simply providing the information, however, rarely successfully achieves the objective of ensuring that those most affected are aware of it. The creation of a website with the results of research is apparently sometimes considered to be the major effort in reaching the target audience. As with any means of publication of results, care must be taken that the material is communicated in a clear manner for the target audience or audiences. With the proliferation of websites dealing with a huge range of issues, those seeking scientifically valid information on which to act are faced with finding their way through what can be a confusing maze of information. The best way, therefore, to ensure that Web-based material reaches the correct audience is to use it as a supplement to other means of communication; a link to a website within a brochure or hand-out, for instance, allows interested readers to gain access to a more detailed presentation of results.

The British Geological Survey (BGS) has had an increasing role in providing geohazard information to a variety of user groups. With the regulatory regime in place in the UK, geological information on hazards has become relevant to homeowners, planners, engineers and others. The extensive datasets available in the past were presented using conventional means, mostly standard geological maps. There has been recognition that products need to be tailored to users' needs and level of geological understanding. The 'Georeports' system provides a report specific to a given residential site, with information on hazards (radon gas, subsidence, etc.), and a listing of relevant information in the national data archive. Map legends have been redesigned tailored to particular users, with relatively complex legends for geoscientists and engineers, and simpler legends for farmers, householders and planners (Walsby 2008). In the simplified legends technical terms are avoided, and specific recommendations for possible remedial action incorporated.

In further recognition of the challenges posed in communication of hazard-related science, the BGS has published a guide to geoscientists (Forster & Freeborough 2006). This emphasizes directing communication at specific audiences, identifying three main groups: professionals, informed members of the public, and potential or actual victims of a hazard. Perhaps the most important conclusion of this report relates to empowerment: 'It is essential that any publication that tells people that they have, or may have, a problem should include guidance on how they may, themselves, take action to: determine if they have such a problem, avoid such a problem or minimise the effect of the problem. Telling them to contact a professional for advice is not sufficient' (Forster & Freeborough 2006).

Other efforts have focused on different means of presenting complex datasets. Computer technology offers the ability to present 3D datasets in innovative ways (Parks et al. 2005, Royse et al. 2008). Traditional methods of presenting 3D data (e.g. contour maps and isopach maps) require experience to understand and visualize. Generation of images of surfaces and structures that can be rotated and viewed from different angles allows easy understanding of complex information, especially when combined with animation. Further efforts include redrafting of standard geological diagrams to match more familiar graphic styles, and generation of tactile models of 3D surfaces. Parks et al. (2005) made the point that the generation of such images requires more work and effort on the part of the geologist, but they convey information far more effectively.

A useful method of translating complex scientific research into tools for decision-making is that of indicators. The indicator concept has been outlined by Berger (1997) and consists of the selection and monitoring of carefully selected variables to indicate changes in a complex system. Environmental indicators are commonly used in State of the Environment reporting, and Berger (1997) showed how such methods can be applied in the geosciences. The International Union of Geological Sciences Geoindicators Initiative developed an annotated check-list of 27 such indicators (Berger & Iams 1996). Indicators are a useful communication tool; they are designed to avoid complex terminology, and portray change so that policy-makers and decision-makers can gauge the effects of their actions. The success of this concept is demonstrated in the adoption of geoindicators in, for instance, the US National Parks system (Higgins & Wood 2001) and in the Lithuanian state of the environment report (Ministry of the Environment of the Republic of Lithuania 2001).

Distribution and dissemination

Marker (2008) has emphasized the importance of appropriate dissemination of information. Although it is rarely the environmental geoscientist's direct responsibility, the task of ensuring that well-produced, appropriate material actually gets into the hands of those who might best use it is often overlooked.

When planning the distribution of the results of environmental geoscience, it is useful to consider it as a continuous process, not a one-off exercise. Elected bodies (governments, municipal councils) change frequently, and efforts to provide information on, for instance, flood risk need to be continuous. Supplying a flood risk map to a local council may have immediate impact, particularly after a major flood. It is important to follow up over time, however, to ensure current decision-makers and planners are aware of the existence of the scientific work. It is equally important to include some means of measuring the effectiveness of the efforts in communication.

Environmental geoscientists working within government agencies usually are restricted to existing institutional means of distribution or communication with external agencies or the public. They may, however, have direct internal access to those making policy; understanding the decision-making structure within the institution can assist in ensuring that results reach those who can act upon them. Academic researchers have more freedom to use the media to distribute important findings (see Nield 2008) but may have more difficulty gaining access to policy-makers and politicians.

Target audiences

One vital element in effective communication is identifying and understanding the target audience.

The target audience in many parts of the world is itself changing as local or community bodies are becoming increasingly involved in decision-making. In Australia, for example, researchers working in the field of soil salinity gave up some time ago trying to reach the public at large, and now focus on the 'leading farmer/agronomist' groups, and other target audiences (Lawrie & Price 2007).

'To contribute effectively in the policy arena, environmental geoscience information should be communicated in the right form, at the right time to the proper channel for a specific purpose' (Pereira 2006). One of the challenges facing a scientist who wishes to see appropriate scientific input to policy is identifying the 'proper channel': the target audience. To be effective, a sound understanding of governance, and the linkages between policy and the various organizations that provide direction, is required.

One approach is to analyse the structure of institutional science and the pathways by which scientific input is provided. Understanding such structure allows the environmental geoscientist to direct communication towards the area in which it is most likely to be effective. Simpson (2008) has provided such an analysis of Australian public science and policy, and pointed out that 'Such pathways are not generally taught or explained during the formal scientific education process and as a consequence it may require considerable experience for individuals to understand the processes involved'. Once the pathways are understood it is, of course, by no means certain that scientists will have access to the appropriate level of policy-making.

Cultural context

A 2002 report to the International Council of Scientific Unions stated 'The World Conference on Science recorded the remarkable progress of science and technology, but pointed at the same time to the challenges ahead to use this knowledge in a responsible manner to address human needs and aspirations. To meet this challenge scientists need to be aware of the cultural setting of their trade. To translate scientific and technological knowledge into meaningful actions requires knowledge and awareness—both of the local arenas of action and of the general assumptions and value issues implied in science and technology' (International Council of Scientific Unions 2002).

Although many physical scientists have no training in social science, and often have difficulty coming to terms with the methods, terminology and concepts expressed in the social science

literature, some understanding of the social context of conventional science, and how it varies between cultures, is essential. Investigation of such cultural differences is a fundamental area of study in anthropology, and geoscientists working on environmental issues that affect communities need to be familiar with the concepts and research methods of anthropologists, both to communicate their results to such people, and to learn from them.

One of the most effective ways to overcome the cultural divide between Western science and non-Western societies is the acknowledgement of the importance and usefulness of traditional knowledge. The value of traditional knowledge and oral history is illustrated by the study of McAdoo et al. (2006), who demonstrated that knowledge of stories of a major tsunami in 1907 resulted in immediate community response to the Sumatra earthquakes in 2004 and 2005 in Simeulue Island, Indonesia, saving countless lives.

Many societies, particularly those closely tied to the land, show strong appreciation and understanding of the problems studied by environmental geosciences. Understanding the insight that these cultures may offer allows the scientist to present their own findings in a format that may be more accessible. For example, in one such study, Cronin et al. (2004) demonstrated that integrating volcanic hazard mapping with traditional knowledge allowed a more effective communication of hazard on Ambae Island, Vanuatu. Rautela (2005) showed how local societies act to mitigate landslide and other hazards in the Himalayas, and suggested that hazard and risk mapping might accommodate these practices. Catto & Parewick (2008) have demonstrated that conventional means of presenting scientific results were ineffective when dealing with Inuit communities in the Canadian Arctic. Becoming involved in the community, and learning about their perceptions and knowledge, and the problems they faced, eventually allowed the community to become aware of the scientific study, and how they might use the scientific results to help the community respond to environmental change.

Other examples, of course, exist, but in general understanding and use of traditional knowledge in the environmental geosciences lags behind that in other areas of science, particularly ecology, and in medical research, where ethnobotany has arisen as a distinct field of study.

Incentives to communicate

There is a need for institutional change to address these issues. Scientists themselves have identified ways in which institutions might encourage them to, at least, attempt to engage with the public. In the UK survey, 81% of respondents felt that bringing more money into their organization was the best incentive to engage in communication with the public. The same survey suggested that 70% agreed with the statement that funders of scientific research should help scientists to communicate with the non-specialist public, and 83% said that they would participate in public engagement if it assisted their career (Royal Society 2006). Other proposals included using professional scientific communicators to assist in organization of events, providing grants to cover staff time for such activities, and the development of institutional support systems to guide and provide structures for public engagement.

Nield (2008) has described successful partnerships between scientists, university public relations professionals and journalists. This method works well when dealing with general interest news stories, effectively a public relations exercise for institutional science. He also emphasized that developing good working relationships with journalists and professional scientific communicators allows scientists to be much more effective in influencing media coverage. Institutions can encourage the development of these types of relationships through innovative programmes. The Royal Society in the UK arranges 'pairings' of scientists and Members of Parliament. The paired participants spend time in each other's place of work, and the scheme aims to further understanding and dialogue between scientists and politicians. A number of fellowships and intern schemes allow scientists to spend time in media organizations; for example, the British Association for the Advancement of Science BA Media Fellowships. The Geological Society of America has a number of initiatives, including the Congressional Science Fellowship (part of the American Association for the Advancement of Science fellowship programme). This fellowship allows geoscientists to spend a year working in the political and policy-making system.

Conclusions

There is a divide between environmental geoscientists and those who might use their work in decision-making, and this is in part caused by a lack of awareness of the body of research in communication of science, and in particular communication of risk, amongst environmental geoscientists.

Barriers to communication include the medium of communication chosen by scientists, the technical language of science, lack of experience and training in dealing with the media, inability to tailor communication to audiences, lack of understanding of decision-making structures, and the lack of incentive to engage outside the scientific community.

Scientists should take responsibility for informing the wider audience of their work; they tend to be trusted by the public, and understand their own work better than any third party. They thus need to develop the skills, and use appropriate venues and methods to communicate effectively with the target audience, whether it is the general public, planners or policy-makers.

There is a need to educate environmental geoscientists on how to ensure their scientific expertise is used effectively by improving their communication skills. Environmental geoscientists spend many years developing the skills and experience to perform scientific research. They need the encouragement and opportunity to add the skills required to communicate their results effectively. University programmes in environmental geosciences should include mandatory courses in communication with public and the media. There needs to be an increased awareness of research in the social sciences. Geography and environmental studies programmes are well placed to provide such interdisciplinary training.

Training in communication and media should be provided or expanded to assist scientists develop their skills. Institutions need to encourage and reward engagement with the non-scientific community, and provide the structure and support to enable scientists to do so.

This paper perhaps has emphasized failures of communication but much can be learned from examples of successful integration of communication into geoscience programmes. This current volume attempts to document some of these.

The IUGS Commission 'Geosciences for Environmental Management' established a working group 'Communicating Environmental Geoscience' in 2006. The working group attempts to develop and improve the tools and skills environmental geoscientists need to communicate effectively with non-specialists: politicians, policy-makers, regulators, educators and the public at large. The group directs a programme of workshops, training courses, meetings and publications. The group is building on existing efforts, as to effectively reach a world-wide community of environmental geoscientists is challenging.

I thank the members of the IUGS GeoIndicators management committee and the IUGS GEM Commission for their encouragement to develop a working group to deal with this issue, and for much interesting discussion and feedback. C. Pereira and A. Berger reviewed the manuscript, and provided much needed direction for its improvement. The Geological Survey of Newfoundland and Labrador is thanked for its support in my involvement with the activities of the working group.

References

ALVERSON, K. 2005. Watching over the world's oceans. *Nature*, **434**, 19–20.

BERGER, A. R. 1997. Assessing rapid environmental change using geoindicators. *Environmental Geology*, **32**, 36–44.

BERGER, A. R. & IAMS, W. J. 1996. *Geoindicators: Assessing Rapid Environmental Changes in Earth Systems*. Balkema, Rotterdam.

BERNKNOPF, R. L., RABINOVICI, S. J. M., WOOD, N. J. & DINITZ, B. L. 2006. The influence of hazard models on GIS-based regional risk assessments and mitigation policies. *International Journal of Risk Assessment and Management*, **6**, 369–387.

BOYKOFF, M. & BOYKOFF, J. 2004. Bias as balance: global warming and the U.S. prestige press. *Global Environmental Change*, **14**, 125–136.

CALDWELL, B. K., CALDWELL, J. C., MITRA, S. N. & SMITH, W. 2003. Tubewells and arsenic in Bangladesh: challenging a public health success story. *International Journal of Population Geography*, **9**, 23–38.

CATTO, N. R. & PAREWICK, K. 2008. Hazard and vulnerability assessment and adaptive planning: mutual and multilateral community–researcher communication, Arctic Canada. *In*: LIVERMAN, D., PEREIRA, C. P. G. & MARKER, B. (eds) *Communicating Environmental Geoscience*. Geological Society, London, Special Publications, **305**, 123–140.

CAVAZZA, W. & SASSI, F. P. 2004. A strategic vision for the Earth Sciences. *32nd IGC Informs (conference newspaper)*, **9**, 1.

CHOI, B. H., PELINOVSKY, E., KIM, K. O. & LEE, J. S. 2003. Simulation of the trans-oceanic tsunami propagation due to the 1883 Krakatau volcanic eruption. *Natural Hazards and Earth System Sciences*, **3**, 321–332.

CLELAND, C. E. 2001. Historical science, experimental science, and the scientific method. *Geology*, **29**, 987–990.

COGEOENVIRONMENT 1995. *Planning and Managing the Human Environment: The Essential Role of the Geosciences*. Commission on Geological Sciences for Environmental Planning. IUGS, Haarlem.

CORRADO, M. & DUTHIE, T. 2006. *Opinion of Professions—Trend Data*. Report for the Royal College of Physicians. Ipsos MORI, London.

CRONIN, S. J., GAYLORD, D. R., CHARLEY, D., ALLOWAY, B. V., WALLEZ, S. & ESAU, J. W. 2004. Participatory methods of incorporating scientific with traditional knowledge for volcanic hazard management on Ambae Island, Vanuatu. *Bulletin of Volcanology*, **66**, 652–668.

DEPARTMENT OF HEALTH 1997. *Communicating about risks to public health: pointers to good practice*. Department of Health, London.

DI GIULIO, G. M., PEREIRA, N. M. & DE FIGUEIREDO, B. R. 2008. Lead contamination, media and risk communication: a case study in the Ribeira Valley, Brazil. *In*: LIVERMAN, D., PEREIRA, C. P. G. & MARKER, B. (eds) *Communicating Environmental Geoscience*. Geological Society, London, Special Publications, **305**, 63–74.

ETKINS, D. & HO, E. 2007. Climate change: perceptions and discourses of risk. *Journal of Risk Research*, **10**, 623–641.

FISCHETTI, M. 2001. Drowning New Orleans. *Scientific American*, October, 77–85.

FORSTER, A. & FREEBOROUGH, K. 2006. *A guide to the communication of geohazards information to the public*. British Geological Survey Internal Report, **IR06–009**.

GLANZ, J. 1997. Cut the communications fog say physicists and editors. *Science Magazine*, **277**, 895–896.

HANDMER, J. 2000. Are flood warnings futile?: risk communication in emergencies. *Australasian Journal of Disaster and Trauma Studies*, **2000-2**. World Wide Web Address http://www.massey.ac.nz/trauma.

HARTZ, J. & CHAPPELL, R. 1998. *Worlds Apart: how the distance between science and journalism threatens America's future*. First Amendment Center Publication, **98-FO2**.

HIGGINS, R. & WOOD, J. 2001. Geoindicators: a tool for monitoring the ecosystem and understanding the resources. *In*: HARMON, D. (ed.) *Crossing Boundaries in Park Management: Proceedings of the 11th Conference on Research and Resource Management in Parks and on Public Lands*. George Wright Society, Harmon, MI, 239–244.

INTERNATIONAL COUNCIL OF SCIENTIFIC UNIONS 2002. *Science and Traditional Knowledge*. Report from the ICSU Study Group on Science and Traditional Knowledge, Paris.

LASKA, S. 2005. Science as the whistleblower for catastrophic disasters; what went wrong with Hurricane Katrina? *American Geophysical Union Fall Meeting Supplement*, **86**, abstract U33C-07.

LAWRIE, K. C. & PRICE, R. 2007. Communicating science is not a one-way street: how science helps communicate science. *Geophysical Research Abstracts*, **9**, A-10588.

LIVERMAN, D. G. E. 2007. Communicating environmental geoscience—a challenge for the geoscientific community. *Geophysical Research Abstracts*, **9**, A-01602.

LOKUGE, K. M., SMITH, W., CALDWELL, B., DEAR, K. & MILTON, A. H. 2004. The effect of arsenic mitigation interventions on disease burden in Bangladesh. *Environmental Health Perspectives*, **112**, 1172–1177.

MARKER, B. 2008. Communication of geoscience information in public administration: UK experiences. *In*: LIVERMAN, D., PEREIRA, C. P. G. & MARKER, B. (eds) *Communicating Environmental Geoscience*. Geological Society, London, Special Publications, **305**, 185–196.

MCADOO, B. G., DENGLER, L., PRASETYA, G. & TITOV, V. 2006. Smong: how an oral history saved thousands on Indonesia's Simeulue Island during the December

2004 and March 2005 tsunamis. *Earthquake Spectra*, **22**, S661–S669.

MCCLOSKEY, J. 2007. John McCloskey speaks. Online article, EGU today 2007. European Geosciences Union. World Wide Web Address: http://www.egu-media.net/content/view/118/68/1/1/.

MILETI, D., NATHE, S., GORI, P., GREENE, M. & LEMERSAL, E. 2004. Public hazards communication and education: the state of the art. *Natural Hazards Informer*, Issue 2 (update), 14 pp.

MINISTRY OF THE ENVIRONMENT OF THE REPUBLIC OF LITHUANIA 2001. *State of Environment of Lithuania, 2001*. Government of Lithuania, Vilnius, Lithuania II.

MORI/SCIENCE MEDIA CENTRE 2002. Science and the media. Survey conducted for the Science Media Centre. World Wide Web Address: http://www.ipsos-mori.com/polls/2002/science.shtml.

NIELD, T. 2008. Altered priorities ahead; or how to develop fruitful relationships with the media. *In*: LIVERMAN, D., PEREIRA, C. P. G. & MARKER, B. (eds) *Communicating Environmental Geoscience*. Geological Society, London, Special Publications, **305**, 5–10.

OGLE, R. 2004. Communicating what the 1% chance flood means. *In*: *Reducing Flood Losses: Is the 1% Chance (100-year) Flood Standard Sufficient?* Association of State Floodplain Managers, 2004 Assembly of the Gilbert F. White National Flood Policy Forum, background papers, 136. http: www.floods.org/foundation/Forum_2004.asp

PARKS, K., ANDRIASHEK, L. & ATKINSON, N. 2005. Lowering barriers to public communication with 3D groundwater mapping at Alberta Geological Survey: examples from Canada's oil sands areas. Abstracts from Workshop, 2005 Annual Meeting, Geological Society of America, Salt Lake City, UT. http: www.isgs.uiuc.edu/research/3Dworkshop/2005/pdf_files/parks2005.pdf

PEREIRA, J. J. 2006. Improving environmental geoscience communication—a policy perspective. Abstracts of a Workshop in Communicating Environmental Geoscience. British Geological Survey, Keyworth. World Wide Web Address: http://www.mun.ca/canqua/ceg/notts.html.

RAUTELA, P. 2005. Indigenous technical knowledge inputs for effective disaster management in the fragile Himalayan ecosystem. *Disaster Prevention and Management*, **14**, 233–241.

ROYAL SOCIETY 2006. *Survey of factors affecting science communication by scientists and engineers*. Royal Society, London.

ROYSE, K. R., REEVES, H. J. & GIBSON, A. R. 2008. The modelling and visualization of digital geoscientific data as a communication aid to land-use planning in the urban environment: an example from the Thames Gateway. *In*: LIVERMAN, D., PEREIRA, C. P. G. & MARKER, B. (eds) *Communicating Environmental Geoscience*. Geological Society, London, Special Publications, **305**, 89–106.

SAUCHYN, D. J., BARROW, E., HOPKINSON, R. F. & LEAVITT, P. 2002. Aridity on the Canadian Plains. *Géographie Physique et Quaternaire*, **56**, 247–259.

SHACKLEY, S. & WYNNE, B. 1996. Representing uncertainty in global climate change science and policy: boundary-ordering devices and authority. *Science, Technology, & Human Values*, **21**, 275–302.

SIMPSON, C. J. 2008. Communicating environmental geoscience; Australian communication pathways. *In*: LIVERMAN, D., PEREIRA, C. P. G. & MARKER, B. (eds) *Communicating Environmental Geoscience*. Geological Society, London, Special Publications, **305**, 179–184.

SNOW, C. P. 1993. *The Two Cultures*. Cambridge University Press, Cambridge.

TURNER, R. J. W., CLAGUE, J. J., VODDEN, C., WYNNE, J. & FRANKLIN, R. 2002. The Geoscape Canada project: Raising public geoliteracy across Canada. Geological Association of Canada and Mineralogical Association of Canada Joint Annual Meeting, 27–29 May 2002. Saskatoon, Sask. Programme and Abstracts. http://gac.esd.mun.ca/gac_2002/search_abs/program.htm

TRAVIS, J. 2005. Scientists fears come true as Hurricane floods New Orleans. *Science*, **309**, 1656–1659.

WALSBY, J. 2008. GeoSure; a bridge between geology and decision-makers. *In*: LIVERMAN, D., PEREIRA, C. P. G. & MARKER, B. (eds) *Communicating Environmental Geoscience*. Geological Society, London, Special Publications, **305**, 81–87.

Index

Page numbers in *italic* denote figures. Page numbers in **bold** denote tables.